BOONE AND CROCKETT CLUB'S
18TH BIG GAME AWARDS

Boone and Crockett Club's 18th Big Game Awards

A BOOK OF THE BOONE AND CROCKETT CLUB
CONTAINING TABULATIONS OF OUTSTANDING NORTH AMERICAN
BIG GAME TROPHIES ACCEPTED DURING THE
18TH AWARDS ENTRY PERIOD OF 1980 - 1982

EDITED BY WM. H. NESBITT

1984
THE BOONE AND CROCKETT CLUB
ALEXANDRIA, VIRGINIA

Boone and Crockett Club's 18th Big Game Awards

Copyright © 1984 by the Boone and Crockett Club.
All rights reserved, including the right to
reproduce this book or portions thereof in any form
or by any means, electronic or mechanical, including
photocopying, recording, or by an information storage
and retrieval system, without permission in writing
from the Boone and Crockett Club.
Library of Congress Catalog Card Number: 84-071676
ISBN Number: 0-940864-05-3
Published July 1984

Published in the United States of America
by the
Boone and Crockett Club
205 South Patrick Street
Alexandria, Virginia 22314

FOREWORD

Over the years, the Boone and Crockett Club has become well-known for its records-keeping activities in behalf of native big-game of North America. Interestingly enough, the club's records keeping didn't start until 1932, with the first edition of the Boone and Crockett Club records book. This was a half-century after the club's founding in 1887 by Theodore Roosevelt and a group of his hunting companions. A major intent of forming the club was to encourage sportsmanship afield and to bring about needed changes for the welfare of the big game of the continent. The club and its individual members have fullfilled this stewardship role admirably during the club's first century.

Faithful followers of the Boone and Crockett Club system of trophy measurement will know that this is the *first* time a records book for a single three-year entry period has appeared. It should certainly prove interesting, settling some arguments and no doubt starting others. The recognition of five new world's records in this book is strong proof that the big ones are indeed still out there. Moreover, the acceptance of nearly 1,000 trophies during the period points to the overall high quality of big-game hunting currently available in North America.

Thanks are due to a number of persons for bringing this volume to fruition. It was Hal Nesbitt's idea to do this book. He and his assistant, Jack Reneau, have not only gathered the stories and carefully checked the trophy data, they have also been responsible for the book design and proofing at every stage. Dr. Philip L. Wright and his Records Committee members deserve thanks for their tireless work in setting standards and settling the more difficult questions of trophy measurement technique. Dean Murphy, Chairman of the 18th Awards Judges Panel, and each of the Judges and Consultants, all spent a solid week, without pay, to carry out the judging activities. We especially thank our nearly 400 Official Measurers who love trophies so much that they volunteer their efforts to serve as measurers.

You'll find a lot of photos in this book. With the exception of some of the bears and cats, there are photos for all 68 trophies receiving awards. I'm sure that they'll help give an even greater appreciation of these top trophies and their hunting stories. We've also included a number of photos of fine trophies that qualified for the records book, although not quite high enough in score to be invited to the Final Judging. It's really an accomplishment to make the book and we hope you the reader agree with us that including these in this book adds extra flavor. All told, there are over 100 photos in this book.

You may have noticed the beautiful Bob Kuhn painting of whitetail deer on the dust jacket of this book. This is the painting used on the Boone and Crockett Club's first ever Conservation Stamp and Conservation Stamp Print (1982). Sales of the stamp and print provide monies to be used in support of the various conservation and big-game projects of the club. Write directly to the club office if you'd like more details about this program and the currently offered stamp and print.

We've greatly enjoyed bringing this book to you. No doubt, you'll enjoy it just as much. Good hunting and happy memories.

William I. Spencer
President
Boone and Crockett Club

CONTENTS

Foreword v
The Story of This Book 1
An Overview of the 18th Big Game Awards 3
The Stories Behind the Award-Winning Trophies
    Columbia Blacktail Deer, Lester H. Miller 7
    Mule Deer (Typical Antlers), Mark A. McCormick 11
    Mule Deer (Typical Antlers), Wesley Bruce Brock 13
    Mule Deer (Non-Typical Antlers), Ronald S. Holbrook 15
    Mule Deer (Non-Typical Antlers), Eddie Stephenson, Jr 17
    Mule Deer (Non-Typical Antlers), Heritage Gun Room 21
    Whitetail Deer (Non-Typical Antlers), Missouri Dept. of Cons. 23
    Whitetail Deer (Non-Typical Antlers), McLean Bowman 25
    Coues' Whitetail Deer (Typical Antlers), Kim J. Poulin 27
    Coues' Whitetail Deer (Typical Antlers), Jay M. Gates III 29
    Coues' Whitetail Deer (Non-Typical Antlers), Carl E. Fasel 33
    American Elk (Wapiti), Aldon L. Hale 35
    Roosevelt's Elk, Pravomil L. Raichl 37
    Roosevelt's Elk, Floyd M. Lindberg 41
    Roosevelt's Elk, Dave D. Godfrey 43
    Roosevelt's Elk, Carroll E. Koenke 45
    Canada Moose, Michael E. Laub 47
    Canada Moose, Albertoni Ferruccio 51

Canada Moose, George A. Sinclair 57
Canada Moose, William R. Lee 61
Alaska-Yukon Moose, Melvin R. Spohn............................ 63
Wyoming Moose, Aldon L. Hale.................................... 69
Wyoming Moose, Robert S. Mastronardi 73
Mountain Caribou, Clark A. Johnson................................ 77
Mountain Caribou, Mike J. Chirpich 81
Mountain Caribou, James V. Bosco, Jr.............................. 83
Woodland Caribou, Timothy E. Fiedler 85
Woodland Caribou, Richard P. Navas 87
Woodland Caribou, James J. McBride 91
Barren Ground Caribou, Q. Odell Robinson 95
Barren Ground Caribou, Lavon L. Chittick 99
Quebec-Labrador Caribou, Charles E. Wilson, Jr. 103
Quebec-Labrador Caribou, Maurice Southmayd 107
Pronghorn, Roger B. Heemeier 109
Pronghorn, Margery H. T. Torrey.................................. 113
Pronghorn, Dwayne A. Anderson 115
Pronghorn, Andy Van Patten....................................... 119
Bison, James Fredrick 121
Rocky Mountain Goat, Jackie O. Arnold........................... 123
Rocky Mountain Goat, Robert A. Hewitt........................... 129
Rocky Mountain Goat, John M. Mitchell........................... 133
Muskox, James M. Domokos....................................... 137
Muskox, Toby J. Johnson 141
Muskox, James W. Owens 145
Bighorn Sheep, Armand H. Johnson................................ 149
Bighorn Sheep, James A. Walls 153
Desert Sheep, Javier Lopez del Bosque 155
Desert Sheep, Claude Bourguignon 159

Desert Sheep, Robert P. Miller	165
Desert Sheep, Carl A. Mattias, Sr.	171
Dall's Sheep, Charles H. Rohrer	173
Dall's Sheep, William E. Medley II	177
Stone's Sheep, David C. Coleman	181
Stone's Sheep, Robert M. Case	183
Stone's Sheep, Robert L. Williamson	187
Cougar, Charles M. Travers	193
Cougar, Donovan W. Ellis	194
Cougar, Jack Harrison	196
Black Bear, Calvin Parsons	199
Black Bear, Harry Kushniryk	200
Black Bear, Robert P. Faufau	203
Black Bear, Thomas C. Middleton	207
Black Bear, Gary G. Johnson	209
Grizzly Bear, Harry Leggett, Jr.	213
Grizzly Bear, Fritz A. Nachant	217
Grizzly Bear, William G. Underhill	220
Alaska Brown Bear, Leon A. Naccarato	223
Alaska Brown Bear, James S. Fogel	225
Tabulations of Trophies Accepted for the 18th Awards Entry Period	227
Black Bear	229
Grizzly Bear	230
Alaska Brown Bear	232
Cougar	233
Pacific Walrus	234
American Elk (wapiti)	235
Roosevelt's Elk	236
Mule Deer, Typical Antlers	238
Mule Deer, Non-Typical Antlers	239

Columbia Blacktail Deer 240
Whitetail Deer, Typical Antlers 242
Whitetail Deer, Non-Typical Antlers 246
Coues' Whitetail Deer, Typical Antlers 248
Coues' Whitetail Deer, Non-Typical Antlers 249
Canada Moose 250
Alaska-Yukon Moose 252
Wyoming (Shiras) Moose 253
Mountain Caribou 254
Woodland Caribou 255
Barren Ground Caribou 256
Quebec-Labrador Caribou 258
Pronghorn 260
Bison 264
Rocky Mountain Goat 265
Muskox 266
Bighorn Sheep 268
Desert Sheep 270
Dall's Sheep 272
Stone's Sheep 273
Charts of the Official Scoring System for North American Big Game 275

ILLUSTRATIONS

Boone and Crockett Club Big Game Award Certificate	xiv
Columbia Blacktail Deer, New World's Record	6
Mule Deer (Typical Antlers), First Award	10
Mule Deer (Typical Antlers), Certificate of Merit	12
Mule Deer (Non-Typical Antlers), First Award	14
Mule Deer (Non-Typical Antlers), Second Award	16
18th. Awards Judges and Consultants	19
Mule Deer (Non-Typical Antlers), Certificate of Merit	20
Whitetail Deer (Non-Typical Antlers), New World's Record	22
Whitetail Deer (Non-Typical Antlers), Certificate of Merit	24
Coues' Whitetail Deer (Typical Antlers), First Award	26
Coues' Whitetail Deer (Typical Antlers), Second Award	28
E. Stephenson, M. McCormick, and W. Brock With Their Award-Winning Trophies	31
Coues' Whitetail Deer (Non-Typical Antlers), First Award	32
American Elk (Wapiti), Certificate of Merit	34
Roosevelt's Elk, New World's Record	36
P. Crocker and J. Elmer With Their Trophies	39
Roosevelt's Elk, Second Award	40
Roosevelt's Elk, Third Award	42
Roosevelt's Elk, Fourth Award	44
Canada Moose, New World's Record	46
K. Price, P. Raichl and B. Hofmann With Their Trophies	49
Canada Moose, Second Award	50
J. Burman, J. Reneau and R. Nolin With Trophies	55
Canada Moose, Third Award	56
Canada Moose, Honorable Mention	60
Alaska-Yukon Moose, First Award	62
Wyoming Moose, First Award	68
J. Kovac, Jr. and A. Peterson With Their Trophies	71
Wyoming Moose, Second Award	72
Mountain Caribou, First Award	76
Mountain Caribou, Second Award	80
Mountain Caribou, Certificate of Merit	82
Woodland Caribou, First Award	84
Woodland Caribou, Second Award	86
Woodland Caribou, Third Award	90
Barren Ground Caribou, First Award	94
M. Chittick and G. Holderman With Their Caribou	97
Barren Ground Caribou, Second Award	98

xi

K. Knutson and J. Conklin With Their Caribou	101
Quebec-Labrador Caribou, First Award	102
Quebec-Labrador Caribou, Second Award	106
Pronghorn, First Award	108
Pronghorn, Second Award	112
Pronghorn, Honorable Mention	114
M. Torrey and L. Chittick Accepting Awards	117
Pronghorn, Honorable Mention	118
Bison, Certificate of Merit	120
Rocky Mountain Goat, First Award	122
M. Duby, R. Sturgeon and W. Nesbitt With Trophies	127
Rocky Mountain Goat, Second Award	128
Rocky Mountain Goat, Certificate of Merit	132
G. Sinclair and A. Ferruccio Accepting Awards	135
Muskox, First Award	136
R. Bartlett, S. Johnson and M. Laurent With Their Trophies	139
Muskox, Second Award	140
K. Gerstung and B. Hartel With Their Caribou	143
Muskox, Third Award	144
D. Hoth and D. Rittenhouse With Their Sheep	147
Bighorn Sheep, First Award	148
Bighorn Sheep, Second Award	152
Desert Sheep, First Award	154
J. Zenz and C. Palmer With Their Sheep	157
Desert Sheep, Second Award	158
V. Clark and T. Martin With Their Sheep	163
Desert Sheep, Third Award	164
Desert Sheep, Certificate of Merit	170
Dall's Sheep, First Award	172
Dall's Sheep, Second Award	176
Stone's Sheep, First Award	180
Stone's Sheep, Second Award	182
M. Helland and J. del Bosque Accepting Awards	185
Stone's Sheep, Honorable Mention	186
G. Mann and G. Dieruf With Their Cougars	191
D. Ellis and J. Harrison With Their Award-Winning Cougars	192
M. Steliga With His Black Bear	198
R. Faufau With His Award-Winning Black Bear	202
G. Johnson With His Award-Winning Black Bear	208
H. Leggett, Jr. With His Award-Winning Grizzly	212
F. Nachant With His Award-Winning Grizzly	216
R. Fisher and J. Zubia With Their Bears	221
L. Naccarato With His Award-Winning Brown Bear	222
L. Miller With His World's Record Columbia Blacktail	226

BOONE AND CROCKETT CLUB'S
18TH BIG GAME AWARDS

BOONE AND CROCKETT CLUB
NORTH AMERICAN BIG GAME AWARDS

This is to certify that the

Quebec-Labrador caribou 429-2/8

entered by

Charles E. Wilson, Jr.

in the 18th. North American Big Game Awards was awarded

First Award

this 30th day of July 1983

Wm. H. Nesbitt
Secretary, Records of North
American Big Game Committee

Philip L. Wright
Chairman, Records of North
American Big Game Committee

The Boone and Crockett Club Big Game Award Certificate. The Certificate and the Boone and Crockett Club Medal (pictured at the top of the certificate) are both given to those trophies certified by the Final Awards Judges Panel for a place award. The Certificate only is given to trophies qualifing for other awards such as the Certificate of Merit and Honorable Mention.

THE STORY OF THIS BOOK

Wm. H. Nesbitt
Administrative Director
Boone and Crockett Club

For over a half-century, the Boone and Crockett Club has maintained the records for native North American big-game trophies. The club's system has been universally accepted for North America, and generally is the standard by which all other systems are judged. But, the records books come out on a regular, six-year basis, leaving a void in determining the best trophies for an individual entry period. This book fills that void by listing and ranking all trophies accepted during the 18th Awards Entry Period of 1980-1982.

The final scores and data shown in this book supplement those of the latest edition of the records book, *Records of North American Big Game* (1981). In the case of asterisked trophy scores, the asterisk indicates that the score shown is tentative, subject to final confirmation by either a Judges Panel or additional verifying measurements. Obviously, rank indicated for such trophies is then also tentative. Only when the asterisk is removed by the additional scoring(s) can the score and rank be finalized. For example, if the number one trophy of the category has an asterisk, it is thus a "tentative number 1." The current or actual number 1 would be the next one without an asterisk. It is assumed that such asterisks will be removed by the time of publication of the next edition (9th) of *Records of North American Big Game*, expected publication date 1987.

Editing this book was both pleasure and challenge. Many of our contributors proved to be just as able with pen or typewriter as they obviously are with gun or bow. Others are obviously "do-ers" rather than journalists. This is the direct cause of the noticeable variety in length and details of the stories in this book. We have included all stories submitted by the trophy owners. Editing has been kept at a minimum to preserve the flavor of each hunter's story. In the cases where the owner failed to submit a story, we have developed a third-person narrative, based upon the data submitted with the trophy entry. There is thus a story for each of the 68 trophies receiving an award at the 18th Awards in Dallas, Texas, in 1983.

For those of you who could not attend the 18th Awards display and banquet in 1983, let me describe, in concise form, the major activities.

The 18th Awards display of invited trophies was at the Dallas Museum of Natural History during the month of July 1983. It was followed by the Awards Banquet at which the 68 trophies featured in this book received their awards. The banquet was held on July 30, 1983 in the Great Hall of the Texas Hall of State, located near the museum.

The Awards Banquet was preceded by two full days of activities that gave trophy owners, club members, and the public a chance to get to know each other and to enjoy the fine trophies on display. The activities began on Friday with a "get acquainted" Mexican luncheon that was certainly memorable for the food. Dr. James H. "Red" Duke of Houston, Texas, presented a very entertaining talk on sheep hunting and high altitude problems, based upon his research in Nepal. Through the courtesy of the Dallas Ecological Foundation and the Dallas Safari Club, we enjoyed an excellent western style buffet barbecue on Friday night. Two special sections of the museum were dedicated prior to the meal, and a beautiful Tom Tishler bronze of a grizzly bear was presented to the museum by the Dallas Ecological Foundation. I'm sure everyone remembers both the food and the camaraderie of the night.

Saturday morning was "Press Day" for the working outdoor press, with the display closed to the general public. The trophy owners, Boone and Crockett Club members, and outdoor writers and editors were the only folks allowed in the trophy display area. There were representatives of a half-dozen major outdoor magazines, several newspapers, and also a number of free-lance writers. The writers and editors got their stories, "true" hunting tales were swapped, and more than a few future hunts were planned. The rest of the day was free time to enjoy Dallas and the trophy display.

The Awards Banquet on Saturday night featured great food and reasonably short speeches. Presentation of the awards was by Dr. Philip L. Wright, Chairman of the Records Committee, and myself as committee secretary. Slides of the trophies were shown as the awards were made. The genuine applause and good natured kidding indicated that everyone had indeed become friends, and they were having a good time.

The display of invited trophies proved quite popular with the general public. Thousands of men, women, and children toured the display during the month of public viewing. Many returned several times to enjoy the trophies and the other fine exhibits of the museum, one of the best in America. It was, as always, an unparalleled opportunity to see exceptional big-game trophics and marvel at their beauty. The display was perhaps the only chance many of the visitors will have to see some of the animals on display. The memories of the display and the sportsmanship represented just might help those folks better understand hunting and conservation and their important roles in proper management of our natural resources.

We'll hope to see you at the next Awards (1986); in the meantime, I wish you many pleasant evenings with this book.

AN OVERVIEW OF THE 18TH BIG GAME AWARDS

Philip L. Wright, Chairman
Boone and Crockett Club Records Committee

This is the first time the club has prepared a records book based on the entries from a single 3-year entry period, the 18th. From early comments, we anticipate that it will be well received.

This book summarizes all of the entries for the years 1980, 1981, and 1982. Each entry has been measured by one of the Club's official measurers. The hunter has submitted a sworn statement that he took the trophy animal in both legal fashion and also according to the Club's Rules of Fair Chase. At the end of the entry period on 31 December 1982, the Club office staff reviewed the top entries, and in consultation with me, invited the top five (or more) entries in each active category to be sent to Dallas, Texas, for the 18th Awards Judging session held in late June 1983. There, the Judges Panel rescored each of the trophies received and decided which awards to make.

In an effort to keep the entries current, the Club's policy is that awards are given only for trophies taken within the past five years. Trophies taken earlier, those where the hunter no longer owns the head, and pick-up heads, are all eligible only for a Certificate of Merit. In those cases where the invited trophy was not sent to be rescored by the panel, the score is shown with an asterisk. Only an assembled Panel of Judges is authorized by the club to designate a new world's record. Five such records were named by the 1983 panel and they are described below.

With entry numbers at an all time high, interest in trophy hunting in North America was never higher. A total of 179 whitetails was entered; 110 in the typical and 69 in the non-typical. Over 2/3 of these were taken in the past five years. What is also striking is that no less than 31 states and provinces are represented in the entries, an all-time high. Minnesota and Wisconsin lead the list with 23 and 22 trophies. Perhaps the most outstanding trophy in the program is the new world's record non-typical whitetail from Missouri. This animal was not taken by a sport hunter, but it exceeds the old world's record by over 47 points. Unlike the previous world's record which is extremely irregular and freakish in configuration, this new record shows in quite symmetrical fashion four normal points on each antler.

The next largest class is that of the pronghorn, with 108 entries and an even half of them from Wyoming. This reflects on the increased numbers of pronghorns in recent years in many parts of the range of the species.

Of considerable interest is the total of 44 entries in the newly established class for Roosevelt's elk. Surprisingly, 30 came from Oregon. Some 29 of the 44 were taken more than five years ago, to be expected in a new class, since these heads were not eligible for entry earlier.

British Columbia moose dominated the Canada moose class, as they usually have in the past. The old world's record, which stood for three decades, was broken by two magnificent British Columbia specimens. The new world's record is a tremendous trophy taken by Michael Laub of Ryetown, N.Y. In addition to its high score, the rack weighed 60 lbs., a very heavy head. Albertoni Ferruccio's trophy, which is wider and lighter in weight than the Laub trophy, also exceeded the previous world's record. Three moose specimens taken from recent hunting in Maine also are listed in the book. These are of particular interest since until 1981 moose had not been legally hunted in the state for many years.

In the muskox class, 2/3 of the entries are from Northwest Territories with the rest from Alaska. All of the heads that placed came from N. W. T. Sport hunting has been reinstated only recently in northwestern Canada and it is gratifying to see generally larger heads from N. W. T. than are being taken on Nunivak Island, Alaska. This latter island has been for several years virtually the only place where muskox trophies could be legally taken.

An increased number of bighorns was entered, with 16 from Montana. This state has had great success in recent years in reestablishing the species in ancestral ranges where sheep had been nearly or completely extirpated. In a number of cases the transplanted rams apparently grew bigger horns at younger ages than the original sheep stock, and faster than the transplanted ones would have grown had they not been moved. A bighorn taken in Montana by Armand Johnson is the largest reported from any area of bighorn sheep range in a number of years.

The new world's record Columbia blacktail deer was taken by Lester Miller 30 years ago in Lewis County, Washington, some 25 miles west of the mule deer/blacktail boundary. This fine trophy, only recently entered, breaks the old record by over 11 points. The old record was taken in Lincoln County, Oregon, in 1962 and it scored 170-6/8.

The long-standing cougar world's record was replaced by a tremendous specimen taken in British Columbia by Douglas Schuk. It supplants Garth Roberts' trophy that was taken in 1954. Roberts' trophy replaced Theodore Roosevelt's trophy that had reigned as the world's record since the current records keeping began in 1950. Whether Schuk's trophy will enjoy a similarly long reign will have to be answered in future years. It does appear that the big trophies are still out there.

In using this book you will no doubt enjoy seeing trophies ranked for the first time for an awards period. Where trophy scores are shown with an asterisk, they are *not* considered as final due to the unanswered questions represented by the asterisk. This is true even if an asterisked trophy is shown as first on the list (and presumably No. 1). To do otherwise would be unfair to the other trophies whose owners complied with the Judges Panel requirements. It is presumed that asterisks will be removed by the owner submitting two additional official scorings (total of three) from which the Boone and Crockett Club Records Committee *may* decide to accept one as final and remove the asterisk insofar as listing in the next regular edition (1987) of the records book, *Records of North American Big Game*.

The next (19th Awards) records book of this type will include two additional categories approved by the records committee in December 1983. The two new categories are Sitka Blacktail Deer with a minimum score of 108 and Central Canada Barren Ground Caribou with a minimum score of 345. The Records Committee is constantly reviewing the subjects of categories and minimum entry scores, in addition to settling the more difficult measurement interpretation questions. New categories are started only if it can be demonstrated that the proposed new category is separate, or can be separated from other, existing categories, and if indeed there is a sufficiently high harvest and interest in the category. Obviously, more categories are proposed than are approved. For further information on the two new categories, or the records keeping and trophy entry in general, write to the club's office for the latest details.

Finally, the large number of entries, the several new world's records, and the excellent quality throughout the entries shown in this book, all point to the truly outstanding job being done by our state and provincial game departments. All sportsmen owe them a debt of gratitude and support for preserving our wildlife stocks in such an obviously healthy and well-managed fashion.

Photograph by Wm. H. Nesbitt

NEW WORLD'S RECORD COLUMBIA BLACKTAIL DEER
CERTIFICATE OF MERIT
SCORE: 182-2/8
Locality: Lewis Co., Wash.   Date: October 1953
Hunter: Lester H. Miller

COLUMBIA BLACKTAIL DEER 182-2/8

Lester H. Miller

From the very first moment that I saw this buck, I knew I had to have him, no matter the cost in time or effort.

He was standing at the back-end of an open hay field, near a patch of second growth timber. His horns glistened in the morning sun and he looked almost like an elk. I had been walking up an old railroad grade that was half obscured by willow and alder. It appeared that I might be able to get close enough for a clear shot at him, but that was not to be. I was carrying my Winchester Model 94 30-30 carbine, not capable of making clean kills at any great distance. My deer hunting had been limited to heavy brush shooting at ranges of 150 yards or less, and this big buck stood at least 300 yards away. I carefully moved to a small opening and peeked out. The buck either saw me or heard me. He was into the second-growth in a flash.

For the greater part of every day of every legal hunting season in the years of 1950, 1951, and 1952, and until that all-important day in October, 1953, I stalked, drove thickets, and took stands in the Upper Lincoln Creek Area of Lewis County, Washington.

On as many as a dozen different occasions during that period, we were able to see him in the vicinity of Lincoln Creek. At Grange meetings, livestock auctions, and wherever people gathered in the nearby towns of Chehalis, Centralia, Fords Prairie, or Adna, it was not unusual to hear someone mention this majestic animal. Mostly, they would talk about his huge antlers, four points or bigger. Of course, the stories grew in the telling and soon he was almost a legend. Although I had twice jumped this deer out of his bed, and had seen him running down a runway on three or four different occasions, I still had never fired a shot at him, fearful that I might wound him and not make a clean kill.

And so it went. The sightings continued to be reported, with an occasional shot fired at the buck. He was seen often in the company of two other large bucks in late summer and early fall. He was seen in many different places (sometimes at the same time), from Doty Lookout to Adna, up Bunker Creek Road to Lincoln Creek. To hunt and to take this fine buck became an obsession with me. As the 1953 season approached, a gnawing kind of fear grew in me that a poacher might kill him or someone else would get him during the coming season.

I began to look for him on foot, cold-tracking him mostly, but many times hot on his trail. The purpose of this was for me to get familiar with his whereabouts and his habits, and hopefully to catch a glimpse of him and rid myself of a little of the "buck fever" I usually felt when I would see him. I covered a lot of ground during this period as I was not hampered by carrying a gun or being heavily dressed. This game came to an end two days before the general buck season opening in 1953. For the greater part of that day, I had been travelling along the creek bottoms and alder swamps, hoping to cut sign.

The day was rainy and the brush was wet. I was wearying of the game, when right in front of me in the muddy crossing, I saw the unmistakable tracks of several large deer and one smaller one.

My pace quickened as I began to follow the very fresh tracks. They led me up the side of a small hog-backed ridge, covered with thick hemlock. I worked my way through this wet brush and emerged on the other side to look down into a large, open alder bottom. There, not 50 yards away, were two large bucks, one a fork-horn and one a very nice four-point. But the size and majesty of a third buck dwarfed the other two. Here was my prize buck! He was nuzzling the neck of a young doe, occasionally watching the other two deer as they sparred with each other.

As quietly as I could, I worked myself back into the heavy cover and made my way down to the creek bank where I sat down. I noticed that my hands were trembling and they continued to do so for some time. Naturally, my mind was full of thoughts and plans for opening day of the buck season, 36 hours away.

My plan for the hunt was fairly simple. As I saw it, I would drive up the forestry road to a point where I could park. As soon as it was daylight, I would walk to the creek, which I felt certain would be an excellent place to start hunting. However, I reasoned that those deer could move some distance in any direction since my sighting of them two days before. Daylight found me parked on the forestry road, preparing to enter the woods. My pack contained a hatchet, knife, whetstone, rope, first-aid kit, lunch, a water-proof tube of "kitchen" matches, a liver bag, and a handful of 30-30 shells.

Arriving at the crossing where I had picked up the tracks before, I discovered more tracks in the mud. They indicated that the deer had returned on their back-track to this creek bottom. It took me quite awhile to figure out the direction the deer had gone when they left the bottom. After several false starts, I finally found the right trail and proceeded to follow the tracks. The deer were obviously following a well established game trail to another locality.

Although it was once-again raining so that any sounds I made were muted, it was difficult to travel this muddy runway without making considerable "sloshing" sounds. I had left the runway, walking in moss, grass and rotting wood parallel to it, when I rounded a bend in the trail and found myself face-to-face with a huge four-point buck.

He was no more than 25 feet from me! I don't know to this day what kept me from shooting that deer. He was a prize in any man's language. I guess instinctively I must have known that he wasn't the one. He whirled half-around and bounded 30 feet away to the creek, jumped it, and disappeared into the woods.

At the same time, a short way up the creek, I saw the ghostly figures of two other deer cross the creek and disappear. The relatively small clearing in which I was standing came to an abrupt end about 50 yards upstream. At that point, a fringe of sapling spruce made an almost solid wall. The runway went through this spruce thicket. As I moved up to peer through it, I saw the rump of a very large deer disappearing up the trail. I bent over and began to trot as best as I could after the now running animal. My pursuit slowed, faltered, and came to a stop after a time, as I became winded and needed rest. I felt that unless the deer entered a clearing or an area of sparse timber, and stopped, I had lost him.

As I sat there, I could see a fairly high ridge-top over the tops of the alder trees and what appeared to be an opening on the side of the ridge. I got to my feet and began making my way toward that clearing. It was only about 150 yards through the bottom to the base of the ridge. When I arrived at the opening, I found that the clearing had been created by a massive debris torrent. Supersaturated dirt and debris had let go to slide down the ridge. In the middle of the clearing, 80 yards away, stood my buck! He was quartering away from me, looking downhill right at me. I raised my gun and fired. The bullet struck him behind the shoulder and went into the heart. He went down in his tracks and never moved.

I have killed many bull elk in my lifetime. But, no animal has ever had the impact on me that this huge buck had when I looked down on him as he lay there on the side of that ridge.

The antlers were awesome to see with their spread and color and symmetry. In addition, they were hanging heavy with moss and lichen that he had accumulated while feeding or "horning" the alders and willows along the creek.

I placed the Game Department seal on a horn and field-dressed him, putting the liver and heart in my liver bag. With my hatchet, I cut alder poles, turning the carcass belly-down on them to cool-out while protected from the rain.

With one last look at my magnificent (to me) buck, I hurried downstream to try and get help to get him out to the road. By my reckoning, the road was about three miles away.

Although this hunt began over 30 years ago, certain things are as clear now in my mind as they were then: the first time I saw him; the times he out-smarted me; and, of course, the day his luck ran out.

One of the things that keeps the hunt fresh in my mind is the never-ending stream of visitors that come to see and admire "The King", and the letters I have received from those who have pursued him in vain.

Photograph by Wm. H. Nesbitt

MULE DEER (TYPICAL ANTLERS)
FIRST AWARD
SCORE: 205-6/8
Locality: Eagle Co., Colo.   Date: November 1981
Hunter: Mark A. McCormick

MULE DEER, TYPICAL ANTLERS
205-6/8

Mark A. McCormick

Mark McCormick hunts with his dad and two brothers. Although dad McCormick has a bad leg and can't get too far from the vehicle, he still enjoys getting out in the woods with his sons. He was with the boys the year Mark got the huge mule deer.

It was November 1981. They had arrived at their hunting area on the 8th. They were hunting the Red Dirt Drainage near Eagle, Colorado. The first couple of days, Mark saw lots of deer, mostly does and fawns and no big bucks.

Then, just about 10:30 a.m. on the 10th, Mark saw him. Mark was watching a meadow when the big buck ran into view. The deer stopped broadside, offering a good shot. Mark shot twice with his 280 Rem. pump to bring him down. Then the work began.

It was a rough two miles back to the road and the truck. Several inches of snow made the footing treacherous. By the time Mark and his brothers got the buck skinned and out to the truck, it was nearly 8:30 p.m.

A tired, but very happy, McCormick family made its way home with the big buck and some very special memories.

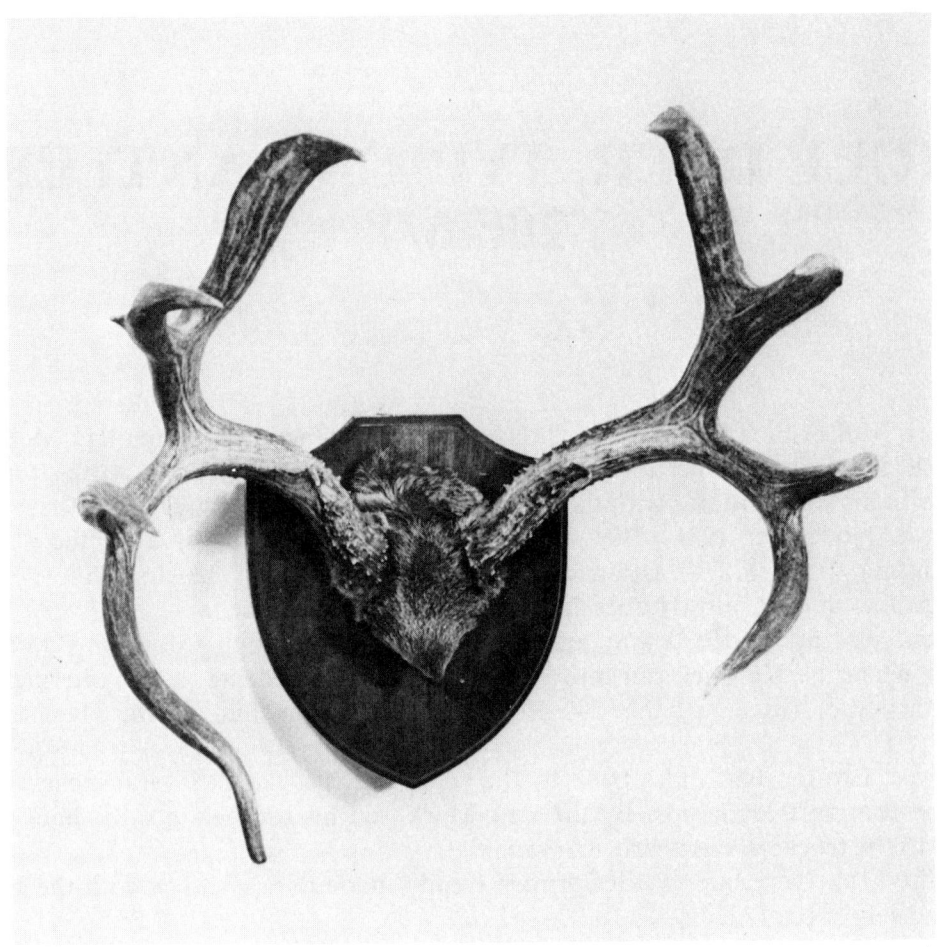

Photograph by Wm. H. Nesbitt

MULE DEER (TYPICAL ANTLERS)
CERTIFICATE OF MERIT
SCORE: 212
Locality: Grand Co., Colo.   Date: October 1963
Hunter: Wesley Bruce Brock

MULE DEER, TYPICAL ANTLERS 212

Wesley Bruce Brock

Wesley Bruce Brock resides in Florida. But, like many hunters, he travels to Colorado whenever he can to hunt. Therefore, it was no surprise that opening day of the 1963 Colorado deer season found Brock heading up a mountain at daybreak. His hunting party was tent-camped on the western slope of the Continental Divide, due east of the town of Tabernash. Opening day generally provides a good opportunity to see deer, but Brock could not have anticipated what was in store for him.

Brock moved along slowly but steadily, checking the surroundings for deer sign as he moved. After 45 minutes of alternately climbing and stopping to listen and look, he began to notice sounds ahead of him, sounds possibly made by another hunter or maybe a deer. It seemed as though something was moving along ahead of him and off to the left.

When Brock reached the mountain crest, he found some 50 yards of flat area with fairly open brush, but no sign of a deer or another hunter. He quickened his pace to reach an outcropping of rocks that would allow him to view the next valley.

To his amazement, he saw a great buck, about 100 yards below, travelling from left to right across his field of vision. The deer was "sneak-walking", not frightened but wary.

Brock waited until the buck reached the single opening that would allow the shot he wanted. A single shot dropped the buck.

As Brock field-dressed his buck, he realized that Lady Luck had indeed been smiling on him. His single killing shot, delivered at a downhill trajectory, had been intended as a heart shot. But, he had underestimated the elevation drop and the bullet hit the deer's backbone, knocking a single disc down into the heart.

After initial field-dressing of his prize, Brock returned to camp to get help and the best 9 a.m. second breakfast a hunter could ask for.

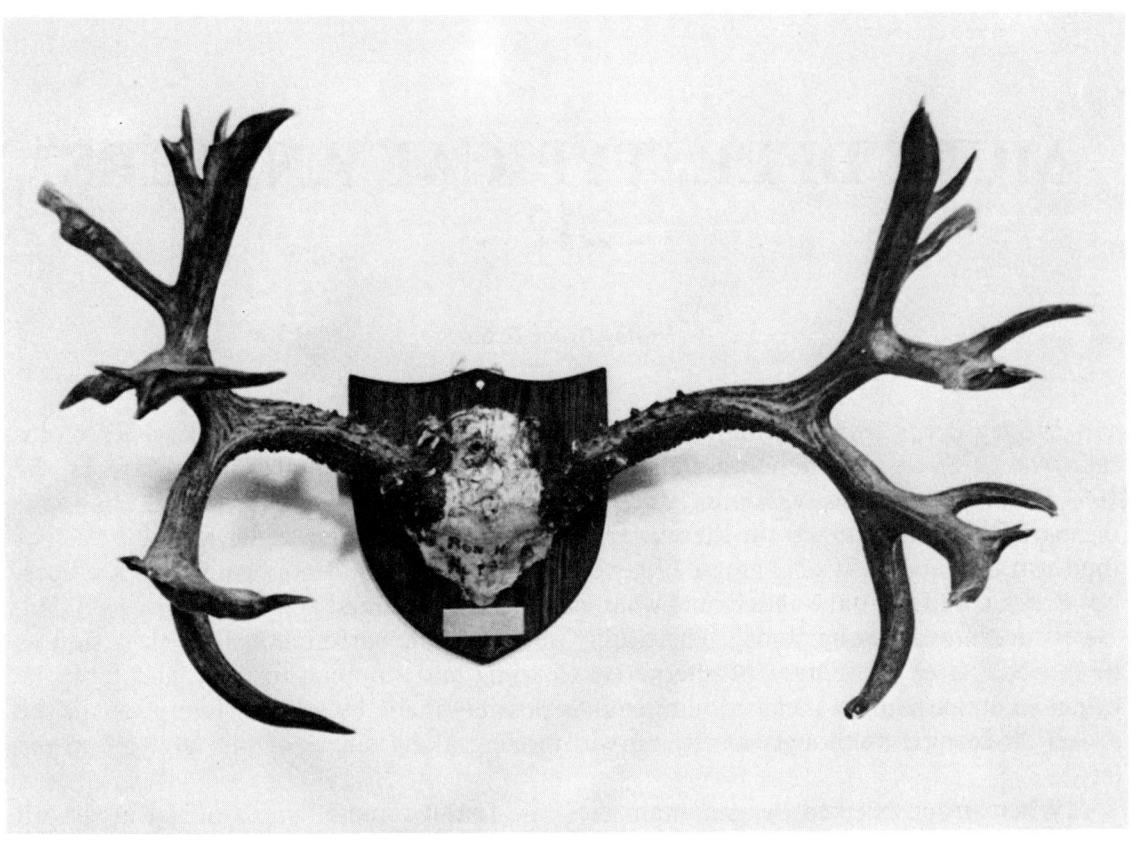

Photograph by Wm. H. Nesbitt

MULE DEER (NON-TYPICAL ANTLERS)
FIRST AWARD
SCORE: 280-4/8
Locality: Gem Co., Idaho   Date: October 1982
Hunter: Ronald S. Holbrook

MULE DEER, NON-TYPICAL ANTLERS 280-4/8

Ronald S. Holbrook

I live on a ranch southeast of Ola, Idaho. The 1982 deer hunt started like many previous hunts I've had, as I have lived and hunted in the same country all my life.

On the hunt I was with Scott Waldner, Monte Jensen and my son Todd, who is 11 years old. The canyon we were hunting (Salmon Gulch) runs east to west and is a tributary to Little Squaw Creek. Scott, Monte, and Todd were to hunt the bottom of the canyon and the north side, while I hunted to the south where the hillside is steeper. I climbed the hill, approximately 400 yards, and started hunting the sagebrush and thorn patches. When I got to the crest of a finger ridge, I stopped and watched the progress of my hunting partners, hoping they would have some success.

I was nearing the head of the canyon and I decided to cross over to the opposite ridge and join my partners. While dropping down the hill, I was watching the draw ahead of me and observed a buck coming up from the bottom. The buck stopped broadside to me, at approximately 100 yards. He was behind a cottonwood tree where he watched me. All I could see was that he was a big buck. I couldn't get a shot at him from where I stood. I started easing up the hill for a better vantage point. But, of course, the buck wasn't as patient as I was, and he broke up the hill to the left, running hard. I shot offhand twice, missing both times. Knowing I had only one shot left, and seeing that he was getting close to the top of the finger ridge and out of sight, I bedded the rifle down across a clump of bunch grass and found my target. I hit him behind the right shoulder at 250 yards. The hunt was over and the work was about to begin.

I didn't realize the buck had such a fine rack until he was on the ground. I've always been more inclined to hunt for the love of hunting, the meat, and the size of the buck, rather than the rack. My partners, hearing the shot, came to where I had downed the buck. We all marvelled at the old boy's horns but didn't realize he would measure like he did. We were more concerned with getting the meat down to the house. We elected to pull him to the top of the ridge with a rope and haul him home in a truck.

After entering the rack in Sunset Sports Center's Big Buck Contest, I was awarded the Grand Prize, a trip to Mazatlan, Mexico.

Photograph by Wm. H. Nesbitt

MULE DEER (NON-TYPICAL ANTLERS)
SECOND AWARD
SCORE 272-4/8

Locality: Eagle Co., Colo. Date: November 1978
Hunter: Eddie Stephenson, Jr.

MULE DEER, NON-TYPICAL ANTLERS 272-4/8

Eddie Stephenson, Jr.

It was November 1, 1978. My father-in-law, Charles Linder, Monty Jr., and I left Oak Grove, Louisiana, headed for Burns, Colorado. Two days later, after driving day and night, we finally reached Burns. In Burns we met Darryl Galloway and two of his friends, who we got to know better at camp. Darryl had been hunting several times on the Luarks ranch, where we had permission to hunt. We all drove from Burns to the Luarks ranch and visited with them for awhile. We then packed all of our camping equipment on our four-wheel drive truck and homemade utility trailer and left for our camp site.

Our camp site was six miles from the ranch and it took about two hours to get there. At our camp we had to set up our tents. We had two 8 x 10 tents where we slept, and one large 20 x 25 tent where we cooked and stored our gear. We were camped on King Mountain, about 8 miles from the Colorado River.

The next day, after we got the rest of the camp set up, we all went scouting to find a place to hunt for the next day when the season opened. That night in camp we all discussed the directions in which we would be hunting. The season was the combination elk and deer. I had hunted here one year before, and had killed a nice five-point bull, western count. I knew the general area where I wanted to hunt, so I went there the opening morning. I hunted that area the first day and didn't see any good bucks or any elk at all. I saw two small bucks, a four-point and a six-point, and several does.

I went to the camp to eat dinner. One of the men that came with Darryl had shot at a big bull and a big deer in the same spot and hit them, but couldn't find either of them. So we all ate dinner and went with Denny, who had done the shooting, down the mountain to where the big buck and the big bull crossed.

We looked for two hours and came up with nothing. Everyone left but Denny and me. I followed the blood trail one more time and found something that we had overlooked. The deer had stopped bleeding, and about 10 yards ahead of the way he was going, I found where he ran into an aspen. I figured that when he got up, he may have gone in any direction. So, I went back up the mountain, 100 yards off the trail which he came down. I found him lying in a gully about 100 yards from where Denny had shot him. We never found the bull. We were lucky to find the deer. He was a good 10-pointer with a 29-inch spread.

That night at camp, we all decided to hunt in the area around the camp the next day. All we saw were some more small bucks and does. So, on the third day we decided to ride in the Blazer across the mountain and hunt near some beaver ponds on B.L.M. land. I didn't see anything over there, but Charles shot at the biggest buck he ever saw in his life. Darryl was with Charles when he shot at the deer and both of them said he had at least a 35 to 40-inch rack. Little Monty had gone the third day with a friend from Glenwood Springs, and he killed a nice 11 point buck with a 25-inch spread. That night at camp we heard on the radio that a winter storm was moving into the mountains, so the next day we hunted close to the camp.

I was about 400 yards from the camp on the fourth day and the front was moving in. Out stepped the biggest deer I had ever seen in my life. He was about 500 yards away and moving right toward me. There were four does standing in front of me, 75 yards away. That big buck was coming straight to them. He stepped into a trench about four or five feet deep and all I could see were his antlers. He had 16 or 18 points and about a 35-inch rack. He stopped in front of a little knoll and the four does walked in front of the knoll with him. They all stayed there for an hour or so, and all I could see was those antlers. I never could get a clean shot. I thought of every angle I could, and finally decided to sneak toward them. I figured that any way he ran I could get a good shot. I was fooled when he went back down the same trench he came up. He came out of the trench about 500 yards away and stopped. I scoped him and fired. He ran toward an open park and I ran to the end of the park where I took five more shots at him. I never hit him.

I went back to the camp and ate dinner and told everyone about missing the biggest deer I had ever seen. After dinner, Little Monty and I went back down to where I had shot at the big deer. By this time the storm was getting close, it was getting colder, and it started clouding up. We had started back to the camp when I saw another big buck walking down the mountain in a thick aspen thicket. I could tell he was a big buck, but after missing such a big one earlier I wasn't too shook-up. He was about 350 to 400 yards from me. I found a small hole through the aspen thicket and waited until he stepped in it. I fired and he fell.

Little Monty and I ran toward the big buck, jumping a barbed-wire fence. The closer we got, the more antlers we saw. When we got up to him I couldn't believe my eyes. My deer had so many points. I started counting points; when I got to 50, I quit.

Photograph by Wm. H. Nesbitt

The 18th Awards Panel of Judges and Consultants. From left to right are: Steve Kubasek (J), Alberta; George K. Tsukamoto (J), Nevada; Dr. Philip L. Wright (C), Montana; Dean Murphy, Chairman of Judges Panel, Missouri; Dr. Glen C. Sanderson (J), Illinois; Ed Williamson (J), Oregon; Glenn St. Charles (C), Washington; and, Frank Cook (C), Alaska. Also shown are the new world's records in cougar, non-typical whitetail, and Columbia blacktail deer.

Photograph by Wm. H. Nesbitt

MULE DEER (NON-TYPICAL ANTLERS)
CERTIFICATE OF MERIT
SCORE: 311-6/8

Locality: Kaibab, Ariz.   Date: November 1941
Hunter: Vernor Wilson   Owner: Heritage Gun Room

MULE DEER, NON-TYPICAL ANTLERS 311-6/8

Heritage Gun Room, Owner

It's a beautiful rack, one to quicken any hunter's pulse. The numerous extra, abnormal points quickly identify this as a non-typical specimen. Unfortunately, little is known about the hunt.

Heritage Gun Shop now owns the trophy and displays it where customers can fully appreciate it. The best information available indicates that Vernor Wilson shot the big deer near Kaibab, Arizona, in 1942. No other details of the hunt are known.

Its high score for entry qualified it to be invited to the Final Awards Judging where it was certified for the Certificate of Merit, the only award available for trophies no longer owned by the hunter.

Photograph by Wm. H. Nesbitt

**NEW WORLD'S RECORD WHITETAIL DEER
(NON-TYPICAL ANTLERS)
CERTIFICATE OF MERIT
SCORE: 333-7/8**
Locality: St. Louis Co., Mo.   Date: Picked Up 1981
Owner: Missouri Dept. of Conservation

WHITETAIL DEER, NON-TYPICAL ANTLERS 333-7/8

Missouri Department of Conservation, Owner

On November 15, 1981, David Beckman met Conservation Agent Michael Helland along a road in northern St. Louis County, Missouri. Beckman had killed a deer and he asked Helland to officially check and seal it, to save the drive to an official check station.

They talked for a few minutes after sealing the deer, and then Beckman drove away. Not long after leaving Helland, Beckman saw a dead buck with a very large rack, lying inside a fence along the road. Knowing that the deer was on private property and that he would not be able to retrieve it, Beckman decided to find Helland and tell him of his discovery.

Agent Helland obtained permission of the landowner to recover the carcass. With the help of friends, he skinned the deer and removed the rack which weighed over 11 pounds. It was estimated that the deer weighed over 250 pounds. Examination of the teeth revealed that the monsterously large deer was 5-1/2 years old. Cause of death could not be determined, but it did not appear to have been shot.

Winter is a busy time of year for conservation agents. The rack was forgotten until after the first of the year, when Helland took the cape and rack to a taxidermist friend. The taxidermist to whom he took it of course recognized its outstanding trophy character. Helland arranged to have the trophy scored by Dean Murphy, Boone and Crockett Club Official Measurer. With the help of Wayne Porath, Deer Biologist for the Missouri Department of Conservation, Murphy scored the trophy for entry into the 18th Awards Entry Period at 325-7/8 points.

All persons involved agreed that a trophy of this stature should be held in public ownership and on public display for everyone to enjoy. Consequently, the Missouri Department of Conservation became the owner of the trophy.

Is there yet another huge whitetail out in the back reaches of Missouri? Probably. Remember that several of the all time top five trophies in typical whitetail are also from Missouri. Missouri is the "show-me" state, and when it comes to whitetails, they really can!

Photograph by Wm. H. Nesbitt

WHITETAIL DEER (NON-TYPICAL ANTLERS)
CERTIFICATE OF MERIT
SCORE: 248-5/8
Locality: Snowy Mts., Mont.　　Date: Unknown
Owner: McLean Bowman

WHITETAIL DEER, NON-TYPICAL ANTLERS 248-5/8

McLean Bowman, Owner

McLean Bowman is a Texas native who has been collecting deer antlers as a hobby for many years. His extensive collection is among the best known today. When he had a chance to acquire this specimen, he quickly closed the deal.

Although details about this trophy are few and sketchy, it apparently was taken some years ago in the Snowy Mountains of Montana.

As Bowman puts it, "If racks could talk, this one would surely have some interesting tales to tell."

Photograph by Wm. H. Nesbitt

COUES' WHITETAIL DEER (TYPICAL ANTLERS)
FIRST AWARD
SCORE: 130-4/8
Locality: Pima Co., Ariz.   Date: November 1981
Hunter: Kim J. Poulin

COUES' WHITETAIL DEER, TYPICAL ANTLERS 130-4/8

Kim J. Poulin

The beautiful little Coues' deer resides in the arid portions of several southwest states and Mexico. It is a popular game animal in Arizona, although occurring there, as elsewhere, in limited numbers.

Kim Poulin resides near prime Coues' deer habitat in Arizona. Little wonder that November 21, 1981 found him hunting the whitetail's little brother in the Catalina Mountains.

Poulin found his trophy at a distance of 125 yards. His 30-06 performed well, as it always did. He admired his trophy and then set about the work of field dressing it and getting it back to his truck.

Later measurement of the rack showed it to be record-book size. At the end of the entry period it was among the top entries for the category and was invited to the Final Awards Judging. It's become one of Poulin's favorite hunting memories.

Photograph by Wm. H. Nesbitt

COUES' WHITETAIL DEER (TYPICAL ANTLERS)
SECOND AWARD
SCORE: 110-2/8

Locality: Hidalgo Co., N. M.   Date: November 1981
Hunter: Jay M. Gates III

COUES' WHITETAIL DEER, TYPICAL ANTLERS 110-2/8

Jay M. Gates III

Few days in my hunting life have dawned as bright and as beautiful as did the morning of November 20, 1981. The rolling hills and rocky peaks that are typical of the landscape of Southwest New Mexico, 20 miles south of Animas, seemed brand new and shining in the warm light of the early sun.

I was on the third leg of my second consecutive "Slam" hunt. I needed the Coues' and Virginia whitetails to fill the '81 card, having already killed a desert mule deer and a fine Columbia blacktail. After this Coues' hunt, I would go directly to Montana for the final buck.

Having scouted the Gray Ranch in September, I was sure that my hunt would be successful - at least as far as getting a buck went. I also had a feeling that a record Coues' deer buck roamed those hills.

When the first light of that late fall day found us, my hunting companions, Jim Travis and Bob Lebo, and I had been in the field for more than an hour. We had left camp at five to drive the truck to the area where we knew there would be Coues' deer doing their early morning feeding. Jim and Bob shared my enthusiasm for the hunt and we soon were roaming the canyons and ridges of the Animas Mountains. Jim and I went into a canyon and Bob took the next ridge, paralleling our course.

The rocky canyon bottom made for difficult walking as we moved into the upper reaches of the mountains. After a short while we spotted a few deer, including a couple of smaller bucks - small enough to attract our attention for only a moment. The sighting provided more basis for our belief that we would find trophy deer on this hunt. Upon spotting the small bucks we joined and hunted together for a while.

It was after 9:30 when Bob and I spied a mature 8-point buck which was up and running away from us about the time we saw him. Bob had time only for a quick off-hand, 200-yard shot. He threw up the gun and squeezed off the round. The buck crumpled into a heap just over the top of the ridge. We good naturedly teased Bob about his "lucky" shot as we dressed the animal and made it ready for packing.

I was on the north side of the ridge, away from Jim, when I first saw "my buck". The greatest Coues' deer hunter I know, John Doyle, once told me that I would know for certain when I saw a record-book Coues' buck - he was absolutely right. As I looked down the steep slope right into the eyes of this buck, there was no question in my mind that he was a true trophy, a Boone and Crockett book buck.

The other ironic thing was that just like other hunters who I had read about or had listened to, I was in a most improbable position when I saw my record animal. I was caught on an open rock slide with nowhere to go, nowhere to hide, and nothing to brace my gun on. The buck was over 200 yards away - too far for an offhand shot from a basic falling-down position.

I decided to sit down on the rocks and try to slide to a rock about 40 feet away. My slide not only moved me but it moved a lot of rocks, which made a lot of noise. The big buck started to move away - I started shooting. It was something akin to a fighter pilot laying down strafing fire from an aircraft in a tailspin. As three rounds from my 270 Remington kicked up rocks and dirt and put the deer in no danger what-so-ever, he broke into a run and moved over a saddle, out of sight.

With my bottom now firmly planted on the rock, I sat back disgusted at the comedy but thanking the Lord for letting me see the buck. I cussed myself for a few minutes and got my head cleared before starting after him again. My experience told me that the Coues' deer is one of the craftier animals to hunt, almost impossible to circle and cut-off or even spot once you have fired on him. Although I was nearly certain I would never see the buck again, I had to make the effort to find him once more.

The next half-hour was nerve-wracking. I let three more excellent bucks go their way while I searched for "big daddy". I trekked into the canyon where he seemed to be headed when I last saw him; but after a few minutes, I had a gut feeling that he was not there. As the sun rose toward the top of the sky, I turned back toward the saddle through which the buck had run.

My hunch was right. As I trudged up the hill and the proverbial clock struck high noon, I jumped the buck again - he had come only about 30 yards over the ridge and when he got up this time he was only 30 feet away. He was so close I couldn't even get my scope on him - I had to wait for what seemed like an eternity for him to get 40 yards away so that I could see him and get off a shot. When the figure focused in my scope, I let the round go - he went down while my pulse rate went up.

I walked to the fallen animal and just stared at him. I must have looked at him for 20 minutes or more, admiring the beauty and feeling the respect for this magnificent specimen. He was the most beautiful animal I had ever seen, bar none. This Coues' buck was a king, even in death. I made quick mental calculations and measurements as I surveyed the rack, I just knew it would make "the book".

There was time for a brief party that night to celebrate the hunt. I rose early the next morning for the 12 hour drive back to Kingman, and then Las Vegas, to catch a plane for Montana and the final hunt for the 1981 season.

Photograph by Jack Reneau

Three very happy trophy owners pose with their award-winning trophies at the 18th Awards Display at Dallas, Texas in 1983. From left to right are: Eddie Stephenson, Jr., non-typical mule deer; Mark A. McCormick, typical mule deer; and Wesley Bruce Brock, typical mule deer.

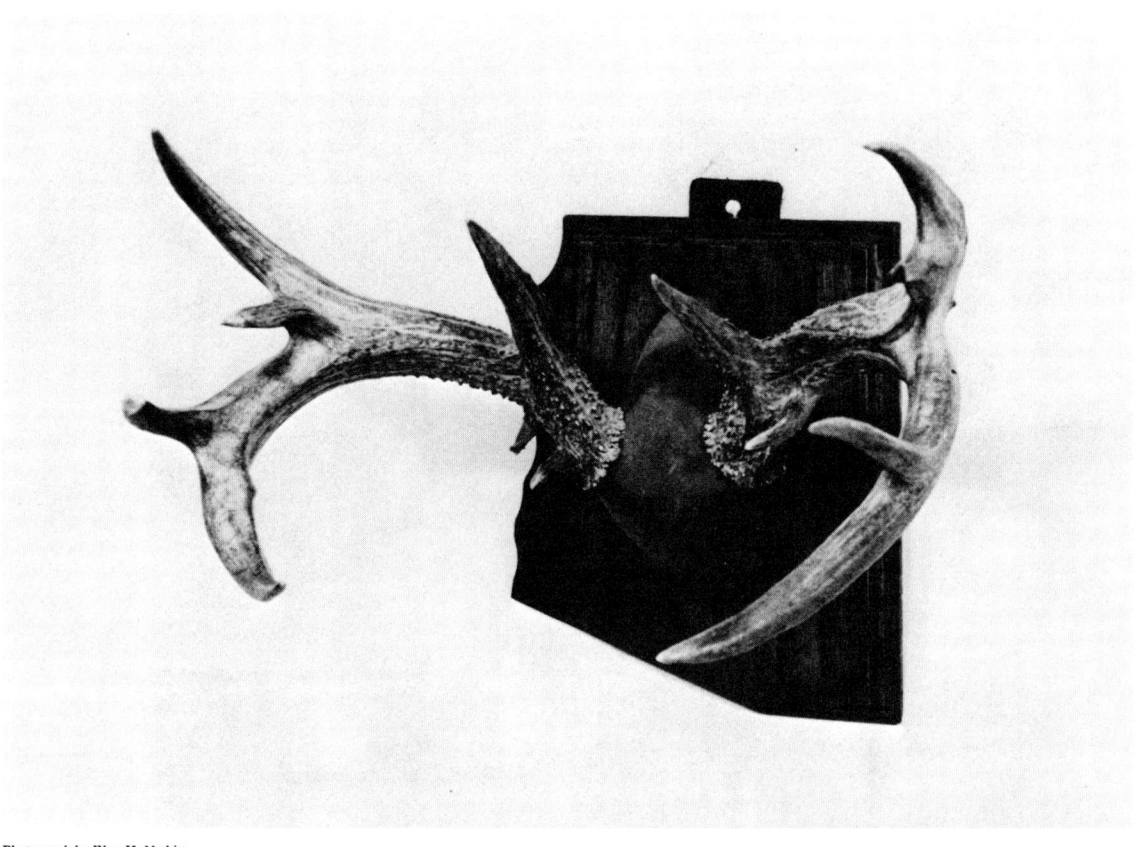

Photograph by Wm. H. Nesbitt

COUES' WHITETAIL DEER (NON-TYPICAL ANTLERS)
FIRST AWARD
SCORE: 120-7/8
Locality: Pima Co., Ariz.   Date: November 1981
Hunter: Carl E. Fasel

COUES' WHITETAIL DEER, NON-TYPICAL ANTLERS 120-7/8

Carl E. Fasel

Carl Fasel hunted Coues' deer in 1981 in the Patagonia Mountains of southeastern Arizona, 20 miles east of Nogales. On the second day of the season, he selected a stand overlooking an opposite canyon wall. In the distance, he could see the peaks of some of the higher mountains in Old Mexico.

Fortunately for Fasel, he missed the first buck he saw that morning. It was fortunate because he got a second chance a little later. While observing the opposite canyon wall, he spotted another, much larger buck heading downhill approximately 80 to 90 yards away.

The shot Fasel had was less than ideal. He had to stand on his tip-toes on a rock six foot high and sight through a small opening in the trees. At the bark of the rifle, the buck vanished. Fasel then waited a couple of minutes before going after his deer.

After a brief and fruitless search, Fasel returned to his stand to better pinpoint the spot where he had last seen the buck. After another 20-minute search, he found the deer dead under some brush. The single shot from his 270 Win. had stopped the buck in mid-leap.

Fasel's previous deer hunting experience was limited to several of the much larger mule deer he had taken in the White Mountains. He therefore wasn't overly impressed with the size of the antlers of his first Coues' deer. In fact, it was his son-in-law who took the antlers to get them officially scored by John Doyle, nearly a year after the kill. Doyle's initial score of 121 points indicated that Fasel's buck indeed belonged in the book.

Photograph by Wm. H. Nesbitt

AMERICAN ELK
CERTIFICATE OF MERIT
SCORE: 397-7/8
Locality: Sublette Co., Wyo.   Date: October 1950
Hunter: Ray Daugherty   Owner: Aldon L. Hale

AMERICAN ELK 397-7/8

Aldon L. Hale, Owner

Ray Daugherty was hunting in Sublette County, Wyoming, in October, 1950. Wyoming is great elk country, and Sublette County always produces some fine racks.

The day was overcast, with a light wind blowing. By sunup, it was lightly snowing. Fairly typical weather for Wyoming at that time of year.

Daugherty came upon the big bull about 8 a.m. The distance was over 100 yards, a long shot under the conditions. But, his aim was true and the big bull became his trophy.

Daugherty had a nice shoulder mount made of his trophy. Over the years, many folks admired the huge elk, including Aldon Hale, owner of a local sports shop. Hale thought that the elk mount would fit very nicely on the wall of his store and provoke comments from customers. Daugherty finally agreed and sold the elk mount to Hale.

Hale had the trophy measured in 1980. At the end of the entry period, it ranked among the top few for the category and was invited to the Final Awards Judging. There, the Judges Panel certified it for a Certificate of Merit award, the only award available for trophies no longer owned by the hunter. Today, the big bull looks just right in Al Hale's store.

Photograph by Wm. H. Nesbitt

NEW WORLD'S RECORD ROOSEVELT'S ELK
FIRST AWARD
SCORE: 356
Locality: Clatsop Co., Oreg.   Date: November 1959
Hunter: Pravomil (Milo) L. Raichl

ROOSEVELT'S ELK 356

Pravomil (Milo) L. Raichl

I came to green Oregon from my former home in Czechoslovakia, where in my youth I had been a forestry man and a game warden. Now escaped from Communist oppression, I sought here peace, and memories of the green home I had left. An ardent hunter, I was delighted with the beauty and bounty of this new home. Now I give thanks to St. Hubert, patron of hunters, for the opportunity to hunt this lovely land full of trophy game, especially the Roosevelt's elk, the "King of the Forest".

On the first hunting day of November 1959, I was only four miles from my own house, in the Saddle Mountain area of Clatsop County, near the North Fork of the Necanicum River. I had my Enfield 303 rifle, with 220 grain Norma cartridges. Being in western Oregon, we had just had plentiful rain but none was falling now. Snow was visible at about the 2,000-foot level of Saddle Mountain's 3,283 feet. The soft ground made for easy, quiet cold tracking.

For a long time, I had known about the large herd of Roosevelt's elk here, and I had admired the great bull with his whitish antlers and huge, bulky body. It didn't take long for me to locate them, for you can hear and smell them long before they are visible. Even in thick brush, when they are quiet, they can be located by the steam rising from their great bodies.

The herd was moving slowly, and I followed them quietly for about a quarter-mile along the North Fork of the Necanicum, toward the 300-400 Line road of the Crown Zellerbach Tree Farm. I had not taken a pickup on this hunt, for at that time, in this location, there were no good roads. It was the old, hard-time hunt on foot.

Presently, I came up to the herd. With my old Enfield at the ready, I started looking for "my" bull. With a "good" front wind, the herd didn't sense that I was near them, behind a huge, overgrown stump, searching for "my" trophy. Already, I felt he was mine although I hadn't seen him yet. With the trained eyes of a hunter, sharpened by too many years of bitter war, I watched the herd grazing the side of the hill before me. Not counting, just watching, I estimated between 50 and 60 elk in the herd.

Finally, he stepped into view, with his lovely white antlers and beautiful black neck, standing perhaps 60 yards ahead of me, close to a small creek.

How quick and easy it was. My firm hand did not tremble when I lifted the old British army rifle and took aim at the beauty before me. "Diana, please be my patron and let my bullet go directly into the heart of this majestic animal, that he may not suffer." The old hunters' prayer was my last thought as I squeezed the trigger.

The sound of the shot seemed to have frozen the herd for a moment, and the black necks moved the heads to face me as the huge body of my trophy crashed to the ground. What a triumphant feeling, known only to the hunter who has experienced it, and impossible to describe to one who has not. "Thank you Diana, and St. Hubert too!" Pagan goddess and Christian saint, we hunters take help where we can get it. That moment will be with me for all my life.

Now the hard work of the hunt lay before me. Before it was over, I would spend the better part of three days packing the animal out the four miles to my home. The work was very demanding and I was exhausted. But, I am still proud that it was all done the proper way. There was no waste.

While I was skinning my trophy, a forester from Crown Zellerbach Company came to the scene and congratulated me. He had probably been after the same bull. We both tried as hard as we could to estimate the live weight. An Oregon Department of Fish and Wildlife booklet reports that the bull Roosevelt's elk grows to a maximum of 1,300 pounds. But I believe, and the forester agreed with me then, that this bull was close to 1,700 pounds, with 1,780 pounds as the top estimate as it lay on the ground in front of us.

What a huge animal! And what a lucky new citizen of my new land, Oregon and America, where anyone can go hunt for a small amount of money. In Europe, hunting is a privileged pleasure for the few who can afford it. Even today, some rich Americans are going to Communist Czechoslovakia to hunt West European stag or Carpathian elk, paying up to $2,000. *for one shot*, hit or miss. Here the fee is only $25. for a resident and we don't have to travel across the sea. I am saddened to think of how little appreciation some hunters have for this privileged land, how they waste the game and trophies, the thrill and the *beauty*. But I know, and care, and I shall be happy hunting in Oregon forever, with friends who care.

Photo Courtesy of Peter F. Crocker, Jr.
Peter F. Crocker, Jr. with his fine non-typical whitetail taken in Isle of Wight Co., Virginia, in 1963. When finally measured for the 18th Awards Entry Period, his trophy scored 216-5/8, easily qualifying for the records book.

Photo Courtesy of Jay E. Elmer
Jay E. Elmer shot this outstanding American elk on the Kaibab National Forest, Arizona, in September 1979. With six points on the right antler and seven on the left, his bull scores 383-2/8 points. The rack weighs 32-1/2 lbs.

Photograph by Wm. H. Nesbitt

ROOSEVELT'S ELK
SECOND AWARD
SCORE: 352-6/8
Locality: Columbia Co., Oreg.   Date: November 1962
Hunter: Floyd M. Lindberg

ROOSEVELT'S ELK 352-6/8

Floyd M. Lindberg

On the particular day I got my bull elk, I had decided to hunt an area about seven miles from my home in Clatskanie, Oregon. That day of November, 1962, it was an area of about 20 square miles, without roads, but since then it has gained a few logging roads around the edges, with more planned. I was walking along an old railroad grade left from the first time this country was logged in the steam power days.

I had walked about a mile, when I found where two elk had crossed the grade. The tracks were not fresh, but I decided to follow them anyway. I followed them down and across the creek and up the opposite hillside. About halfway up the hill, there is a bench where I found elk tracks and beds all over. I crisscrossed the hillside in the drizzling rain until I found their tracks leaving the area. I followed them to the top of the hill where I found another place that they had fed and bedded down. I knew they were in no hurry to go anyplace, so I kept following them, finding several more places where they had milled around making lots of tracks and beds.

I followed them into mid-afternoon. I was going down an alder-covered side canyon, the kind that when your line-of-sight gets under the tops of the trees, you can see the opposite hillsides pretty well in otherwise very brushy country.

I just got down to where I could see through the trees when I spotted the head and front shoulder of an elk about 100 yards away. Looking through my binoculars, I saw that it was a bull with long eyeguards. I couldn't see the rest of his antlers because of the cedar tree limbs in front of him.

I knew he was a nice bull, so I slipped the safety off my 30-06 and aimed behind his front leg. At the shot, he whirled and ran up the hill, directly behind the cedar, where I couldn't see him. I waited awhile. I couldn't hear any noises, so I headed up the canyon. I circled around to the top of the hill, coming down toward where I had shot at him. I was about 200 feet from where I first saw him when I saw his yellow body, lying in the ferns.

As I eased down closer, I heard a noise off to my left. There was the other elk I had been cold tracking. He was a smaller five-point. I watched him run off. Then, I went down to my bull, dead with a shot in the lungs.

Photograph by Wm. H. Nesbitt

ROOSEVELT'S ELK
THIRD AWARD
SCORE: 344-2/8
Locality: Jefferson Co., Wash.   Date: November 1966
Hunter: Dave D. Godfrey

ROOSEVELT'S ELK 344-2/8

Dave D. Godfrey

It was Saturday morning of the second weekend of elk season, November, 1968. A hunting party of my Dad, my cousin, my brother-in-law and I headed for the hills east of the Kalaloch Lodge. Turning east on the first road past the Kalaloch Lodge, we travelled alongside the Kalaloch Creek for about five miles on a gravel logging road where we set up camp on a hill overlooking the area we were to hunt. I took time to check my rifle, a Winchester Model 88 in 308 caliber.

We hunted the downhill side towards the Clearwater River area; a compass was not necessary. As we headed downhill through virgin timber, the weather was cloudy and cool. We decided to split up, with my Dad and I staying together. We went down one ridge to the left, which took us to the lower end of a clear cut, still inside the timber. While heading down the main ridge, the terrain started to "bench out". At this point, my Dad was about 15 to 20 feet in front. I kept looking around, and out of the corner of my eye I saw legs moving slowly through the "dog hair" behind us. I bent down on one knee with my rifle in hand, waiting to see what it was. A few seconds later, I determined it was an elk. So, I spotted an opening in the direction that it was headed. As it appeared in the opening, I could see that it was a "bull". I fired immediately, knocking it down with the first shot.

I ran up to it as fast as I could and noticed that I had broken its back. When he fell, he wedged himself between a log and the ground. He was hitting his head against the log, and trying to get up when I got there. I had to shoot him again to finish him.

Dad and I started dressing and skinning out the elk. Then my brother-in-law and cousin arrived. This all happened around 9:00 a.m. I hiked out to my pickup, carrying the largest set of antlers that I had ever seen! It wasn't an easy trip out, as the antlers kept getting stuck on tree branches and brush, knocking me down several times. I had to be very careful not to break off any points on this magnificent trophy.

By the time we finished quartering and tying meat to our packs, it took us another six hours to finish packing everything out to our pickups.

We tied the antlers to the front of my pickup and headed for home - four very proud hunters!

Photograph by Wm. H. Nesbitt

ROOSEVELT'S ELK
FOURTH AWARD
SCORE: 340-4/8
Locality: Jefferson Co., Wash.   Date: November 1966
Hunter: Carroll E. Koenke

ROOSEVELT'S ELK 340-4/8

Carroll E. Koenke

Jefferson County, Washington, is prime habit for Roosevelt's elk. And, Noland Creek was a favorite place of Carroll Koenke to hunt. He had seen the large elk on several days. In fact, he had been trying to get close to this big bull for nearly a week.

The day was November 12th, 1966. It had been a long day, but one that Carroll would remember forever. It was getting near dusk, almost 7 p.m. He finally spotted the great bull at a distance of 300 yards. It was heavy overcast but there was no wind. He knew his 348 Win. would do the job.

Hunting alone as he usually did, Carroll did not even bother to save the cape. Later, when he found out what a trophy he had, he had to purchase a cape to have his trophy mounted. With the establishment of the Roosevelt's elk category, Carroll's fine trophy is recognized as one of the very best ever taken.

Carroll still hunts each fall and is hoping to see an even bigger one.

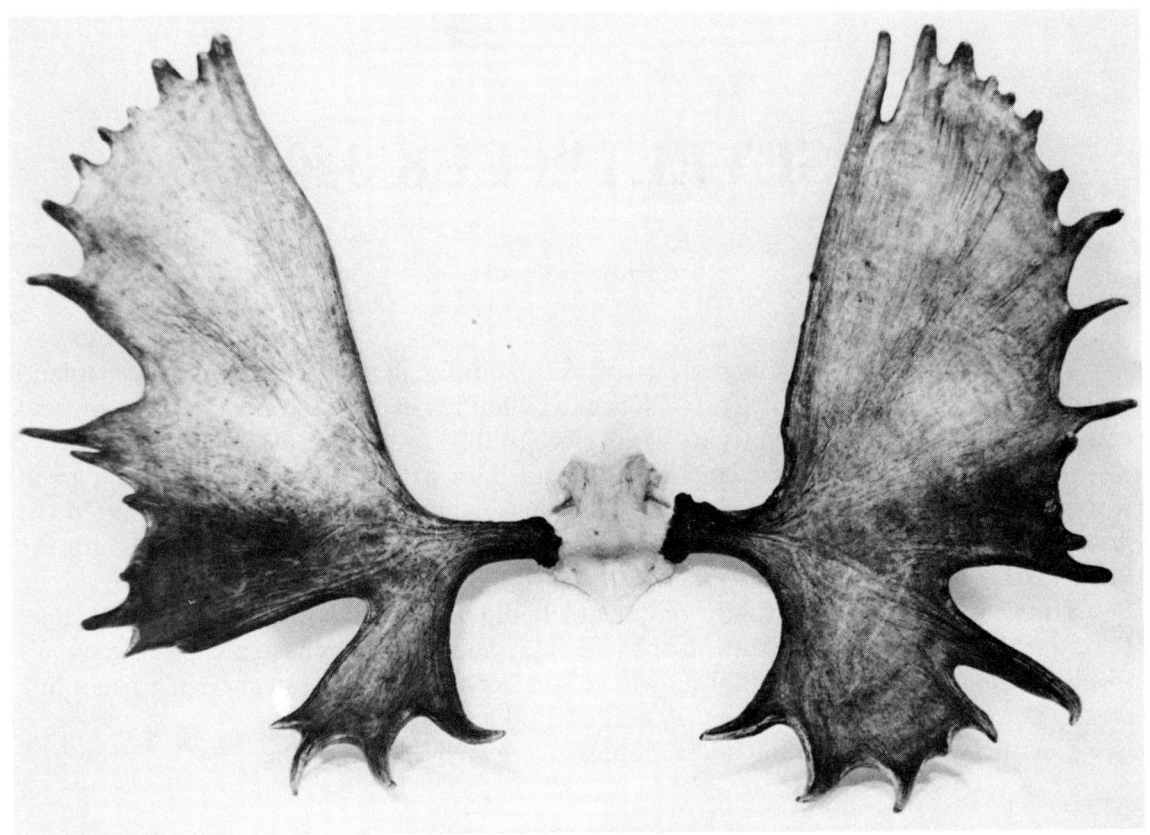

Photograph by Wm. H. Nesbitt

NEW WORLD'S RECORD CANADA MOOSE
FIRST AWARD
SCORE: 242
Locality: Grayling River, B. C.   Date: October 1980
Hunter: Michael E. Laub

CANADA MOOSE 242

Michael E. Laub

On October 10, 1980, my childhood dream of a big-game wilderness hunt came true. My friend, Sal Casino, had asked me to join him and his hunting buddy, Angelo Brocatello, on a moose and grizzly bear hunt in British Columbia. As a child of nine, my dad had started taking me hunting for deer on our property in Pennsylvania. I am now 40 and I have taken many whitetails over the years.

I was anxious about my adventure and prepared myself mentally for four months. I even went horseback riding at the stable near my home to get my butt calloused a little. To my surprise, it didn't matter. I had many sleepless nights thinking about the dangers of the bears. As it turned out, the most dangerous part was riding the horses through the rough terrain. If a person gets hurt out there, it is pretty tough getting a plane or other transportation in to get him out. Many times we had to blaze a trail through the thick brush and woods with a hatchet.

On October 10th we left Kennedy Airport in New York for Toronto. We then flew to Fort Nelson with various stops on the way. In Fort Nelson, we were met by Gil Weins' wife. Gil was our outfitter but was out at the campsite, about a half-hour away by Piper Cub.

The small plane landed on an airstrip about 300 yards long at Vizer Creek, British Columbia. In addition to being nervous about the hunt, I was afraid of flying. After October 10th I was cured of that fear. I was most impressed when we landed. Two hunters from Wyoming were going home with nice moose racks. I had been expecting to see herds of moose running by, and I would just pick out the one I wanted. Was I naive!

Gil Weins and his three Indian guides took us to our camp through the muddy trail; there are lots of mud streams in British Columbia. Our quarters were what I had expected: a tent which slept three, with a wood-burning stove to keep warm. We were surrounded by horses and howling wolves at night. The first night I lay awake with my 300 Savage at my side.

The first day out was tough on my legs and butt. I grimaced in pain from eight hours in the saddle and swore a lot at the guides, but that was all part of the adventure. I loved riding back to camp in the moonlight. I drank water from the cold running streams, just as I had seen in western movies. I kept both a movie camera and a 35mm camera in my saddlebag and filmed our entire trip.

On our fifth day another hunter, Glen Deringer, from Saskatchewan, bagged a big grizzly, his prize coming on his last day. On October 19th, after a couple of days of fly-camping, we were pretty demoralized. We hadn't even seen a rabbit. I was able to call my wife Carol via short-wave radio to tell her of our misfortune.

After I spoke to my wife, Sal and I went out again with our Indian guides. We had lunch around a lake, and then we split up. My guide, George, was on the trail of a moose. We got to the top of a mountain and looked down. To my surprise I saw a bull, just grazing with his horns glittering in the sun. The moose was at least 400 yards away, so we began the descent on our horses.

I was so excited; but, I didn't realize how big the bull was because I had never seen a moose before. I started shooting at 350 yards, but the shots were not even coming close. We kept moving down the mountain and I stopped again to shoot, but missed again. The moose took off into the brush and we continued down the mountain. I then saw the moose standing, his back toward me in the thick, high grass at about 250 yards. I shot, hitting it in the left rear leg. He went down, got up again, and moved off. We got on our horses and galloped through the brush. We were behind and above the moose, the sun to our back. I was now 25 feet from my moose. I grabbed my rifle out of its scabbard and downed him with a shot right through the head with my last bullet.

We then set about dressing it, chopped the rack off, and butchered some meat. Since we only had one pack horse with us, we couldn't take too much meat. The rest probably would go to the bears.

George was so excited that he jumped up and down like a little boy. He knew what I didn't, that this was a world-record sized moose.

Then, we heard shooting on the other side of the mountain. As we made our way up the mountain to see what luck Sal or Bronk had, George realized he had left his binoculars behind. I took the packhorse up the mountain while George said he would meet me at the top. The trail was rough, so I took a side trail. I waited on top for George but he didn't show up for 40 minutes. I had no bullets left and it was getting dark. I was scared, not knowing if George would find me. I had my whistle and I started blowing it. George appeared just above me.

We met Bronk who had just bagged a moose. I then realized why George was so excited about mine. Bronk's moose had a 52-inch spread; mine was 64-3/4 inches.

We only had one packhorse, so we left the meat and both racks to be picked up the next day in the midst of a snow storm. (That was a sight seeing those horns making their way through the snow-filled mountains and woods.) On the way back, Sal was crossing a bridge to our camp when his horse lost its footing and dumped Sal into the water. My adventure was complete, but the excitement has never ended.

Photos Courtesy of Kevin P. Price and Pravomil (Milo) Raichl

Two fine trophies and two happy hunters. From left, Kevin P. Price was hunting on White Mountain, Utah, when he found his mule deer that scores 199-4/8 points. Pravomil (Milo) Raichl was hunting near Saddle Mtn. in Clatsop Co., Oregon, when he shot his huge Roosevelt's elk bull in 1959. Years later, when a category was established for Roosevelt's elk, Raichl's trophy was recognized as the new world's record.

Photo Courtesy of Bart Hofmann

Bart Hofmann was hunting in the Sawtooth Wilderness of Blaine Co., Idaho, in October of 1980 when he found this fine mule deer. The big buck scores 197-2/8 points.

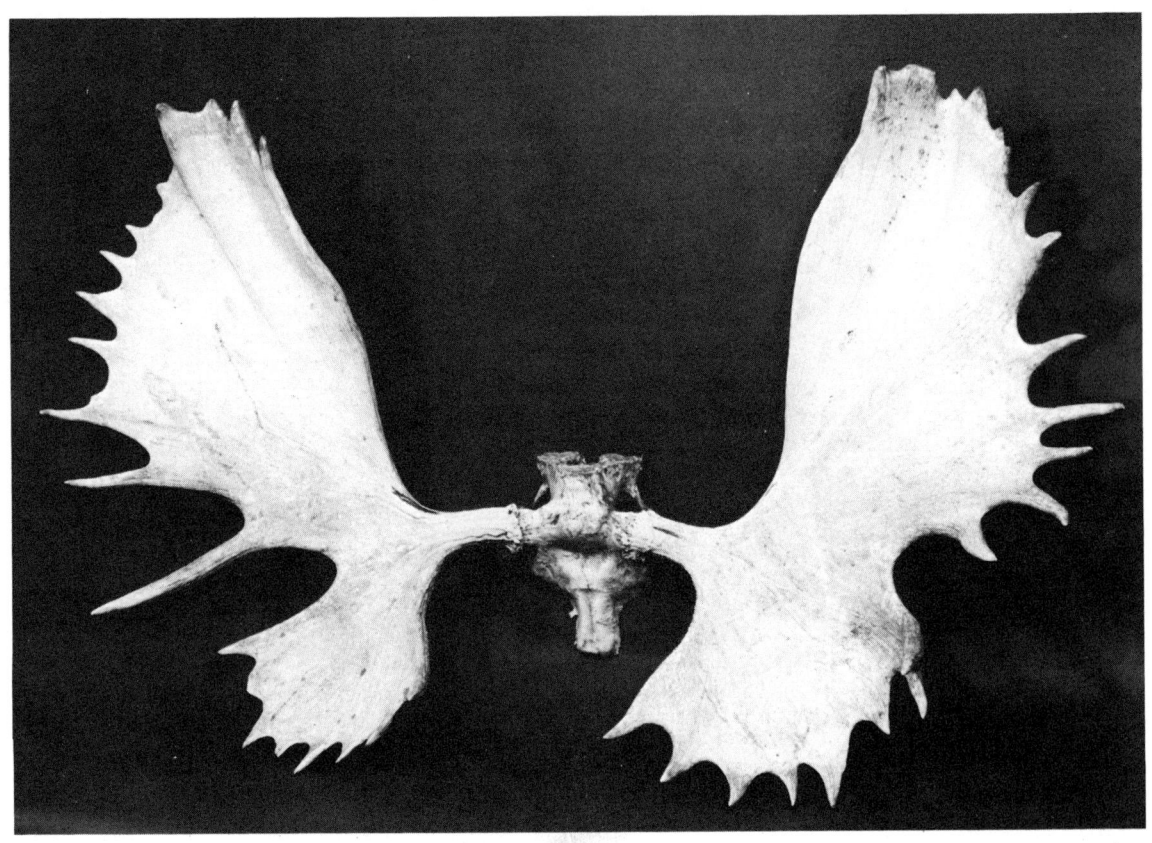

Photograph by Wm. H. Nesbitt

CANADA MOOSE
SECOND AWARD
SCORE: 240-2/8
Locality: Teslin River, B. C.   Date: September 1982
Hunter: Albertoni Ferruccio

CANADA MOOSE 240-2/8

Albertoni Ferruccio

My hunt took place in the Cassiar Mountains of Northern British Columbia. We were about 100 miles south of the Yukon/B. C. border, in the Glen Kilgour hunting area of Region 6. On August 31, 1982, I left Watson Lake, Yukon, with my hunting companions Urs, Kurt and Adolf by means of a float plane. We reached Kilgour Lake (alt. 400 feet) at around midday. The camp was very well organized, and there were 15 horses at our disposal. It was planned that Kurt and I would hunt in the immediate area, while the others would go on horseback for a day to reach another camp. We were in a remote, untouched and fantastically beautiful land. I felt as if I had returned back in time. This sensation increased day by day during my stay.

In the afternoon, we carried out a shooting test. My rifle was a Mauser 375 H & H Magnum using Remington 270 grain soft point bullets. I had been advised to use such a large caliber because of the danger of grizzly bears. I got tags for moose, caribou, grizzly bear and wolves. My greatest ambition, however, was to bag a bull moose which I had only seen in pictures.

On September 1st, at 8:30 a.m., I started my first day of 21 days hunting. I set out with my 21-year old Indian guide, Joseph Allick, on horseback. I had heard that his father had been the best guide in the country. It was drizzling when we started, and the rain gradually increased in intensity. We made our way to a hill in typical moose country. Once there, we roamed up and down, through pine trees and streams, carefully looking everywhere for game. The visibility was becoming steadily worse but did not prevent Joseph's sharp eyes from spotting two bull moose on a hill in front of us, a few miles away in a small glade. I could not make them out.

We advanced on foot in a direct line to a knoll about 500 yards away, which gave us a better viewpoint. The bulls were still there, but they disappeared and then reappeared again. This took about a half-hour, and in the meantime, the weather was getting even worse. This was the moment it seemed appropriate to have a spot of lunch. As it was still raining heavily after lunch, we decided to return to camp and revisit the same place on the morrow.

Kurt and his guide, Martin Lamoureux, returned to camp at around 7:00 p.m. They had been luckier than us, having taken a good moose trophy. The next morning the weather had improved, no rain but it was cloudy.

Returning to the same hill, hoping to see the two bulls again, we were delighted to pick them out once more. We descended the hill and made our way to another. The going was uphill and tough. I experienced mounting excitement as the time passed by and the quarry became nearer. Joseph also seemed to sense this and smiled at me. After about an hour we almost reached the hilltop. There we stopped and tethered the horses. Here I prepared my rifle and began cautiously making the final approach. Joseph seemed very sure of himself and was to show exceptional intuition. After about a half-hour, we spotted a bull lying down at a range of about 250 yards. Partially obscured by brush, we could make out the head and antlers, from which Joseph deduced that it was not our prize. Squatting behind a large rock, we observed this bull continuously. There was a pallid sun in the sky, with intermittent drizzle.

After about a half-hour, the bull rose to its feet and remained without moving. To me, who had never seen a moose before in the wild, its bulk seemed enormous, as indeed it was. In order to make the bull move, we started to whistle and shout. It took a few minutes for it to understand something was wrong and move off. As this happened, we had a surprise. Its companion rose to its feet about 40 yards away on the left. We only glimpsed them for a few seconds before they dissolved into the woods. Without warning, Joseph told me to ready myself pointing out the boundary of the wood at almost the summit of the hill.

After a few minutes, the two bulls appeared in the open walking slowly towards our right, one behind the other, about 20 yards apart. The range was perhaps 400 yards. Joseph urged me to shoot at the leading bull; but for me this was quite impossible. I was unable to focus it well and in order to aim at it, I had to climb up on the rock, where I obviously had no arm support, and where I was also unstable on my feet. Meanwhile, the bull had stopped in its tracks. I could not shoot. Shooting at that range and under those conditions, I would have only risked wounding the animal, for which I could not have forgiven myself. All this happened in a few moments. Then, both moose disappeared into the pine woods. We returned to our horses without saying a word. We then had some lunch. Joseph seemed out-of-sorts with me for not attempting a shot and remained a bit taciturn. Afterwards, he told me that the bull was a very good trophy and such opportunities happened very seldom.

After a very brief lunch we continued riding to the top of the hill and went towards our right, carefully looking above all at the glades in the woods below us. Joseph was riding about 60 yards in front of me. After about three-quarters of an hour, he pulled his horse to a stop. I joined him and was glad to see that he was calm again. He told me that he had found two bulls a little lower down the slope. They were not the same pair of bulls that we had seen previously. We quickly reached the cover of the woods and tethered our horses. The two bulls were very near us now.

Edging carefully forward for about ten minutes, we reached the boundary of a large flat glade between two pine woods. The two bulls were standing almost at the other extremity of the glade, at an approximate range of 300 yards. They were side-by-side, quite close together, and seemed to be at ease. "Take the one on the left!" Joseph whispered.

Strangely, now that the great moment had come, I felt quite calm and collected. The only available means of arm support was a small dry pine, but that was sufficient. I took careful aim and almost at once pressed the trigger. "Click." I had made the classic mistake of leaving the safety catch on! I quickly fired again. The bull remained almost immovable but reared ever so slightly and moved a little back, remaining firmly on its feet. I fired twice more, shooting free-standing because I was so elated by my first shot which I was sure had struck home. Still, the bull did not collapse but started instead to drag itself slowly towards the woods about 20 yards away. As he was moving away, I fired a final round, still free-standing. As soon as the bull entered the woods, it still made a few steps and then collapsed. Then it started to whirl its antlers like a windmill. After a few minutes it remained motionless.

The date was September 2nd, 1982 and the time was around 3:00 p.m. The location was near the headwaters of the Teslin River. Now I was very happy, and strong emotion filled me. My heart seemed ready to burst out of my chest. Joseph was triumphant. As we approached the woods he told me that in his career as a guide he had never seen such a large bull and that he was as happy as I.

Just before we reached the woods, we saw, about 60 yards away on our right, the other moose. After the first shot, he had speedily gone away and now had returned. It would have been a mediocre trophy. He noticed us and started to move away. I managed to get a bit nearer, perhaps 10 yards, and took a couple of photographs.

We then entered the wood and there was my bull. It was of immense size and a truly splendid trophy. Its antlers were just out of velvet, showing a few small residues on the inner palms. I looked at it in ecstasy for some seconds, in silence. Joseph was exultant. He said that the spread of the antlers was over 60 inches. We then took some photographs, which finished the roll of film.

I went to collect the horses and then we began the skinning. Joseph did the cutting and I assisted him. This was difficult and took quite a long time due to the animal's size. After a summary butchering, the head was detached along with the skin up to the shoulders. While doing the skinning, we discussed the shots I had made. The first shot, just on the shoulder, was a little below the point I had aimed at. I had underestimated the range by about 80 yards. Nevertheless, it had been the decisive shot, striking vital spots. We recovered the bullet. In that environment I found it difficult to evaluate the range, perhaps because of the light effect. Probably, the size of the animal had also deceived me. We did not investigate the result of the other three shots, mainly because of the impossibility of turning over this great mass of weight.

Meantime, our horses, which had been left just outside the wood, suddenly became restless. Taking my rifle I went to see what was wrong. The reason turned out to be that the other bull had returned, perhaps in search of its companion. In any case, it did not seem to be in a friendly mood. It was about 30 yards distant from me when it started to go away. I would have like to take some clear photographs but unfortunately, I still had not changed the film.

It was almost 6:00 p.m. when we decided to go back to camp. We would have to return the next day with an extra horse in order to complete the skinning and carry home the trophy.

We arrived back in camp at around 8:00 p.m., as it was growing dark. I was very tired and mighty hungry as well. I appreciated the delicious and savory supper of moose meat (the moose shot by Kurt) that was cooked by Sharon, the pretty wife of guide Martin.

The next day we all admired the fantastic trophy. The spread of its antlers measured almost 67 inches. Martin said it was the biggest that he had ever seen in that vast area. We had no idea at that time that it would turn out to be one of the largest trophies of the Canada moose category to be officially recognized. During the remaining days I saw only a few moose, including a cow, as I was hunting predominantly in caribou country.

After ten days, we returned to where I had made the kill hoping to find that the carcass had attracted grizzly bear, but no tracks were in evidence. However, we did see wolf signs. All the meat had disappeared.

I saw a lot of caribou but only a few with reasonable antlers. However, on the third-to-last day I managed to bag a good trophy.

My hunt ended on September 20th, 1982. My only regret was that I had not seen a grizzly bear. But I did see some wolverine and a wolf that did not give me enough time to fire.

Apart from the trophies bagged, I had a marvelous and unforgettable experience, and was also lucky with the weather.

I was most impressed by the great competence and seriousness of Glen Kilgour and all his staff for the helpful advice and friendliness they showed me; and, for this I sincerely thank them.

Flying back to Switzerland, reading an American hunting magazine, I knew that the present world record for the Canada moose was obtained in 1914. Reflecting on the unbelievable luck I had enjoyed on my first hunting trip outside Europe, I felt a little guilty in front of the numerous North American hunters. As I read, they spend a lot of time and money hoping to bag a trophy such as mine.

Photos Courtesy of John C. Burman and Wm. H. Nesbitt

(Left) John C. Burman was hunting in Marsh Creek of Elko Co., Nevada, in October 1980 when he shot this fine mule deer that scores 196-2/8 points with a minor subtraction for two abnormal points. (Right) Jack Reneau, Asst. Secretary of the Boone and Crockett Club's Records Committee, admires the fine Coues' deer shot by Jay M. Gates III that received Second Award at the 18th Awards, 1983.

Photo Courtesy of Robert D. Nolin

Robert D. Nolin shot this good Wyoming moose in Grimms Meadow of Lincoln Co., Montana, in September 1979. Nolin's bull scores 155-5/8.

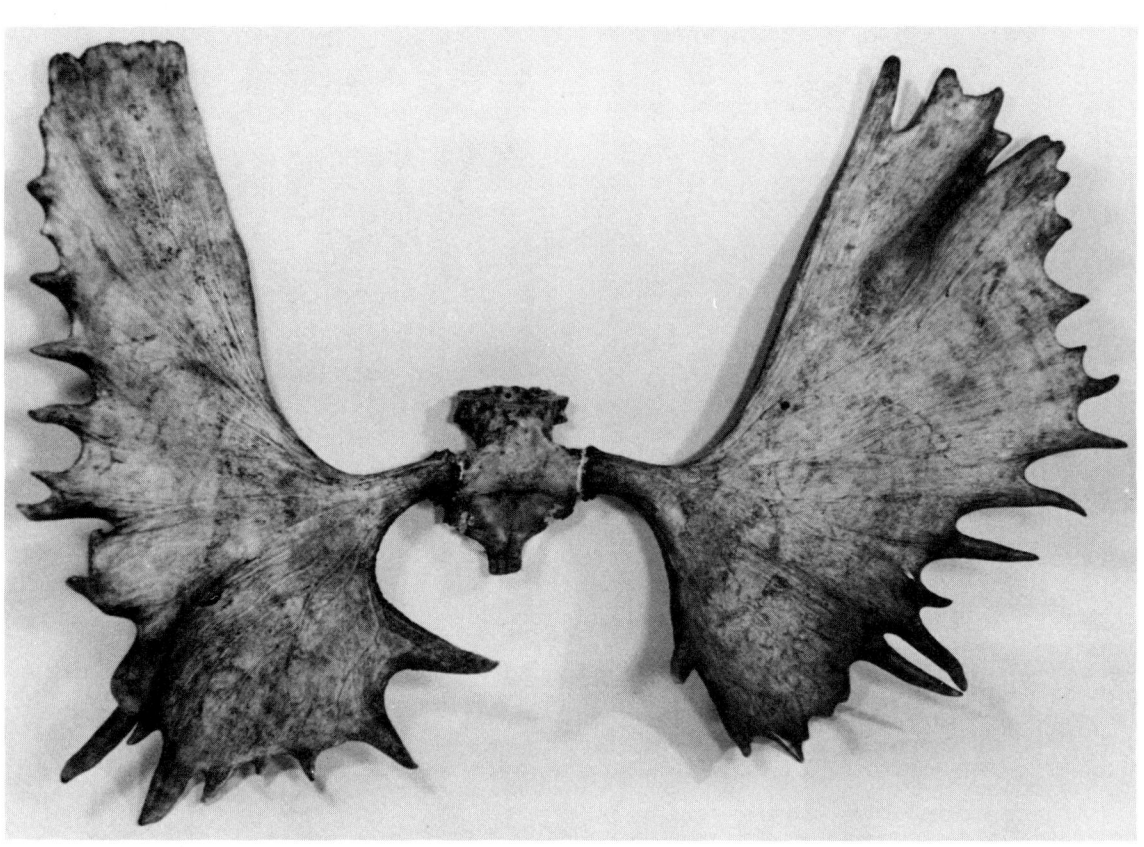

Photograph by Wm. H. Nesbitt

CANADA MOOSE
THIRD AWARD
SCORE: 216-1/8
Locality: Dease Lake, B. C.   Date: September 1981
Hunter: George A. (Sandy) Sinclair

CANADA MOOSE 216-1/8

George A. (Sandy) Sinclair

My lucky moose was the third I've shot. The first was with Herb Anderson and it was shot at Fox Creek, Alberta. It scored a whopping 180 points and weighed almost 1,700 pounds on the hoof. The second was with Ross Mann and Brad Wilkerson. We were hunting elk in the Kootenays but ended up getting a one-antlered bull moose and four deer. At night, while we were heavy into crazy eights, we fantasized flying into some remote lake and hunting big moose and caribou. It sounded so good we made plans for the next year's hunt.

We ended up with a party of four, Ross Mann, Ted Marson, Bill Walton and me. We reserved flights for the second week in September, with a return ten days later. On September the 11th, we caught the first ferry from Vancouver Island and started driving north. I had two 45 gallon drums for gas in my pickup and Ted had all the gear in his truck. The last 300 miles to Dease Lake was gravel road. The bumps were so bad my false teeth were chattering.

We were booked to fly out at 10:00 a.m. the next morning. But, when we got to the plane dock, Cameron (the pilot) said the ceiling was too low so we would have to wait. What a disappointment. We came back later and persuaded the pilot to try taking only Ted and Bill. Ross and I watched as they flew off low over the mountains and out of sight. We turned to each other and expressed our eagerness to get out there. Just then we could hear the plane motoring back. Too socked-in, drat!

We waited around a couple of hours and they tried again. This time, they were gone close to an hour. We thought for sure they'd made it, but wait, there's still three heads in that plane and six white eyes. Boy, were they shook up! The pilot told us they were just coming up to the lake when a down draft threw them down, pinning them all to the ceiling. The pilot pulled her up and headed back. He said he hadn't felt one like that for years.

So, the choice was ours, wait till tomorrow or take another lake. The pilot suggested a lake where he had seen moose, so we took it. I promised the group I'd keep the name a secret, but I can tell you it was west of Dease Lake.

We landed on the lake a short time later, unloaded the gear and started to work. The plane left and all of a sudden the silence and solitude were there, no one for miles. Everything was wet and mushy, so we got set up and went straight to bed after setting-up camp.

During the night I was awakened by a grunting, snorting sound. So I swung my arm over, hit poor Ross in the stomach and yelled "Bear!" Ross flung himself up and turned his head to hear. It was only Ted's snoring.

We got up about 9:00 a.m. It was still drizzling. All of us headed out in different directions and all came back wet and cold. No one saw anything. Boy, was this our great hunt?

Well, the next day we did get up early. The weather was better and we were optimistic. We got in the rubber raft and headed down the lake. The going was rough with four in the boat, so I got out and they went further down the lake.

I checked the wind and headed into it, up a hill. When I got to the top, I looked around and down. About that soon, I saw one-half of a moose rack. I moved over a bit to see better. It was a huge moose rack with the moose still attached! I knelt down on the rock and brought my Parker Hale 7 mm Remington magnum up to my eye to get a better look through my Redfield 3 x 9 power variable scope. Yes, he was a beauty.

I Accutracked him in at only 250 yards. I looked again and fired. It was all over. I walked over to my moose and fired one more shot to ensure the kill. As I was struggling to field-dress it, I heard some shots. The others must have found something.

After finishing up and punching my game tag, I started down the hill with the head and rack. The others were coming up to see what I got. Their chins dropped. Ross said right away, "It's book". Bill had gotten a young bull. After getting all the meat back to camp we had a good meal by the fire.

Ray Wilson flew in that day, alone, and camped by us. He was planning to get the world record moose with a bow. If he'd shot mine, he would have made it. He has a goat and a black bear in the book. He measured my moose at 221 points. Wilf Klingsat measured it officially after the drying period at 217-4/8.

The next day while the others were out hunting for more moose, I fixed up camp and built our meat pole. That's when I decided I was going after caribou. They told me not to but I was going anyway. It just seemed too easy.

The next morning I put on my 50-pound pack and started for the plateau alone. I walked 13 miles across two streams, hills and buck brush. I even had to crawl across one muskeg bog. I got to the plateau the next day and camped.

The next morning I decided to go out onto the plateau just for a look. I went light and only took my rifle, five cartridges and glasses. After going two miles, I stopped, thinking I'd better get back as the plane was coming the next day. But wait, something moved.

I looked through the glasses to see a couple of caribou crossing the valley. I started toward them. I went about a mile and saw a herd of about 200, some lying and some standing. I got as close as I thought I could, about 450 yards. I picked out a nice bull and fired. I missed him. I fired three more shots and he went down. The herd barely moved. I got closer and he got up. I only had one bullet. But what about bears? My fear of bears seemed to be gone, so I finished him off. It was a nice double shovel.

I caped the caribou out and started back to get my pack and bullets, when there he was. A beautiful, shining, silver-tip grizzly, running across in front of me about 600 yards away. I watched a bit, then started around the other way at a trot. He disappeared.

There was a creek bed ahead so I stopped and followed it up with my glasses. They ended up right on the bear, standing on his hind legs, looking at me about 70 yards away. God help me, no bullets! He was sniffing the air and my hands were covered in blood. I froze. He sniffed and looked, and then he laid down. I wasn't going to pass up the opportunity so I ran.

Every time I ran, he sat up and looked. Finally, off I went nonstop for three miles back to my camp. While stuffing my tent and other gear in my pack, I watched the bear rolling the caribou over. That was one meal he wouldn't have to fight for. I was so spooked I almost ran back to the main camp, but I collapsed only a half-mile away. It was dark, so I couldn't go on. I rolled myself up in my tent and fell asleep.

The next day I made my way into camp just as the first plane was taking off. Ross had shot a moose scoring 180-4/8 and Ted shot one totaling 190-3/8 while I was gone. It took three flights to get our 2,000 pounds of meat out.

I looked at my grizzly bear tag, thinking to myself what a trip this could have been if I only had taken my pack with my bullets. But, who could complain with a moose like that. I can only thank God I'm alive and give Him the glory for the honor of being able to take home such a beautiful specimen.

Photograph by Wm. H. Nesbitt

CANADA MOOSE
HONORABLE MENTION
SCORE: 199
Locality: Trout Lake, B. C.   Date: September 1982
Hunter: William R. (Bill) Lee

CANADA MOOSE 199

William R. (Bill) Lee

My ten-day Canada moose hunt started September 1, 1982 with a drive from my home in Chehalis, Washington, to Vancouver, British Columbia. From B. C., I flew to Whitehorse in the Yukon Territory. From there, we travelled by float-plane to Line Lake, a base camp out of Atlin in Northern British Columbia. The hunt was handled by Wynn's Outfitters Ltd. (Barrett Wynn, owner), who headquarters during the season in Atlin.

My guide, Hank Foley, is an experienced horseman; I am not! Our first day out was a 20-mile ride to an area near Trout Lake, where we set up a fly camp. The horseback ride was so miserable, I can't really describe it. My horse was large and wide, and my 60-year-old hips were not designed to be spread so far for so long! I often thought, "What am I doing here?"

After a long day, we set up camp. We were supplied with a rather new-looking tent; but, when the rains came, the seams all leaked. However, wet or not, I was pleased to be off the horse.

Each day, we rode and hiked several miles, particularly watching an area at the mouth of a river which flows into the north end of Trout Lake. We saw several cow moose during the week, but not a bull. With only two more hunting days left, I thought I was about to have another "dry run". Then, on the tenth day while watching the edge of the lake from a rock-covered knoll, I heard twigs break in the woods behind me. We stayed absolutely still for a few minutes. Soon, this magnificent animal came into view several hundred yards to my left and waded along the shoreline of the lake toward the mouth of the stream below us.

As the big bull veered across the mouth of the river, in shallow water toward the far shore, I fired just as he approached land. Luckily, he dropped immediately before reaching heavy brush.

There were no heroics - no charging bull - just the immense thrill all hunters feel when they get their animal. The big bull was so heavy that we had to quarter him to move him for cleaning and boning of the meat. Then, to avoid wasting any meat, I rode that damned horse those torturous 20 miles back to base camp to get more pack horses to carry the meat back to camp for the other guides and hunters to enjoy.

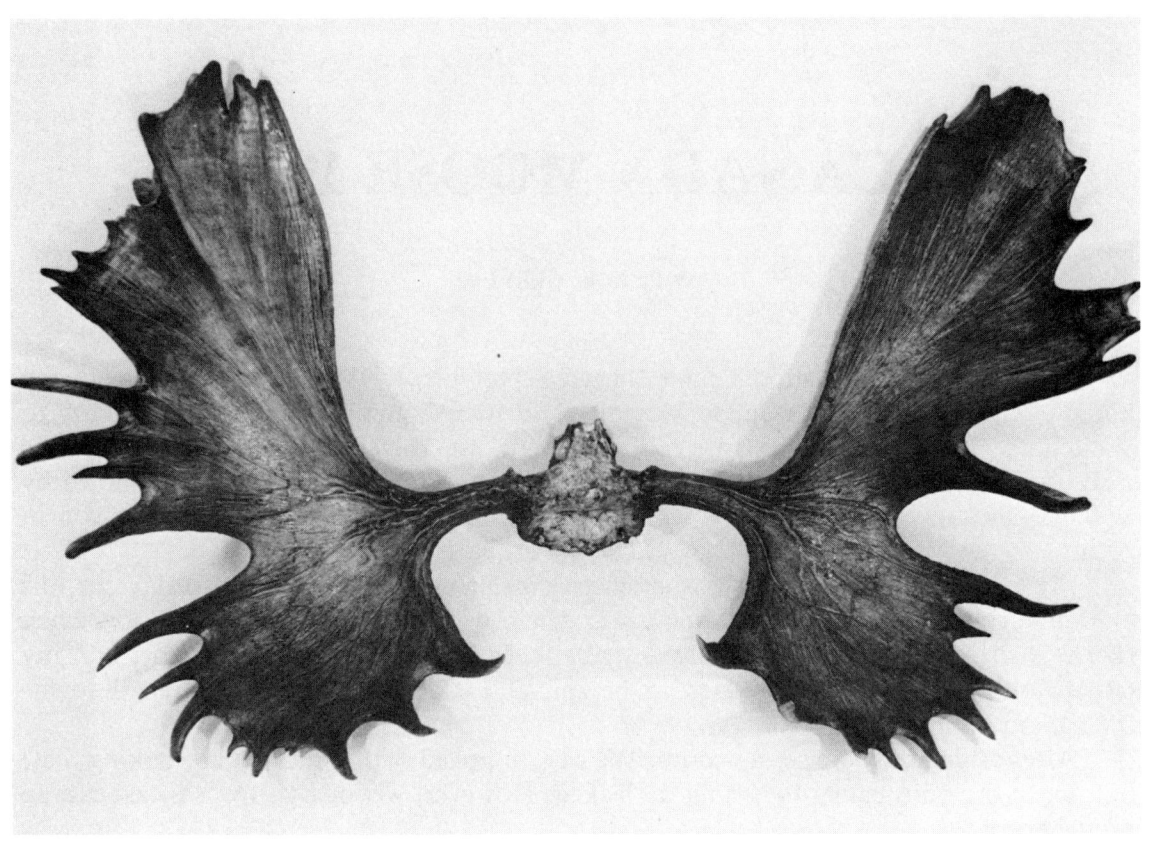

Photograph by Wm. H. Nesbitt

ALASKA-YUKON MOOSE
FIRST AWARD
SCORE: 242
Locality: Grass Lakes, Yukon Date: September 1981
Hunter: Melvin R. Spohn

ALASKA-YUKON MOOSE 242

Melvin R. Spohn

My hunt started in February 1981, when a friend of mine in the Chicago Chapter of Safari Club International told me he would not be able to make a hunt he and two other members had booked with Teslin Outfitters of Teslin, Yukon. He asked me if I would like to take his place. After thinking about it for a few weeks, I decided I would.

All the arrangements were made, and I waited for the summer to pass. We made a couple of trips to the rifle range that summer to check our rifles. I live about 50 miles from the Fox Valley Rifle Range where I shoot, so I was only able to practice a couple of times that summer. I load all my own ammo, and my shot groups were pretty good, so I felt real confident.

Finally, the big day came. We left Chicago on August 29, 1981, and flew to Vancouver, B. C. We all had high hopes and were really excited. My hunting partners were John Kotan and Richard Orban (also members of the Chicago Chapter of S.C.I.), and a good friend, Gene Stanley, of Hammond, Indiana. The next morning we left Vancouver for Watson Lake, arriving in the late afternoon. We checked into the Watson Lake Hotel and went for a walk around town.

Next morning we awoke to cloudy skies and rain. There was also a lot of smoke in the air from forest fires miles away. We checked in with the Watson Lake Flying Service and were informed that they were not flying due to the bad weather. We went to the local office of the D.N.R. to purchase our hunting licenses and seals. We checked with the flying service every two hours, but with no luck; a day lost to weather. The following afternoon the weather had cleared enough to fly. We left Watson Lake in a single engine Otter float plane. We headed north and slightly west to Fire Lake in the Simpson Range of the Pelly Mts., the location of our base camp. We were met by Doug Smarch, our outfitter; his wife, Jane; and four guides. We stowed our gear, had lunch, and checked our rifles. That night at dinner, we decided that Peter Fox, a guide with many years experience, would be my guide. John would be guided by Doug, and the four of us would hunt together. Dick, Gene, and Hans Georg Geisel, a hunter from Germany, would hunt together. They would leave the next day; my group would leave the day after. We hunted around the base camp the next day and saw some sheep, but no mature rams.

The next morning we left for the spike camp, planning to hunt our way to it. We rode all day, spotting only a few moose and caribou. John and Doug stalked one moose, but he gave us the slip. Towards evening it began to rain and sleet, so we had to pitch camp in the rain. Little did we know then that it would rain, sleet, or snow for the rest of the hunt. We made a fire and cooked dinner. It really hit the spot! Somehow, food always tastes 100% better when cooked and eaten in the great outdoors.

On September 4th we left camp in the rain and rode down a long valley. The going was real hard as there were no trails and the undergrowth was very thick. The horses really had to work hard. The ground was spongy and they had a hard time pulling their feet out. After a couple of miles we headed up and over a saddle to the next valley. Just beyond the saddle we stopped to have lunch and to do some glassing. Caribou! They seemed to be everywhere! They appeared in spots where a few minutes earlier there were none. At the head of the valley we spotted two bulls that looked real good, so we decided to make a stalk.

We started out riding until we ran out of cover. We tied the horses and took off on foot. We stalked to within 200 yards. Suddenly, the wind shifted and the caribou started to get real spooky. They started to move off. Quickly, I took a shot and hit one in the neck. He went down. He got up and I shot again. He went down again and stayed down. The other caribou took off around the mountain. John and Doug took off on horseback after them.

Peter and I climbed up to my bull. We took some pictures, then field-dressed and caped him. Later, I would find out that I had taken a Boone and Crockett mountain caribou that scored 393-1/8 points. What luck! John had caught up with the other caribou and made a good shot on a real nice bull. Both bulls were secured for the night as we would have to come back the next day with packhorses to retrieve the meat, hides and antlers.

The next morning we left camp with a couple of packhorses. The going was just as bad. It took all morning to reach the caribou and pack them up. We stopped on the way back to have lunch and do some spotting. We made a fire to warm up and have some hot soup and tea. Doug was looking through the spotting scope when he said he thought he saw a good moose about two miles away. We all took a look and agreed that he was a real good bull, but it was too late to go after him. We decided to go on to camp and give him a try in the morning. On September 6th, we awoke to very bad weather. We were socked-in by rain all day. We worked on the caribou capes and tried to dry our clothes and boots by the fire.

September 7th, my birthday, started out sunny and clear, so we left camp. John and Doug went back after the big moose while Peter and I went the other way. We rode all morning down a beautiful valley, around a crystal clear lake, and up a draw where Peter said he had seen sheep. The draw led up to a saddle. We stopped for lunch and while there spotted some sheep, but no rams. The skies were getting very dark. We climbed up into the saddle where we could see the next valley and the mountains around it. By now it was pouring rain again. We spotted a few caribou and more sheep, but no rams. We headed back to camp in the rain. A real wet birthday! Back at camp, we learned that John and Doug didn't have any luck.

It rained all night, but we awoke to a sunny, clear day. Peter and I left camp, crossed the river, and headed straight up. We reached a bench on the side of the mountain about three-fourths of the way up. We rode around the mountain on the flat bench, stopping to glass often. We spotted sheep across a valley, mostly ewes and lambs, and a couple of small rams. We spotted more sheep and lots of caribou. The caribou were at the top of the mountain in last year's snow, higher than the sheep. We crossed many berry patches as we rode and were very careful. We saw many signs of grizzly bear, although we did not actually see any bears. The bench led to a saddle between two mountains. We continued through the saddle to take a look in the next valley. It was beautiful with a long lake in the bottom. We stopped to have lunch and to do some glassing. We were unable to spot any game, so we decided to work our way down a little to improve our line of sight.

We came to a small ridge and tied up the horses. We set up the scope and started glassing. After glassing for an hour or so, my eyes got tired. I stopped for awhile and just took in the beauty of the valley. Nothing seemed to be moving. All of a sudden, I saw something move just up from the lake, about a mile-and-a-half away. I picked up the glasses and quickly tried to find what had moved. About 200 yards from the lake on the far side, I saw a bull moose in the tall dark timber. He was a giant and I could hardly tell Peter in my excitement. Peter couldn't see him at first. I set up the scope and he took a good look. He couldn't believe his eyes. The only thing he said for some time was, "Big Moose! Big Moose!" We watched the moose move slowly through the timber. He seemed to just glide. Finally, he laid down. Peter asked me if I wanted to go after him now because it was getting late, and we were still a long way from camp. I told him I wanted *that* moose *now*!

We worked our way down through the timber on our side to just above the lake. Peter said it would take too long to go around the lake, so we tied the horses in the timber and worked our way down to the edge of the lake. There was a point of land that extended out into the lake for 50 feet or so. We worked our way through the shoulder-high willows to the end of the point to cut down the length of the shot. We looked hard, but could not find the moose. Looking up into the timber was not as good as looking down into the timber.

Finally, Peter located one little point on one of the antlers. I looked and looked and even with all of Peter's directions, I just could not see that point. Peter told me to rest, and he directed me to a spot in the timber to shoot at. With the roar of the rifle, the moose stood up. All I could see were the antlers above the heavy ground cover. At least I knew he was there and which direction he was facing! I guessed about how far down to hold and fired three shots as fast as I could. After the third shot the antlers instantly disappeared. A loud crash sounded as he fell. We hurried back to the horses and rode around the lake.

Even with good landmarks we had a hard time finding him in the heavy undergrowth. We found him about 30 minutes later. What a moose! I couldn't believe my eyes! I couldn't believe that this was happening to me! Peter looked at me, shook my hand, and very calmly said, "Happy Birthday one day late." I then realized how he had wanted me to be successful the day before. If Peter had not found that one antler point in all that heavy growth, I would surely not have connected with this great moose.

We took some pictures. Since we did not have a measuring tape, we held a string and tied a knot at the widest point. Gutting him was a real job, he was so big and heavy. It had rained continuously since I shot him, and it continued to rain until we had retraced our route back to camp, arriving about midnight. Doug heard us ride in and was relieved that we had made it back. Peter and I ate and then sat around the fire celebrating our success with a bottle of scotch. Sleep came easy that night.

The next morning we woke to rain and fog. It was so bad that Doug decided not to go back after the moose until it cleared-up. We stayed in camp all day. After our tremendous ordeal the day before, the rest was a welcomed and much deserved break. I was worried about a bear getting into the moose and ruining it. Doug wasn't sure how big the moose was. Hunters and guides have a way of stretching the truth. After lunch, I remembered the string and got it out of my saddle bag. We put a tape to it and it measured almost 70 inches. Doug asked if we could have made a mistake with the string. In all his years, he had never seen a moose that big in this area. He decided that if the moose was that big, we should move the camp closer to the moose instead of moving the moose to our present camp.

The next day dawned cloudy, but dry. We packed camp and moved to the side of the lake I had shot from. As we were moving along the same bench, passing through the berry patches, I spotted a grizzly bear. It turned out to be a sow bear with two cubs. We just watched her as she led her cubs away. What a sight she was! Her long, dark fur rippled in the wind with every movement. Late in the day we finally reached the spot where we had tied the horses the day we stalked the moose. It was raining again and we had to pitch camp in the rain. John said he would stay in camp, get supper ready, and keep the fire going. Doug, Peter, and I went after my moose.

We rode around the lake again and it took us a few minutes to locate the moose. Doug couldn't believe his eyes! He proclaimed it a record moose. I started to get excited again! We took some more pictures, shook hands, and set about the task of caping, butchering, and boning the moose. About four hours later we returned to camp with the meat, hide, and antlers. The horses looked so small under their heavy, wide loads. Doug estimated that the shot must have been 400 to 450 yards, but a moose is a big target and not too hard to hit, even at that distance.

The next two days were spent mostly in camp, working on the moose. A couple of times a day we climbed the mountain behind camp to glass for sheep and bears. It rained and snowed during those two days so I was very content to stay close to camp and stay dry. I walked down to the lake a couple of times and did some fishing. I caught a few lake trout in the four to five pound category. They were delicious and a welcome change from meat.

We hunted hard the last few days looking for sheep and grizzly. We saw only ewes and lambs and one sow grizzly with cubs again. No more luck, but how much luck can one man have? Two Boone and Crockett animals on one hunt! Both trophies were later scored by John Batten, a good friend, a great hunter, and a gentleman. After John scored the moose, he said it was the largest moose he had ever seen. Coming from John, this was quite a compliment as John is a living "Hunting Legend".

On September 14th, we packed the horses, broke camp, and headed back to base camp. It rained all afternoon. Many times, we had to cut trees so the horse carrying the moose antlers could get through. I felt sorry for the horse and told Doug how I felt. He said the horse was strong, even though he was very old. His name was Scotty. Doug told me that Scotty was the last horse that Jack O'Connor had ridden in the Yukon. A very famous horse! We got back to base camp just before dark, soaking wet. Dick, Gene, Hans, and their guides, and Doug's wife, Jane, were surprised to see the big moose. Hand shakes were in order.

The 15th dawned clear and the plane arrived to take us back to Watson Lake. Doug and the guys were all kidding me that they would have to cut the antlers to get them in the plane. I told them the first one to touch those antlers would meet the same fate as the moose!

We flew back to Watson Lake. The local taxidermist, John Devries of Laird Basin Taxidermy, met the plane. I made arrangements with him to resalt the capes and dry them out, and then ship them, along with the antlers, to my home in Downers Grove, Illinois. What a hunt!

The following spring, I was notified by the National Rifle Association that my moose had won the Leatherstocking Award. A real honor! I also won the third award from S.C.I. for the America's category. Both awards were presented to me on the same weekend: the Leatherstocking in Philadelphia, Pennsylvania; and the S.C.I. Award in Las Vegas, Nevada. I became a proficient air traveler. It was a memorable weekend, recognizing a hunt not soon to be forgotten.

Photograph by Wm. H. Nesbitt

WYOMING MOOSE
FIRST AWARD
SCORE: 200-3/8

Locality: Lincoln Co., Wyo.   Date: September 1981
Hunter: Aldon L. Hale

WYOMING MOOSE 200-3/8

Aldon L. Hale

After applying for over 15 years for a permit to hunt moose in the great hunting state of Wyoming, I was beginning to feel Lady Luck was against me. It seemed like everyone else at one time or another had drawn a permit but me. Then one day it happened! As I pulled letters from my mail box, an unfamiliar, large and bulky business envelope dropped onto the floor. I noticed it was from the Wyoming Game and Fish Commission. I instinctively knew it contained my long awaited, coveted permit.

After anxiously waiting for some four months, the opening of the Wyoming moose season finally arrived. My hunting companions consisted of three older brothers: Ted, Lyle and Kay. Ted, who also had a moose permit and who had bagged a moose five years previously, was our appointed guide. He earned this distinction by being a big-game guide and outfitter in Wyoming for 28 years. Both of our permits were good for the Greys River-Salt River Drainage area in extreme western Wyoming, where the elevation ranges from 6,000 to 9,000 feet.

During the first three days of the hunt, our four-wheel drive vehicles covered dusty roads and trails to reach the willows and marsh that are feeding grounds of the Shiras moose. Having arrived at their habitat by daylight, their slow moving, bulky, black bodies soon attracted our attention. We were disappointed, however, when all of these turned out to be either small bulls, cows, or calves. Ted and I were both hunting for "horns", so we passed up these smaller trophies. After three days of hunting, and experiencing more hunters than moose, I decided to try a different location.

It was a few days later when I recollected stories from various hunting, hiking, and fishing acquaintances that had stopped at my sporting goods store, who reported sighting a huge bull moose that ranged in the Spring Creek area near the Wyoming-Idaho border. I visited with a few of them who had recently been in the area and decided that this bull hadn't yet been harvested. There was a distinct possibility that it still roamed there!

After two days of hunting, not a trace was to be found. Then one morning, Lyman Clark said that while deer hunting he had seen an extremely large moose and thought this might be the one I was after. At noon that same day, he and Steve (his father) and I saddled three riding horses, and loaded three packhorses, and began our four-mile ride up Pack String for the elusive "Big One".

The afternoon sun began to fade quickly and the farther we rode, the more the trail steepened and the elevation increased. Soon we were on the high ridge and a cool fall wind was blowing briskly. Reaching the top of the drainage area, we looked north into Spring Creek that overlooks the Afton-Star Valley area. The wind velocity began to increase and the temperature began to drop; truly "fall was in the air."

I positioned myself at a good vantage point, after tethering my horse and the three packhorses, while Steve and Lyman rode through some timbered areas. I was looking to the east, when from behind me I heard some loud grunting noises. As I turned around and looked across the canyon, the "Big One" was making his way slowly down the hillside. The grunting sounds came with each labored step. I watched him through my rifle scope until he lumbered out of sight. As I anxiously waited, two cow moose passed within 30 yards of me. A few minutes later the big moose again appeared coming directly toward me. As he trudged down the trail, his head was low and he was sniffing and following the scent of the two cows. My heart quickened and my muscles tightened as I watched him proceed closer and closer toward me.

After laboriously walking to within 50 yards of me, he raised his head as if sensing my presence. It was then that I squeezed the trigger of my 300 Magnum and the "Big One" dropped in his tracks, not taking another step. My hunt of a lifetime had come to an end.

The moose produced a few hundred pounds of tough, chewy, "shoe leather tasting" meat. However, the jerky we had made was excellent, beyond compare. Duane Hyde, Warden for the Wyoming Game and Fish Department, tentatively scored the moose at over 200 points. The biologists at the department studied the jawbone and estimated it to be 13-1/2 years old.

Photo Courtesy of Johnnie Kovac, Jr.

Johnnie Kovac, Jr. was hunting south of Mer Rouge in Morehouse Parish, Louisiana, in December 1979 when he shot this fine whitetail that scores 170-1/8 points, making the records book.

Photo Courtesy of Arden L. Peterson

Arden L. Peterson hunted the Seward Peninsula of Alaska in September 1979 where he found his prized bull. With a spread of 71-4/8 inches, this fine Alaska-Yukon moose scores 234-4/8 points. It was a heavy load to pack out; the rack weighs some 80 lbs.

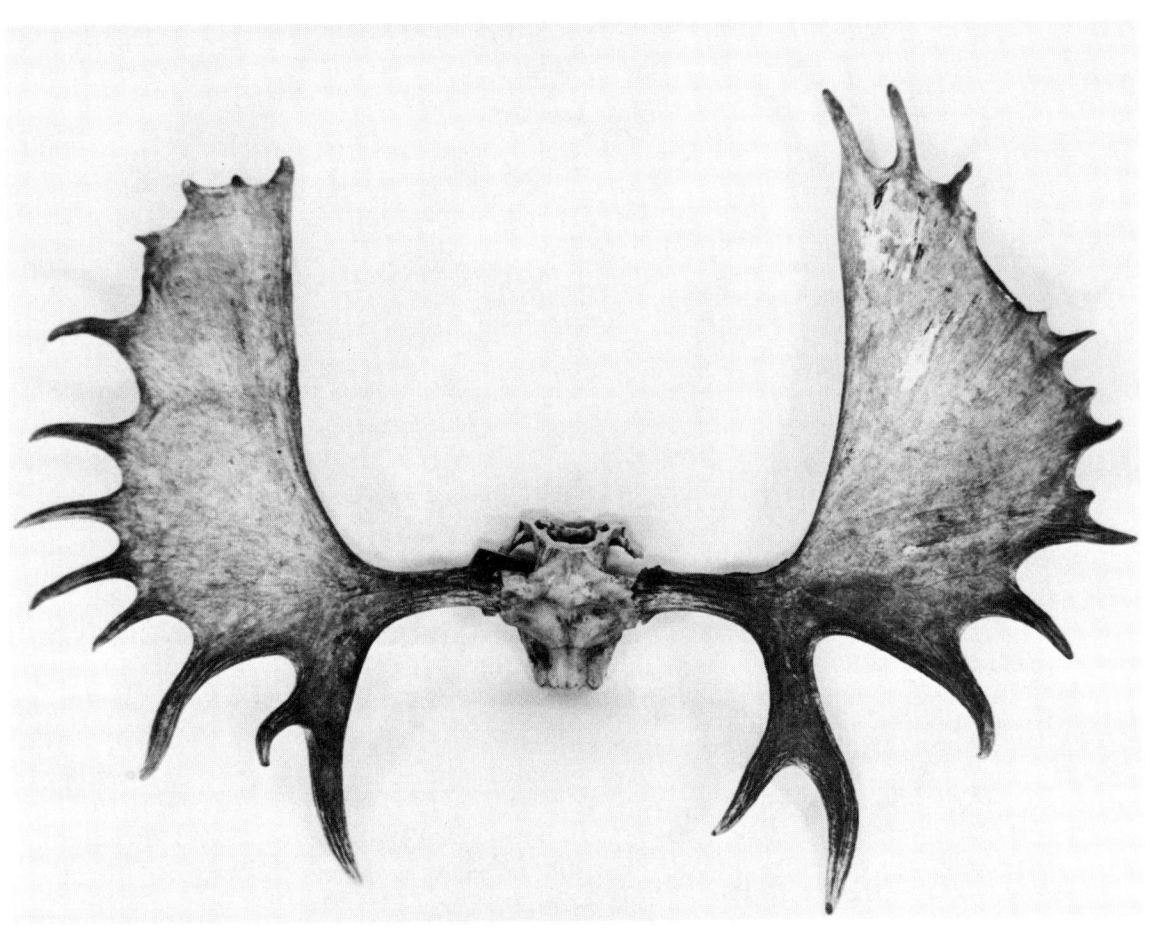

Photograph by Wm. H. Nesbitt

WYOMING MOOSE
SECOND AWARD
SCORE: 180-2/8
Locality: Weber Co., Utah   Date: October 1981
Hunter: Robert S. Mastronardi

WYOMING MOOSE 180-2/8

Robert S. Mastronardi

The hunt for my Wyoming moose took place on October 31st, 1981, on the South Fork of the Ogden River about 30 miles east of my hometown of Ogden, Utah. Along on the hunt were my son, Steven, who was 14 years old; my best friend and constant hunting partner, Ross Messerly; and a friend of Ross', Roydel Norris, whom I had met a few days earlier.

I am employed at Hill Air Force Base as a mason. While in the cafeteria one day, I saw Ron Meyers, a fellow I used to work with. Knowing that I like to hunt a lot, Ron asked what I had been hunting lately, and we went on talking. I mentioned that I had drawn a moose permit. There was a fellow having coffee with Ron, Doug Sorenson, whom I had seen but never met. Doug asked what area I had drawn. I told him and he said, "I'm going deer hunting in that area this weekend and I'll keep my eyes open for moose." Upon leaving, I told Doug to spot me a big bull. The next week, I was working on some freshly poured concrete when someone said, "Hey, I found your bull!" I looked up and it was Doug. He said he had seen several bulls while deer hunting, and one particularly large one, the largest he had ever seen. After he described the area where the large bull was spotted, I thanked Doug and he left.

I had a feeling of excitement after hearing the news. So, three days before the opening day, my partner, Ross, and I took off work to go do some looking. Leaving home early in the morning, we got to the area at daylight, left the paved road and headed into the hills. It had snowed the night before, leaving four to six inches, our first snow of the year. We had previously received a lot of rain, so the roads were slick and muddy. We spotted three or four cows and calves on the way up the mountain. After getting on top, the road travels parallel to the area below, where we were to hunt. Off quite a distance, in a different drainage, we glassed a small bull and a couple of cows. I knew I had to make a right turn from Doug's directions, so I took the first road I came to. This should take us to the upper part of the area we were looking for. As we went down the road, it started to drop off quite a bit. Finally, I came to a hill I knew I couldn't get back up without chains on my four-wheel drive. Since my chains were home in my garage, I turned around and went back to the top, continued to the next fork, and turned down again. This road was passable.

On the way down, a small bull crossed the road right in front of us and, going further, I saw a cow feeding. I got out of the truck and was about 40 yards away from her when I snapped her picture. She didn't mind at all. We were at the side of a large basin with pines at the top, dropping into aspen and further down oak brush. There were patches of chaparral here and there. This is a favorite diet for moose at this time of year. Glassing the basin, we spotted several moose, with two or three bulls that were of interest to me at the head of a basin about two miles across. The road we were previously following on top goes right to the head of this basin. I wanted to go over there and get a closer look at the bulls. Going back up the ridge, we stopped to look over some cows in another drainage we had looked at before. We looked for a bull but didn't see one, so we continued up.

All of a sudden, I caught movement about 300 - 400 yards across the hill. I stopped and looked - it was a cow coming out of the pines. Directly behind the cow came this large set of antlers. I knew I had found the bull I wanted and probably the one Doug had seen. We didn't even go look at the other bulls we had spotted. More snow had fallen by Saturday (the opening day) and I knew this was beneficial both for seeing fresh tracks and also large black bodies against the white blanket that covered the hills. Leaving for home, I had a lot of optimism. But, hunting is hunting and you never know how things will turn out. Being only 30 miles from home, we didn't plan on making a camp but to drive back and forth from home to hunt.

Opening day was to be a clear, sunny day. Ross was going to pick up Steven and me at four o'clock in the morning and we would meet Roydel at a local cafe. Ross' truck was equipped to haul a horse trailer, so he would drive his truck and haul our horses. My son and I rode with Roydel, who volunteered to take his truck because it was equipped with chains and a winch. When we reached the place where we would leave the pavement, we didn't try to drag the horses and trailer through the steep, muddy roads. We unloaded the horses and tied them up. All four of us got in Roydel's truck and took off. Half-way up the mountain, we had to put chains on the four-wheel drive to go any further. Arriving on top, about a half-hour before daylight, we had hot coffee and sweet rolls.

At daylight, we drove toward the area where we had seen the large bull. On the way there, a respectable-sized bull was feeding about 75 yards off the road. He raised his head and looked at us. What a temptation! But, I wanted the big bull we had seen. Stopping the truck a good distance from the canyon where we had seen the large bull three days earlier, Steven and I got out of the truck and walked down the hill, getting to a good vantage point so I could glass the canyon. No moose in sight; just my luck, I thought!

Continuing down the ridge brought us in view of the large basin we had glassed before. I looked down the canyon and saw a small bull and a couple of cows. While we glassed the moose, Ross and Roydel arrived. We were looking the valley over when, topping a hill about 1,000 yards away, a few moose came out of the trees. Ross said he had heard grunts over the hill, thinking it might be the large bull. Sure enough, out he came! I knew it was our bull and I figured we would have no trouble getting him. He was in an excellent place for a good stalk.

Steven and I went after him, while Ross and Roydel stayed back to watch. Dropping down the hill and then up the other side, put us about 125 yards away. The bull was facing away from us. After quite a long time, he finally turned broadside. My shot rang out and I looked at him. He was just standing there, so I fired another round. I looked again and he still stood there; but it looked like he was starting to move, so I fired a third shot. The bull laid down on the spot, probably dead from the first or second shot.

Two rounds from my Sako 7 mm Magnum loaded with 160 grain Speer handloads had entered the brisket right behind the shoulder. The third shot was a little forward and entered through the shoulder blade. After taking pictures (that didn't turn out well) and cleaning the bull, the chore of getting him out came next. I figured we would have to go back to get the horses, quarter him, and carry him out. I didn't know that Roydel had 3,000 feet of nylon rope in his truck. He said he had dragged elk out with it before. He hooked a snatch block to a clump of oak brush next to the road and we strung out the rope - all 3,000 feet. It just barely reached the moose. We attached the rope around the neck of the bull and started pulling with the truck. The moose just started to move when the rope broke. We cut the bull in half, just in front of the hind quarters, retied the broken rope and gave the signal to try again. The bull started sliding along.

Ross and I guided his antlers through the trees and brush. We had to go down the hill and then up the other side. I thought we wouldn't make it through all the aspen and the steep hill. After three or four rounds of breaking the rope and re-tying it, we finally got the first half up to the road. We then hauled the rope back to the hind quarters, hooked them up, and dragged them out. They were easier than the front half, since there were no antlers to worry about. This was a new way for me to bring out an animal, but it worked. We loaded the two halves in the truck and, after stopping to get the other truck with the horses, we left for home. We arrived at my house about two o'clock in the afternoon.

I found out later that there were three "record-book" bulls taken out of that area that year!

Photograph by Wm. H. Nesbitt

MOUNTAIN CARIBOU
FIRST AWARD
SCORE: 419-3/8
Locality: Mount Mye, Yukon   Date: August 1981
Hunter: Clark A. Johnson

MOUNTAIN CARIBOU 419-3/8

Clark A. Johnson

As Peter and I left spike camp just over two hours earlier, we had found it hard to believe that we were 13-1/2 days into my 16-day hunt. I was hunting with "Big Dan" Swank and his guide Ron Koser. Ron is the son of Werner Koser, who operates "Koser Outfitters" of Ross River, Yukon. I had hunted with Werner Koser along with three good friends from Somerset, Pennsylvania, in September of 1976. We hunted that year on Werner's northernmost camp around the Keele Peak area. That was the year! I was very fortunate in taking five beautiful trophies: a fine, full-curl Dall's sheep; a caribou; two wolves; and a 60-inch moose. My companions also did real well with grizzly, sheep, moose, and caribou. A first class hunt with excellent guides, food and quality game.

This hunt was different. We found that out as soon as Roy Hemminger, John Thomas, Big Dan, and I landed at Ross River. To our pleasant surprise, we were met by a beautiful, blonde young lady who took charge immediately. Monique turned out to be Ron Koser's wife and she doubled as Koser Outfitters' expediter at Ross River. She informed us in no uncertain terms that John and Roy were going to Keele Peak while Dan and I would hunt the Blind Creek area. We disliked splitting up but I assured my buddies that Werner was thinking of our best interests. My assurance turned out to be true, as we found out later. Dan and I said "So long, good luck-and we'll see you in 16 days".

Our fly-in took only 25 minutes to get us to "Pickup Mountain". Nestled at its base was a beautiful lake with only one way to land and just the reverse to take-off. No mistakes allowed! One need not worry, as it seems those pilots handle these problems as easy as a cabby driving a VW Bug. Looking down, we saw our guides, Ron and Peter Edzel, with the string of horses to take us to Blind Creek Camp. Watching them pack our gear, and the way they made us feel comfortable, assured us we again had first class guides. This assumption again turned out correct. They are Number One in my book! Two German hunters were taking the plane on its return to Ross River. Dan and I felt encouraged as they both had full-curl rams along with moose and caribou. We couldn't understand their language, but their smiles said it all. Two hours of riding brought us to base camp where Arno, the cook and wrangler, delighted Dan and me with moose steak, rice and gravy, bannock, and Jello topped off with fruit. Tomorrow we would start the hunt.

Next day started our hunt, as opposed to the many fantasies we had enjoyed after engaging Koser Outfitters almost two years prior. Dan's priority was Stone's sheep and grizzly; mine would be Stone's sheep and a caribou, if it were bigger than my 1976 bull. A great surprise lay in store that I would fully comprehend 13-1/2 days later. There were many spike camps, different areas, much game, but no kills until the fifth day when Dan took a real fine 400 lb. black bear. Two of our days were smoked-out, as the high areas were all but obscured. However, Peter and I did see 18 rams in one herd, but after our climb, we found only one trophy ram. We backed off after Peter recognized the very tight curl wouldn't exceed 35 inches. We saw moose of the 60-inch class but Dan and I would want one of these monarchs only if in record class. The days wore on and the midriff wore off.

Then, high anxiety on the evening of the 11th day. Ron and Dan returned to camp to announce they had spotted seven rams, three full-curl and one huge broomed ram. Dan had suggested to Ron, "Let's wait 'till tomorrow, pick up Clark and Peter and try for a double."

The longest day of our hunt started at 4:30 a.m. the next morning. The day was filled with the hardest riding (mostly leading) and climbing I have ever encountered. We returned to camp that night about 11:30 p.m. After enjoying sheep ribs and lots of hot tea, we hit the sleeping bags with the warm satisfaction of two ram capes outside our tent. The next day was recovery for Dan and me, as Ron and Peter finished taking care of the capes of our sheep.

We were then 13-1/2 days into our hunt when Peter saw a lone bull caribou about two miles up on Lone Mountain. When Peter got excited, I realized it just might be that special bull I wanted. Grabbing his spotting scope for a closer look and zeroing in, he said, "Maybe you should look". Peter couldn't mask his feelings and I knew my looking wasn't necessary. The antlers looked massive and he was alone. Of course at this distance, even with the scope, there was nothing for sure. A closer look? Let's go!

Fortunately, we were able to ride all but 500 yards of the stalk. The expertise of Peter will always be remembered on this stalk. He thought the bull, which had lain down earlier, might get up and feed out of range as it was about 2:30 p.m. He said, "We ride fast, we climb fast, we get close, decide, and then you don't miss." I wasn't sure if his words were advice or a threat! We did just that.

After leaving the horses in a blind ravine, we started our last 500 yards. After 400 yards, Peter crouched to almost all-fours and he motioned for me to do the same. With my nose next to his rump, I noticed he had his cigarette lighter out. Every few yards he would light it to check the air currents. Neither Peter nor I could see the bull for the last 70 yards. Not to worry as Peter's know-how now had us only 50 yards from the bull. As Peter slowly raised up, I did also. There, the tips of his velveted antlers started to show. We were below him and a few jumps would put a rock formation between him and us. I pointed toward my Weatherby 7 mm Mag. but Peter shook his head. He then crouched down to lead us in a circle to our left to put me above the bull and give me a clear shot.

I'll never know to this day why that bull didn't hear my heart thumping. After our little semicircle, Peter's lighter told us the bull would soon wind us for sure. All of a sudden, not more than 35 yards away, he came up on all fours in full view. I needed no second look to know he was record-class.

Instantly, I had the cross hairs on the heart area. I fired and missed! My sight through the scope had appeared clear, but the bullet's path wasn't and the bullet ricocheted. The bull whirled in a half-circle, took about two steps, and dropped dead with my second shot. The significance of those few seconds have reminded me time and time again of the need for an expert guide. Thank you, Peter. I don't believe there are words that can encompass the feeling between hunter and guide at that moment. The warm handshake and bearhugs are the outside dimension but the internal feelings are what are cherished and remembered forever.

We had our coldest temperature, about 15 degrees F., that August 29, 1981. The ride back to base camp was a little saddening. We would not be hunting any more in the rugged Anvil Range, just a little north of Faro, Yukon.

Photograph by Wm. H. Nesbitt

MOUNTAIN CARIBOU
SECOND AWARD
SCORE: 413-2/8
Locality: Livingstone, Yukon   Date: August 1977
Hunter: Mike J. Chirpich

MOUNTAIN CARIBOU 413-2/8

Mike J. Chirpich

It was my second hunting trip to the Yukon Territory. With three friends, Jimmy McKay and Larry Dossman of Houston, and Romeo Hinojosa of Alice, Texas, we proceeded to our hunting destination on horseback, with our guide, R. G. Hassard on August 16th, 1977.

We were camped ten miles east of Livingstone, Yukon, and the four of us were hunting Stone's sheep. After a successful sheep hunt, we proceeded to hunt other game.

On August 27th, we first spotted the caribou from our base camp with a spotting scope, and he looked good. The next day, Hassard and I decided to take a closer look.

After travelling for awhile, we stopped and had lunch at the bottom of a creek. A little over two hours later, we spotted the caribou again, lying down. We had overrun him, so Hassard was going to go around on the backside to throw rocks at him to get him up. He told me that if I thought the caribou looked good, and I wanted him, to take him.

The kill was made at approximately 75 yards with a 7 mm Weatherby Magnum. It wasn't until we returned to camp and started measuring him that we realized this caribou was records book size.

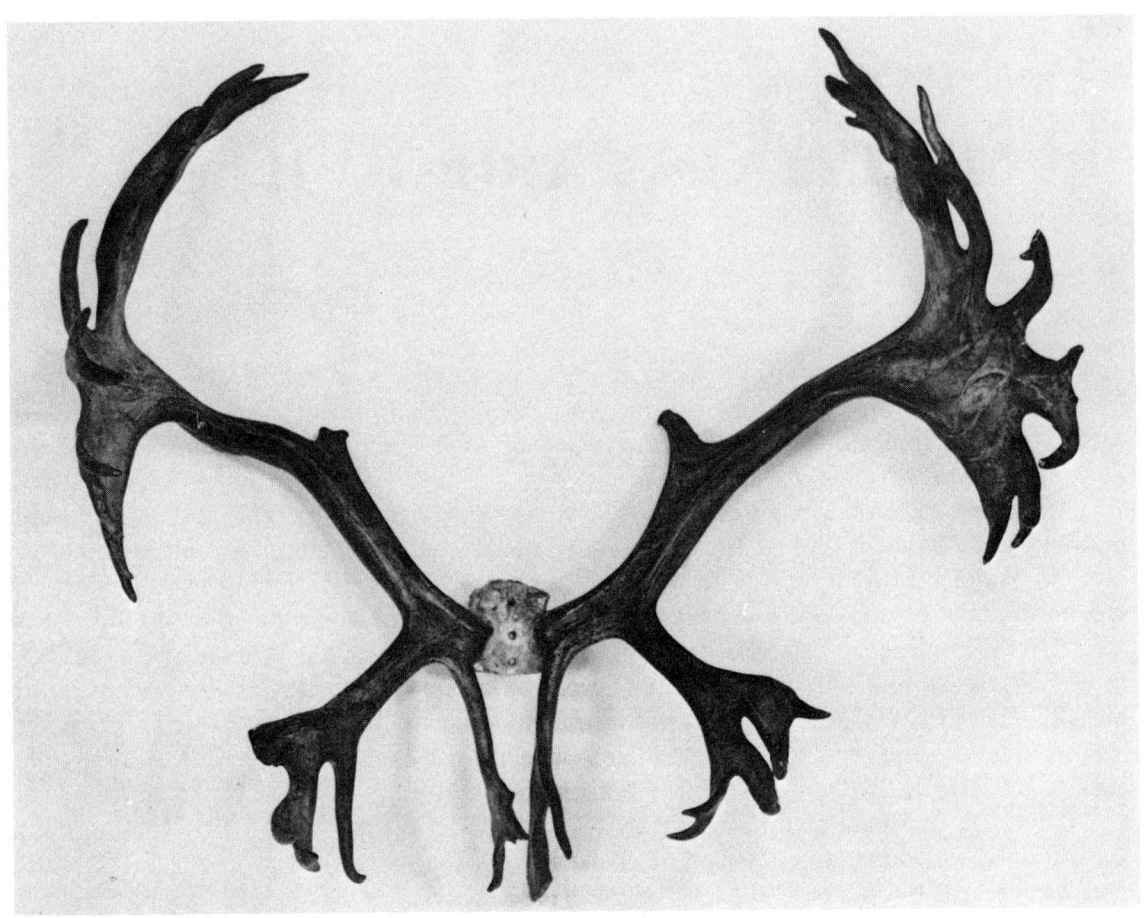

Photograph by Wm. H. Nesbitt

MOUNTAIN CARIBOU
CERTIFICATE OF MERIT
SCORE: 413-2/8
Locality: Nisutlin Lake, Yukon   Date: 1935
Hunter: James V. Bosco, Sr.   Owner: James V. Bosco, Jr.

MOUNTAIN CARIBOU 413-2/8

James V. Bosco, Jr., Owner

Like many of us, Dr. James V. Bosco, Jr. was fortunate enough to have a father who hunted and who passed-on his love of the outdoors. One of the most memorable hunts by the senior Bosco was for caribou in 1935 in the Yukon.

In those days, float planes were not yet a common means of travel, and the roads ended short distances from town. Horses were therefore used to get the party into the Pelly Mountains.

It was near Nisutlin Lake that Bosco found his big caribou. He was probably using his 270 Win. on this hunt. His guide told him that it was a very old caribou, and it sure was a big one.

Many years later, Dr. Bosco had his dad's trophy measured and found that it easily made the records book. In fact, it placed among the top few entered during the 18th Awards Entry Period. Its outstanding trophy character was recognized with the Certificate of Merit Award, due recognition for an outstanding trophy from yesteryear.

Photograph by Wm. H. Nesbitt

WOODLAND CARIBOU
FIRST AWARD
SCORE: 329-4/8

Locality: Robinsons River, Nfld.   Date: October 1980
Hunter: Timothy E. Fiedler

WOODLAND CARIBOU 329-4/8

Timothy E. Fiedler

It's a long way from Illinois to Newfoundland, but Timothy E. Fiedler relished each mile that brought him closer to hunting the beautiful woodland caribou.

Fiedler had booked his hunt for the fall of 1980 with Don MacInnis of Highlands, Newfoundland. He arrived in Newfoundland in early October to begin the final flight to the hunting area. They arrived near La Poile on October 4th. The next several days failed to produce the trophy they wanted. But, on the 8th, good fortune sent the caribou trophy of Fiedler's dreams.

The weather was overcast and very foggy, although it was already 10:30 a.m. They had worked their way to within 200 yards of the big caribou. It was time to take him. Fiedler's shot rang-out and he had a trophy to gladden any hunter's heart.

Photograph by Wm. H. Nesbitt

WOODLAND CARIBOU
SECOND AWARD
SCORE: 322-2/8

Locality: Lloyds River, Nfld.   Date: September 1980
Hunter: Richard P. Navas

Woodland Caribou 322-2/8

Richard P. Navas

It had been a long summer. Finally I was at Corner Brook, waiting to be flown in to meet my guide for my long-awaited caribou hunt. After arriving at camp, which was about a half-hour flight, I met Joe Shephard, my guide for the week. I squared away my gear and talked with Joe and the other guides for awhile. Then, I decided to go on the ridge behind the camp and glass the area which I would be hunting the next week. It was late Saturday afternoon. Although my hunt didn't start until Sunday, I thought I would get some idea of the terrain through my field glasses. My hunting partner had arrived and he accompanied me to the ridge.

We were up and out of camp early on the first day. With a slight rain falling, we figured the animals would be bedded down for the day and our chances of getting a good head were slim. We glassed and walked most of the morning, hoping to find something. But by lunch we had seen nothing.

After lunch, we went to the top of the ridge and started to glass once again. We had glassed for about a half-hour. It was amazing how many bushes and rocks look just like a caribou. I had been glassing an area to the east when my hunting partner said he had found a caribou lying down. I glassed the area where he saw the animal and sure enough there lay the caribou. Tom was there for meat, and so was I, so we took off, trying to stay down wind and out of sight.

We finally came to a small wooded area in front of where we had seen the caribou. After moving to the edge of the woods, Tom had a clear shot at this animal. We were both using muzzleloaders, so we figured we had to get a little closer. We had agreed that if the caribou started to run and Tom could not get reloaded, I would fire when the caribou crossed in front of me.

When Tom fired, he struck the caribou just behind the shoulder. It ran about 20 feet and fell. Both guides were amazed that a muzzleloader could bring down a caribou that cleanly. We spent the next two hours cleaning, quartering, and caping Tom's trophy. By this time, I was really hot for my turn.

After returning to camp the first day and having carried my quarter of the caribou back, I was plenty glad to see camp. The next morning came quickly and we were off again. Let me say this about Newfoundland, you can stand at Point A and see Point B a half-mile away, but it takes over two miles of walking to get to Point B. We hunted a rock-covered ridge called, appropriately, Little Rockie Ridge. There was nothing little about it. About 9 a.m. we glassed a couple of good sized caribou on this ridge and by 1 p.m. we were at the top. The weather was still damp and the going was slow. I had seen one of the two caribou moving to the north side of the ridge. I was determined I was going to get a shot.

I watched that son-of-a-gun walk through some tall grass and lie down by a pond. He then got up and looked around, lying back down and looking right into my field glasses. After moving back behind the ridge, and circling about 300 yards to the east, I moved back to the top of the ridge. When I looked down to see him, he was standing, looking at where I had been. I had a nice shot, although a bit far for a muzzleloader. I figured that if I aimed just a little high, I could put that .50 caliber bullet where it should be. When I tripped that muzzleloader, it both looked and felt good.

When the smoke had cleared, I could see the pond, the tall grass, and where the caribou had been standing. Needless to say I was beside myself. My hunting partner and the two guides were oh *so* consoling with their laughter. They told me that when the gun went off, the caribou was already down the other side of the ridge and probably waiting on the ferry at Port-Aux-Basque.

That was the first time I had ever missed with my muzzleloader and I figured, it was due to my being over anxious. I could have said my powder was wet or a raindrop fell on my sights, but it was just buck fever.

Going down the ridge was much easier and the rain had stopped. We hunted our way back to camp. We were about a mile from camp when my guide pointed out a large caribou coming across a boggy area. He told me you can get pretty close to caribou before they would run. After my earlier experience, I could hardly believe that. But why not, I would give it a try.

While the two guides and my hunting partner stood at the edge of the trees, I started off straight at the caribou. After closing the distance between us by about 50 yards, the caribou turned and widened it by 300. So much for caribou letting you get close.

We all had a good laugh at camp that night. With just four days to go and only one tag filled, I said I would hunt with the muzzleloader one more day.

The next morning we were off early again. The sky was grey, but no rain. We loaded the camp boat and headed down Andrews Lake, ready to hunt the Lloyds River area.

We hunted along the river most of the morning, working our way up a ridge when my hunting partner's guide yelled, "Moose." The next thing I heard was Tom's 270 Win. and the moose began moving smartly up the ridge. Tom fired again and now had both his licenses filled. It was a small moose, but it was meat in the freezer. After cleaning and quartering Tom's moose, we hunted the rest of the day but I came up empty again.

By this time, I was beginning to doubt my guide's ability. He told me not to worry, the right caribou had not yet come along. I had seen quite a few that I thought were good animals, but they were moving in the wrong direction and too fast to be caught.

With two-and-a-half days of rain, they were up and on the move. I had seen quite a few good-looking heads Wednesday and I felt that my best bet would be to go back and hunt hard Thursday in the same area.

Thursday morning, after a good breakfast, we were off once more to the far end of the lake. This time I had my 30-06. Time was getting short and I knew I could make a longer shot with this gun. The sun finally came out and created a beautiful morning. We had glassed for about an hour when I saw a nice bull heading for the river. I decided I would try for him.

I had moved a half-mile closer to some higher ground where I thought I could see the bull again. He had turned and started to move up the ridge. I told Joe that we would have to move fast to catch him coming down the other side. As we got up to move, I saw something move off to our right. I told my guide to get down, for we were silhouetted against the skyline. I didn't want to spook what I thought I had seen. We both glassed that area and sure enough I could see the rump of a caribou. He apparently was feeding, so we decided to move around to get a better look.

We moved down the ridge to an area of heavy brush. At this time, I could see it was a nice bull, but still about 400 yards away. I wanted to close the range as much as possible for a good shot. We started moving closer. All I could think about was the one I missed on the ridge and how fast they can open up ground when they see you. I was determined to let neither of these things happen again.

By now, I was not using the field glasses anymore, I was using the scope on my rifle. We had moved within 175 yards and my guide had told me two or three times to take a shot. But, I was determined to get as close as possible. The range now was approximately 150 yards. I felt this was as close as I was going to get without exposing myself to full view of the caribou.

I slid the bolt back on my 30-06 and worked a round into the chamber. As I looked through the scope, he picked his head up and I could see one shovel very clearly. It seemed as though I looked over every inch of his rack before I noticed he had double shovels. I adjusted my scope from nine to three power, slid off the safety, took aim at his shoulder and tripped the trigger. To my amazement he was still standing. I knew I hadn't missed, but I couldn't understand why he was still standing.

I cranked my scope up to six power, chambered another round, and sighted on his shoulder again. I could see where the first bullet had hit him. It struck him well in the shoulder. I squeezed off the second round and watched the hair spin on impact. Two rounds, about one inch apart, and he was still standing. My guide was telling me to shoot, shoot, shoot again.

I chambered another round and aimed again. This time I could see steam coming from both bullet holes. Before I could trip the third round, he collapsed. This was one animal I was happy to clean and quarter, for it was mine.

Photograph by Wm. H. Nesbitt

WOODLAND CARIBOU
THIRD AWARD
SCORE: 314-7/8
Locality: Long Range Mts., Nfld.   Date: October 1982
Hunter: James J. McBride

WOODLAND CARIBOU 314-7/8

James J. McBride

In early January 1982, I decided to book hunts for the woodland and Quebec-Labrador caribou in eastern Canada. The best times would be late September or early October according to my booking agent, who also recommended Gerry Pumphrey of Long Range Outfitters Highlands, Newfoundland, as a guide for woodland caribou.

I reviewed old Boone and Crockett Club awards booklets and found that Thomas Phillipe had taken a big woodland caribou with Gerry in 1975 and it received the coveted First Award at the 16th Awards (1977).

Despite the long flight from California, the weather on arrival in Stephenville was similar. I was met at the airport by Gerry's wife, who said the weather was too bad to fly to the camp today, but that we would go tomorrow.

That night, a group of caribou hunters bound for Gerry's camp came by my motel room in Highlands. They were from New York, on their first hunt for caribou. They said they had seen a couple of mounted heads and wanted to know how to tell a good head. We talked for awhile and I explained that two long top points, good bezes, and shovels with plenty of points were important.

After breakfast, the three of us piled into their truck and headed to the pond where Gerry and the plane were located. The morning air was cold as we met Gerry in his supply shack/airport terminal building next to the lake.

There were five moose hunters, in addition to the three of us after caribou. Gerry distributed the proper licenses to each of us. Gerry asked how the hunt had been in Quebec. I told him I was fortunate enough to take a giant bull that met minimum requirements for the Boone and Crockett Record book. "De ye fel luky?" Gerry asked. I said yes. "Du ye lik te tek a gambol?" I asked what he had in mind. "I've seen a stag dat luks lik a moose, ef ye wan te try fer im." I've heard stories in the north that can be a bit exaggerated, but this was hard to comprehend.

Gerry went on to say that last year one of his guides saw a monster caribou stag in his territory. They had not gotten it, because it was near his moose camp and not near the main caribou camp. Gerry said there were not many caribou near his moose camp, but that is where the monster was seen. I said that I'd take a chance and try to find the big one.

After a short flight with the moose hunters from the air base to the moose camp at Hungry Grove, I met Ron Biggin. On the way in, about six moose were seen from the air, including a big bull of about 50 inches. Needless to say, sleep would not be easy for anyone that night.

After dinner, Gerry and Ron told me more about the big stag. Ron told me of a moose hunter the previous year who was approaching the brow of a hill covered by stunted pines. As he approached, he thought he could see the brow palms of a good moose. They waited, and out stepped the giant stag. The hunter didn't have a caribou tag, so they both simply marvelled at the most massive rack Ron had seen in his 15 years of guiding. Ron said a hunter who was out two weeks before saw what Ron felt was the same stag across a big valley, as there couldn't be two stags with racks like that. Gerry said that he too had seen the stag while flying supplies to his distant caribou camp and felt it was the largest he had seen.

After an early breakfast, one of the moose hunters looked through the door of the lodge and saw two moose in the bog at the end of the lake. Excitement ran high as boots crunched the frost on the front porch, signaling the departure of the hunters.

Gerry said we would head for a high point some distance away to try to locate the stag. The tundra was dotted with small lakes and streams, while the spongy ground supported small stands of stunted evergreens. Ron called the stunted evergreens "tanglebush", and they really earned their reputation. Gerry said the caribou were now in the rut and the stags would be out trying to gather a harem of cows or does.

While working toward the knoll, a single stag was seen off to the left. Gerry quickly checked the wind and we stopped. Off to the right on a small hill were four does coming out of some pines. "Let the stag go by. If we spook him, there will be nothing but running caribou and that could spook the big one if he is anywhere around," said Ron. The stag trotted over a low ridge and disappeared as we made our way toward the knoll.

As our trio neared the top of the knoll, Gerry said to freeze. About 500 yards away was a small hill with three white dots on it. Gerry said they might spook if they detected any movement. Raising my 15 x 65 binoculars, the white dots were transformed into two cows being followed by a big stag. I could see long beams with six points on each side over a good shovel. The stag moved to the side of the cows and began twisting his head from side to side. Gerry looked through the glasses and said, "Don't load yer rifle, that's not im!" For the moment, we were pinned-down in the open so we decided to watch the bull.

The top of the knoll was about 150 yards to our left with the bog beyond obscured by the line of the hill. A few moments later, a white dot appeared from the area of the bog we couldn't see and started moving toward the bull. The cows seemed unconcerned as the two stags began to square off. Ron said the second stag was a double-shovel bull, and would probably be in the book, but he wasn't the one we were looking for. We were still caught in the open, where we could hear the sounds of antlers clashing over the bog.

From the obscured bog where the last bull appeared came yet another white dot. Ron took the glasses and said, "Oh my son, my son, there he is. The moose caribou!" Gerry took the glasses and said it was the same one he'd seen. All I could see through the glasses was the most massive set of chocolate antlers I ever imagined. There seemed to be a brown box over the head, of two beams with points attached. The giant stag slowly sauntered past the two fighting stags and herded the two cows of the first stag back into the hidden bog.

After the giant stag and cows were out of sight, Ron felt it was safe to move as the other two stags were still concentrating on their fight. We slowly made our way to a point overlooking the bog by crawling on hands and knees through the low pines and small dips on the knoll. Ron didn't want to take any chances on spooking the giant he dreamed of seeing down.

There in the bog, 450 yards away, was the giant stag and his harem of 16 cows. "Any one of those 34 eyes can ruin it if we make a mistake!" said Ron. We slowly backed away, and using the concealment of the hill line, made our way carefully to a stand of stunted trees about 200 yards closer.

Ron peered over the pines, saw the stag, and ducked down. Gerry was both excited and nervous. Gerry jokingly said, "Unda Nufi law, da guide is allowed to shoot 'n bury the hunter that misses a shot on a stag dat big!" About 20 feet ahead in the pines was a dead snag sticking above the tops of the other pines that would make a good rest from which to shoot.

The Ruger 7 mm Mag. came up to the snag with no problem. However, the Redfield 3x-9x Accu-Trac just wouldn't settle down as I felt a slight touch of buck fever. "Ron, git the shovel!" said Gerry. I took a deep breath and held it, as the stag turned broadside and the cross hairs settled behind the shoulders. The silence of the tundra was shattered as the rifle roared in the pines. The giant stag took one step and stopped, as all heads came up to see where the noise came from. Just as Ron said to shoot again, the stag crumpled to the ground. "My son you got im! Good shot!" said Gerry.

Ron and Gerry seemed to go into a trance as they lifted the antlers. "En al my yers of chasin stags, dis es the granpa," said Gerry, as he ran his fingers along the massive bez points. The bezes seemed to be large triangles crowned with points, over double shovels. The main beams arched up, with two long points on each side. The 150 grain Nosler solid base had done its work. It had taken out both lungs, nicked the spine, and smashed through the right shoulder before resting under the skin.

The load of the cape and head on my shoulders seemed weightless as we headed back to the lodge. The moose hunters killed two bulls on their hunt that day. As the group of hunters sat down to dinner that night in the lodge, Ron said, "Today is Thanksgiving Day in Canada and we have much to be thankful for, Lord!" His eyes then strayed to the window where the tops of the stag's antlers rested on the sill.

Photograph by Wm. H. Nesbitt

BARREN GROUND CARIBOU
FIRST AWARD
SCORE: 451-4/8
Locality: Wood River, Alaska   Date: September 1980
Hunter: Q. Odell Robinson

BARREN GROUND CARIBOU
451-4/8

Q. Odell Robinson

Bill Perry, from Talladega, Alabama, met me in Mobile on the 25th of August, 1980, for our prearranged hunt with L & S Outfitters of Wood River, Alaska. From Mobile we travelled to southeast Alaska, up through the Yukon, visiting old friends of mine, arriving in Fairbanks on September 2nd. The next day we met our chartered flight out to base camp. Seeing Lynn Castle and his staff brought back great memories of a prior hunt when I took a grizzly bear and a full-curl Dall's ram the year before.

On September 4th, we flew out to our spike camp with great excitement and anticipation of our hunt to begin the next day. We awoke to a cold, frosty morning with about eight inches of snow covering the mountain from a prior storm. We downed our breakfast, saddled our horses, and headed up the valley to look for caribou, moose and sheep.

In the following two days, Bill took two fine trophies, a massive near-record moose and a nice full-curl Dall's sheep. We had planned to split up into two hunting parties, as Bill was going for a grizzly. But, things were going so well, we all decided to hunt together for my caribou.

We wanted to take a spike camp and go over to the high tableland slopes of the foothills where we planned to spend at least several days looking for a real trophy. Expecting to see caribou in every draw, we had run into only one small band of young bulls and cows with calves when we finally topped-out on the back side of the high mesas overlooking the river valley. Almost immediately, we spotted caribou about a mile ahead of us, and we quickly set up the spotting scope.

After looking at the animals, Lynn turned to Bill and me and said, "Get a look at this bull." I quickly looked through the scope and saw the caribou's high, palmated top points and tremendous shovel, but the bez looked skinny. He had the heaviest rack I had ever seen on a caribou, but we decided against taking him so early in the hunt. We had not gone more than 100 yards, when I glanced over my shoulder and saw another small herd of animals lying in a shallow depression, not yet exposed to the rising morning sun. I used my binoculars and then dismounted to set up the spotting scope. There were 12 mature bulls with good racks.

One of the animals in particular stood out from the rest, with his exceptionally wide spread and long beams. Lynn asked Hans (Lynn's helper) and Bill to go get the horses and join us. We moved the scope to a rocky outcropping where we would not be silhouetted to the bulls. After looking at this animal, we guessed he had a spread of 60 inches and beams six inches longer. We were mentally adding up the points and comparing the big bulls to each other. We estimated the larger would go to at least 430 Boone and Crockett points. Lynn said, "That's one hell of a caribou bull." But, there was one we kept going back to that was not nearly as wide nor as long overall. He had magnificently palmated top palms and equally impressive bez and shovel development. We estimated he would go 425 points.

By this time, I was getting real excited as we inched down off the rock knob toward the now feeding animals. We still had not made up our minds as to which bull I would take. When we were within 100 yards of the animals, these two bulls squared off and began sparring. There are few things that compare to the beauty and grandeur of these old white-necked bulls, with their chocolate colored backs, punctuated by the white strip down their flanks, and their polished antlers reflecting the spectacular reds and golds of Alaska's autumn tundra. Lynn said, "Odell, let's take the palmated bull; he is prettier and more representative of this area. Besides, you can always get a big, spindly bull down on the peninsula if you ever hunt down there."

At that point, I squeezed the trigger on my 7 mm Remington Magnum. As the bullet went home, he hardly flinched. But, with the second shot, he collapsed. We ran to the fallen bull and began measuring him, realizing that we had a bull that would go in the top two or three all-time records. As it turned out, the larger spindly bull was not spindly at all. It was so big it just looked that way. So, out there somewhere is a bull that would score 15 points better than this one.

After picture taking and caping and loading the trophy on our saddle horses, we started down the mountain and met Charlie (another guide working for Lynn). We were glad to see him and the packhorses which he brought to us after hearing the shots from across the mountain.

We met several small herds of caribou, and saw a grizzly and moose across the mountain on the way back to our camp. After getting our trophies back to camp, Charlie and I went on to take a real fine moose and a 40-inch, full-curl ram, thus ending the hunt-of-a-lifetime.

Photo Courtesy of Max E. Chittick

The Chittick family loves to hunt caribou and they have a great hunting area on the Alaska Peninsula. Max E. Chittick shot this fine barren ground caribou bull in September 1980. It scores 415-3/8 points.

Photo Courtesy of Gail W. Holderman

Well-developed shovels were an obvious feature of this Quebec-Labrador caribou bull that Gail W. Holderman shot near the George River of Quebec in September of 1979. It scores 408-6/8 points.

Photograph by Wm. H. Nesbitt

BARREN GROUND CARIBOU
SECOND AWARD
SCORE: 425-5/8
Locality: Becharof Lake, Alaska   Date: September 1981
Hunter: Lavon L. Chittick

BARREN GROUND CARIBOU
425-5/8

Lavon L. Chittick

The year was 1981. My husband, Max, my son, Gordon, and I hunted in Alaska on the Alaska Peninsula from September 10 to 26. We set up our camp on the shore of an unmarked lake that we call Rainbow Lake because of the many rainbows in that area.

We had hunted there two years previously, and we had done quite well. These hunts are non-guided. The first year(1979), my husband shot one that scored 403-5/8, my son's scored 397 and mine scored 385. The next year my husband's scored 415-3/8, my son's scored 406-6/8 and mine scored 410-4/8. This was to be the last year that we would be hunting barren ground caribou, since our trophy room was nearly full. The second year we saw one that was almost totally black. We would have shot him, but we couldn't get close enough to shoot without alerting the herd.

It is our custom to choose who shoots first before we reach our hunting area. On our flight to Anchorage my son had said, "Mom, you're going to shoot first. Dad and I want to look over the herds for ones that score high in the records book." I said, "Gordon, I really don't want to be first." He said teasingly, "Sorry Mom, you're first." Never in my wildest imagination would I have believed that I would end up with the largest bull that would score so high.

We have found that the three of us can hunt together to an advantage. After the kill, we are able to back-pack meat, cape, antlers, and equipment back to camp in one trip. Each day we back-pack out five miles to an area we have found suitable for glassing herds. It is high ground between two mountain ranges, where caribou must cross. We are hunting the wintering grounds, not the migration route. We can see quite a distance because the area is treeless. I enjoy glassing these animals nearly as much as stalking them. They are all different.

On the third morning of our caribou hunt we backpacked the five miles to our favorite spot to glass the mountain ridges. It was a windy, brisk morning. Sitting under the tarp, glassing the hillside, we saw a herd of about 300 way up on top. Half-way down, we could see hunters shooting at the herd, scattering them somewhat. We glassed them for about two hours. Using a 60 power spotting scope, we found one part of the herd that had a rather nice bull.

Max and I went down towards the gorge, while Gordon went the other way. We didn't know which way the caribou would go. If Gordon had a chance, and it was one he wanted, he would shoot. When Max and I got to the gorge, there were no caribou in sight. Obviously, they had changed their route.

We back-tracked to high ground to find where they went. As luck would have it, the herd was passing below us at about 200 yards. As I positioned myself to shoot, the herd stopped, then turned back in our direction. At about 100 yards, I placed the crosshairs on the big bull's shoulder and touched off a shot. He dropped immediately. When I saw that he was going to stay down, I ran up to see how large he really was.

It is almost impossible to see double shovels through binoculars. You can see how far the antlers extend over the nose, but that could mean one large shovel and nice bezes. I said, "Max, he has double shovels." He said he wasn't surprised. I was not just a little bit excited. We still didn't know that it would score so well. It was not a wide head, and the animal was not large in body.

When we got back to camp, we measured the head. It had almost no subtractions. It was the most symmetrical head that we had ever shot.

As we were field-dressing my caribou, we noticed a red fox watching us. This was not startling as we saw quite a number of them. They watched us as a dog would, only moving when we walked too close.

A moose walked close to camp, as we were leaving to hunt one morning. He watched us until we were out of sight. He was a fine trophy bull, but we were hunting caribou.

We saw a sow Alaska brown bear with two 300-pound cubs on a number of occasions. When we were walking out to hunt the morning after Gordon shot his caribou, we saw the sow and cubs cleaning up the carcass. In watching them, we could tell when they got close enough to get a whiff of it.

On the eighth day of our hunt, Gordon shot a caribou that scored 414-5/8. The spread was wide and he was large-beamed, but he was weak in the shovel and bezes.

Max didn't see any bulls he liked until the last day. He decided he wasn't going to shoot one unless it would make the book. That day, as we were sitting and glassing, we saw a lone bull (which is rare) coming over the hills. For quite awhile we saw parts of antlers now and then. He was a beautiful animal. He scores 407-5/8.

Max, being a taxidermist and a hunting consultant, soon had our animals mounted. We have a caribou kingdom in our trophy room. We enjoy the Alaska Peninsula and the challenge of hunting for the book.

I hear Max and Gordon saying, "Just one more year and this must be our last year. There must be a new world record out there." Time will tell.

Photo Courtesy of Kurt K. Knutson

Kurt K. Knutson was hunting in the Talkeetna Mountains of Alaska, near Watana Lake in September 1981. His big barren ground caribou bull scores 415-4/8 points, with a rack weight of over 23 lbs.

Photo Courtesy of James E. Conklin

Dr. James E. Conklin shot this fine woodland caribou in October 1981 near Alex Lake in Newfoundland. It scores 309 points.

Photograph by Wm. H. Nesbitt

QUEBEC-LABRADOR CARIBOU
FIRST AWARD
SCORE: 429-2/8

Locality: Mistinibi Lake, Que.   Date: September 1980
Hunter: Charles E. Wilson, Jr.

QUEBEC-LABRADOR CARIBOU 429-2/8

Charles E. Wilson, Jr.

My trip to Mistinibi Lake was not my first try for the Quebec Labrador caribou. In September of 1978, my wife and I, along with three other couples, booked a caribou hunt at Ilkalu Lodge in the Ungava Bay area of northern Quebec. We flew to Montreal, spent the night there, and the following morning flew on to Fort Chimo, just south of Hudson Straights on the lower tip of Ungava Bay. Here my party transferred to an ancient P.B.Y. flying-boat and headed east toward the camp on Ford Lake.

The flight was to take a little over an hour, so we became somewhat apprehensive about being lost when more time than that had elapsed and the pilot began to make ever-increasingly large circles. However, at length he spotted some tiny cabins and we were relieved to get ashore. It was only the beginning of a disastrous one-week hunt in which only one of our group of eight took a caribou. When we arrived, a group of hunters that had been in the camp previously refused to leave, stating their hunt had been cut short by bad weather. We were short on guides, places to sleep, and food. Later in the week, a man from a camp further down the lake suffered a heart attack and died on a small hill clearly visible from our camp. The Eskimo guides would not move the body, saying that only the Canadian Mounties had that authority. They merely threw a blanket over him and he remained on the hillside during the rest of our stay. When we flew out of camp, too late to make our connection back to Montreal, we discovered that the P.B.Y. pilot had brushed the side of a mountain with one wing, tearing off at least six feet of wing. With quite incredible luck he was able to fly back to Fort Chimo with his full load of passengers without crashing. When I later viewed the damaged plane, my feeling of having been unlucky all week was instantly replaced by relief that our group had not been aboard during that flight.

I have gone into this lengthy resume of an earlier trip only to indicate that these thoughts were on my mind as I again flew north out of Montreal in the fall of 1980. This time the date was September 13th and my destination was Mistinibi Lake, about two-thirds of the way up Quebec along the western border of Labrador. I was travelling alone but knew there would be a number of other hunters in camp.

To reach Mistinibi one flies commercially to Schefferville, Quebec, and then by charter into the hunting camp. I had arranged this hunt through outfitter Gerry Poitras, who calls his organization Tuktu. After obtaining my license and tag, I joined an enthusiastic group of hunters and boarded an Otter pontoon plane for the flight into camp.

Until one has flown over this type of terrain, it is hard to imagine the desolation of northern Quebec. You see only mile after mile of bog interspersed with rivers, lakes, and rocky, small mountains covered with caribou moss and stunted scrub pines. Upon landing, we were each carried to shore by guides in hip boots. The heavily loaded Otter, without a dock, had its pontoons stuck on the bottom far short of the beach. The ten hunters waiting to fly out quickly assured me that this would be a different outcome than my trip two years before. All had taken caribou, with one exception and he had chosen to be extremely selective. The weather had turned blustery and cold with traces of snow in the air. The caribou were now restless and really starting to move. It seemed to the guides that the migration was definitely underway. I knew I had arrived at the right time.

The Tuktu camps are well-run and the people are experienced. The dinner that night was substantial and nicely prepared. We each selected a bunk in a dormitory-type room and got our gear ready for the first day of hunting in the morning. In a separate room there were chairs where we could sit around and get to know each other over a few drinks of whiskey. There were nine of us hunting, all Americans, and we were from five or six different states. I found that the hunting experience of our group members varied from practically zero to African safaris.

We drew lots for guides and I came up with a young French-Canadian who was far from bilingual. His native tongue was French, every bit as much as mine was English. Mistinibi Lake is enormous and the usual method of hunting it is for two hunters and their guides to travel some distance up or down the lake by boat and then go ashore. They use large, square-stern cargo canoes for this purpose. If the water is rough, these canoes powered by outboards are a pretty wet way to travel.

I ended-up being the odd man in our group of nine and my guide decided to head out on foot up the half-mountain/half-hill back of camp. We left shortly after breakfast and climbed steadily until we came out on an even plateau above most of the surrounding countryside. We could see great distances, although there were many ravines, patches of scrub growth, and outcroppings of rock that effectively obscured our view.

We soon saw bands of caribou, mostly moving in our general direction, although somewhat to one side of us. I have taken excellent trophies of the three other species of caribou, two of which are record class, and my guide knew I wanted a top head on this trip. I had gotten the camp manager to explain in French at breakfast what I was hoping for. We kept glassing the caribou as they seemingly appeared from nowhere. We kept moving to new ridges and vantage points to best cover the country.

My guide, Antoine, headed me back the same way the following morning, although when we reached the plateau we struck-off in a different direction. The weather was misting and foggy, making the spotting scope and binoculars hard to use. I was a little disappointed at seeing many fewer caribou, but felt that perhaps the different type of day was the reason. We holed-up in a partial cave for lunch to get out of an increasingly persistent rain. At length it did quit, and about 3:00 in the afternoon we headed back for a warm camp.

As we moved along, we came to a small gully where we could see a bull caribou feeding. Only the tips of his antlers were visible as he moved his head, while busily working on some caribou moss or lichen growth. I had no impression of size, and handed my rifle to Antoine while I got out my camera, thinking that I could get very close for a good picture.

Suddenly, having winded us, the caribou bolted down the gully and out into the open. I have spent many hours watching and trying to judge caribou. Those of you who have hunted them know that any fully mature bull is a most impressive looking trophy. Despite this, I instantly recognized that this caribou was certainly out of the ordinary. Fortunately, my guide was quickly there shoving my rifle into my hands. I quickly sat down for the running shot and promptly wasted two shells before knocking him down with my third try. He was at least 200 yards away when I finally connected.

I knew he was good as we hurried up to him. But, I was frankly surprised and excited to see a beautiful double shovel. We had the head and cape back in camp by sundown and my guide went back for the meat the following day. I believe that this was the only truly solitary caribou I saw on the entire trip. What a great stroke of luck to catch him feeding where I did.

In camp, one more hunter had been successful. The following morning I opted to go along with a young hunter from Wyoming for the day. We had a super day with him collecting a record-class head. I saw more caribou than the first day and thought that they were in an even more compelling migration. They all came from the same direction at a determined trot that really covered the country. It would have been impossible to follow the herds and the only way to hunt them was to try to intercept an advancing herd. I was astounded at the speed with which they plunged into the rivers and lakes. They would hit the water with a great splash, swim strongly across, and immediately sprint up the opposite bank and be on their way again.

By the end of the fourth hunting day, all of our hunters had taken caribou and they were mainly excellent trophies. I green-scored most of the heads for my new hunting friends and we were a happy lot. I noticed that Antoine seemed particularly jovial with the other guides and mentioned this to the camp manager. He said, "Don't you know why? They all have a pool with each hunt and put in $25.00 apiece. The guide whose hunter shoots the biggest caribou takes all, and Antoine thinks he's going to win!" He did. My caribou when officially measured scored 430-3/8.

Photograph by Wm. H. Nesbitt

QUEBEC-LABRADOR CARIBOU
SECOND AWARD
SCORE: 421-4/8
Locality: George River, Que.   Date: September 1979
Hunter: Maurice Southmayd

QUEBEC-LABRADOR CARIBOU
421-4/8

Maurice Southmayd

It was the fourth day of a five-day hunt, and we had seen caribou continually from the first day. The hills were moving with them. The migration was definitely at its peak. We had hunted this area from Twin River Lodge since 1972 and had always seen game, but never in numbers like this. On almost every barren ridge there were hundreds of them moving. In four days we had looked at, conservatively, 8,000 to 10,000 animals.

My hunting partner, Bruce Markham from Constableville, New York, had taken an exceptional bull on the second day. It scored 395-2/8 and I was hoping for one at least as good.

We were glassing from a barren hill approximately 100 yards from the west shore of the George River, near the mouth of Indian Creek. The major migration pattern seemed to be from the east, across the river, and continuing west along or near Indian Creek. The rough terrain naturally funneled most of the trails to this point. From our vantage point we could see the caribou for about a mile before they reached the river, as they crossed the river, and then as they passed us on one of the three or four trails that were within 200 yards of our position. It was a constant parade, sometimes slowing to only a few animals and then growing to hundreds.

Mid-afternoon of the fourth day, we saw a tremendous herd of large bulls approaching the river approximately a quarter-mile north of us. But, as they crossed, they angled south. When they reached the west shore, they were directly in front of us. The lead bull picked a trail that passed within 50 yards of us. As they were crossing the river, I counted 82 bulls. There may have been more; most were mature animals and carried respectable antlers. It was truly an unforgettable sight.

My trophy bull was the third from the end of the long line. As he approached, one shot from my 300 Weatherby Magnum put him in the records book.

There were 12 men in our party. Of the 12 bulls taken that week, six qualified for Boone and Crockett and one for Pope and Young.

Photograph by Wm. H. Nesbitt

PRONGHORN
FIRST AWARD
SCORE: 85-4/8
Locality: Mora Co., N. M.   Date: August 1982
Hunter: Roger B. Heemeier

PRONGHORN 85-4/8

Roger B. Heemeier

My hunt actually began in May of 1979 when The American Hunter magazine published an article called "A Is For Antelope." It was about a ranch near Wagon Mound, New Mexico, noted for its trophy pronghorns. Since moving to Colorado in 1974, I had successfully hunted pronghorn in Wyoming and Colorado, but without the opportunity to take a buck over 16 inches. Needless to say, shortly after reading about the Diamond A Ranch, I fired off a letter to begin the preparations for a 1980 hunt. Much to my disappointment, I learned that the ranch had decided to allow a two-year management period with no pronghorn hunts, in order to improve the trophy quality of the herd.

In February of 1982, I learned that the management of the ranch was planning a hunt for that fall. When I received the basic hunt information at the end of May, I began making definite plans for vacation, finances, and related matters. I phoned Tony Dickinson (the Diamond A Cattle Company Game Manager and Biologist) to inquire about the terrain, accessibility of the herds, and other details to better prepare myself for the coming hunt. Having learned that the shooting distance could be very long, I decided to use my Remington 700 in 7 mm Rem. Magnum. I also started a weekly regime of range practice at distances up to 400 yards, utilizing a Harris bipod and Federal Premium ammo loaded with the 150-grain Sierra boat-tail bullet.

The evening before my departure, I double-checked my equipment and tried, with some difficulty, to get a good night's rest. After a pleasant, though seemingly endless six-hour drive, I arrived at the entrance to the Diamond A on August 27th to begin my three-day hunt. I was met at the ranch headquarters by Tony, who showed me where to stow my gear in the bunkhouse. He then introduced me to the other 16 hunters who were from various states and Canada. Along with several fellow sportsmen, we drove to a makeshift rifle range to check our rifles' zero and then made a pre-opening day tour of part of the ranch. After a bountiful steak dinner, Tony assigned hunters to their guides.

Shortly after sunrise, Charley, the retired ranch foreman, and I headed for our assigned pasture. During the drive I learned that I would have to rely on my eyesight, as Charley had cataracts. I soon realized, however, that what Charley lacked in his ability to see, he made up for in his knowledge of the ranch. We spent the day in a pasture of about 7,000 acres, glassing numerous bucks in the 14-16 inch class. We saw nothing exceptional, so we headed back to headquarters about 5 p.m. Upon our arrival, we learned that 13 of the 17 hunters had successfully taken bucks ranging from 14-1/2 to 16-1/2 inches, including three which green scored 82 or better. That evening was spent listening to the successful hunters recount their hunts.

At breakfast Sunday morning Tony informed me that he would take me to a pasture located at the base of a dormant volcanic mountain, Cerra Palon, in which several exceptional bucks had been sighted. The morning's hunt was frustrating for me in the sense that not shooting a 16-inch buck (over 20 glassed while searching for the trophy I was after) can be to someone who has hunted for years where a 16-inch buck is an exceptional trophy.

At about noon, we met two hunters from Michigan who were having lunch. One of them proudly displayed his 17-incher. This only heightened my anticipation.

After lunch, we left the Michigan hunters and proceeded onto the side of Cerra Palon in the vicinity where a herd with a big buck had been seen the previous day. Travelling through the trees, interspersed with meadows, I spotted an antelope about a half mile below and ahead of us. Through an opening in the timber, we could see the herd. It had a buck that our glances through the spotting scope told us was the trophy I was seeking. Since the wind was quartering toward the herd, we began a stalk through the trees to put the wind in our favor. Due to the open timber, we were able to easily approach within 600 yards. Then, we began the slow and difficult stalk through mountain meadow grass, using the scattered trees as additional cover. Although the trees were beneficial to our stalk, they also prevented us from seeing the entire herd, especially the buck.

When we had advanced to approximately 400 yards from the does we could see, I left Tony at the base of a small evergreen. I then began to crawl to his right and forward, so he could alert me if we were spotted. After travelling about 20 yards, I saw that the herd was moving some, but I still could not see the buck due to several intervening trees. Suddenly, I could see his black horns through the branches. As he stepped into the open, I tried to settle the cross hairs, but couldn't as he was walking and my heart was pounding. Knowing I had to get control of my breathing, I blew like an old horse. Just as he stopped broadside, at what I estimated to be 400 yards, I settled the cross hairs at the top of his back and squeezed off. Losing sight of him in the recoil, I sat up, chambered a second round and breathlessly scanned the meadow.

I couldn't see the buck or the herd through the trees. I looked to Tony, but he hadn't even seen the buck before I shot. Then, we saw the herd running about 500 yards to our right, no buck visible among them. We headed for where he had been standing when I fired and, from about 100 yards, we saw a horn tip curling above the mountain grass. Whooping and hollering, we did that 100 yards in under 10 seconds.

After sharing congratulations, we admired my trophy. We found that my shot entered about two inches behind the shoulder and exited about the same location on the far side. The shot had totally destroyed both lungs. It's no wonder I lost him in the recoil, he had dropped in his tracks. Grinning to myself, I realized those weekly sessions on the range had really paid-off with a perfect shot at a paced distance of 375 yards.

Back at the ranch headquarters, we green-scored my trophy at over 88 points; not only the largest taken during this hunt, but the largest known to ever be taken from the ranch.

Thinking about 17 happy, successful hunters, and remembering the two bucks we saw on our way back to the ranch that afternoon that would push 17 inches, I hope to once again hunt the Diamond A.

Photograph by Wm. H. Nesbitt

PRONGHORN
SECOND AWARD
SCORE: 85-2/8

Locality: Natrona Co., Wyo.   Date: September 1981
Hunter: Margery H. T. Torrey

PRONGHORN 85-2/8

Margery H. T. Torrey

Central Wyoming is the pronghorn capital of the West. Having lived 20 miles outside of Casper, Wyoming, for several years, I am used to seeing herds of pronghorn in record numbers. During 1981, like any other year, reports of sightings of big bucks were constantly filtering in to the taxidermy shop where I worked.

The buildup to hunting starts around June, with dedicated hunters spotting and comparing the finer points of bucks' horns.

My hunt area was located 40 miles west of Casper, east of the Rattlesnake Mountains and north of Pathfinder Reservoir. Opening day was windy, with gusts up to 40 mph and the pronghorns were extremely spooky. Added to this was the fact that it was opening day and hunters were everywhere, with four-wheel drives galore. I was out by myself, just glassing the area, and I headed off the plains and up into the big draws, in no hurry.

In the late afternoon, a small group of pronghorn, about 800 yards out in a draw, caught my eye. The buck's massive horns were outstanding, even at that distance. I worked down a ridge to get a closer look, which confirmed my belief that it was a big buck. Then, the group wheeled off in a circle of several miles. I watched them disappear, knowing I could find them again, as there were no roads in the area and pronghorn are, essentially, creatures of habit.

Four days later, on September 29th (which coincidentally was my birthday), I took the day off to go hunting and take advantage of the midweek lull. I was accompanied by my friend, Gordon Crawford.

We started before dawn. As the sun rose, it was a perfect fall day - clear, crisp and calm. We drove as close as we could to the area where I had seen the pronghorn; then we left the truck. We struck out for a ridge where we glassed the terrain, hoping to catch a glimpse of the buck I had seen. There was nothing.

We worked our way over to the next ridge and surprised the group of pronghorn at 200 yards. There was no doubt that the buck was the biggest I had ever seen. I was using my favorite rifle, a Remington 7 mm Magnum, with a four power Weaver scope. I shot him right behind the shoulder and he dropped.

While I was field-dressing him, I could see he was of remarkable size and had inch-long ivory tips on his horns. What a birthday gift!

Photograph by Wm. H. Nesbitt

PRONGHORN
HONORABLE MENTION
SCORE: 83-2/8
Locality: Campbell Co., Wyo.　　Date: October 1982
Hunter: Dwayne A. Anderson

PRONGHORN 83-2/8

Dwayne A. Anderson

The old 300 Savage, bored to 308, was originally given to my father by my grandfather. Then, somehow, I ended up with it. After refinishing the dilapidated stock and replacing the old steel scope with a new Leupold, I was ready for the trophy every hunter dreams of but rarely finds.

This was to be my second pronghorn hunt since moving to Gillette, Wyoming, three summers before. I teach Vocational Agriculture at Campbell County High School and my wife, Lynn, is a geologist with a local oil company. We live on a ranch southeast of town, ten miles by the road but only five miles as the crow flies. The past winter had been mild, and plentiful rain during summer provided the cattle and pronghorn with ample grass, even into the fall months.

That particular autumn, as the days shortened and the nights cooled, I found myself driving to work more slowly - scouting the pronghorn herd for the one I would put into my sights. After weeks of stopping and looking and glassing, I spotted him. On September 30, the night before the season opened, I sighted the buck just before dark. He was grazing in the meadow with five other bucks, not seeming to notice me as I drove to within 200 yards of him. I guess it was more the unusual shape of his horns that attracted me to this buck than their size (which is always difficult to tell at a distance). Clint Pickrel (my landlord, neighbor, friend and guide) had mentioned seeing this buck, "The one whose horns curled together and almost touched". He suggested hunting the next morning, before the herd was stirred-up. Unfortunately, I couldn't fit in a hunt before work. So, we planned the hunt for the next afternoon.

We were all set to go the next day at about 3:45 p.m. With us were two successful hunters that Clint had guided earlier in the day. Within a mile from the house we spotted my buck moving northeast with several other "goats". Since Gillette and the surrounding area is very busy with energy development, the pronghorns have grown accustomed to the traffic. But, motionless vehicles, or a person walking, will cause a stampede that would impress a herd of Texas Longhorns.

Before dropping my trophy, I had him in my sights two other times. The first time, Clint had let me out of the pickup in a thick sagebrush stand where the buck should cross on his present course. However, he must have sensed my presence because he changed direction 90 degrees. He was moving away from me and I didn't want to risk a shot that would only wound him or spoil a good part of the meat.

The second time, Clint and I had crawled to the crest of a hill where the herd was passing on the other side. With a stiff, 25-mph wind blowing into my face, and shooting downhill, I neglected to compensate and shot over him twice. By then he was out of range.

The third and final assault found me crawling through the sagebrush to get within range. This time, at 200 yards, I nailed him just as the herd ran out of sight behind a small rise. Thinking I had missed him, I walked over the hill to intercept the herd, only to find that the buck wasn't there. After searching for 20 minutes, we found him. My shot had brought him down in a buffalo wallow, making him hard to see from any distance.

The old 308 had again found its mark, even though it belongs to the third generation of hunters. It has dropped one bear, two moose, 15 elk, 13 deer, and countless pronghorns, and now, finally, a true "trophy" animal.

Photograph by Brad Spencer
Margery H. T. Torrey receives the Second Award for pronghorn at the 18th Awards, Dallas, Texas, in 1983. Presenting the award is Dr. Philip L. Wright, Chairman of the Records of North American Big Game Committee.

Photograph by Brad Spencer
Lavon L. Chittick receives the Second Award for barren ground caribou at the 18th Awards, Dallas, Texas, in 1983. Presenting the award is Dr. Philip L. Wright, Chairman of the Records of North American Big Game Committee.

Photograph by Wm. H. Nesbitt

PRONGHORN
HONORABLE MENTION
SCORE: 83-2/8
Locality: Natrona Co., Wyo.   Date: September 1981
Hunter: Andy Van Patten

PRONGHORN 83-2/8

Andy Van Patten

First of all, I'm from Waltman, Wyoming, which is in the heart of pronghorn country. We are 50 miles west of Casper.

We are surrounded by lots and lots of pronghorns. They love our trees and garden. We are entitled to one landowner's permit every year. I told my wife to take the landowner's permit because we always have a bunch of hunters from Iowa and I decided to apply for a different area with them. (We can apply for five areas.) When the license came back, I had our home area.

When our hunters got here, they had brought a muzzleloader. The first day of the season they talked me into using it. I had never shot one before. We jumped a pronghorn at about 75 yards and I missed. The second day I missed the same buck again. That was the end of muzzleloading hunting for me.

The last day of the season, my family and I went out and jumped the same old buck. This time I used the 25-06 and got him. The location was 16 miles south of Waltman, near the old town site of Urvay.

Our son said he was a record but I didn't think so. We threw him in the back of the truck and went sage chicken hunting. When we got home and measured him I, decided maybe I did have something nice. And sure enough, I did.

I am a Government Trapper and the outdoors and hunting are my life. I was born and raised in Wyoming and have worked on ranches until becoming a trapper. It is a great life.

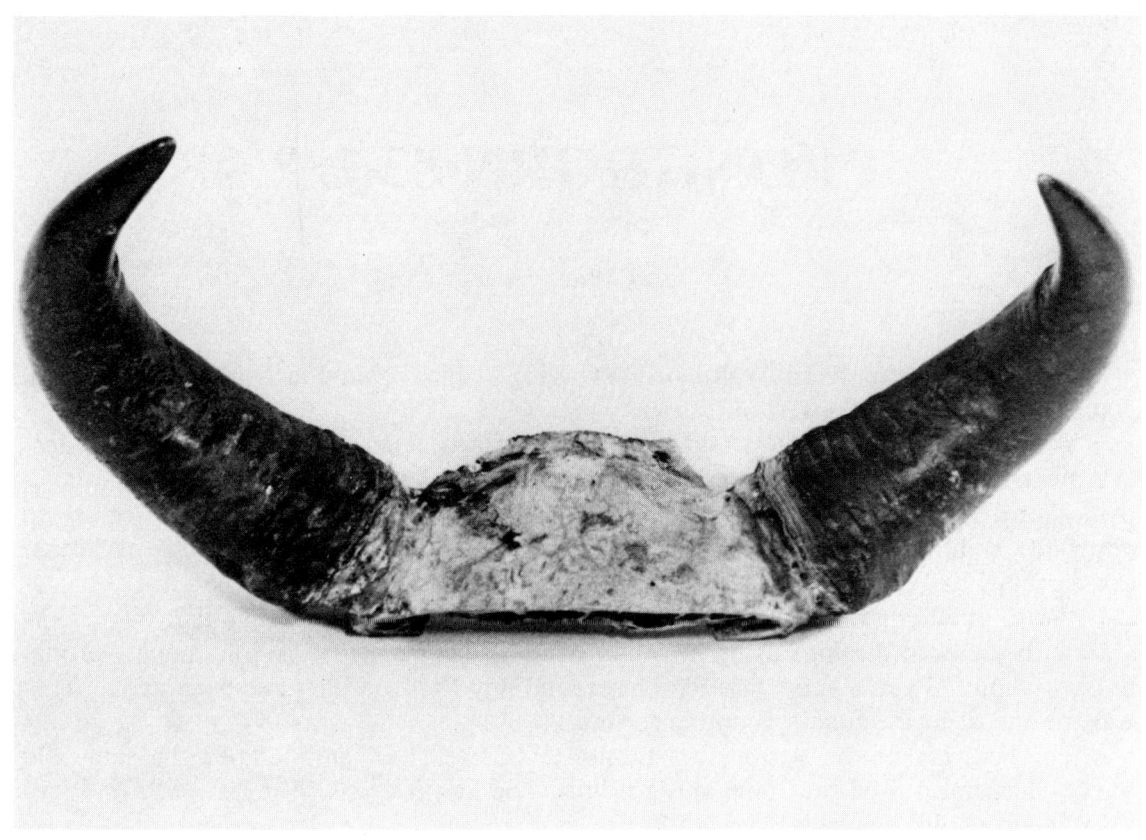

Photograph by Wm. H. Nesbitt

BISON
CERTIFICATE OF MERIT
SCORE: 125
Locality: Manitoba   Date: 1928
Hunter: Unknown   Owner: James Fredrick

BISON 125

James Fredrick, Owner

The bison that once covered virtually every available foot of suitable prairie habitat in North America and even extended to near the eastern seaboard are found today in a wild, free-ranging status only in Alaska, Canada, and a few herds in the lower 48 states.

James Fredrick lives in Wisconsin. He acquired the big bull's horns but very little information about its death. It is believed that the bull was killed by a hunter in 1928 in Manitoba. Whatever the details now lost, it was certainly big enough to measure for the records book.

The great horns scored well enough to easily qualify it for invitation to the Final Awards Judging. There it was certified for a Certificate of Merit, the only award available for pickups and unknown hunter tropies.

Photograph by Wm. H. Nesbitt

ROCKY MOUNTAIN GOAT
FIRST AWARD
SCORE: 53-4/8

Locality: Mount Horetzky, B. C. Date: September 1980
Hunter: Jackie O. Arnold

ROCKY MOUNTAIN GOAT 53-4/8

Jackie O. Arnold

This was my third hunt in Kemano, British Columbia, but my first time to try for Rocky Mountain goat. The two previous hunts had been for grizzly and black bears, but I'd come to realize that goat hunting was a challenge of a different kind.

My guide for this hunt (as for the two previous ones) was Red Fern Guiding Service, owned by Cy Ford, as fine a gentleman and hunter as you'll ever meet. He had personally guided me on my previous hunts (both successful) that I thoroughly enjoyed. On my first hunt with Cy, he had tried to interest me in a goat hunt in his area. I had declined as I was determined to get a "grizz". At the end of my second hunt he had convinced me to make a try.

In September of 1980, I arrived at Terrace, British Columbia, and caught a floatplane. I was picked up at the dock at Kemano by Cy and Spencer Ford. As another hunter was in camp, "Spence" was to be my guide for this trip. Spence and I hit it off right away, and we started out glassing the mountains for a good goat.

We returned to Cy's camp and had an excellent supper, cooked by Cy's wife, Norma. In all my other hunting trips I had always lost weight, but I'd actually gained five pounds on both of my other hunts with Cy because of Norma's excellent cooking.

We spent the first several days glassing for goats and bear, as I also had a black bear and grizzly tag. The weather was unusually warm, with drizzle being common on most days. We spotted several "blacks", but most were smaller than the ones I'd taken on the two previous trips with Cy.

Goats were abundant also, but many were nannies or else on peaks impossible to get to without wings. After seeing where the goats were staying in the warm weather (on top), I was beginning to have second thoughts about this idea. The mountains in this area are not particularly high, ranging around 7,000 feet above sea level. But they're so damned steep they make the use of horses impossible. "Straight up" is probably a good adjective for this area.

After several days of glassing the slopes and eating Norma's home cooked meals, I was becoming quite satisfied to sit for hours in the warm sun with a pair of binoculars in my hands. I think that Spence sensed this and decided it might be the time for a climb just for exercise.

Bill, the other hunter in camp, and I had passed up a chance at a good goat because the climb looked nearly impossible. I know now that it wasn't impossible, just a tremendous amount of work. Bill scored on a goat first, making a good shot on a goat from a logging road. I was to find out later that it's not always that easy.

Spence was really ready for a climb after Bill got his goat. We glassed all the next day, with nothing exceptional or in reach, until fairly late when we spotted a good goat on top, on his way down for some reason. We watched him a long time, until he had dropped down low enough to be reachable. Then, we started our climb.

The first problem we (or rather I) encountered was a log bridge across a rain-swollen stream. The tree was 25 feet above the stream, without a handrail. Spence trotted across with no problem, telling me not to look down.

I made it to midstream before deciding that crawling on my hands and knees would be better; at least I wouldn't have nearly as far to fall. Spence waited patiently on the far side, expecting the worst.

The footbridge was the easy part. For the remainder of the afternoon, we were slipping and sliding around on the rock face. It started drizzling on the way up and everything was as slick as glass. Just before dark we reached a rounded rock face that was very difficult to climb. Spence made it over and scouted ahead. I was near the top, when I lost my footing and slid some 20 feet down the side, losing my gun in the process. The fall scared the hell out of me, but I realized that nothing was injured, save for bruised knees and pride.

Spence had scouted ahead, encountering a steep face that wasn't impossible to climb, but extremely difficult. Due to the lateness of the day, the drizzle, and our failure to spot the goat, Spence called a halt to the climb, much to my relief. The climb down was bad, but a lot easier than going up. When we finally reached the stream, we found an easier place to cross. We did get wet up to the waist, that not being too important because it had been raining all evening anyhow.

The next day was bright sunshine but still fairly warm. Around ten o'clock in the morning we spotted a goat in a patch of snow, fairly high-up. After we glassed for awhile, the goat bedded down for a noon nap on a ledge not too far from the top. After considerable discussion Spence and I decided to give it a try, hoping to get close enough for a shot before the goat spotted us and took off.

Six grueling hours later, at four o'clock, we were resting on a 12-inch wide ledge approximately 350 to 400 yards from the goat. The previous six hours had nearly killed me, the climbing being steep and rough. Had it not been for Spence's determination and help, I would have quit 15 times. On several occasions Spence had pulled me up steep places after I had passed the rifles up to him. As Spence peeked over the ledge and glassed the goat, I tried to catch my breath. After a short, five-minute break, Spence told me to get ready as the goat was standing and was getting ready to bug-off.

Four shots later, the goat was down and Spence and I were dancing a jig on our 12-inch ledge. Little did I know that the hard part was just beginning.

It took Spence about 30 minutes to reach the goat and start caping it out. It took me over an hour and the climb was as bad or worse than anything I'd seen so far. The goat was lying on the ledge, with a large portion of his body hanging off into space. We took turns hanging-out over the ledge, trying to skin him, as he was too heavy to pull back onto the ledge. After some time, the goat's body slipped further off the ledge and was becoming impossible to hold. Deciding to let him fall rather than risk a bad accident, Spence threw the caped-out hide over his horns as the goat slipped off the ledge.

My goat fell some 300 feet, struck a ledge, bounded-out into space, and then fell completely out-of-view some 1,000 to 5,000 feet below us. The goat's fall suddenly made me realize that while the climb up had been hell, the climb down was going to be worse. I was sure that the horns had been reduced to toothpicks anyway, and I was beginning to wish that we had never started this ordeal.

The climb down was just as bad as I had thought. The rocks and shale were loose and footing was nearly impossible. The weight of our guns tended to pull us away from the mountain and give the sensation of falling. Once, Spence slipped and fell some 25 to 30 feet, losing his gun and scaring the hell out of me. I thought he was a goner for sure. After what seemed like hours we reached the goat. Spence arrived first and gave out a yell when he discovered that neither horn was scratched. We finished the caping job, rested awhile, and then continued down.

Dark caught us as we reached a cliff just above the tree line. It was straight up and we had gone around it on our way up; but, this was the fastest way down. Fear of falling from the cliff was replaced by loud cussing on my part as the brambles growing out of the cliff prevented falling for more than a few feet at a time. Spence was carrying the hide and head and was managing fairly well. I spent most of my time unhooking my gun and his from the limbs. It was totally dark now, and there was no way to tell what was below us; whether a limb to grasp while searching for another, or pure open space.

We finally reached a waterfall on a steep slope. It was great to find something solid to stand on besides limbs and open air. As we rested, Spence spotted a fire down the mountain. We knew it had to be Cy trying to guide us down.

As we headed for the fire we heard Cy shout out to us, and we met him on a small trail. It was great to have a flashlight to lead us back to the fire where we rested for a short while. We then headed down to the logging road. We finally reached the truck some 14 hours after we had left it. Exhausted and beat, but extremely happy, we headed back to camp.

Spence and I "slept in" the next morning. I could have stayed in bed, but I got up around eight o'clock to help Spence flesh-out the hide. This is a hard chore, but every hunter should always help his guide, so I pitched-in. I think Spence would have preferred that I not help, as I was doing an excellent job of punching holes in an otherwise perfect hide.

For most of the day we worked on the hide, ate, and enjoyed just sitting around. There was not a spot on my body that didn't hurt, or that wasn't blue from falls and limbs. I was very pleased with our goat, but I was also quite happy just to still be in one piece. My excitement was enhanced at supper that night as Cy told us that the goat's horns would make the book. Spence and I were elated and had a few victory drinks to celebrate before going to bed.

A perfect hunting trip became even better a few days later when I killed an 800 pound "grizz" with help from Spence. It took five shots to finish him off at 35 yards; three from me, and two from Spence. This was a hair-raising experience in itself that would take too long to tell here. It was quite a thrill; it was great.

My trip back home was rough, as usual, but I finally arrived safely in Texas. Some months later, I received my goat head back from the taxidermist and immediately had it measured for both the Boone and Crockett Club and the Safari Club International records. The goat placed number one in Safari Club on preliminary scoring. I was excited beyond words. I received a gold award from S.C.I. in April at the 1981 Las Vegas Convention. I couldn't attend due to business pressures; but, Jack Jonas, my good friend, picked-up the award for me.

I've made hunts in Montana, Idaho, and again with Cy and Spence in September 1981, and each has been a thrill in its own right. But, I'll never forget the feeling of achievement in Kemano on that first goat hunt. I'd never have made it except for "Spence", as good a guide as I've ever hunted with and a true "mountain man" of the toughest kind. "Our" goat head decorates my office and has been the conversation piece for many hunting stories.

I'm currently planning another trip. Where? To Kemano! And, I'll keep going back there as long as Spence can drag this fat-old-body up-top to have a chance at a better goat. The pain, exhaustion, aching muscles, and stark fear were all replaced with a sense of joy, camaraderie with Spence, and a wonderful feeling of achievement that I'll never lose. As Cy Ford always says, "That's hunting".

Photos Courtesy of Michael W. Duby and Ronald A. Sturgeon

(Left) Michael W. Duby shot this fine Rocky Mountain goat that scores 51-2/8 points in Kittitas Co., Washington, in October 1980. (Right) Ronald A. Sturgeon hunted the area of the Chitna River, Alaska, in September 1979 to take this bison bull that scores 115-4/8 points.

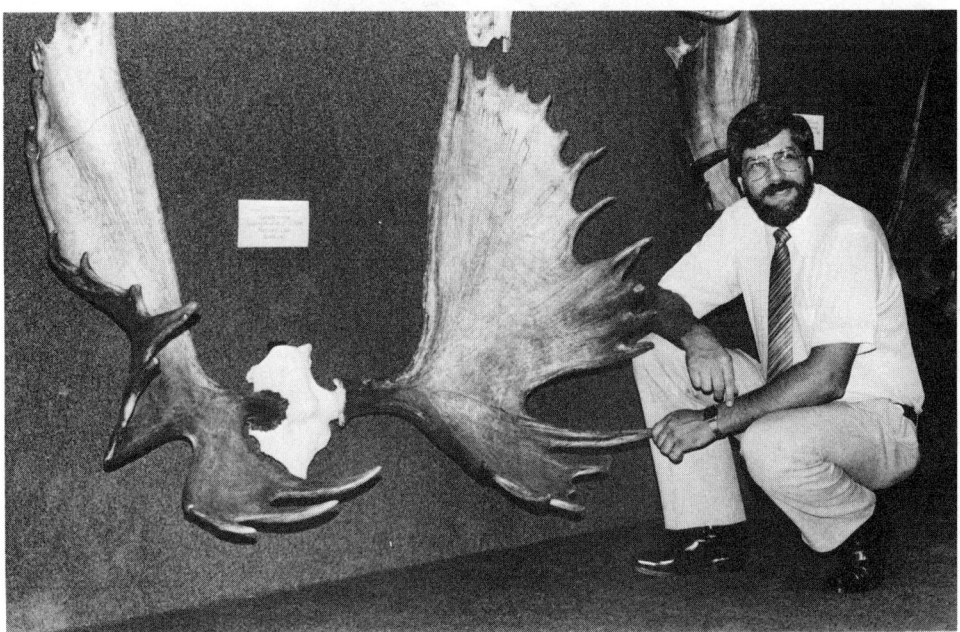

Photograph by Jack Reneau

The new world's record Canada moose, scoring 242 points and taken by Michael E. Laub near the Grayling River, B. C., in October 1980, is admired by Wm. Harold Nesbitt, Administrative Director of the Boone and Crockett Club.

Photograph by Wm. H. Nesbitt

ROCKY MOUNTAIN GOAT
SECOND AWARD
SCORE: 53-2/8

Locality: Half Moon Lake, Alaska   Date: October 1980
Hunter: Robert A. Hewitt

ROCKY MOUNTAIN GOAT 53-2/8

Robert A. Hewitt

After planning our goat hunt for several weeks, my two fellow teachers and I could hardly wait for the final bell to ring October 1st. Bob Hammer, Kurt Kuehl, and I made tracks to Southeast Air, where our friend Jeff Carlin would be our pilot.

We loaded our gear in the De Haviland Beaver. Our destination, about 50 miles from Ketchikan, was the Twin Rift Lake area. Kurt had done some research and found that this area seemed to be a likely spot for goats.

Since Jeff was ahead of his busy schedule, he offered to fly us over several places to scout for goats. It was a stroke of luck because, about ten minutes from Twin Rift, Jeff called, "There's one on that ledge!" We all leaned to the left to see the goat - this was a first for Kurt and me. Bob had hunted goats before, but the closest Kurt and I had ever been was seeing pictures in the Alaska Geographic magazine.

We continued on to Twin Rift Lake only to find no goats in that area. We decided to re-check the place we'd seen the goat. Jeff said he could drop us off at the high, small, un-named lake but he couldn't pick us up there with packs loaded with game. (He was optimistic!) The obvious problem then was, how do we get out, if we get in? Jeff said he'd be able to pick us up at a larger lake (Half Moon) that was about two miles down the mountain from the small lake. We flew over the ridge that we would take down to Half Moon Lake. It looked so feasible (from the air) and we were so excited to land and start planning our goat strategy, that we decided to have Jeff drop us off at the small lake.

Jeff suggested we leave some of our extra supplies at Half Moon Lake. Looking back, that was a grand idea. We dropped down on Half Moon Lake, unloaded some of our gear in the selected spot, and jumped back in the plane. As we went up and circled the upper lake, I remember Jeff saying, "I don't know, guys, she's starting to look pretty small!" (The lake *wasn't* very big; no wonder we can't find a name for it on any map.) We finally did land on the lake, taxied to shore, and unloaded our remaining gear.

Jeff exhibited some real flying skills getting out of that lake. He circled once slowly to check things out, then a second time to buildup speed. The third time around, he was on one float and banking the plane hard to the left. All of a sudden he disappeared right over a waterfall. A few minutes later, he flew over on his way back to Ketchikan. After seeing that, I was glad we were walking out.

We set up camp and Kurt cooked a great dinner of fried potatoes and hamburgers. We sat around the camp fire and swapped hunting and coaching stories, *most* of which were true. About 9:00 p.m. we turned in, eager to get on with the hunt the next morning.

We were up at daybreak. Just as we were finishing breakfast, we spotted a goat on a cliff at the other end of the lake! He was a couple of miles from us, and, needless to say, had a real advantage in location.

We quickly planned our strategy and decided that one person would try to get above the goat while the others waited at camp. We flipped a coin to see who the lucky one was, and I won the toss. I got a half-hour start while Kurt and Bob did the dishes. (Not only would I have the best position on the hunt, I got out of doing the dishes!)

As I reached the top of the hill where we'd seen the goat, I could see Bob and Kurt around the other side of the lake. Kurt was taking the right flank. I found out later that he'd spotted another goat to the right of the first one. Bob was coming up the middle, under both goats.

I was on top of the hill now and could see nothing but Bob moving up the cliff. Then, he suddenly fired three shots. I could hear the goat down below me, but I couldn't see him. I got my scope on Bob, and he started waving at me to move down. I did so, but not easily. The terrain was really rough. I looked to Bob again for help, and he signaled that the goat was right below me. I leaned over a tree to look below; there was the billy coming towards the top. I put my right shoulder on the tree, with my 300 Win. Magnum sideways, and fired two shots. The goat disappeared. It soon became apparent that my last spring's marathon training wasn't in vain, for I was in a foot race to the top of the mountain. As I ran back up the path, I was huffing and blowing from excitement rather than fatigue.

As I climbed, I loaded two more cartridges in my rifle. Minutes later, I had almost reached the top of the peak. Suddenly, right out of nowhere, stood a big billy goat. It was my lucky day because he was standing broadside, looking at Bob. I stepped behind a rock to catch my breath. I pushed the safety forward and started around the rock. I put the cross hairs about an inch behind the goat's left shoulder and squeezed off a round. The goat lurched forward and was gone. I couldn't believe it! Maybe I should have scratched the marathon training and concentrated on target practice. The goat had entered a short canyon about 20 yards long that opened to the top. We had another short foot race, this time all the way to the top. As I came into the canyon, I didn't see the goat. Where had he gone? He wasn't on the top . . . maybe he'd back-tracked and gone down the face of the mountain. I was feeling a little sick at this point.

I jumped down into the small canyon and walked towards the other end. There, about six feet from the end, was a big, beautiful, billy lying dead. He'd only taken a few steps before dying. It had only been about two hours since I left camp, what a fantastically lucky day!

I ran out of the canyon and signaled to Bob that I'd killed the goat. I owe that kill to Bob Hammer for the tremendous job he did in sending the goat right into our trap.

As I later learned, he could have killed the goat, but he couldn't have gotten to it because of the cliff. So, he scared it up the hill to me.

I skinned and boned the goat and loaded the meat into my pack. It took about an hour to get back to camp. As I caught my breath and prepared to make a second trip for the hide and horns, Kurt came into camp. Here was a surprise. Kurt's pack was full of goat meat too! While circling the right side of the mountain, he had spotted another big billy. Kurt pursued him onto a grassy knoll and made that knoll the billy's last stand. Kurt estimated that his goat was around 280 pounds, about 50 pounds heavier than I'd figured mine to be.

We were both really excited. We swapped stories and half-heartedly discussed going back for the hides and horns. We debated leaving them, figuring we'd done enough walking for one day. Finally, Kurt boasted that his horns were bigger than mine. Now, I couldn't let that go unchallenged! We got a new burst of competitive energy and off we went.

We wound down that exciting day by relaxing by the fire and telling every detail of our separate hunts again. We went to bed about nine so we'd be able to bounce-up and tackle our big hike back down to Half Moon Lake, with our overflowing packs!

Sunday, October 3, we arose at daybreak after spending a damp night in the rain. It was hard to get motivated, but we had to be at Half Moon Lake by 4:00 p.m. We ate and then broke camp, heading up and over the mountain behind us. The muskeg trail was mushy and slippery, and we fell several times. After taking several rest periods along the way, we reached the top. Not much conversation took place, just moans and groans and an occasional curse when one of us fell. We were glad that there were three of us to carry out two goats!

Once on top, the going was smoother. Our only difficulty was having to do some zigzagging to find the way down. Kurt was the trailblazer. He did a good job, with one minor exception. We hit one place where we had to lower the packs with ropes and then lower ourselves with prayers!

We finally reached Half Moon Lake about 2:00 p.m. Fog had set-in and it looked questionable as to whether Jeff could fly into the lake to pick us up. We set up camp and prepared ourselves to stay a few days until the weather cleared. About 4:30 p.m. we heard the throb of airplane engines and were delighted to see a plane coming in. As we packed one more time, Jeff landed and taxied to the shore. We were loaded-up and out of the lake in an hour, headed for Ketchikan.

Our goat trip was a great success due to Jeff Carlin, our excellent pilot, and Kurt Kuehl and Bob Hammer, two good friends and hunting companions, and lots of luck!

Photograph by Wm. H. Nesbitt

ROCKY MOUNTAIN GOAT
CERTIFICATE OF MERIT
SCORE: 51-6/8
Locality: Snohomish Co., Wash.   Date: November 1981
Hunter: Michael J. Simon   Owner: John M. Mitchell

ROCKY MOUNTAIN GOAT 51-6/8

John M. Mitchell, Owner

For John Mitchell and Michael J. Simon, the killing of the huge mountain goat was largely being in the right place at the right time.

For the 220-pound mountain goat, who had lived to a ripe old 13-15 years, it was apparently his destiny to become the trophy-class mount Mitchell had long coveted for his chalet.

It was October 11, 1980. Mitchell and Simon had started the day about 6:30 a.m., parking their car at the end of No Name Creek Road on Mount Persis in Western Washington. The weather was clear and crisp.

It was Simon's plan that day to hunt for goat, while Mitchell had come along as a companion with hopes of getting a deer. After zigzagging for a couple of miles up Mount Persis, the pair split up. Mitchell hiked west toward a rock bench that dropped abruptly some 800 feet into a canyon.

Looking over the edge, Mitchell spotted what he figured was a granddaddy of mountain goats. He raced back to get Simon, who had a goat tag and the binoculars. The glasses confirmed Mitchell's suspicions.

"The goat is no bigger than an eighth-of-an-inch high to the naked eye. If you can hit that, he's yours," Mitchell teased Simon.

Simon meticulously cleared a perch atop the shelf of rubble, clearing away some of the six inches of snow that had accumulated the night before. After creating a makeshift gun rest out of coats, Simon aimed his 243 Winchester at the goat and studied the animal's movements.

Mitchell and he discussed the possibility of not hauling the goat out if Simon did manage to hit him. Mitchell was confident they could, so Simon took aim and fired. The goat went down. He rolled over once and then struggled to stand, his haunches still on the ground.

Simon fired four more rounds but none apparently found their mark. After trying for 10 minutes to stand, the billy finally got up and staggered toward some nearby timber. Simon got off another round, but the goat continued about 60 yards before collapsing near a tree.

Mitchell elected to go down the cliff while Simon stayed above to act as a spotter. With Simon's directions, Mitchell found the goat. But, as he drew near, the goat agonizingly stood one last time. Mitchell quickly put him out of his misery with a shot to the neck from his 30-06.

Hearing the shot, Simon headed down the cliff with the packs. While skinning and quartering the goat, Simon discovered his first shot had hit in the back, severing the spine.

The two men then divided the meat into two equal packs of about 90 pounds each and Mitchell asked for the head. Simon agreed, and the pair headed for a lake about a half-mile away. By the time they arrived it was nearly 1:00 p.m.

After a brief lunch by the lake, the two loaded their packs and hiked west for what they thought was the trail back to their car. This error took them over sheer rock walls, forcing them to pass their packs between them with a 20-foot rope. They had to crawl down the cliffs like mountain climbers, a talent neither could claim.

Mitchell and Simon had descended some 700 feet when they realized their mistake. It took another couple of hours to crawl back. Exhausted by the time they again reached the lake, they decided against setting-up camp for the approaching night, since Mitchell was dressed only for a day trip.

However, the Pacific Northwest weather didn't help them. Within moments, a storm came up, dumping buckets of water on them and the terrain, water-logging everything. They knew this would make travelling though the brush even rougher. They decided to hide their packs by the lake, planning to come back for them early the next day.

Upon leaving the lake, their real troubles began. Already exhausted and wet, it took them 7-1/2 hours to travel the three miles to their car. The hours were spent busting through water-soaked brush, crawling up and down rain-slicked rocks and dirt, and falling into timber slash hidden beneath quilts of pine needles. Their journey was further hindered by the cold which came with the deepening darkness. It was a hell Mitchell and Simon would never forget.

Around 11:00 p.m., they reached No Name Creek Road, having crawled the last yards on their bellies. Later they recounted that at times during that night they feared they wouldn't make it. More experienced hikers have died of exposure on Mount Persis.

Once back at their car, the two men started for home, almost too numb to be thankful for their kill or their own survival.

As planned, the next day they rounded up some friends and went back for the goat and the packs. Under daylight, they realized they had been crawling through brush only yards from a logging road that would have spared them much of the previous night's miseries.

But, this was a new day and they had the billy to celebrate. Today, he graces the wall of Mitchell's home.

Photograph by Brad Spencer

George A. (Sandy) Sinclair receives the Third Award for Canada moose at the 18th Awards, Dallas, Texas, in 1983. Presenting the award is Dr. Philip L. Wright, Chairman of the Records of North American Big Game Committee. Visible in the background is William L. Searle of Skokie, Illinois, long-time Secretary of the Boone and Crockett Club.

Photograph by Brad Spencer

Albertoni Ferruccio travelled from his home in Switzerland to receive the Second Award for Canada moose at the 18th Awards, Dallas, Texas, in 1983. Presenting the award is Dr. Philip L. Wright, Chairman of the Records of North American Big Game Committee.

Photograph by Wm. H. Nesbitt

MUSKOX
FIRST AWARD
SCORE: 109-4/8
Locality: Banks Island, N.W.T.   Date: March 1981
Hunter: James M. Domokos

MUSKOX 109-4/8

James M. Domokos

It was in the late 1970's that I became interested in hunting muskox. Alaska had been issuing a few permits. But, the chance of getting one didn't seem the best, so I gave up on the idea of a hunt. It was a couple of years later that I received a newsletter from Jack Atcheson of Butte, Montana, telling of muskox hunts that were going to open soon in the Northwest Territories of Canada. It did not take me long to call Jack to get a hunt arranged for the spring of 1981.

Finally, the time for the hunt arrived, so I left Ohio in route for the Northwest Territories and hopefully a meeting with a muskox. After a night in Edmonton, Alberta, I caught a plane for Inuvik, N. W. T. After some hours flying, and several stops along the way, the plane arrived at its destination of Inuvik.

At Inuvik I met some of the other hunters and John Matson. John is the representative of the Iniut Development Company, which takes care of the muskox hunts. After spending the night in Inuvik, and taking care of last-minute details, the other hunters and I left for the hunting camps.

Our plane touched down at a small Eskimo village called Paulatuk. Here, about half the group departed. One of them, Ron Kolpin, was going to try for muskox with a bow. After one other stop to drop off two hunters from Italy, we arrived at our destination of Sachs Harbour, located on Banks Island, N. W. T. Everyone put their gear into the back of a four-wheel drive truck that drove us to a house that served as base camp during the hunt. I think there must have been only two or three vehicles in the small village, and I can't recall any roads leaving town.

There were three other hunters in camp besides me. One was Bill Poole of San Diego, who does quite a bit of big-game hunting. The others were from Nevada and Ohio.

After getting our gear put away, a couple of the guides came over. Each of us had our own guide. Frank Carpenter was to be my guide and his brother would be his assistant. Frank asked if I wanted to sight-in my rifle to make sure it was still on after the long plane trip. That sounded like a good idea, so I put on some heavy clothes and we left. About a half-mile from the village, we went out on the frozen bay and stopped the snowmobile. I fired a couple of shots, which were right on, so we then returned to camp.

The next morning found everyone getting into their heavy clothes as the temperature was around 30 below. The transportation we would be using was a snowmobile. Frank and his brother each had one. A sled was attached by rope to each snowmobile for carrying gear and the hunter. The ride was quite rough, to say the least.

Before long everyone was leaving camp. We went up a frozen river, then headed in a different direction. I noticed some piled stones on some of the higher elevations, which were probably used as landmarks. Frank stopped to check a fox set he had put out. In it was an artic fox that had a very pretty white coat. A few of these would make a nice coat, I thought. We had also seen caribou now and then. They are called Peary's caribou and hunting them at that time was not allowed.

About two hours from camp we came upon a small herd of muskox. We walked in to have a closer look and discovered one large bull in the herd. As it was early in the hunt, I wanted to look around some more. Before we left, I got some close-up pictures of the muskox herd. Later in the afternoon we came across a herd of 15 to 20 muskox. They ran off in different directions. Frank and I moved in on one small group, as there was a nice bull among them. After looking them over carefully, I decided to try for the large bull.

We were quite close to them. Frank was a little too close, I guess, as the bull charged him. I then noticed that Frank can move quite fast. Anyhow, I fired the 338 and the big bull dropped in his tracks. A second shot was not needed. I helped Frank and his brother skin-out my muskox and load it onto a sled. We then headed back towards camp. A break down with one of the snowmobiles took over an hour to fix, and it was quite dark when we arrived back at the village.

The next morning I walked down to the game department trailer to get an export permit for the muskox. I then spent the rest of the day getting my things together as a plane was coming the next day to fly us out.

Hunting in the artic with the Eskimos is a different experience, and very interesting. It is certainly not for anyone who dislikes cold. But, for those who don't mind the cold and would like to try something different, I would strongly recommend a muskox hunt.

Photos Courtesy of Robert J. Bartlett and Samuel C. Johnson

(Left) Robert J. Bartlett was hunting near Savoonga, Alaska, in May 1979 when he took this walrus scoring 102 points. (Right) Samuel C. Johnson hunted the Egegik River Drainage of Alaska in October 1978 where he shot this fine barren ground caribou that scores 424-2/8 points.

Photo Courtesy of Michel Laurent

Michel Laurent travelled from his home in Vancresson, France, to Sachs Harbour of Banks Island, N. W. T., to hunt muskox in March 1982. His reward was this big bull that scores 104-6/8 points.

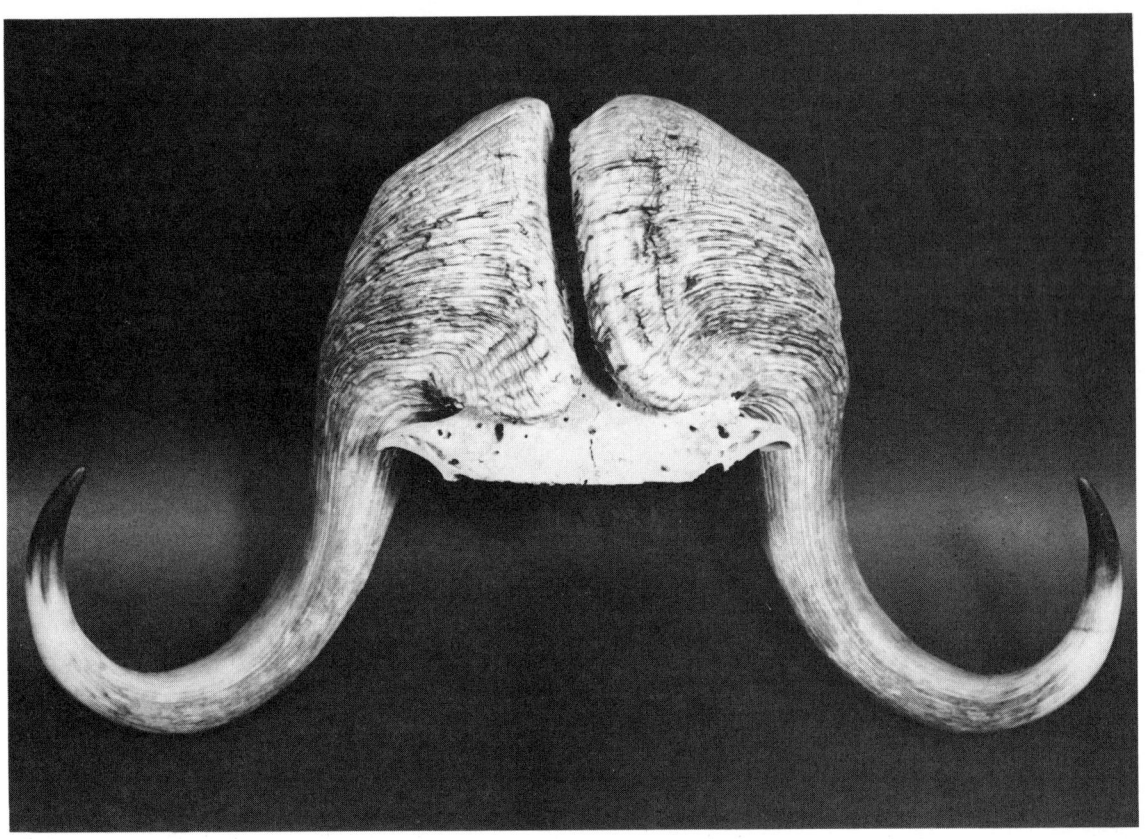

Photograph by Wm. H. Nesbitt

MUSKOX
SECOND AWARD
SCORE: 108-6/8

Locality: Banks Island, N. W. T.   Date: March 1981
Hunter: Toby J. Johnson

MUSKOX 108-6/8

Toby J. Johnson

In 1981, Norman Taylor and I hunted muskox together out of Sachs Harbour on Banks Island in the Northwest Territories.

When we arrived in mid-March the weather was typical for that time of year. It was windy and the thermometer hovered around 40 degrees below zero. There were about 12 hours of daylight each day.

The first day of the season turned out to be a bust. It was windy that morning and the guides, Floyd Sydney and Frank Kudlak, indicated that it wouldn't be safe hunting under those conditions. Instead, we all spent the day keeping warm and entertaining each other with stories of past hunting trips.

The next day the weather cleared and everyone assisted in loading the sleds for a noon departure. The sleds, each about ten feet long by four feet wide by three feet high, are pulled by snowmobiles. The boisterous, barking sled dogs, which one normally expects in remote parts of the world such as this, have been replaced by advanced technology. Gear loaded by the Eskimos on the sleds included food, sleeping bags, tents, stoves, gasoline, tools, and spare parts for the snowmobiles. The Arctic is no place to get stranded.

We were out for six hours before we sighted our first herd of muskox feeding about two miles away. Upon seeing us, the herd formed the defensive circle characteristic of the species. The adults all face outward, with the younger animals inside this protective ring. However, as we approached, the animals broke and ran. We saw two other herds during the remainder of that day, but nothing that Norman or I was interested in taking. Other wildlife sighted that day included Arctic fox and hares, ptarmigan, and caribou.

That night was comfortably spent in the double-walled tents furnished by the Eskimos. Two-burner Coleman stoves were used for cooking; they also provided heat for the tents. Sleeping gear consisted of muskox-hide sleeping bags and ground cloths, also provided by the Eskimos. The next day Norman was able to score with a muskox that should place high in the records book. We saw five different groups of muskox that day. Norman collected his trophy from a group of two bulls and one cow.

Early in the afternoon of the following day we stopped the snowmobiles on a high point to check the area for game. Immediately, we spotted three different herds that ranged in size from 12 to 36 animals. All the animals of the smallest group were of the same approximate size, indicating that they were probably all bulls. There were no smaller or younger animals that usually indicates a herd that includes cows and calves. We decided to stalk this herd.

Once we had moved to within 80 yards of the herd, the difficulty of selecting the finest trophy presented itself. Since the Eskimos had been guiding trophy hunters for only two years, and also since they take only the younger animals to meet their daily needs, the guides were not entirely familiar with what constituted a records book trophy. Ultimately, however, I took the bull that everyone agreed was the largest.

My trophy is now mounted life-size and displayed at the Big Horn Wildlife Museum in Buffalo, Wyoming.

(Left) Kenneth J. Gerstung hunted the Tunulik River of Quebec in September 1979, 70 miles east of Chimo. His Quebec-Labrador caribou scores 391-4/8 points. (Right) The famed George River was the setting for Bruce Hartel's hunt in September 1981 for Quebec-Labrador caribou. His fine bull scores 401-2/8 points.

Photograph by Wm. H. Nesbitt

MUSKOX
THIRD AWARD
SCORE: 108-4/8
Locality: Banks Island, N. W. T.   Date: March 1981
Hunter: James W. Owens

MUSKOX 108-4/8

James W. Owens

After flying over ice floes and open water for two hours, the small Eskimo village of Sachs Harbour was a welcome sight. Having booked a muskox hunt the previous year, I had done enough reading to know that the inhabitants of Banks Island were closer to the North Pole than any inhabited area of North America. We were warmly welcomed by the Eskimos at Sachs Harbour and taken to the town meeting hall. There, guides were assigned to each hunter, my guide being David Nasogalvak. I had specifically requested to be allowed to hunt with David, as my usual hunting buddy, Bud Callahan, had hunted with him the previous year and said he was the top hunter and trapper in the village. David invited me to stay in his home rather than the town hall and I quickly accepted. When I arrived at his house I learned why David was considered the best trapper in the village. He had just returned from running his trap line and had 50 white arctic fox. I watched in awe as David and his family skinned foxes, doing the complete job in about 2 minutes per fox. I asked David what animals we could expect to see during our hunting trip. He informed me that Banks Island had arctic hare, arctic fox (both blue and white), Peary's caribou, ptarmigan, wolves, polar bear, and muskox. Further questioning of David revealed that the fox were the main export of the island, and that he had personally taken 2,250 pelts during his best year.

That evening we began gathering our gear for the hunt and David went over my equipment. I had a quality down expedition parka and pants which, to my surprise, he declared inadequate and discarded. He provided me with an Eskimo parka with wolverine around the hood, about three layers of wool, and a nylon exterior. I had previously sent a request to get size 13 mukluks and large mittens and they were waiting for me. They had muskox hides on the outside and arctic hare fur on the inside. All during the hunt I can honestly say I was never cold. The light, yet warm, mukluks and mittens served me well.

The next morning we were up at dawn to begin the 8-10 hour trip out to the hunting area. David's brother, Henry, and my hunting partner, Don Corley of Fort Worth, were to hunt with us. Once out on the tundra you can understand why hunting and travelling is done in pairs. It's very cold (50-70 degrees below zero), and there are absolutely no landmarks, only a vast tundra of snow and slightly rolling hills. Any equipment break down could be a serious problem. We went into the hunt area on double-track snowmobiles pulling large freighter sleds. While the sled was bumpy and uncomfortable, I was never cold but surprisingly warm, considering we were over 300 miles inside the arctic circle.

Camp consisted of a canvas wall tent with snow packed around it for insulation. We had a double-burner Coleman stove. When we were cooking, everyone had to shed his parka and leggings as it was hot - well, at least warm - in the tent. The guides supplied us with Woods Five-Star sleeping bags and these were adequate for sleeping in the arctic, although the thought of the next day's hunting made it a restless night.

The next morning, March 13, 1981, we arose early, anxious to begin the hunt. While we had bacon, David cooked us Peary's caribou steaks which tasted so good no one asked for any "store bought" meat after that. Our hunting plan was to follow the ridges until encountering the muskox, then beginning a stalk. Don and his guide went one way and David and I the other. I reflected back on the reading I had done on muskox and the Boone & Crockett requirements for what a mature muskox should be. I wanted one with a straight boss and a rounded, full-looking crown, with horns dropping down and swinging well back up.

We looked over one herd but the bulls didn't measure up to those requirements. After travelling on the ridge another two or three miles, we saw a group of muskox with 15 in the herd. David said five were males and we looked them over carefully for the traits I desired. In the middle of the herd was a bull that looked exactly like the prototype of what I was looking for. We followed the ridge, and then a snow covered draw, keeping low and watching the wind. As is the case with many well-executed stalks, David took me to within 100 yards of the bull and a shot with my 375 H & H Magnum (270 grain bullet) ended my quest. I wanted to mount my animal life-size and I was amazed at the speed with which David took off the hide in 50 degrees below zero temperature.

Back at camp I asked David if I might accompany him running his trap line, as I was enjoying the arctic and had a number of days left on the hunt. We decided to run about 20 miles of his trap line that was in the general direction of Sachs Harbour. The traps are set by a rock or caribou antler, and some scraps of muskox meat are put on all four sides of the trap. To set the trap, he would place a piece of toilet paper over the jaws and then sprinkle soft snow over that.

In the 20 miles of trap line we followed, David had 18 white fox and one beautiful blue fox. Also, we saw a number of muskox and Peary's caribou. David said there are 22,000 muskox on Banks and 6,000 to 8,000 caribou. He said that the muskox need to be reduced as they have no natural enemies and the natives far prefer the caribou for food. The hunting of muskox gives the hunters and trappers of Banks a source of revenue and the hunter a unique hunting experience.

As our plane flew toward Inuvik, and back to our civilization, I could not help but look back toward the interior of Banks Island and reflect on the unspoiled beauty being protected by the ice, snow, and sub-zero temperatures. This is a land where the Eskimo can still exist and make a living off the land.

Photo Courtesy of Dale W. Hoth

Rock Creek in Granite Co., Montana, was the location of Dale W. Hoth's hunt in September 1981 for bighorn sheep. His huge ram scores 186 points.

Photo Courtesy of David D. Rittenhouse

David D. Rittenhouse also hunted Rock Creek in Montana to bag his ram in September 1980. His big ram scores 181-3/8 points.

Photograph by Wm. H. Nesbitt

BIGHORN SHEEP
FIRST AWARD
SCORE: 197-1/8
Locality: Sanders Co., Mont.   Date: November 1979
Hunter: Armand H. Johnson

BIGHORN SHEEP 197-1/8

Armand H. Johnson

I began applying for a permit to hunt bighorn sheep in 1957. Twenty-one years later my persistence paid off. In August 1979, the Montana Department of Fish, Wildlife, and Parks issued me a permit to hunt the Cabinet Mountains surrounding Thompson Falls, Montana, an area well-known for its sheep population.

I live in Missoula (which is about 100 miles southeast of this area) making it possible for me to hunt on weekends with my son Kenton. In the month before I began hunting, Kenton and I mapped-out the area and decided that Priscilla Mountain would be our central point.

Our first hunt was on September 23, 1979. After hunting four weekends, I was discouraged at not having seen more sheep. However, the opportunity to hunt bighorn sheep had come once in a lifetime for me, so I scheduled two full weeks of vacation to hunt. I hunted 12 out of 13 days of vacation.

It was November and Kenton was in school, so I hunted alone. The days were warm, to the mid-forties, but cooled quickly as the sun went down. I decided that my camp trailer would be much more comfortable than camping-out for two weeks. On November 9, I pulled the trailer up the Thompson River to the West Fork and parked it in a camping area. This would serve as my home for the duration of my stay.

The next morning I began an expedition which spanned ten days that I will never forget nor tire of telling. The mountains the sheep inhabit are rugged and rocky, with shale rock and steep ledges covering Priscilla Mountain. I glassed the area surrounding this mountain every day to see any sheep I could spot. That first day, I saw a ram with a 3/4 curl. It was exciting for me because I knew the sheep were there; it was just a matter of finding them.

I met a hunter who told me of a bunch of sheep at a log landing near the highway. I went back to the Jeep and, after reaching the site, discovered the hunter wasn't exaggerating. There were at least 50 sheep, just 50 feet away from me. I recorded their activities with my camera, watching for hours with awe.

The morning of the 12th, I glassed four rams a mile above me. I climbed through the shale rock and ledges to get a closer look. However, when I got to a vantage point they were gone and I didn't catch sight of them again. Across another ridge, I spotted a 3/4-curl ram. I watched as he worked his way across the ledges to within 50 yards of me. Quietly, I waited until he moved on. I hadn't moved when I saw a little ram coming toward me, using the same route. He got within 40 feet of me and then just stood there. It seemed as though he had been run out of a bunch and was merely looking for a friend. He stayed with me as I worked my way down the ridge.

The next few days I observed several sheep in their natural habitat, fighting, feeding, and bedding down. I spotted a couple of 3/4-curl rams and a few that were better than 3/4, but I decided to take pictures rather than shoot as I had plenty of hunting time left.

Tuesday, November 13th, I called home. Kenton needed help packing out a spike elk he had shot, so I returned home.

I resumed my quest on Thursday morning, climbing the ledges and shale rock where I had seen a big ram a few days earlier. I had no luck, but I continued searching.

Saturday was rainy and foggy, with visibility only about 100 feet. I climbed the slide rock to a small bench. The fog wasn't lifting and it was so cold that I built a fire, quite a feat since all the wood was wet. Just after noon the fog lifted, allowing me to glass the ridges. However, the sheep were under cover from the weather also.

The rain held through the next day which meant fog again. By noon the dreary gloom started to move out of the valley but it was too late to climb into the canyons. I tried a trail I had used earlier that week, seeing a couple of 3/4-curl rams with a group of ewes and lambs. Darkness set in before I could reach the Jeep. The main ridge along this trail changes directions several times, going up and down. Because of the rain clouds I was unable to use the moonlight to see. After both sets of flashlight batteries had gone dim, and I had crossed my tracks in the half-inch of snow now on the ground, I decided it was time to build a fire and spend the night.

I cut pine boughs and built a shelter between the fallen timber to stop the wind. I then cut more boughs to lie on, but this proved very uncomfortable due to the icicles frozen on the needles beneath me. The temperature had already dropped to about 20 degrees, so I kept a fire going and took short cat-naps throughout the night.

Dawn was a welcome sight next morning. I started walking at about 7:00 am, and found I was only about 100 yards from the ridge that led into the main ridge. I went back to the camper to eat and fix a lunch, starting again about 11:00 a.m.

I drove east, following a four-wheel drive road. Then I followed sheep trails on foot which led me into the steep slopes and ledges the sheep love. Below me, I saw some sheep grazing in a meadow. I took off my packboard and set-up the spotting scope. I studied a couple of 3/4-curl rams in the bunch. Falling rocks above me turned my attention to a fairly nice 3/4-curl ram coming down the trail. He came close to me and watched me for a few seconds, then turned and looked out over a ledge. I picked up the camera and rifle, hoping to see the large ram that had been so elusive. The rocks above me again stirred. This time another 3/4-curl ram and a ewe followed the trail. A few minutes later, the rocks started falling and a big ram followed where the other three had come down. I could see that his horns were better than a full curl, protruding well below his jaw. He was in no hurry and luckily he hadn't seen me.

When he reached the trail the others had taken, he stopped and looked at me.

Again I could see that he had exceptionally large horns. I wasted no time; this was the ram I had seen and I didn't want to risk losing him again. I shot, felling him instantly.

I knew he was a very good ram, but he was better than I had anticipated. November 20th I returned to Missoula and called the office of the District Fish, Wildlife, and Parks Department. I wanted to talk to Jim Ford, District Supervisor, because he is an Official Measurer for the Boone and Crockett Club. I made a 2:00 p.m. appointment. Jim's green score of my ram was: left horn - 46 inches long, 16-5/8 inches around the base; right horn - 44-6/8 inches long, 16-4/8 inches around the base. The total green score was 200-6/8 points by the Boone and Crockett scoring system.

On January 22, 1980, Jim Ford measured the horns officially after the 60-day drying period required by the Boone and Crockett Club rules. His scoring showed my ram to be the biggest recorded in Montana since 1955, and the biggest ram taken by a hunter since 1924. It was also a dream come true for me.

Photograph by Wm. H. Nesbitt

BIGHORN SHEEP
SECOND AWARD
SCORE: 186-3/8
Locality: Simpson River, B. C.   Date: October 1979
Hunter: James A. Walls

BIGHORN SHEEP 186-3/8

James A. Walls

This was the second trip my partner, Mike Moroni, and I had made for sheep in three years. The previous hunt had been unsuccessful for a ram.

I was raised in Montana and now live on a cattle ranch in the Cariboo region of British Columbia. I've been fortunate to have enjoyed tremendous hunting on both sides of the border.

Our hunt started on the 5th of October on the Simpson River Trail, in the mighty Kootenay Mountains of southeastern British Columbia. We'd ridden the horses for about six hours to a place overlooking Eohippus Lake, where we made camp and thought about tomorrow.

Daybreak found us riding along the bottom slopes of a high range, stopping now and then to glass the high country. About ten o'clock, we paused once more. With thoughts of giving-up for the day, I glassed the area one last time, and spotted the biggest ram I'd ever hoped to see! There were two others bedded down with the big one on an outcropping of rock.

We quickly rode on past for a half-mile, where we picketed the horses. We then started a tough, 2-1/2 hour climb from an elevation of 4,500 feet up the east slope of very rugged Cathedral Mountain. Wondering all the while if our rams would still be where we'd spotted them, we finally crested this 9,000 foot hunk of granite. When we glassed below us, there they were, about 300 yards away.

They still had not gotten wind of us nor detected our movements. We watched for 10 minutes or so, deciding on our targets. Then, we crawled some more to a point overlooking the rams. Our shots would be over 200 yards, straight downhill.

We both shot on the count of three, and to our amazement, neither ram fell! We apparently hadn't crawled far enough over the rim of the ledge, and both bullets hit the dirt in front of the barrels. The sheep bolted downhill, but then, instead of going away from us, for some reason ran towards us. We stood up and fired again. That time both rams fell, and fell, and fell!

We watched with dismay as our hard-won trophies cartwheeled for about 2,000 feet, before crashing to a stop in a narrow canyon. Naturally we assumed the horns would be completely destroyed after such a battering. We were overjoyed to discover, when we finally caught up to them, that the horns weren't damaged except for a few gouges and a shattered tip.

Photograph by Wm. H. Nesbitt

DESERT SHEEP
FIRST AWARD
SCORE: 192-5/8
Locality: Baja Calif., Mexico   Date: November 1979
Hunter: Javier Lopez del Bosque

DESERT SHEEP 192-5/8

Javier Lopez del Bosque

On the 31st of October 1979, I left Saltillo for Mexicali along with my brother, Isidro, to look for a big desert sheep. We arrived there at 11:00 a.m. and had lunch at the Lucerna Hotel. At 4:00 p.m., we set out in the direction of the Main Camp (Arroyo Grande), about three hours by jeep. Once we got there, each of us settled in our own tent. Later, we had dinner, talked, and came to an agreement as to the hunting ground.

Very early in the morning on November 1 (5:00 a.m.), I started to climb the Sierra El Borrego. My hunting team was made up of guide Juan Antonio Romero; two scope spotters, and two helpers. All of them carried backpacks with food, water, and light sleeping bags. During our second day, in the afternoon, we saw a group of five ewes and one ram. We watched them about 20 minutes with the 60 power telescope, and we deduced that it was a 165 point ram. As I already had one that size, we decided to pass it by.

On November 3, we descended from the rocky mountain and again refilled our packing bags with food and water. On the same day we moved to "La Mina" mountain.

We hunted La Mina on November 4 for rams, but we did not find any big ones. We were very happy to see large flocks of ewes and rams; but, none were what I had in mind. I said to Juan Antonio that I wanted a 180 point one. He responded: "We will do our best to get it."

November 6 found us coming down from "La Sierrita" mountain, after exploring it.

We went to a place named "La Tinaja Colorada" by jeep on November 7. We went as far as a large waterhole at the foot of a high mountain. We took our knapsacks, filled them with cans of food, "gordas de harina", and water. We started to climb the mountain at 6:00 a.m. When we reached our destination it was 12:00 noon. Juan Antonio and his son, who was a scope spotter, separated to watch with binoculars, soon seeing various flocks of ewes. At 1:00 p.m., we had lunch and began to worry, for we had not seen any rams even of regular size.

All afternoon, we continued watching with binoculars. About 20 minutes before sunset, Juan Antonio threw a little stone toward me so that I would turn my head and look at him. With one of his arms he made signs indicating that he had seen a big ram. I went up and looked through the telescope. When I saw the ram, I felt my pulse quicken. I liked this ram very much! It was grazing with another ram of very regular size. The wind was blowing strongly and did not allow me to fix my sight well, but we realized that it was a trophy ram. I asked Juan Antonio for his estimation and he answered, "180 points."

The rams were about a mile away from us. Unfortunately, daylight was fading fast. We left the rams grazing.

We came down about 200 yards, to where we had left our knapsacks, and then had dinner. We went to sleep about 7:00 p.m. Near midnight, the wind began to blow strongly and it started to rain. We rushed into a cave, taking our sleeping bags. We stayed there until dawn.

Next morning, we left the cave nervously, hoping to spot the rams again. We knew that rain and wind could have made them move to another place, far from where we had seen them. But, I felt much better when Juan Antonio mumbled, "They are over there." The two rams soon separated; the bigger one moved down and in 10 minutes was lost behind a hill.

Juan Antonio and I made up our minds to leave everybody and the equipment, except my rifle. We had to come down from the high mountain and climb another one of the same height, in order to be able to reach the place where the big ram had laid down. We began to climb down at 6:00 a.m. By 9:00 a.m. we were positioned and looking for it, when Juan Antonio whispered: "It is lying over there."

The ram showed just his right horn. We checked the wind, planning to shoot from a window that allowed me a shot from 250 yards. We got near the window, carefully, about 10:00 a.m. When I looked through the window, I had the most beautiful spectacle that a hunter can see. The ram had risen; it was at the edge of a cliff. I raised my 300 Weatherby Magnum and I put the one minute dot on his shoulder and shot. The ram turned around and began to run. I shot again but the animal was already running dead. It was so strong that went up and then down about 200 yards.

The helpers had come down when they heard the shots. When they reached us, we took some photos. All of us were very happy. We arrived at the Main Camp (Arroyo Grande) just in time to have dinner. There I learned that my brother Isidro, who was with Jorge Belloc, had not been lucky. They had passed-up a 170 point ram.

I returned to Mexicali on November 9, taking along the ram's horns. I took them to the Director of Fauna in Baja California, Eliseo Araujo. He sent the horns to the two biologists of the Secretary of Agriculture, in the same building. We were having a cup of coffee when one of them came in and gave us the score of 196 points. Then, Eliseo told me: "It is the largest desert sheep ever taken by a hunter."

Photo Courtesy of John Virgil Zenz

John Virgil Zenz hunted Clark Co., Nevada, in November 1980 for desert sheep. This huge ram that scores 180 points was his reward.

Photo Courtesy of C. R. (Bob) Palmer

Arroyo Grande of Baja Calif., Mexico, was the setting for C. R. (Bob) Palmer's hunt for desert sheep in December 1979 that resulted in this fine ram that scores 168-1/8 points.

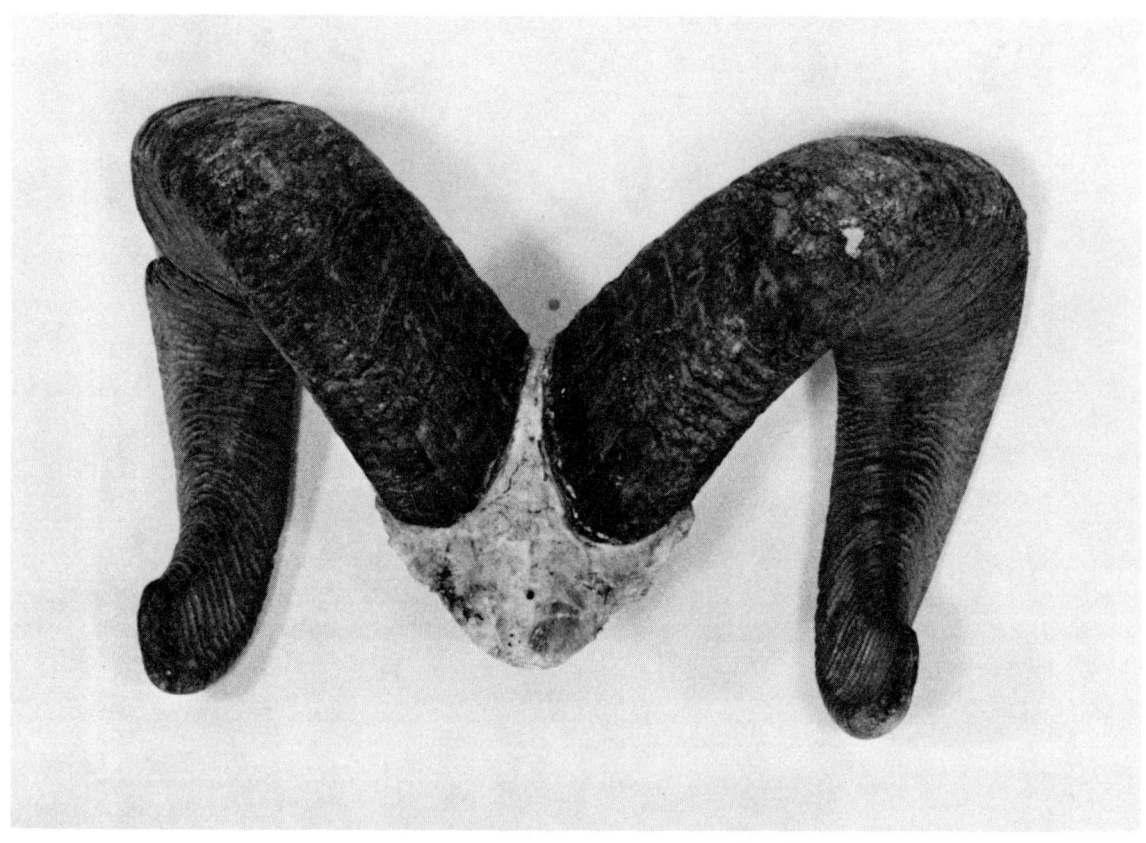

Photograph by Wm. H. Nesbitt

DESERT SHEEP
SECOND AWARD
SCORE: 191-2/8

Locality: Baja Calif., Mexico Date: February 1979
Hunter: Claude Bourguignon

DESERT SHEEP 191-2/8

Claude Bourguignon

I departed San Diego at 1:30 p.m. on Sunday, February 21, 1982 in my Cherokee Jeep. I arrived in Mexicali, Mexico, at the Hotel Lucerna, that afternoon. Manuel Cerdas, a good friend with whom I hunt quail and doves south of Ensenada during the fall of each year, introduced me to Melchor Aguiar, my guide. Manuel was going to act as translator, and also cameraman, for this hunt. I have a little knowledge of Spanish but the conversation would have to be very slow. During the hunt there would be times that I couldn't have slow conversation, especially when a trophy is standing there.

I offered Manuel and Melchor a drink before we departed for the desert. They started explaining to me approximately where we were going. It was the mountain range on the west side of the highway between Mexicali and San Felipe. The mountains are approximately one to two miles from the main highway. I had hunted the same mountain range for quail, approximately 60 miles toward Ensenada. They also told me that some 50 hunters since October had been successful in obtaining their desert sheep. The scores were good, in the lower 180's and average was around 170. I said that this was my first sheep for the grand slam and I would be happy with an average-sized one.

Manuel drove my jeep. Once we left the highway, we were on a desert road and I wondered how the guide, whom we were following, could know the desert so well. There were many tracks made by various dune buggies, motocrossers, and other vehicles. We drove the desert for approximately 1-1/2 hours, reaching the base camp around 8:00 p.m. I had a good-sized tent for my camp, with a cot for my sleeping bag. We had a couple of beers and all sat around talking. There was a chef, just a wonderful lady of 68 years, who spoke only Spanish. We got along fine with my little bit of Spanish. I was introduced to two assistant guides who would carry my sleeping bag, extra shirts and socks, and, of course, the food and drinks for the hunt.

Monday morning, we had breakfast at 6:00 a.m. and left at 6:45 a.m. in the pickup truck. I decided to carry my 338 rifle instead of my 7 mm, as I was more used to it. I knew it was not the best for a long shot, but I had sighted-it-in at 200 yards the previous Sunday. We arrived at the base of the mountains. Needless to say, they appeared all rocks and cactus, and looking at the highest peak, approximately 10,000 feet tall. From that base, everybody was scoping for sheep. We didn't see any and decided to take the trail (which was a riverbed), as the snow was melting from the top and water was running. It was pure and drinkable water.

It was a bright, sunny day with a temperature of 70 degrees. We kept a fairly good pace, jumping from one rock to another, sometimes needing help from a guide to grab my hand after certain jumps. Neeless to say, it got hard on the legs as I was not used to this type of walking day-in and day-out. After two hours, we stopped to have an orange and decided to scope around for sheep; we still didn't see anything.

We kept on walking until around noon, when we arrived at a large waterhole where we decided to stop for lunch and, of course, a little siesta. From that spot, we scoped but didn't see any sheep. Around 2:00 p.m. we departed and walked for another two hours. At that time, I figured we had travelled approximately six miles and were up 5,000 feet in that riverbed.

We came to a large sandy area between two mountains and decided that this would be a good spot for camping overnight. It was around 4:00 p.m. Manuel informed me that the guides were going up the canyon 1,500 feet to scope for sheep. He asked me if I wanted to go. He said that I didn't need to go, that we could set up the sleeping bags and wait for their return. Since this was the first day, and my legs were weakening on me, I decided I would rest. So, Melchor and his two assistants went up the canyon.

Manuel and I sat around and discussed some of our quail-hunting trips, and some of the enjoyment of the day so far, and hoped they would see some sheep. He said, "Don't worry, you have 10 days and before the end of those 10 days you will definitely have your sheep." He was prophetic.

They came down at 6:00 p.m., just about dark. They all had big smiles on their faces. They had seen a sheep that had very large horns, with tremendous base size. The large sheep was with two smaller sheep. They said the big one had approached to approximately 50 yards. Needless to say, if I had gone up with them, the hunt might be over. Melchor said it was the biggest set of horns he had ever seen. He figured they were at least 190 points. That got my heart pumping. All night, I could hardly sleep thinking that if I had gone up with them, I probably would have shot that sheep.

The next morning, we got up very early. Manuel, Melchor, and the two assistants went to the opposite mountain where they had scoped six sheep the day before. This time, they wanted to look at the one with the big horns to see if it was still where they had spotted it the day before. About an hour later, they came down and said they had spotted him. He was on the way down toward the desert. We packed and went down the riverbed, stopping to scope the sheep. I had not yet seen the sheep. Melchor located him, and said he was moving down. We kept going down; at that time the sheep were nearly 4,000 to 5,000 feet above us.

We kept going down. We stopped for lunch at noon, when we scoped the three sheep. I could not see them through my binoculars, due to the sameness of their color and the terrain, which hides their appearance. They blend in with the background of rocks, cactus, and other features. We finally worked our way down to where our truck was parked. Still, Melchor could see the sheep on the mountain, about 6,000 feet above the desert. He said that we should go up there tomorrow, prepared for at least three days. We would take two additional assistants to carry the food, drinks, and everything else necessary. I kept saying to myself that I should have gone up with them. Manuel said, "Not to worry, if that sheep is meant for you, you will get it." It started to rain at 9:00 p.m. and didn't quit all night.

It was still raining when we woke, so our hunt was canceled for that morning. The rain brought snow to the 7,000-foot level. Manuel said that was good because the sheep would not go to the snow; they would remain where we saw them last. The rain stopped at 3:00 p.m. and we decided to go with the pickup. This time we took a spotting scope. We put the scope on the pickup, so I could see the sheep if we spotted them. We arrived at the base of the mountain and, sure enough, Melchor could see the sheep in his binoculars.

They installed the scope on the hood of the truck and I saw those sheep for the first time. I could see the one with the big horns, and I said to Melchor, "I want that sheep." Melchor said that next morning we would go up the mountain early. I looked at the mountain. It appeared straight-up for 7,000 feet. So, we went to bed early, planning on getting up at 5:00 a.m. The two additional guides arrived and spent the night with us.

The next morning, we packed sufficient food and drinks for three days. Manuel said that if we had to stay on the mountain, we would have the two additional assistant guides go down to get more food and drinks. I thought this was a very organized group. All I had to carry was my body and my rifle. They carried everything else.

As we reached the foot of the mountain, we tried to locate the sheep with the binoculars but couldn't see them. The rain had left beautiful snow peaks at 7,000 feet and the weather was 70 degrees. We started up, which was definitely harder than climbing up the riverbed. This time we were at more like a 30 degree angle versus a 4 degree angle. In two or three areas on the way up, they had to drop a cable to me so I could pull myself up the rocks. Looking back, we could see the desert areas and the mountains to the east of us, approximately four miles away.

Every hour or so, we stopped for an orange and a drink of water. I had to catch my breath, but the guides were like the sheep we hunted. They had no problem carrying the packs and walking. Melchor was leading the way, with an assistant guide behind him. I was behind him, followed by an assistant guide in case I needed help. Manuel was closing the trail with my camera, taking all the pictures he could take for souvenirs of this great hunt. At 11:00 a.m. we sat and had an orange. Everyone had their binoculars out, trying to locate the sheep; we couldn't see anything. Melchor indicated a knoll approximately 1,200 feet higher than we were, saying that we had to reach that knoll which would give us a great view of the plateau. The plateau was all rock formation, not just the beautiful flatland on top of the mountains in Colorado.

As Melchor reached the knoll at noon, he said in Spanish, "They are there." Manuel behind me said, "Claude, be ready!" I put a cartridge in the chamber, took my hat off, and leaned my rifle on my hat. Sweat was running into my eyes, and my heart was pumping fast. I could see the three sheep, 300 yards from us. Manuel changed from wide angle to telephoto lens on my camera and started shooting pictures. All six of us stood and looked at the sheep. The big sheep was walking toward us but there was a big valley between us and the sheep. I could hear Melchor saying, "Shoot," and my friend Manuel saying, "Don't shoot; he is approaching." I fired and missed.

Manuel said I shot behind him. I think the scope had banged on some rocks and it was off from left to right. I loaded another cartridge and aimed at its neck, as it was broadside. My shot hit him in the lungs. He took five steps and fell approximately 35 feet from the cliff. We could see him still breathing, so we decided to stay quiet for five minutes. Melchor couldn't wait. He walked slowly toward the animal, knowing the ram would be dead by the time he reached him. When he did reach him, Melchor screamed in Spanish, indicating that my ram had the biggest set of horns he had ever seen in his guiding life, which was about 20 years. I arrived second, my heart still pumping fast, but now with pleasure rather than fatigue. All of a sudden, the mountain didn't look so high.

Needless to say, we measured and re-measured the ram, with scores of 194 to 195. Manuel kept screaming, "This is number one," and I kept saying, "I hope so." I told Melchor I wanted the skin, since I was going to do a full-mount of that animal. He skinned it and packed the skin and horns. The other guides took the meat. My guide said it was 1:30 p.m. and we didn't have to stay up there. So, we started going down, which is a lot more difficult than going up.

We took a different route on a slope of 15 degrees. We jumped from one rock to another, which is a lot harder on your legs as you feel the impact from the hard rocks on the bottom of your feet and knees. I still have a cracked bone from that hunt. We reached camp, where I had a couple of bottles of wine and a bottle of Crown Royal. I have to admit they went around the table in no time. I said that next day I would go to San Felipe and get all the necessary food (fresh shrimp, beer, tequila, etc.,) and treat everyone to a "Grande dinner", which I did.

The entry measurement for Boone and Crockett was 191-5/8, which places it very high in the records book. The measurement for Safari Club International was 194-3/8, which placed it first in the last issue of the S.C.I. records book. At the S.C.I. Convention in Las Vegas, I was awarded the first trophy for the North American species.

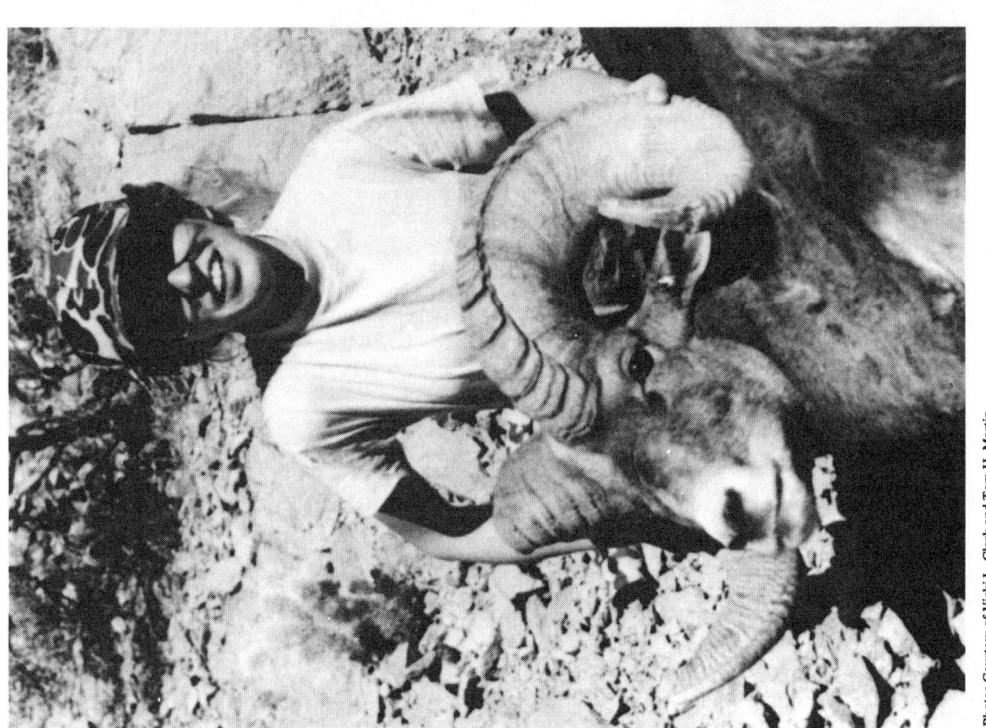

Photos Courtesy of Vicki L. Clark and Tom H. Martin

(Left) Hunting the Kofa Mountains of Arizona in December 1980, Vicki L. Clark shot this fine desert sheep that scores 176-2/8 points. (Right) Tom H. Martin shot this desert sheep in December 1980. He was hunting in Mohave Co., Arizona, and his trophy scores 168 points.

Photograph by Wm. H. Nesbitt

DESERT SHEEP
THIRD AWARD
SCORE: 186-2/8
Locality: Baja Calif., Mexico   Date: February 1981
Hunter: Robert P. Miller

DESERT SHEEP 186-2/8

Robert P. Miller

Growing up in southwestern Pennsylvania, Robert Miller learned how to hunt, fish, and trap. He spent many days afield learning from his father, Paul Miller, about the great outdoors and the joys that it holds for the hunter. Like many hunters, he harbored a passion to hunt the elusive desert sheep. In 1981, he got his chance and fortune smiled brightly his way.

Miller's outfitter was George Belloc. Their base camp, La Palamita, was about 200 miles south of Mexicali. Unfortunately, the Spanish-English translator who was to accompany them had taken ill. Since the Mexican members of the hunting party could not speak English, and Miller couldn't speak any Spanish, it promised to be an interesting trip.

Guadalupe (Lupe) was designated as chief guide and Rafael as camp chief. At the base camp, Miller was introduced to the spotters, Cuauhtemoc and Jose, the packers Mario and Francisco, Reyna the cook, and Adolfo, the camp guard. Miller learned very quickly that there was a communication gap. Dinner was a field cooked Mexican meal. Miller did not know exactly what went into the dinner, but it was very good and extremely hot. After dinner, everyone sat around the camp fire, laughing and telling stories. Miller found he could communicate somewhat, using sign language.

The camp was alive before sun-up with the sounds of clanging pots and pans and the aroma of fresh meat on the grill. After breakfast, everything was loaded into the pickup truck. Cuauhtemoc then took a cardboard box and taped a target to it. He stepped-off a hundred paces and placed the target so Miller could sight-in his rifle. Miller's shots looked good; one in the small bull's-eye and two inside the first circle.

Everyone except the camp guard climbed into the two trucks to head farther south and higher in the mountains. In three hours they came to the mouth of a ravine where they stopped to unload the trucks. A small outcamp was then set up. Taking minimum gear and sleeping bags, the party left the small camp on foot. They were prepared to spend the next several days in the mountains.

Trudging up the ravine, Lupe led the way, followed by Miller, then the others. This same "pecking order" would be followed throughout the hunt. Lupe, who appeared to be in his early fifties, was beginning to gray and had a paunch over his belt. But, he was tough as nails. He easily led the pack, literally walking them into the ground. After gaining several thousand feet in elevation, they stopped for lunch.

Franciso reached into his pack, looked at Miller and offered, "Pepsi?" The sun beat down hot and bright. Each man was given something to drink and a plastic bag. The bags contained burritos, wrapped in foil. After a fire was built, the Mexicans unwrapped the aluminum foil and placed the burritos on the hot ashes. When cooked, they retrieved them with their bare hands from the ashes. As Miller bit into his first burrito, he found scrambled eggs, just right for a late breakfast.

After lunch, Mario and Francisco indicated they were going to build camp on the spot and that Jose would accompany Miller up the mountainside.

The panorama at the crest stunned Miller. He had hunted throughout the United States and the Canadian Rockies, including the Mackenzie Mountains and the Brooks Range of Alaska. But, each time he reached the top of one of these magnificent sculptures, he felt overwhelmed by the view. He always had the feeling that man is really insignificant when compared to the expanse of such vistas.

Due north from them was a large plateau, perhaps two miles long and one mile wide. Due east, a huge valley lay on the opposite side of the mountain they had just climbed. The long, narrow ridge on which they were standing extended due south, and extending westward was the slope of the mountain they had climbed.

The guides began glassing while Miller rested, trying to shade himself from the merciless sun. After a few minutes rest, Miller stayed in a crouch and worked himself to a position to glass, keeping his silhouette away from the skyline. The party remained there for several hours. Lupe indicated to Miller that there was a big sheep in this area, an animal he called "Borrego Grande". Back in Mexicali, George Belloc had told Miller that Lupe would take him to the area where a hunter had missed a great sheep the previous year. This was obviously the area, but no ram to be seen. They saw only two ewes and three kids. The sinking sun prompted the party to start back to their camp, several thousand feet below.

At camp, the burritos were already on the fire and the sleeping bags laid out around it. Francisco assisted Miller in removing his backpack. He made signs to ask if Miller had seen the Borrego Grande. Miller indicated no. Francisco said "Bull ——". Miller now knew that Francisco knew at least two words of English.

Dinner consisted of three burritos, one each of egg, hot dog, and very hot chili. A can of beans, cooked on the fire, and a can of peaches for dessert, rounded-out the meal. Desert sand was the detergent used for washing the dishes; water is precious in the desert.

Next morning's breakfast was another one of those hot chili burritos. During breakfast, Miller began to notice the aches and pains caused by the previous day's activities. Although well-conditioned prior to the hunt, he was finding these mountains to be steeper than imagined. As they broke camp, the sun was beginning to brighten the sky and no clouds were in sight - another scorching day!

They were half-way up when the sun began striking the peaks of the western mountains. At that angle, the sun made a brown western mountain turn into orange fire, while mountains to the east maintained their brownish-gray tinge. It was an amazing contrast, and a sight Miller felt privileged to behold.

When they reached the top of the mountain, Miller began to wonder if he had trained enough. His feet had developed blisters the size of half-dollars on the inside of each heel. Even though the Mexicans laughed at his situation, Miller could tell they were also concerned. Sore feet could seriously damage their chances for success.

Miller searched his toilet kit for the blister cure. As he did, Lupe set up the spotting scope. That meant he had located sheep. Miller decided to forget the blisters. He slipped socks and shoes back on, then worked himself around to Lupe's position to see what he had discovered. It was a ram on top of the next mountain, but quickly out-of-view. Lupe used graphic hand signals to tell Miller it was a small ram, probably not legal. Miller worked his way back to his backpack, found the blister cream and moleskin, and doctored his feet.

The party glassed for another hour before deciding to head southeast down the mountainside, across the valley, and up the next mountain. When they reached bottom and removed their packs, Jose discovered he had left his binoculars on top of the mountain. With a shrug of his shoulders, he prepared to go back up the mountain they had just descended. He removed his pack, put his canteen over his shoulder and two burritos in his pockets, and started up the mountain at a pace that was halfway between a walk and a run.

The wind was at the party's back. That meant no fire and cold burritos, cold beans, and warm water for lunch. Jose returned down the mountain at the same pace he had left. Though he had been gone two hours, he was ready to go again without a minute's rest.

The next mountaintop gave a spectacular view in every direction. There was only one peak higher than the one the party was on. It lay across a large saddle to the southeast. The party moved across a little flat area of the mountain to a sheer cliff that dropped straight down for several thousand feet. From this vantage point they could see the valleys to the east, the plateaus to the north and south, and across the saddle and up the peak to the southeast. Miller found a little cave where he decided to stand just inside to get some relief from the blazing sun. His face, hands and forearms were all beginning to burn and blister. But, when he stepped inside, he realized it was hotter there than in the sun. It was later explained to him that when the sun shines into an east-facing cave, it heats the rocks inside, without vegetation to absorb it. Needless to say, Miller quickly exited the cave to rejoin his friends in the sun.

They glassed for only a short time, sending Cuauhtemoc across the saddle and up the peak to the southeast. Miller saw the emotion on Lupe's face when he glassed where Cuauhtemoc had gone. Miller swung his own glasses toward the peak and saw Cuauhtemoc crouched down, motioning for them to come.

They quickly repacked and started at a full trot down the slope, across the saddle and up the peak toward Cuauhtemoc. The pace slowed to a fast climb when they started up the mountain. Everyone was on the peak except Francisco, who had gone back to the outcamp where Rafael and Reyna were staying, to pick up food and water. They were a day-and-a-half from the outcamp, and had only had one day's food supply. Francisco would bring enough supplies for two more days for each of them.

Reaching Cuauhtemoc's position, Lupe looked through the spotting scope, then quickly motioned for Miller. Miller made his way to Lupe's position with his rifle on his back, crawling on hands and knees the last few yards. Lupe signaled for him to remove his hat, take a short look, and get down. He did exactly as instructed. As Miller looked through the scope, his heart fluttered. Although the ram was a mile away, with mirage making the scene ripple, he saw "Borrego Grande".

Lupe and Cuauhtemoc were as excited as Miller. They made plans while Miller tried to keep the broiling sun from his hands and face. After a minute of discussion, Lupe sent Cuauhtemoc to retrieve the scope and motioned for Mario to come there. He instructed Mario to go back to the last glassing area to wait for Francisco. He also told Mario where they were going and how they were going to stalk the great ram.

From that point onward, not a word was spoken in any language. They moved, one at a time, southward along the west side of the ridge, keeping the ram on the east. The wind was blowing from west to east, forcing them to go high on the mountain and hope the wind would blow their scent over the sheep, not down on the plateau where he grazed.

They moved steadily along, until suddenly Lupe came to the end of the mountain, a sheer cliff. Lupe sent Cuauhtemoc down the west side of the mountain to see if there was a way around the sheer cliff. He returned about 40 minutes later. There was no alternate route. Lupe motioned for Miller to join him at the peak of the mountain. They crawled up to the crest, to a little rock ledge on the sheep's side, always keeping their silhouettes from being skylined. They then made themselves as comfortable as possible, clinging to that 24-inch ledge.

Lupe pulled back from the scope slowly and indicated that Miller should take a look. It was adjusted to 35 power, which offered the best visibility in this spotting scope. Miller's first impression was that the entire scope was filled with one pair of horns. But, the ram was a good 700 yards away.

Lupe asked Miller if he could shoot that far. Miller shook his head no. Lupe indicated he wanted Miller to shoot. Miller responded, "Why?" They were both perplexed at this point, and the communication gap was magnified. Then the ram laid down, keeping his head high. Miller was tired and his throat parched. The ledge was too small for them to move to a more restful position. Water and the rest of the gear had been left with Jose. Lupe again encouraged Miller to shoot. Miller declined, hoping the ram would move closer.

The ram got up and gazed slowly in all directions. Then, he started walking briskly straight towards Miller, looking back over his right shoulder as if there was danger in that direction. He came 200 yards closer (still about 500 yards away), then began grazing again. Lupe again urged Miller to shoot. Miller prepared himself to shoot, but then looked at Lupe and indicated that it was too far. Lupe dropped his head as if to say, "What am I going to do with this gringo?"

When Miller looked back at the ram, he had begun to move again. But, this time he was moving away from them to their left. Instinctively, Miller knew it was now or never. Lupe crawled alongside him and grasped his belt and trousers with his left hand to keep Miller from falling from the ledge when he fired. At 500 yards, the ram occupied a very small portion of the center of the 9 power scope. Immediately after the rifle cracked, Miller could hear the thud of bullet on flesh.

The ram dropped, but got up before Miller could relocate him in the scope. Miller's second shot ricocheted off the rocks beneath the ram. Then, the ram paused motionless, looking in their direction. Knowing this would be his last opportunity with darkness falling fast, Miller carefully positioned the cross hairs. This time, the ram went down to stay.

It took an hour to descend the mountain, going slowly to avoid accident. A fire was then built to help Mario and Francisco locate the rest of the party. Lupe and Miller went directly to the ram. A hasty measurement of the horns indicated lengths of well over 40 inches and base circumferences close to 15 inches.

The next morning, they ate breakfast and played catch with rocks while waiting for enough light to take photographs. After photographs, they skinned the ram for a full-mount. Then, they broke camp and began the long journey back to the outcamp. Hunter's joy made their packs lighter and their footsteps quicker.

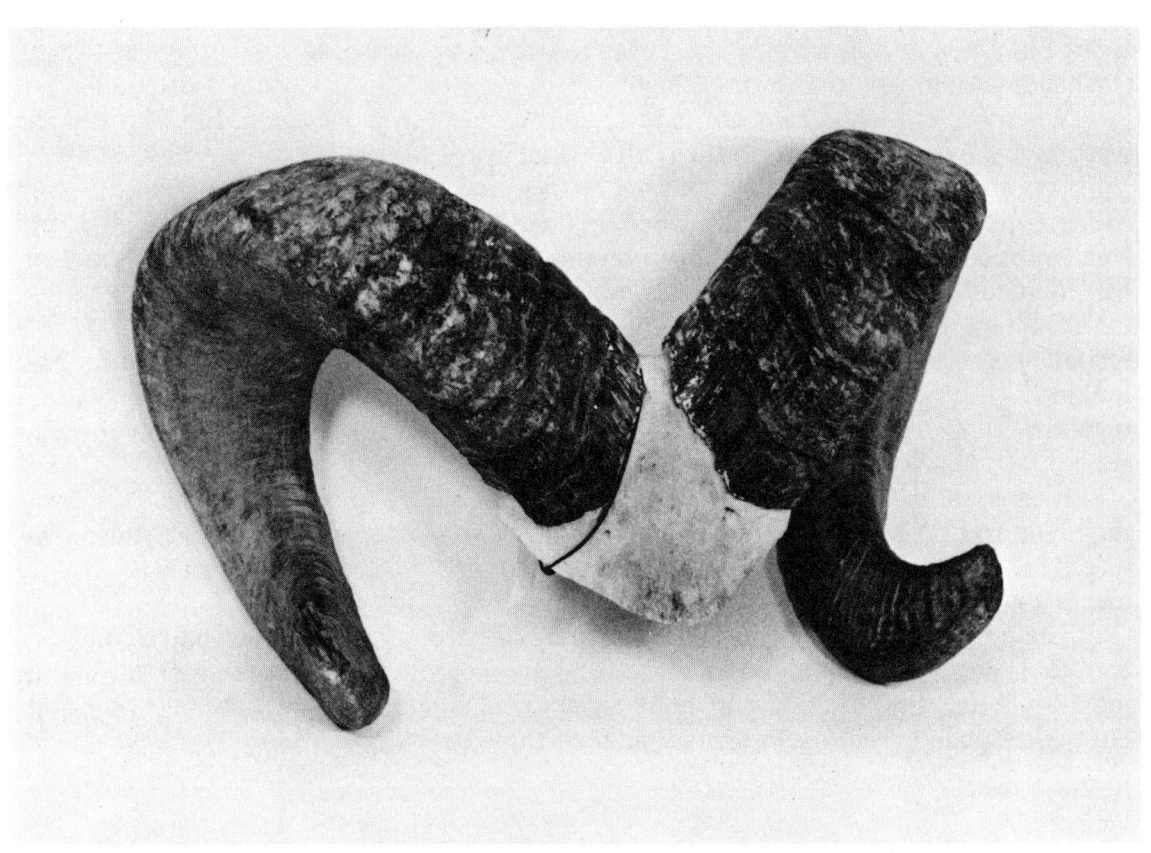

DESERT SHEEP
CERTIFICATE OF MERIT
SCORE: 187-7/8

Locality: Pima Co., Ariz. Date: January 1982
Hunter: Carl A. Mattias, Sr.

DESERT SHEEP 187-7/8

Carl A. Mattias, Sr.

Carl A. Mattias, Sr., is a member of the Papago Indian Tribe of Arizona. The tribal reservation, located near Pima, offers some fine big-game hunting, including the elusive desert bighorn sheep.

Under long-standing agreements, Indian tribes are responsible for management and the regulation of hunting for the big-game found on their lands. The tribal leadership can grant valid hunting licenses to members of the tribe to hunt on tribal lands. Such permission was granted to Carl Mattias to hunt desert sheep on the reservation in January, 1982.

Mattias found his great ram on January 17th on the Quijotoa area. He worked himself to within 80 yards of his quarry. It was nearly 11:30 a.m. when his 243 Rem. brought the sheep down.

After the required drying period, the horns were measured. They easily made the entrance score for the records book. At the end of the period, Mattias was requested to send-in his trophy as it ranked in the all-time top ten of its category. Had it not come in to the Judges Panel, it would be asterisked in future editions of the records book. As a trophy taken under conditions *not* available to the general public (restricted license), it was only eligible for a Certificate of Merit.

Photograph by Wm. H. Nesbitt

DALL'S SHEEP
FIRST AWARD
SCORE: 176-6/8

Locality: Chugach Mts., Alaska   Date: August 1982
Hunter: Charles H. Rohrer

DALL'S SHEEP 176-6/8

Charles H. Rohrer

It hardly seemed possible that only a few short months earlier my brother Dick, who is an outfitter and master guide, called and said, "Let's go for our rams this fall."

I had hunted with my brother in Alaska in 1970 when I took a Kodiak bear, a 72-inch moose, an elk, and three deer. At that time we talked about a sheep hunt. But, it seemed that every time we were going to go, something would turn up for one or the other of us. We would always end-up saying, "Well, next year."

So, here I was descending on Anchorage where Dick was to meet me. (He lives on Kodiak Island.) After a reunion of handshakes and back-slaps, we picked up some supplies and my hunting licenses.

On Sunday we headed for Glenallen, where we were to fly-out at 2:30 p.m. Because of overcast skies and poor visibility over the mountains, we didn't get out until 7:30 p.m. Dick had selected an area in the Tunsena River Drainage of the Chugach Mountains.

We flew up several big valleys, finally finding the lake that we wanted to use as our base camp. The pilot made one circle and we saw several sheep on the hillside. I knew we were in the right place. Throttle back, flaps down, and splash, we were in the water. We taxied to the shore and quickly unloaded our gear.

It was 8:00 p.m. and starting to get dark, so we quickly set up our tent and got organized. We had hoped to do some hiking and spotting Sunday, but were unable to do so. That left only Monday to look around before the season opened on Tuesday, the 10th of August. We turned in early so we could get an early start the next morning.

It was a new area for my brother, and I had never hunted sheep before, so anticipation was high as we crawled into our sleeping bags. I don't remember, but I'm sure visions of rams danced in our heads.

We were up at the crack of dawn and had breakfast as the sun came over the mountains. While we ate, we saw some white spots on the mountain to our north. A look with the binoculars verified our suspicions, sheep.

This called for the spotting scope. After a close-up view we were satisfied that they were all ewes and lambs, about 15 total. We got our packs organized and headed west. We climbed for about an hour, reaching a big valley. We continued to climb and spot all morning. It was very evident that there had been sheep there very recently, but we saw nothing. It was close to noon. We decided to head back to camp to get some lunch before hiking up the valley to the east of the lake. As we came down the mountain, Dick hollered, "Sheep! sheep!" He always gets excited when he sees sheep, even if they are five miles away. Sure enough, we could make out three white spots way up on the side of the mountains to the east of the lake.

The spotting scope told us what we needed to know. Rams! We hurried back to camp, had a quick lunch, and headed east to get a better look at those rams. We were camped near the mouth of the lake, so we could cross it in hip boots. Then, the climbing began. After about 1-1/2 hours of climbing, we were up in the big valley to the east of the lake. We chose a vantage point about a mile from where the rams were seen and put the spotting scope into use. After a close examination we knew that one ram was legal and another one had possibilities.

It was slightly hazy, so we could not determine just how big the larger ram was; but, we were sure he was a full-curl. If he stayed put, we would know for sure tomorrow. We stayed there for the rest of the afternoon, watching the rams. They were joined by four others, none of which was legal.

We returned to camp around 5:00 p.m. and had a first-class supper. Before we went to sleep Dick asked me if I would take a legal ram. I said, "Not until the seventh or eighth day." "How big a ram do you want," he asked. He laughed at my answer, "Not less than a full-curl and preferably about 42 inches." He said, "You don't want much, do you?"

We left camp at 6:00 a.m. the next morning and hiked to the big valley where we set up the spotting scope. There were only three rams there, but one of them was the big one. We had looked at a draw that went the whole way to the top of the mountain. We decided we could stay out of sight and reach the top from there. The wind was in our favor, but we had to get above the rams because it was impossible to get within range from below.

It was quite a climb and I was hoping we would not have to come down this way. It's one thing going up; but when I looked down, it was pretty scary. By 10:00 a.m. we had reached the top of the mountain. Now all we had to do was work our way east until we could see the rams.

We worked our way across rock slides and boulders, and by 11:30 a.m. we were ready to eat some lunch. We knew they couldn't be much farther away, unless we had spooked them and they had left the area. We carefully climbed each ridge, checking out the valley carefully before moving to the next ridge.

On each ridge, Dick would take off his hat and peep over the top so the rams would be less likely to see him. We knew we had to be close to where they were. We kept saying it has to be the next one. Then finally, it was!

Dick quickly slid back off the top and we got rid of our packs. He got his spotting scope and we eased up the ridge and peeped over. There they were beneath us! Dick checked them and said, "The big one is on the right and he's a good one."

We were about 350 to 400 yards away. That was a little further than I preferred for a shot. We checked the ridge and found a point about 250 yards away from the sheep.

Dick said I was to work my way down there. He would stay where he was and cover in case they decided to leave.

I reached the point and looked over to where they were still lying. "Now what do I do," I thought. "I don't want to shoot that ram in his bed." I just did not feel right shooting an animal lying down. I wanted to take another look, and as I did, two of the rams stood up. I remembered that Dick had told me that if they stand up, don't wait too long, because they might leave.

I figured that the ram was about 250 yards away, and downhill at a pretty steep angle. He was standing at an angle to me, so I didn't have the broadside shot that I had hoped for. I was lying down, so I eased my Remington 700 in .270 caliber over the top and put the cross hairs where I thought they ought to be for the most damage. When I squeezed the trigger, three rams turned and left on the run. Dick shot once and I got a second shot at my ram's rump as he went around a small ridge and out of sight.

"I blew it!" I thought. "I missed him!" I waited for Dick to shoot and hoped that I might be able to see them again, but nothing. Finally, I decided to crawl back to where the packs were. As I neared the packs, I saw Dick coming back from the next ridge. When he saw me he lifted his fist in the air and yelled, "You got him!" In amazement I called, "I did? Where is he?" He pointed down to the gully.

He hurried over to tell me what had happened. After he shot, he ran across a rock slide to the next ridge. When he looked for the sheep he saw only two and they were looking back, so he knew the big ram was hit. Just as he spotted him standing, the ram staggered, then fell and slid down the mountain about 100 yards.

It took us a half-hour to get down to the ram. As we got near, we finally realized that we had more than just an ordinary ram. Dick pulled his tape out and we started along the right horn . . . 38 . . . 40 . . . 42 . . . 43-5/8! The left horn was 43-2/8, and the bases 14-5/8!

Dick was even more excited than me. We knew we had a ram for the books. We dressed him out and found that my first shot had hit the right lung. Because of the angle I was shooting from, it had hit the intestines and the bullet was under the skin of his left flank. It was the only hole in him.

By 4:30 p.m. we had him loaded on our packs and we began to work down the mountain. Some 3-1/2 hours later we arrived back at the camp. I was exhausted but very happy. The next day we left camp at noon. By 5:00 p.m. Dick had taken a nice full-curl ram measuring 38 inches on each horn.

This would be a story we would tell over and over, about the big one the *did not* get away.

Photograph by Wm. H. Nesbitt

DALL'S SHEEP
SECOND AWARD
SCORE: 172-3/8
Locality: Granite Lake, Yukon   Date: August 1980
Hunter: William E. Medley II

DALL'S SHEEP 172-3/8

William E. Medley II

My first Dall's sheep hunt in the Yukon was unsuccessful and disappointing because of an accident that cut it short after only five days. I was fortunate enough to return two years later (August of 1980) for a hunt that was much more successful than I had ever imagined.

I left my home in Charleston, West Virginia, on August 14, 1980, arriving at the airport in Whitehorse, Yukon, the following afternoon. The excitement of finally being there was dulled by my luggage and gear not arriving with me. I checked-in at the Taku Motel in Whitehorse and was soon greeted by my outfitter, Dave Young. He had recently acquired the territory that I had hunted on my first hunt in 1978, the same area I would hunt this trip. With Dave was Bailey Peyton, from Hollandale, Mississippi, who was to be my hunting partner. We got our licenses and spent the rest of the day discussing the plans for the hunt with Dave and two of his guides, Rick Guinn and Murray Tennant.

The next morning, Dave picked Bailey and me up at the motel and drove us to his house to look at the Dall's sheep he had taken in 1972. That's about all it took to get a fellow psyched-up for a sheep hunt. Its horns measure 46 inches by 15-2/8 inches, and it scores 185-3/8, placing it fourth in the 1981 records book. Since we were to hunt the same general area in which Dave had taken his ram, it got us pretty excited.

Fortunately, my gear arrived later in the day and we were able to get on our way. We drove with our guides to Dave's horse camp, about 25 miles west of Whitehorse on the Alaska Highway. There we set up tents for the night and later test-fired our rifles.

The next morning we transported the 10 horses we were going to use 14 miles up the highway to a point where we would load all of our gear and supplies and head for the base camp.

When we arrived at the base camp, after five hours of riding, we found that a black bear had made quite a mess of the cook tent. We cleaned things up, then set up our tent for the night.

The next two days of hunting were pretty much the same. We had a good bit of rain at night but the days were clear and we were able to hunt. We rode quite a bit and spotted several groups of rams, although none looked larger than 34 inches.

The third day I took a nice black bear on the mountain just above camp. It turned out to be the culprit that had ransacked the camp and had gotten into the sheep steaks we had hidden in the stream next to camp the night before. At least now we wouldn't have to leave one guide in camp during the day to watch for the bear. By the time we got back to camp, it was too late to try for sheep, so Bailey and I decided to take baths. We walked to a small lake above camp near Granite Lake. Although the sun was shining, it was a frigid experience. After a dinner of sheep stew, we turned in around 9:45 p.m. although it wasn't getting dark until 10:30 p.m.

The next day, August 20th, Bailey and I and our two guides rode back to the mountains where we had seen rams on the 17th. There, Bailey took a nice 37-inch ram and a black bear.

Next morning my guide and I left the base camp and rode for three hours to a spike camp where we planned to hunt for several days. Some nice rams had been seen in the area. We spent the rest of the day setting-up camp and glassing the area.

The following day we spotted 37 rams and a number of ewes and lambs. I thought I had blown my chance for taking a big ram when I missed a downhill shot at 250 yards. My guide estimated the left horn at 45 inches and the right one a few inches shorter. It's hard to explain how disappointed I was.

The rain, heavy clouds on the mountains, and horses all conspired to keep us from hunting the next day. We spent most of the afternoon looking for Rusty and Two-Spot, two of our five horses, who had wandered away during the night. Even though they were hobbled, we found them quite a distance from camp.

Sunday, August 24, found us back in the area where we had seen all the rams two days earlier. As we were working our way up the mountain on horseback, we spotted six rams in the green grass on the far side of a basin. Using the spotting scope, we looked them over. One ram was much larger than the others, although his left horn barely came to the bridge of the nose. We wanted to get a better look at them, so we decided to work our way up the ridge to the top of the mountain and around to the other side of the basin. But, on top it started snowing very hard and the clouds came down, making it impossible to see anything. As the snow slowly let up, we found that the storm had moved the sheep and we did not see them again that day.

August 25th was cool and clear, and a day I will never forget It was the last day we were going to hunt in the area. After having a breakfast of bacon and eggs, we left camp early with three horses. We decided to go back to the area where we had seen six rams. At the top of the mountain, we were again caught in a very hard snow storm but not but not before we saw two groups of small rams. Although the snow slowed us down considerably, we were able to work our way around the mountain.

Later in the afternoon, as we were coming down a mountain side, we spotted the six rams. They were across Van Bibber Creek and down the mountain to our left. We came down the right side of the creek to a point where we crossed and tied-up the horses. Our plan was to make our way across the side of the mountain to come upon the rams. Instead we came out below the sheep. We quickly crawled and ran back to the horses, afraid the rams had winded us. We followed the creek up the mountain another quarter-mile before attempting to reach the sheep again. We only had to crawl a couple of hundred yards before spotting them in the willows. They were no more than 50 yards from us when my guide said, "He's the second one from the top". One look and you could see how massive his horns were. All six of the rams were standing. I fired my 270 Remington just as they looked our way, sensing something was wrong. All of them immediately ran, with my ram slowing down before falling in some rocks.

While my guide went back for the horses, I ran over to the ram. He was a tremendous trophy! After looking at him I could see why it was difficult to judge the size of his horns yesterday. They were a fairly close curl, dropping far below his jaw and the tip of the left horn came just about even with the bridge of his nose. We put the steel tape on the horns. The left one measured 42-2/8 inches and the right one 43-2/8 inches! The feeling of elation that I experienced when I realized the size of this trophy is something I will never forget. After taking a few pictures, we took off the cape and quartered the ram. We loaded the panniers on the packhorse and headed down the mountain toward camp, about a mile below us.

The next morning, we loaded our gear on the horses and started back to the base camp. With the hunt successfully completed we spent the last evening in base camp with Bailey and his guide, talking about our experiences over the past week-and-a-half.

We got an early start in the morning back to Whitehorse where Bailey and I checked into the Yukon Motel and took much needed showers.

Our guides took us to the Yukon Game Branch to obtain export permits for our sheep horns. We then drove to Northland Taxidermy where Charles Buchanan measured my horns for the Yukon Outfitters and Guides Competition. He came up with a green score of 176-2/8. In late November, Dave Young informed me that my ram had won the competition for the top Dall's sheep killed in the Yukon for 1980.

My trophy also won the Gold Medal award presented by the Foundation for North American Wild Sheep in February, 1981, for the best Dall's sheep taken in North America in 1980.

But, the highest honor came in March, 1983, when I was invited to send my trophy to the Dallas Museum of Natural History for the Boone and Crockett Club's 18th North American Big Game Awards (1980-1982), to be held July 30, 1983. There it took the 2nd Place Award for Dall's sheep, with a final score of 172-3/8. The right horn measured 42-7/8 inches, the left horn 41-6/8 inches , and the bases measured 14-2/8 inches.

Photograph by Wm. H. Nesbitt

STONE'S SHEEP
FIRST AWARD
SCORE: 176-4/8
Locality: Gataga River, B. C.   Date: August 1980
Hunter: David C. Coleman

STONE'S SHEEP 176-4/8

David C. Coleman

David Coleman and his hunting partner, Dick Shepard, booked a sheep hunt with Gary Moore of Dawson Creek, British Columbia, in 1980. Coleman had hunted deer and elk in Colorado, New Mexico, and southern Texas, but this was to be his first big-game hunt in Canada. They scheduled a three-week hunt for moose, wolf, goat, caribou, grizzly bear, and Stone's sheep. If they scored on just half, they'd have a memorable hunt.

August 21, 1980, found them flying into Watson Lake, Yukon. From there they were transported by floatplanes approximately 150 miles south to hunt the area around the Gataga River in northern B. C. After landing, they spent another two days on horseback to reach their first spike camp.

Their first day out, they attempted to reach a rocky peak by horseback. However, after four hours of climbing, a snowstorm forced them to abandon their climb and find cover. While they ate lunch and rested, their guides, Ed Calliou and Kenny Napoleon, scouted the area for sheep. Soon, Calliou located four rams feeding in a basin about 1,600 feet below them.

A short stalk brought them to within 800 feet without disturbing the rams. From that distance they could identify what appeared to be two legal rams.

The guides decided that it would be best for the two hunters to stay put while Calliou worked his way around to the other side of the basin with the intention of spooking the sheep toward them.

For once, things worked as they should. When Calliou jumped the sheep, they headed toward the hunters. As the four rams passed in single file, Coleman chose the best ram on the left and Shepard aimed for one on the right, as earlier agreed. When the rams were within 250 yards, they fired together.

Coleman's ram took a few steps and dropped. The other three rams took off at high speed, going out-of-sight over the next ridge. Shepard's gun had misfired. He did get off a couple of ineffective shots before the sheep disappeared from sight.

The group moved down to examine Coleman's prize. The guides proclaimed it outstanding. With unbroomed horns that green-scored 179 points, Coleman had to agree.

Photograph by Wm. H. Nesbitt

STONE'S SHEEP
SECOND AWARD
SCORE: 175-4/8
Locality: Muskwa River, B. C.   Date: October 1980
Hunter: Robert M. Case

STONE'S SHEEP 175-4/8

Robert M. Case

Tom Vince and I sat on top of the mountain, the excitement of the hunt dulling the effects of the cold and wind as we watched and waited. Tom had just spotted four rams below us and about 600 yards away. The rams were peacefully lying down, looking away from us. With the spotting scope we could tell that one looked good, but because of his position we would not know until later just "how good". We settled down to wait, knowing that sooner or later they would be up feeding again.

A half-hour passed and still no movement from below, as fog began settling-in on the mountain. I began to worry that when the fog lifted, if it did lift before dark, would the rams still be there? Tom said we could wait no longer than 4:30 p.m. because we must get down the mountain before dark or be prepared to spend the night on top. I wasn't prepared for that, so I reluctantly agreed to the time.

This hunt started taking shape at the Foundation for North American Wild Sheep meeting in Houston in February, 1980. While there, R. G. "Garry" Vince persuaded me to book an October Stone's sheep hunt with him in British Columbia. This was to be his last sheep hunt for the year. Having been on the "last hunt" with other outfitters, and having my last two hunts end without success, I wasn't, at first, too excited about a "last hunt". I finally agreed to give it a try.

Arriving at Garry's Muskwa River base camp on October 6, I learned that Garry's son, Tom, would be my guide. I also met Jim Gray, an experienced sheep hunter from California, who was working on his second "slam". Jim and his guide, Rick, would also be hunting with us.

The following morning we packed-up and headed to our first camp, arriving that evening. During the next 11 days Tom and I saw over 65 Stone's rams, along with numerous moose and goat. On the fourth day out, I took a 52-inch moose, not a record book entry by any means, but a fair Canada moose.

We stayed in three different camps, hunting all areas thoroughly, then moved on to Beaver Creek Camp so we could hunt the Prophet Bench and the upper reaches of the Muskwa. The first morning out of Beaver Creek Camp, Jim headed for a mountain range past the Bench with his guide, While Tom and I headed for White Ram Mountain. After tying the horses at the base of a small mountain adjoining White Ram, we started up at approximately 9 a.m. We made our way over the small mountain into a basin on

White Ram and then on to the top. Around 2 p.m., as we worked our way easterly along the top of White Ram, Tom spotted the four rams.

An hour passed. It began snowing heavily and the wind picked up. Occasionally, the snow would stop long enough for us to see that the rams were still there below us. I had already decided to take the largest, if he was legal, when Tom suggested the same thing. We both realized that we were on the 13th day of a 15-day hunt and I had already turned down two legal rams (8-year-olds) so the odds of us finding another in the next two days were slim to none. We both knew this was it.

We had to wait for the rams to get up and start feeding. We hoped they would feed around the side of the mountain, because our only stalking route was across and down a wide-open shale slide. Around 4:00 p.m., the snow stopped and the fog began to lift. We were then able to see the last ram feed out of sight. We started our stalk, still not knowing how big the largest ram was, or if he in fact was legal. At 4:30 we spotted the first ram, a small one, about 50 yards to our right and just below us. He didn't spook but seemed to sense that something was wrong. As we eased down a little further, another ram poked his head up. We were travelling down a narrow ridge by this time, with the sheep to our right and below us, under a ledge. Suddenly, the area was full of running rams, the largest one in the lead. Just as suddenly I heard Tom shout, "YES!" Though the ram's horns still didn't look very large to me (I guess because of his tremendous body size) I fired. Later, after I brought him down, Tom estimated him to weigh 350 pounds on the hoof.

My first shot, at 40 yards, missed. The second connected high in the back, although I didn't realize it because he was still running full-blast. The third shot centered his horns at the skull, stopping him for keeps. Not until we climbed down to him did we realize just how big he really was. Tom quickly put the tape on the horns and said he was sure the ram would make the book. I couldn't believe it! Ending what had certainly been a long, dry spell for me, my last two hunts being unsuccessful, with a book Stone's ram was almost overwhelming.

After caping him and boning-out the meat, we packed up and headed down to a cabin about three miles away. It was too late to return to camp, so we decided to spend the night at the cabin and go for the horses and on to camp in the morning. After supper we did an accurate taping job on the ram. His green measurements were 38-7/8 inches on the right and 38-3/8 inches on the left. I was elated to say the least.

We returned to camp the following day to find that Jim had scored on his Stone's also. As a heavy snow began to fall, we all packed-up camp and headed out.

After returning home, I learned from Tom that my ram won the British Columbia Outfitters' Competition for 1980. My ram also received second place (the silver award) for 1980 in the Foundation for North American Wild Sheep Awards.

Photograph by Brad Spencer
Michael Helland of the Missouri Dept. of Conservation accepts the Certificate of Merit Award for the new world's record non-typical whitetail deer, found dead in St. Louis Co., Missouri, in 1981. Making the presentation at the 18th Awards in Dallas, Texas, in 1983, is Dr. Philip L. Wright, Chairman of the Records of North American Big Game Committee.

Photograph by Brad Spencer
Javier Lopez del Bosque travelled from his home in Mexico to receive the First Award for desert sheep at the 18th Awards, Dallas, Texas, in 1983. Presenting the award is Dr. Philip L. Wright, Chairman of the Records of North American Big Game Committee.

Photograph by Wm. H. Nesbitt

STONE'S SHEEP
HONORABLE MENTION
SCORE: 170-2/8
Locality: Townsley Creek, B. C.   Date: August 1981
Hunter: Robert L. Williamson

STONE'S SHEEP 170-2/8

Robert L. Williamson

At noon on August 18, 1981, the second day of my two-week Stone's sheep hunt, I had taken a fine, heavily broomed records book ram. I didn't have the faintest notion that he was even close to the book, much less score over minimum. This was my second sheep hunt, and I had just improved my success ratio on sheep from zero to 50 per cent. My first try for sheep was a backpack hunt for bighorn in Montana where I saw sheep, but no legal rams.

I am a 35-year-old independent geologist in Shreveport, Louisiana. At the time of this hunt, I had developed a good case of sheep fever. I decided to book for Stone's sheep with Bucking Horse and Besa River Outfitters.

On the afternoon of August 13, I departed Shreveport and spent a short lay over night in Vancouver before an early departure to Fort St. John, British Columbia. About 8:30 a.m. on the 14th, I arrived in Fort St. John. But, my luggage, guns, and outfitter did not. Not too much of an eternity later my outfitter, Axel Zarbock, arrived after being slowed down by auto trouble. He informed me we were in no hurry because my hunting partner was not arriving until that evening. Axel told the airline to deliver my gear to the MacKinzie Inn, and we were off to pick up my license and tags. My gear arrived about mid-afternoon and I headed out to find a territorial office in order to buy a topographic map of the area we would be hunting. That map proved to be a key element in the quick success of the hunt.

As I was heading to breakfast the next morning, I met my hunting partner. Bill Cass was a judge from upstate New York who was accompanied by his 18-year-old son, Steve, along as a non-hunter. I was comforted that Bill had also heard good things about our outfitter's operation and that he was here to attempt to close-out his Grand Slam. We met our pilot, loaded up a nice Cessna 206, said a temporary good-bye to Axel and departed north over the Alaska Highway.

Upon arrival, we placed our gear in a cabin, had lunch, and checked out the base camp. That afternoon we fished for grayling and dolly varden, shot our rifles, glassed for sheep, and in general, soaked up the beautiful mountain serenity. We met our Beaver Indian guides who were men of few words, shin-high moose skin moccasins, and excellent eyesight. My guide, Paul Notseta, was in his 50's and more agile than I. Bill's guide was Johnny Bigfoot, who called everybody "Partner" and probably was in his late 30's.

Next morning it was breakfast, organizing gear, and packing the horses for our all-day pack train ride to sheep camp. The pack train totaled over a dozen horses, which included the saddle horses for three sports, two guides, the cook, and a wrangler. We rode through changing terrain into beautiful U-shaped valleys occasionally dotted with ewes and lambs. Our morning was highlighted by a ride down and through a wet, shady mountainside bog protected by an outstanding group of yellow jackets. I discovered how the Bucking Horse River was named, and I certainly am not able to adequately describe the action which occurred.

After a lunch near the Besa River, we crossed over and rode the rest of the afternoon before making the camp which would be home for several days. While making camp, Johnny spotted sheep in the distance and glassed them to find five rams. I never did find them with my glasses. He said we would come back to them later because he had another place he wanted to take Bill and Steve the next day.

After leaving home four days earlier, I was finally hunting. Paul and I had made our way up-canyon from camp and began to hunt a basin. The previous year Paul had put his hunter on four different rams in this basin in as many days; but, he missed his shots. Lunchtime found us in the middle of our basin that now was void of sheep. Paul wanted to ride as high as we could, tie the horses, and climb the backside of the basin where we would be high enough for some distant glassing.

We topped-out in early afternoon to a beautiful panoramic view of purple mountains and distant snowfields of the Richards Creek and Prophet River drainage. Wow! Although overheated from the climb, we were quickly chilled by the crisp wind gushing over the saddle dividing the two drainage areas. I pulled out a down vest from my day pack and settled down for some glassing of the nearby area. While Paul was setting up my 16 to 36 power Bushnell scope, I found a 3/4-curl ram down about 45 degrees and to the right. Although there were abundant sheep trails, he was apparently alone while bedded in a steep talus slope. Further glassing yielded no other sheep, so we checked our backtrail from a better vantage point.

Movement caught our eyes on a southeast ridge. Caribou, moving as usual. Back to the north side, I laid down on the slope, head resting on a rock as I soaked up warm sunshine and munched on a candy bar while steadily glassing. I was enjoying a new pair of lightweight Zeiss 10 x 25 binoculars that Sandra, my wife, had presented to me as a birthday gift. I was checking the shady side of a steep north-south ridge about a mile in the distance when I spotted two white rump patches. After telling Paul of the sheep, I lost them in the poor light. Minutes later, three rams appeared on the skyline, and one was obviously a stand-out. As we admired these rams, a fourth and possibly better ram began walking up the crest of the ridge to join the party! Paul was impressed, but we couldn't make the proper stalk with a shortage of daylight.

We spent the rest of our day studying the sheep as they alternately fed and bedded on the ridge. Two were younger 3/4-curl rams; the other two were mature rams with good bases, full-curl and better. Paul was excited about the fourth ram. He judged the big one was 39, maybe 40; the other was 36, maybe 37. When we left, they had moved off the south end of the ridge and were above a water hole that was in a saddle connecting four ridges. Camp morale was running high that night. Bill found rams also, a group of three, but nothing that Johnny and Bill both agreed to go after.

Next morning Paul and I again rode up-canyon, but farther west past the basin we had previously hunted. We hoped to find a route that would lead us up to the south end of the ridge where we last saw the four rams. By late morning we were where we should be, but nothing looked as we expected from the previous day's view. The topo map showed that we should climb east over a ridge which was probably obscuring our objective area and the water hole landmark. So, we rode to the creek, watered the horses, and ate part of our lunch before climbing.

It was a clear day, and I was sweating under the warm sun as we topped-out to see the water hole and the south end of the ridge where we left the sheep yesterday afternoon. No sheep. We proceeded down by the water hole and made our way to the base of the ridge's south end. If our sheep were still on this ridge, our problem was to find them without being seen first. The ridge itself was long and narrow, with a sharp crest running full-length. There were small erosional depressions in the ridge which could hide the sheep until we were literally a few feet from them. I was already nervous at the thought of a covey shot as I chambered a round from my pouch, leaving my magazine full. I was shooting a Weatherby Vanguard in 7 mm Rem. Mag., with handloaded 160 grain Noslers in front of 63 grains of IMR 4831 powder.

We began a careful ascent, which continuously became more deliberate and nerve-wracking. We worked our way past the depression where the sheep were feeding when we left the day before. For awhile we had to take the right side of the ridge, which was as steep as the average sheep hunter wants to traverse. We inched across a wet shale slide where I found a puddle of clear water deep enough to provide some relief for my dry mouth. We had to cross over the top, and with the wind in our faces, we saw that our ridge connected westward to another peak, which was higher. We inched farther, with Paul looking up and to our left at this new area. We were sitting, with Paul a few feet higher, as I looked to my right and slightly lower. That's when what looked like a bedded ram materialized in the rocks.

Unbelieving, I slowly raised my glasses and confirmed the truth. I tapped Paul on the foot, mouthed, "ram", and nodded in that direction. Paul saw him and we rolled back out of sight while getting out of our day packs. Paul found an observation point while I was killing time with my camera. Paul came to my side and held up four shaking fingers. He said the big ram (longest horns) was number three from the top. Paul calmly added, "They've seen us." As I bellied forward, I found the ram in my scope and then checked my barrel, which was pointed into a rock. As I repositioned my barrel higher to clear the rocks, the sheep bolted. I was forced to take a hurried snap shot. They were out of sight in less than ten feet, and I told Paul I had missed. He agreed. Before I could enter the reality of what had vanished before my eyes, Paul ran pell-mell toward their bed with me scrambling behind. Before reaching their bed, he stopped, then pointed almost straight down over the west side of the ridge and quietly called, "There's the other ram; take him."

There, more than 300 yards below us, was the other big ram and one of the 3/4-curls standing looking up at us. I plopped on my rear, with my arm in the sling and elbows on knees. They were off, but running straight away. I held between the big ram's horns, squeezed, and he rolled. I had gone from the agony of defeat to the thrill of victory in less than a minute! I consider it no small miracle that in running away over the side of a sizable mountain, my ram ran back into view and afforded me such a shot.

I hurried down to the ram while Paul went after the day packs and my camera. I used an insurance round when the ram moved a leg, but it was probably unnecessary. The ram was obviously old, judging from his massive, cracked and weathered horns which were broomed back to the first growth ring. Paul was anxious to get to work, so we hurried some pictures. Then, we skinned and dressed out my trophy. While Paul was working on the cape, I climbed back up and looked for the first ram, just in case Murphy's Law was working that day. I never saw the other two rams or any sign that I had wounded the ram at which I had taken the snap shot. We beat Bill, Steve, and Johnny back to camp.

They arrived with a report of seeing five rams, but no attempts were made to take one. I was congratulated on my sheep, and we enjoyed some fried heart for supper. Believe it or not, there wasn't a tape in camp to measure my ram. Johnny Bigfoot, the man of few words, said what he was to repeat daily, "Partner, that's a damn beeg sheep."

Good fortune continued the next day, as Bill completed his Slam with a fine, full-curl ram taken from a group of 13 rams in the same area where they had seen three rams the first day. After taking that sheep, Bill presented his son Steve with his gun, a Winchester Model 70 in 264 Winchester Magnum. Bill's ram later taped 37 plus on the long horn.

The next morning, we broke camp and had supper back in base camp following a long but enjoyable ride. Johnny was anxious to put a tape on my sheep and said, "Partner, you want to score 'im up?" So we did, and Johnny scored him well into the records book. The only question in my mind about this hunt is, "What if I had taken Paul's first choice?"

Photo Courtesy of George P. Mann

George P. Mann looks properly pleased with the big tom cougar he took with a bow in February 1981 in Taos Co., New Mexico. It scores 15-6/16 points.

Photo Courtesy of George A. Dieruf

The guide, the dogs, and George A. Dieruf all look happy with the result of a cougar hunt in Madison Co., Montana, in December 1980. Dieruf's cougar scores 15 points, meeting the minimum score for entry.

Photo Courtesy of Donovan W. Ellis

Donovan W. Ellis, dog Homer, and hunting companion Allan Strauss admire Ellis' trophy cougar. Taken near Gold Creek, B. C., in December 1981, it scores 15-7/16 points, qualifying it for the First Award at the 18th. Awards, 1983.

Photo Courtesy of Jack Harrison

Jack Harrison hunted the East Fork of the Escalante River of Mesa Co., Colorado, in January 1980 to get his big cougar. Scoring 15-6/16 points, Harrison's cougar was awarded Second Award at the 18th. Awards, 1983.

COUGAR 16-4/16

**New World's Record
Certificate of Merit**

Charles M. Travers, Owner

The top places in the cougar category change slowly. The 1952 records book (the first based upon the current scoring system) listed a cougar scored at 15-12/16 points and taken by Theodore Roosevelt in 1901 near Meeker, Colorado, as the World's Record.

The 1971 records book recorded a new number one, a cougar scoring 16 points and taken in Garfield County, Utah, in 1964 by Garth Roberts. Thus, the cougar taken by Douglas E. Schuk, and now owned by Charles M., Travers, becomes only the third record-holder under the current system (adopted in 1950).

Schuk was hunting near Tatlayoko Lake, British Columbia. It was February 12, 1979, and there were 32 inches of snow on the ground. It was 3:00 p.m.. when the dogs finally brought the big tom to bay. Schuk used his 308 to bring him down.

Charles Travers later acquired the skull of the tom. When he had it measured, it was hard to believe. The entry measurement was well above the long standing record of 16. As a potential record, it had to come before the Final Awards Judges Panel. They too found it to score better than the record and confirmed it as the new world's record for the category. Since it was no longer owned by the hunter, it was eligible only for the Certificate of Merit award.

COUGAR 15-7/16

First Award

Donovan W. Ellis

It was rapidly becoming dusk when we reached the top of the snow-covered ridge in the East Kootenays of southern British Columbia. As we listened, we could hear the sound we had been hoping for all afternoon - the baying of a lone hound dog barking treed.

I had been visiting my parents in Cranbrook, British Columbia, for the Christmas holiday of 1981. For several years I had been interested in getting a cougar. For the past few days, my father, Bud Ellis, and I had been searching for tracks with no luck.

The evening of December 27, Dad called a friend, Allen Strauss, who is a guide for cougar and other big game of the area. Allen reported that he had been out the previous week and had found where a large cougar had killed a fine mule deer buck. We made plans to go out in the morning. Allen was confident that with a little luck we might pick up the large cat's track.

The following morning, Dec. 28, my brother Patrick, my father, and I took my father's two hounds and drove to Wardner B. C. where we rendezvoused with Allen. We drove from there to an area known as the Libby Pondage.

The Libby Reservoir is formed by a large power dam on the Kootenay River in Libby, Montana. The Kootenay River starts in the Rocky Mountains of British Columbia, north of Radium in Kootenay National Park, and flows south to the Libby Dam. The dam backs water up some 60 miles to Wardner, B. C., where it forms Lake Koocanusa. (The lake name is derived from Kootenay, Canada and U.S.A.)

We crossed Lake Koocanusa on a Bailey Bridge and drove southwest to a large logged-off area near Plumbob Mountain. This is an excellent wintering spot for elk, mule deer, and whitetail deer. After several hours of searching around for tracks, we stopped at a small lake (Chain Lake) and ate our lunch.

After lunch, we decided to leash the dogs, buckle on our snowshoes, and head for an area known as Gold Creek Canyon. Most every cougar in the county passes through this area at one time or another, and there are several caves up in the rock bluffs where the female cougar often have their young. We each took one of the four hounds we had with us. Patrick took Zeke (a young male bluetick), I took Tracker, one of Allen's dogs (black-and-tan/bluetick cross female), Dad took his old reliable male Homer (Walker/bluetick cross) and Allen took Rink, his black-and-tan male.

It seemed Lady Luck was on our side. When we hit the end of the lake, we found a large cat track coming from the direction of the canyon and heading northeast towards the Bailey Bridge we had crossed several hours before. The track was about 14 hours old. We had about 3-1/2 hours of daylight left, so we decided to take a chance and turn the dogs loose.

The dogs were baying enthusiastically as they headed up the hill on the track. But, within 20 minutes they were over the ridge and out of hearing. With only three hours of daylight left, we had to put things into high gear. We headed up the hill as snow began to fall slightly. When we hit the crest of the hill, we could see that the dogs were having some trouble staying with the track. The wind had drifted some snow and the cat had passed through a large herd of elk. We split-up into pairs and circled in the timber to try to locate the track. After about 30 minutes, Dad and Allen found the "out" track and fired a signal shot. We regrouped and Patrick and I advised the others we had heard dogs barking in the distance to the north. We headed off on the track as quickly as possible, as we were running out of daylight. The track seemed to have only one dog on it.

An hour and 15 minutes later, we were staring at the large cougar some 40 feet up in a fir tree. Homer was the only dog on the scene, just as the tracks had indicated. I prepared to shoot the cat with my Winchester 22 Hornet, as the rest of the guys made a fuss over Homer who was wildly barking at the base of the tree.

I held behind the big cat's shoulder and squeezed the trigger. The cat instantly toppled out of the tree and hit the ground with a thud. Patrick, who had been holding Homer back from the tree, released him and Homer got his day's reward by being allowed a few good chews on the dead tom.

By the time we had the cougar skinned, the other dogs showed up on the scene. I guess they were lost or chasing something else. It was dark by this time and we were all tired and hungry as we took off towards our vehicles.

A very few weeks later, father's dog Homer ruptured his stomach and had to be put to rest. We were all very sad. But, he had a good long life and we were glad that he had such a successful final hunt.

COUGAR 15-6/16

Second Award

Jack Harrison

After living in Colorado for almost 22 years, it is still a great feeling to be able to work in Denver and hunt the Rocky Mountains. Owning my own masonry business gives me the opportunity to spend a lot of my time in the mountains.

My children have grown up with constant participation in hunting and camping trips with me. All three of my sons have developed into avid hunters. Dan, my oldest son, moved to the western slope of Colorado to live in the small town of Olathe. There he became friends with Cap Atwood, a well-known mountain lion and bear hunter. Under his guidance, Dan became an excellent guide and outfitter.

Dan had been after me for some time to come over for a lion hunt. I finally took him up in January, 1980. We arrived in Olathe on Thursday, January 3, giving a chance to visit with the family. During all my hunts, I had never encountered a mountain lion and I was looking forward to the prospect of seeing one.

Dan knew of a large lion in the Escalante Canyon, not far from Olathe. Friday morning he loaded five of his hounds into the dog box in the back of the pickup. Breeze, Blue, and Bay were his top trackers. Two younger pups were taken along to get in some training. A couple of Dan's friends, Rick Strong and Doug McCarty, joined us, and just as the sun was coming up over the mountains, we headed north.

The East Fork of the Escalante Canyon is located in the Uncompahgre Plateau, 15 miles out of Delta, in Montrose County. This range is known to the locals as "The Big Unc". It was a typical January morning; the sky was clear, and it was cold. There was no snow at the lower elevations, but we could look up and see snow on the higher peaks. Dan said his hounds were good, but it sure would be helpful if we had some fresh snow.

At around 10:00 a.m. we found the track we were looking for. We parked the truck on what is called Saw Mill Mesa Road. The terrain was typical Western Slope. Here on the mesa the junipers and pinons grew profusely and precariously close to the edge of the sheer cliffs that drop down about 100 feet. It was on this jeep road that we released the dogs. Their excitement was immediately obvious. The quietness of the canyon was shattered as the dogs took off. The hunt had begun!

The track they cut could not have been too old. Breeze was off in a flash, with the others not far behind. The four of us jumped into the truck and headed after the dogs. After three or four miles, the dogs changed their tune; we were now at the level where snow was on the ground. We stopped the truck and started following on foot. The pack of hounds had switched direction and were dropping down into the Dry Fork of the Escalante. As expected, the cat was heading for the Escalante Canyon. The hounds, especially the pups, were having difficulty in following, not having the advantage of being able to bound from rock to rock like the lion.

By now we hunters were having more difficulty than the dogs in keeping up. The snow was slowing us down and it was beginning to get dark. We could no longer hear any barking or howling, but we knew the general direction they had been heading. So, we cut cross-country in the truck toward Dry Fork Mesa.

It was about 9:30 p.m. by the time we found the tracks of the dogs and the lion crossing the road. After a few more hours of looking, with no success, we decided to call it off until morning. We headed back to Dan's house to grab a couple of hours of sleep. It had been a long, tiring day.

Next day, we drove around in the canyon for about an hour before we finally cut the tracks of the dogs and the lion heading up the canyon. With no time to waste, we sped on. Eventually, the tracks crossed the road again and Dan pulled over to listen for the dogs. It was like music to our ears; in the distance we heard the faint baying of the hounds. We drove as close to the sound as we could before finally parking the truck. It seemed like the dogs were directly above us. Dan was sure the lion was treed.

The Escalante Canyon is about 30-40 miles long as it winds up to the Big Unc. It is only about a quarter-mile wide and is surrounded by solid red rimrock, 100 to 150 feet high. At this point, we had to find a break in the rim to climb up.

When we made it to the top of the rim, we followed the edge. We rounded a small knoll and there were the dogs howling and dancing around a small pinon. There, about halfway up the tree, was the cat, snarling at the hounds. For all his huge size, he was, as they say, "nervous as a cat". After climbing out on a branch of that pinon, he bailed out like a shot. He streaked past me, so close I could have hit him with a club.

A lion can trot all day through the mountains, but when forced to run fast they tire easily and will look for a tree to climb. This tom was no exception.

He started running down the side of a cliff and disappeared down a 20-foot drop. This was his mistake. He had trapped himself in a small amphitheater. The dogs had him treed again. We all raced after them. While Dan let the dogs enjoy their capture, Doug snapped some pictures.

Dan said, "This is it, Dad." I took the 22 Mag. pistol from my holster, steadied myself and fired. The first shot hit him, but only sent him higher in the tree. The second shot hit home and he came crashing to the ground.

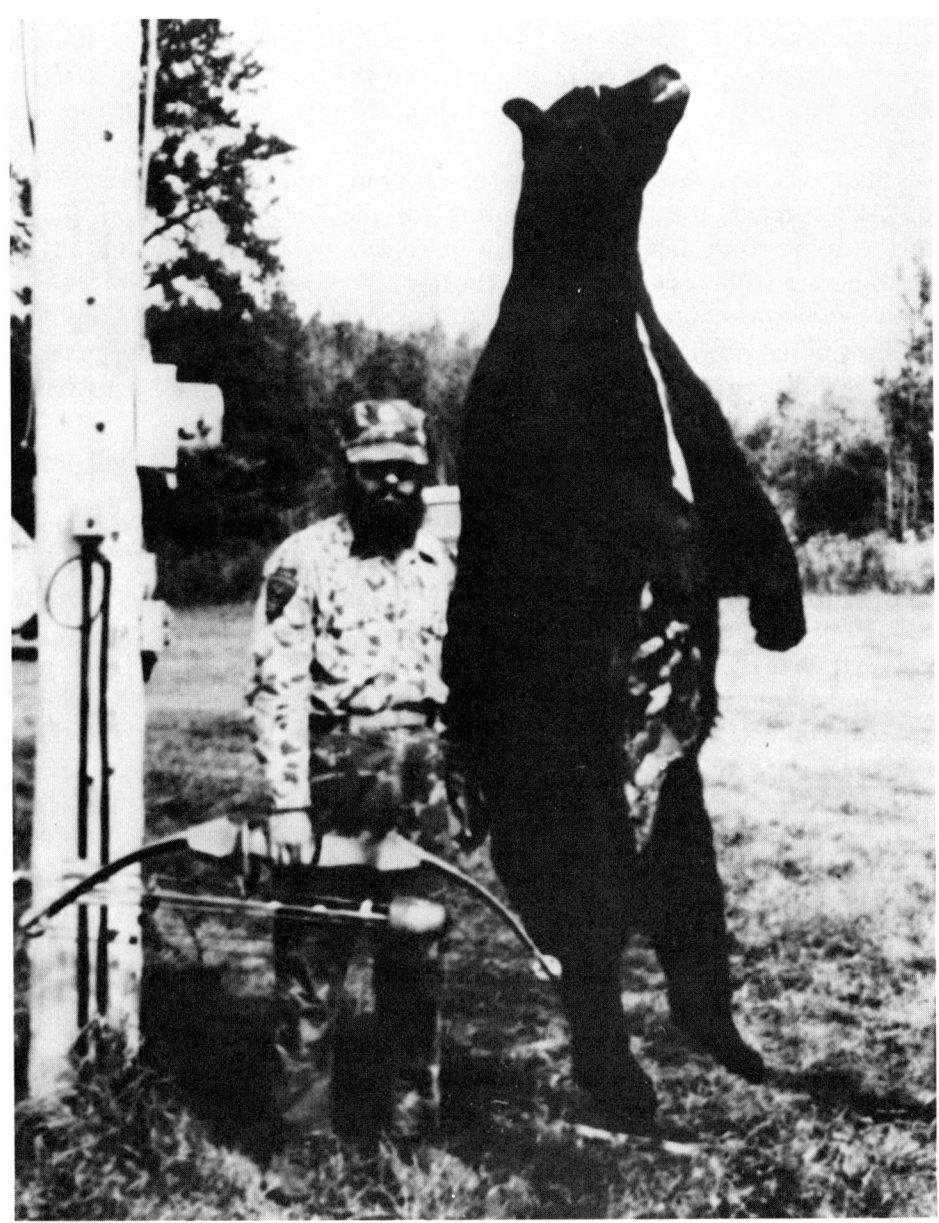

Photo Courtesy of Michael Steliga

Michael Steliga is dwarfed by his big black bear. The bear scores 21 points and was shot in September 1982 in Langlade Co., Wisconsin.

BLACK BEAR 22-8/16

First Award

Calvin Parsons

Raising bees in Porcupine Plains, Saskatchewan, is an uncertain business. Uncertain weather often creates problems with the health of the hive and its sweet store of honey is a constant attraction to bears and other honey loving animals.

The big bear was beginning to make a habit of raiding the hives. Calvin knew that he would have to do something about the bear to avoid severe financial losses.

The date was September 7, 1977. The overcast sky was now beginning to drizzle rain. It was nearly 6 p.m., a good time for the bear to appear under the weather conditions.

As the big bruin made his appearance at some 20 yards, Calvin settled his 308 Win. and put the 180 grain bullet home. Another beehive raider gone to bear heaven.

BLACK BEAR 22-1/16

Second Award

Harry Kushniryk

I've been a farmer for the past 40 years, a big-game hunter in the fall, and a trapper during the winter season. I have never taken time out just to go for a special bear hunt. However, I have always obtained a bear permit, in case one should cross my path during trapping season. I have taken several bears through the years, selling the hides along with my other fur pelts. Not until ten years ago did I realize that there were trophies or awards for certain-sized bears in Canada.

On April 20th, 1981, I was checking the beaver traps on my trap line located eight miles north of Arran, Saskatchewan. I found one of my beaver traps missing, and it was evident a beaver had been caught in it. This seemed strange, as trap and all were now missing. Upon closer inspection, I noticed faint tracks where the leaves were slightly disturbed. I attempted to follow them for about 200 -300 yards into the bush as there were traces of snow here and there.

Suddenly, I heard a crackling sound and a loud growl. A huge black bear was standing on its hind legs, trying to scare me away. There was only about 75 yards between me and this huge-looking animal. I got scared and naturally nervous. Shivers ran down my spine!

I did manage to fire my 30-30 Marlin, which I carry with me on my trap line. Much to my relief the bear dropped to the ground dead, with only the single shot being fired.

I was in a hurry to carry on with my trap line; I still had to check the balance of my traps for the day. With a light drizzle of rain off and on, I wasted no time in starting to skin this huge animal. With a bit of difficulty, I managed to skin the one side. Attempting to turn this enormous beast over proved a bit more difficult. Luckily, I had a piece of rope and some wire with me to re-tie my traps if needed. I tied wire and rope together, then to the bear leg and finally to a long piece of wood. I tried to pry, twist, and force it around a tree that was close by. With a lot of tugging and pulling, I managed to roll the bear over, so I could skin the other side.

Much to my surprise, there was my missing Connibear beaver trap, plus a partially eaten beaver still in it. I was shocked to see this, since by now I had forgotten about the trap.

It was a very tough and big animal to skin. But, I carry a skinning knife and sharpening stone with me at all times on my trap line. It certainly came in handy, as I had to stop and sharpen the knife several times.

Being in a hurry, along with the light drizzle, I never gave a thought to the possibility that I should have gone home first, or even to a neighbor, to get a camera and have some pictures taken. I didn't realize that this bear might be large enough to be near world-record size and that I should take a picture.

I had to walk back about a half-mile to my pickup on which I carried a three-wheel Honda motorcycle. I use the Honda on my trap line, crossing fields or following the edge of the bush, to haul my traps. With my Honda, I went back into the bush to bring out the hide and the head for later skull measurement by our local Pelly-Arran Fish and Game Wildlife Federation Branch. By this time, my nerves were more calm. I figured that this bear would beat the black bear that I had shot ten years ago that had brought me trophies at that time.

It was only after waiting four or five months to have the skull dried and ready to be measured that I actually realized the enormous size of this bear. Our Official Measurer, Mr. John Kuzma, took the measurements, along with a witness. It measured 22-4/16 points. Of course, by this time, I had sold the hide to a fur buyer with no picture of even the hide.

On February 12th, 1982, I received an invitation to attend the banquet and presentation of trophies of the Saskatchewan Wildlife Federation at Prince Albert. There I received a trophy for overall best big game head. I also received an engraved medallion and certificate noting first place in the Henry Kelsey Club competition.

This is where I was told that my bear was only 2/16 short of the world record, to the best of their knowledge. Some two weeks later, I was presented with a local award from our own Pelly-Arran Wildlife Branch.

By this time, I was very upset with myself for rushing to get through on my trap line that day. I should have gotten a fellow with a front-end loader to come and lift the bear, and then have pictures taken, or at least have the animal's weight recorded. But, I guess it's too late to cry over spilled milk.

So after all this, I entered my bear skull into the Boone and Crockett Club's records archives in the U.S.A. I received an invitation to attend the Boone and Crockett Club's 18th Awards Banquet at Dallas, Texas, on July 30th, 1983. I regret even more that I have no pictures, or even the tanned hide, to show, but I have my memories.

Photo Courtesy of Robert P. Faufau

With a dressed weight of nearly 600 lbs., this huge black bear was a fine reward for Robert P. Faufau's careful planning and hard hunting. The bear was taken in Lincoln Co., Wisconsin, in September 1981 and scores 21-14/16 points. It was awarded Third Award at the 18th Awards, 1983.

BLACK BEAR 21-14/16

Third Award

Robert P. Faufau

I first encountered this bear during the season of 1980. A 300-pounder smelled me opening day and spooked before I could make a shot. By the third week of season, I was disappointed to have only small bears using the baits. The area I'm hunting, western Lincoln County, is typical of most of northern Wisconsin, with thick popple and balsams and patches of hardwoods interwoven with marsh elder and and bog swamps, habitat ideal for a good bear population. I was determined I'd get a big bear that year, or nothing at all.

I kept replenishing the baits every two or three days, hoping for a sign of a big one each time. But day after day, only small tracks were there. One day, when I checked a bait that had looked especially promising from the terrain and sign, I noticed more of the bait was gone than usual. I saw what looked like two faint, adjoining hind tracks, but was actually one large hind track. It wasn't hard to follow the trail where a heavy animal had walked through the bog swamp. But, when the prints came out on high ground and still left deep marks, I really got fired up! The huge tracks headed across an open hardwood ridge, leaving deep impressions in the soft clay soil under a new blanket of leaves. I knew this had to be the 500-pounder I'd dreamed of for years.

I was optimistic. The berries were frozen and on the ground by this time, and most other baiters had given up to pursue other game. So with less food around, I thought the bear hit my bait steady, but he didn't come back for a week. Again, the excitement of the big bear hitting the bait was replaced with disappointment as he hit and then disappeared for another week. The really big black bears are supposed to be unpredictable and this one was certainly living up to that theory. Sitting for him when he only hit once a week would be a shot-in-a-million.

The shorter fall days found me hunting deer and scouting for the upcoming rut. I was still baiting at two or three day intervals, hoping the big one would come in more steadily. The bear that had scented me opening day (or one the same size anyway) was hitting that bait daily. Things didn't look very promising for the big one, so I decided to give up on him for the year and try for the other bear. After several days of continued baiting and some impatient waiting for favorable wind conditions, a nice-sized bear came to the bait as I sat. I carefully took aim and seconds later, only 45 yards away, there lay a 350-pound bear with an exceptionally good coat. It later dressed out at 304 pounds and made the Pope & Young Club Records at 18-13/16. Was I tickled! I even forgot all about old "big feet" for awhile. This was my first Pope & Young bear.

In late summer 1980, my good buddy, Jim Lechleitner (who got me started in bear hunting), and I decided to bait in the same area and share expenses. We set baits in many new locations along two sites I'd used the previous year. Within three weeks, there were a few small bears and two bigger ones hitting the baits. But, I was disappointed that we hadn't seen any sign of the hefty fellow with the big feet.

Then in late August, while we were on vacation, Jim and his wife took over the baiting chores. When I got back, he told me about a track that was small dinner plate size with toes as big as silver dollars. The news short changed me on sleep that night. The very next morning I was peering into the mud at a somewhat washed-out track that was incredible!

From that day on, the bait was cleaned out nightly. We baited faithfully and were really getting excited. By this time we had determined that there were three bears using the one bait - a yearling, a 250-300 pounder, and the humongus one. We still didn't know how big, we just knew he was big! And, things looked very promising. With the poor acorn and berry crops, the baits were being hit consistently.

Opening day finally came. As I sat in my stand, hidden in a balsam tree, my thoughts were reviewing the whole situation. I had the stand downwind of the bait and trails leading to it. I was concerned about one small trail that was downwind of me. Not wanting to take any chances on the big one using that trail, I completely bathed in baking soda water and carried my soda-washed clothes in a box full of balsam branches in the open back of my pickup. I changed clothes before I sneaked into my stand. I also put a little skunk scent on a rag to help cover my scent. I kept thinking of those huge tracks and wondering if he would show before dark.

At 5:00 p.m. my pulse slowed down a little when a small bear showed after a long sneak on the bait. He fed nervously for 10 or 15 minutes. After eating his fill, he moved into the shadows. I sat and waited without moving. The noisy red squirrels and bluejays covered the sound of the gentle breeze, but in the distance I could hear the small bear breaking branches as he munched on choke cherries.

The shadows grew and an hour passed. The big balsams blocked the light from the setting sun, making it seem much later than it actually was. I checked my watch and waited. About 6:30 I heard soft squishing steps coming from a bog swamp next to the ridge I was on. My heart stopped. The steps stopped for quite a while. Then from behind a screen of balsams a large bear drifted without making a sound. He looked big and at first I thought 500 pounds. But as he approached, I realized he was closer to 300, and not the big fellow after all. With a lot of gruffing and heavy breathing, he fed. It was tempting, to say the least, but not tempting enough to blow the chance on the really big bear.

I watched him feed for close to a half-hour. He was a little nervous about being there, turning around often to look down a different trail than the one he had come in on. I didn't know why he was so edgy, but time was running out, with only 15 minutes of shooting time left. I decided to sit until the last minute, hoping he would leave on his own. If he didn't I'd have to shake the branches to scare him off.

All of a sudden, without warning, the bear crashed out of the bait as if shot. He didn't stop running until he was deep in the bog swamp. I didn't know if he had smelled me or if something else had scared him. Within seconds I had the answer.

A tremendous bear, twice the size of the other, stepped out of the balsams and stood triumphantly surveying the scene.

He just stood in the trail for what seemed like hours. He finally moved forward, only to stop again after a few steps. Just before he reached the bait, he stepped off the trail and stopped, hidden under a large balsam, only 15 yards away. Many times I've seen a bear lay down in the cover near the bait until he could be sure it was okay. I was afraid the big fella, would too and time was getting short. He stood there, inhaling deeply, trying to pick up a scent. Finally, when he was satisfied the coast was clear, he moved quickly onto the bait.

I knew this was it. I watched with nervous fingers on the string as he scooped up the goodies with his left shoulder and leg. I waited until he switched to his right leg, exposing the entire lung area and reducing the chance of a shoulder hit. All I could hear was his gruff breathing as I told myself to forget everything about the monster and just concentrate on making the shot. Everything felt just right when I released.

I saw the white feathers against the black hide behind his shoulder as the arrow hit. The big bear crashed down the trail, sending the other two bears running for their skins again. I heard him drop in just seconds, then the sigh of his last breath. The entire woods was silent now, except for the wet slosh of a scared little bear high-tailing it through the marsh. I climbed down and headed for the truck. The silence was eerie, and with the shadows creeping fast, everything looked "bear-y". I wasn't anxious to stick around.

When I found Jim, it turned out he'd also taken a nice bear. We gratefully accepted the help of his brothers and decided to bring Jim's bear out first. We were really tickled when we found Jim had bagged a nice 320-pounder, scoring 18-8/16 for Pope & Young. It was the biggest bear Jim had ever taken.

Then we headed back to my bait. With flashlights and lantern, we walked down the slippery mud trail in the direction I heard the bear drop. Only 45 yards from the bait lay 700 pounds of bear. I couldn't believe it! We all laughed and swatted each other on the back. All the baiting and scouting had paid off in a big way, but we didn't realize how big. Our guesses ranged from 475 to 600 pounds.

We hooked a logging chain around the huge neck, then tied knots for grips. Four of us started dragging, three feet at a time, until we hit a clearing and hill. It was the hill that put a halt to things. It was obvious that we weren't going up the steep hill pulling that bear by hand, so we'd just have to think of something else. There was an overgrown skid trail near, so with a lot of maneuvering and a few fancy words, I got my four wheeler over brush and stumps and between trees and down the faint trail. But, I still couldn't quite reach the bear. Finally, we hooked a long chain from the truck to the bear and pulled him up the hill to the skid trail. Then, with two pulling on the chain around the huge head and three lifting from behind, we just managed to get him in the pickup. What a load! Side by side, Jim's and mine, over 900 pounds of bear!

When we got home, we skinned and quartered the bears right away. The temperature was about 60 degrees and we were afraid the meat would spoil. After quartering and skinning, I hopped on the bathroom scale, holding one quarter at a time. As close as we could figure, with the dial going around twice, it was close to 600 pounds total! Two days later, when we put the frozen quarters on the supermarket scale, it was still 555. Using the accepted formula of bear biologists, we estimated the live weight to be 700 pounds.

The meat went into the freezer and I got the hide to my friend Marv Smith, who is an excellent taxidermist. He volunteered to mount him full-size. I told my wife it sure beat buying more furniture for the living room!

After cleaning the skull, I took a green measurement to get an idea of where this bear stood for the book. I couldn't believe it, over 22 inches! I was surprised that it was that big, because the head actually looked small on the body. After the required 60-day drying period, the skull still measured 22 inches on my ruler. There was no doubt that I'd enter it for both the Boone & Crockett Club and Pope & Young Club books. Peter Haupt, from the Wisconsin Buck and Bear Club, performed the measurements for both. It was a strong 22. At present it is the largest in the state for both bow and gun, and second largest in the world for bow.

BLACK BEAR 21-9/16

Fourth Award

Thomas C. Middleton

October 15 was the first day of Colorado's 1978 separate deer hunting season. The ensuing events which would take place would make it one which I will always remember. My father (Tom), my brother (Ron), and two hunting companions from California (Burt Houston and Don Gulickson), and I were hunting on family property 12 miles southeast of Montrose, Colorado. We were on Cimarron Ridge of the Billy Creek drainage of the Uncompahgre River. First weekend weather that year was partly cloudy and warm, although recent storms left the ground damp but not muddy. The only wildlife we observed was mule deer, just does and fawns. However, there was abundant evidence of black bear in the area.

After an uneventful first day, I decided to purchase a bear license when we arrived back in Montrose, just in case I should happen upon the comparatively rare opportunity of getting a shot at a bruin. The second day weather was much as the first. As the day wore on, I found myself walking along a cow trail in the bottom of a small draw. The slopes were covered by Gambels oak brush, typical of the cover at the 7,000 - 8,000 foot elevations in which we were hunting.

My attention was diverted by a commotion in the brush, consisting of rustling oak leaves and grunts. Upon investigation, the source of the ruckus appeared to be a large, dark animal. I peered through openings in the thick brush from a kneeling position to gain a better perspective and saw what I thought to be a yearling cow, the logical assumption since my grandfather's stock was still on pasture. Upon closer scrutiny, I discovered that the animal had small round ears. The feeling of certainty that I was looking at a bear caused a sudden increase in my flow of adrenaline.

I centered the cross hairs of the scope to bring my Remington 300 Win. Mag. onto the bear's neck and shot. The bear collapsed 20 yards from my position. It was mid-afternoon of October 16.

I proceeded to rendezvous with Dad and the others at a small stock pond a half-mile down the draw. My story was met with disbelief by the others. Don brought the jeep and we all headed back up the draw on the cow trail to the scene.

The bear was too large to load in the jeep by hand, but the jeep was equipped with a winch in the back compartment for just such situations.

Photo Courtesy of Gary G. Johnson

From left to right, Gary G. Johnson, Charles H. Johnson, and Dave Diamond admire Gary's black bear that weighed nearly 500 lbs. Taken in Iron Co., Michigan in September, 1982, the bear scored 21-7/16 points and received the Honorable Mention Award at the 18th. Awards, 1983.

BLACK BEAR 21-7/16

Honorable Mention

Gary G. Johnson

The hunt for this bear really started three years prior to the 1982 hunting season. During those years, I travelled north 150 miles on weekends from my central Wisconsin home to the Springsted area. The Flambeau flowage there is home to many bears. There, I would drop bait, returning the following weekend to re-bait. I would begin about seven weeks prior to the opening of the season. I would have preferred to have baited more often, but with a 300-mile round trip, Saturday was the only day I could bait.

I did have bears "hit" my baits. But, it was hard to keep them coming to the bait as a food supply, without being able to keep the supply of bait there at all times.

I was quite sure a very large bear was in the area because of the 2-1/2 and 3-inch diameter choke cherry trees that were broken over. The choke cherry trees were uprooted for their fruit. As a comparison, I thought how long it would take a man of 200 pounds to try to break a cherry tree over, guessing it to be impossible. A close inspection of the trees showed that the bear was using one paw to break them off. With that in mind, I knew it had to be a trophy-class bear.

Unfortunately, it seemed each year that due to my job or some other factor, I was only able to hunt two or three weekends. But that changed with the 1982 season.

In July of 1982, I moved to Minocqua, Wisconsin. This put me only 33 miles from my hunting area and what my father, Charles H. Johnson, and I considered a very large bear. That year, I felt more confident because I was closer to my hunting area. This meant I could bait more often. I think that being confident builds your persistence; and, if you are persistent, success will come.

I started my 1982 baiting in August, prior to the September 11 opening day. My father and I put out three baits and returned three days later to find two of the baits had been visited by bears. I returned every three days thereafter until three weeks before the season. Then, I increased my baiting to every two days. With the many wild berries and natural food in the area, the baits were being hit but not as often as I thought necessary to be considered good baits.

After the first frost killed the raspberries and blackberries, it was a different story. Each time, the bear cleaned the two foot square hole in which I had placed sweet rolls and bread soaked with molasses. (The two by two-foot bait hole is specified by law in my state; depth is not a factor.) I covered the bait with logs so ravens couldn't get to it. For carrying my bait the 1/4-mile, I used a 100 pound cheese box to which I attached shoulder straps.

I couldn't believe my eyes one morning after a rain. I got my first good print of a bear track on the side of the bait. I used a stick to measure the diameter, in order to remeasure it more accurately at home. The track was about 6-1/2 inches across. With these known facts of track size and the amount of bait being consumed, I was very excited about the opening day.

As opening day came, I was not to be talked to all day. I only hunt evenings, because that's when the critters seem to feed, rather than mornings. It's not always true, but as a rule it's worth following.

My father and I headed for our evening hunt about 2:00 p.m. When we got there, I re-baited and sprinkled liquid smoke all around to cover my scent. I sprinkled some on my clothes also. Then I climbed up in my homemade portable tree stand.

There was a lot of action to watch, although some folks may think of sitting in a tree as a boring experience. Canada jays would come down to the bait to take scraps of rolls or bread and fly off with them to a limb. The funniest part was watching the red squirrels as they would go between the logs and discover the bait covered with molasses. The squirrels would get the molasses on their feet and come running out with dry leaves stuck to the bottoms of their feet. You can just imagine all their actions in trying to get the leaves off their feet. I watched them for quite awhile. As the sun set and the northwest wind gradually died, I came back to the reason why I was in the stand. I got myself mentally ready in case the animal I had dreamed of came to the bait. From my deer hunting experience, I felt it was the time game would be on the move. I became excited with just the thought of getting a bear with a bow.

Then, over there was a movement. I could see a fern bush moving. I watched it intently, but then it quit moving. I thought perhaps it had been a deer or other animal, maybe a bird? But then, I could see a black outline coming through the ferns. There he was, padding into my bait. He was about 45 yards out when I first saw him. At 15 yards, the distance of my stand to the bait, I hadn't heard him make a sound. As he got to the bait, the bear looked at it and then came lumbering over to the base of my tree, looking me right in the face. I froze. I could hear him breathing, and his teeth were clicking together. I suppose he was just kind of opening and closing his mouth, like a hog, for no apparent reason. That's what I wanted to think, anyway. Then, he started to turn around very slowly.

When he was broadside, I started to draw. He was about four yards from the base of my tree. As I got to half-draw he looked at me again, and I held 72 pounds of peak weight steady for about five seconds. (It seemed like five minutes!) Then, as if he'd inspected the form on the side of that spruce tree long enough, he started back to the bait. Just as he got to the bait, I drew again and released since I didn't know if he was going to feed or just walk away.

The yellow fletching was like a tracer. I watched the arrow enter on a quartering-away angle, up into the lungs and heart area, to stop against the opposite shoulder. He made one great leap from the bait and then out of sight. Almost instantly I heard the gurgling sound, a couple of low growls, and I knew I had him down. All became quiet again and I was sure he was mine.

Without being overconfident, I went to get my father. By the time I got to the jeep, I knew that lanterns would be needed to track the bear.

My father was coming from his stand as I got to the jeep. I asked if he had seen anything. He'd seen the red squirrels wrestling with leaves. I told him I had too, but I also saw a bear that I shot. He asked if it was the big bear, and I replied I was sure that it was.

Dad and I then went out to track the bear, thinking that enough time had elapsed from the time the bear had been shot so that he should be dead.

With lanterns and flashlight, we got back to the bait. From where the bear had jumped from the bait, to the place he had landed, you could tell it was a very good hit. The blood trail was very easy to follow. All at once, it came to an end. Dad, who was behind me, said, "There's your bear." With the lantern, I couldn't see beyond the shadows, so I held it up and looked ahead. Dad said, "No, beside you!" I looked, and there he was, lying on the back side of a balsam tree about 35 yards from where I had hit him. Evidently, he must have gone down there, while watching his back trail.

After some hand shaking and back slapping, it hit us like a Joe Lewis punch. "How are we going to get this monster out of here?" It was all the two of us could do, just to roll him over on his back. Dad, being the quickest man I know at field-dressing took my knife and proceeded with the job at hand. I steadied the bear while Dad worked. When finished, Dad said, "Let's move him just a little way from the area where we've dressed him out." We each grabbed an ear and rocked back. But he wouldn't budge. We were 400 yards from the nearest logging road and needed help.

From the nearest residents of the area, we got help. The five men were anxious to see the bear. With about ten rest stops, clothes drenched and tongues hanging out, seven of us loaded him onto the hood of my jeep. The bear's weight crushed the hood of my jeep down to the air cleaner.

We took the bear to Phillips, Wisconsin, to be weighed and registered. He weighed 492 pounds, some 16 hours after he'd been shot and put into the cooler. His green skull measurements were 21-12/16. After the drying period, the skull was measured by Michael Steliga, (Pope and Young Club measurer) and by Peter Haupt (Boone and Crockett Club measurer). Both measured the skull at 21-9/16, making him the largest bear in Wisconsin for 1982.

Photo Courtesy of Harry Leggett, Jr.

Harry Leggett, Jr. and Kniebert Stillman admire "their" grizzly bear. It culminated several years of hunting by the pair. Leggett shot the big bear on the Wakeman River, B. C., in October 1980. Scoring 26-13/16 points, Leggett's bear received the First Award at the 18th. Awards, 1983.

GRIZZLY BEAR 26-13/16

First Award

Harry Leggett, Jr.

The quest for this trophy started in 1968 with my first hunt in Canada. While I was in excellent grizzly country, and had a successful hunt for moose and caribou, I never even saw a grizzly. During this hunt I heard many stories from the guides about grizzlies. They were not the typical stories about a snarling, ferocious monster, but about their wariness, sense of smell and hearing, cunning and intelligence, and what a good mother the sow was. I was fascinated.

I returned in 1969 to British Columbia and had a successful hunt for goat and caribou. On this trip I saw my first grizzly. The "die was cast." I wanted a big bear. In 1972, I teamed with a hunting buddy, Kniebert Stillman of Peach Orchard, Missouri. We both had a goal. We wanted a "records book bear", either grizzly or brown. We read, talked to hunters and guides, and decided: (1) A combination hunt might be great but it wasn't the way to get a record book bear -we had to concentrate on one animal. (2) We had to be in the right area - Kodiak for browns or British Columbia coast for grizzlies. (3) To have patience.

On September 30, 1980, we left Little Rock on our ninth hunt. Nine hunts exclusively for bear - 120 hunting days, $$$$ spent, ???? miles walked. We had been cold, wet, hot, dry, wind-blown, sunburned, and fogbound by weather as only this coastal area can produce. We didn't keep a log, but I'm certain we have seen 100 bear, stalked maybe 20, and passed up perhaps ten good, adult animals. We had strained our marriages and at times our friendship. But, in spite of having experienced boredom, excitement, frustration, and even being terrorized, with a *singleness of purpose*- we wanted "one in the book".

We left Little Rock and flew to Campbell River, British Columbia, where we met our guide (and by now good friend), Jack Innes. On the morning of September 30th, we boarded his boat, The Estero, and proceeded to our usual hunting grounds about 100 miles up the coast of British Columbia. The first stop was a quiet, remote area where we had observed a huge, black grizzly the year before.

On October 1st, we spent the morning scouting the area for bear sign. There were a lot of dog salmon in the river and fresh sign of at least two large grizzlies. Since this area was remote and would not be disturbed, we decided to look over another area about 25 miles away. So, we pulled anchor and proceeded to the Wakeman River. About ten miles out from Wakeman, the usual clear ocean waters took on a muddy color, which could only mean a flood in the Wakeman. As we pulled into Wakeman Sound, our confidence level fell to zero. The Wakeman had flooded and washed most of the spawning fish back to the ocean. This would make bear hunting very difficult. But we were there, so we decided to look around.

In the previous years, we had seen several grizzlies here, and a couple we knew were record size. We docked at the logging camp and talked to our friends at the camp. They informed us that while the Wakeman had flooded, another river about six miles up the valley, the Attway, had not. We decided to start in the morning for the junction of the Wakeman and the Attway. After all the years of pursuit, this decision put us on a collision course with *our bear*.

We left the boat the next morning before daylight. It was a beautiful, crisp fall morning. But, the Wakeman was so muddy our confidence level was, on a scale of one to ten, zero. Just about 200 yards below the Attway River, we saw his tracks - a very large bear and the tracks were obviously fresh. Now, one set of bear tracks does not a bear hunt make, but a hunter's confidence level and adrenaline operate somewhat like a yo-yo. Our confidence level went from zero to ten.

After a brief discussion, we decided that Kniebert would stay to watch the riffle at the junction of the rivers. Jack and I would circle around, go upstream, cross the Attway and check the shoals above the junction of the rivers. While this was about a half-mile circle, it only placed us about 300 yards apart, but separated by heavy bush. My parting words to Kniebert were, "If you hear a shot, it will be a stud."

Jack and I circled and crossed the Attway. Just as we approached the junction of the rivers, I saw the bear. He was walking out of the bush onto a gravel bar at the edge of the river. He was about 50 yards from me, standing broadside and up-wind, with perfect lighting. One of the things I have learned on my many hunts is how difficult it is to determine the size of a bear. All adult grizzlies look *big*.

I held that bear in my scope while Jack studied it through his binoculars for what seemed like 20 minutes but probably was only 20 seconds. Jack said, "You better take him." I fired; the bear jumped. I fired again; the bear fell off the bank into the river and sank. All hell then broke loose.

The river at this point was about five feet deep and swift. We were on the opposite side from the bear and Jack had lost a bear right here many years ago. He yelled, "Quick, back to Kniebert!" We ran to the crossing of the Attway and around a thicket, down the Wakeman to where Kniebert was waiting. Jack, being in better physical condition than I, arrived below the bear before I did. He teamed with Kniebert and began looking down the muddy Wakeman River for the bear - nothing. They were both sick thinking we had lost him. Thankfully, I was spared this trauma. About the time I arrived, they saw the bear. He was dead and hung under a snag in about 3-1/2 feet of water, 50 feet from the bank.

Kniebert and I charged out. We grabbed a foot, which dislodged the bear from the snag; 1,000 pounds of bear in a freezing, roaring current will put you to a test. But at this point, we had him and he couldn't have been pulled away from us with a winch truck. Jack scrambled to his pack for a rope and threw it to us. We tied a leg and held on, as the current worked the bear into the bank. Then we realized what a monster we had. We will never know the weight, but the three of us were unable to roll him over. His skull measured 26-15/16 and the hide was 9 feet, 10 inches square. We had done it! Not only did we have a record class grizzly, but perhaps as big or bigger than any other collected in Fair Chase.

Now this story might be more entertaining if I could tell of my superb marksmanship and a three-day stalk for a desert bighorn ending in a 400-yard neck shot just before dusk on the closing day of the season, or if this bear had been a charging, snarling, slobbering beast killed in full charge at only four yards. But, neither tale would be the truth, nor I assure you, would either represent the trophy that this animal represents.

We persevered and we got our trophy. I say "we" because the sighting down the rifle and the pulling of the trigger represents about 20 seconds out of nine years in *our* quest for this animal.

Photo Courtesy of Fritz A. Nachant

Fritz A. Nachant smiles happily over his big grizzly shot on the Iskut River, B. C., in May 1980. Nachant's bear scores 25-15/16 points and was recognized with the Second Award at the 18th. Awards, 1983.

GRIZZLY BEAR 25-15/16

Second Award

Fritz A. Nachant

I am 65 years old and have hunted North American game all my life. I also measure trophies for the Boone and Crockett Club's records. Deer, sheep and bear have been my number one pursuit and I have two slams on sheep, with three rams in the records book.

In the spring of 1980, my good friend and hunting partner, Allen Murray, and I had a hunt booked for grizzly bear in Bobby Ball's territory on the Stikine River of British Columbia.

We arrived in Wrangell, Alaska, on the 19th of May and were met by Big John, who looked like Paul Bunyon. Big John runs a supply and ferry system on the Stikine. On the morning of May 20th we departed for our hunting camp, approximately 40 miles up the Stikine into British Columbia. Upon arrival, after a cold and wet trip, we met our guides. Mine was Robbie Ried, an Indian guide from Smithers, British Columbia.

After settling our gear in camp, we took off separately for an afternoon hunt. We travelled up the Stikine in 16-foot johnboats with jet drives. Robbie made our first stop at the trail to Mud Glacier. We tied up the boat and hunted on foot to the base of the glacier. We picked up some large, 9-inch front pad bear tracks near the base of the glacier, but saw no bears and returned to the boat after about five hours.

That part of the country is heavy with alders, fir, and poplars (cottonwood), and one gets a slight chill up the spine sometimes when sneaking along a fresh track in heavy brush. We moved to a new location near a mountain called the Knob. We hunted a couple of hours in swampy marshes that had bear tracks going every which way and mosquitos biting even through our rubber hip boots. No bears were seen. We decided it was time to return to camp, arriving there at 9:30 p.m. A little toddy for the body, dinner, and then to bed.

Next day, at 4:00 a.m. Al left for Hole-in-the-Wall, while I went to the Porcupine River area. Robbie and I walked, glassed, and scouted, then walked and climbed some more. We saw lots of signs of fresh bear tracks, but no bears. Late in the afternoon we decided to move into a backwater canal where we could watch a long, grassy bench. The canal had lots of overhanging trees and limbs, so it was easier to drift than use the motor. As we were drifting along, I would duck under the trees and limbs. Suddenly, I heard a splash. Robbie was gone. A second later his head bobbed up. I grabbed him by his jacket and jerked him into the boat. It was not easy; hip boots full of water are not light. Robbie's first words were, "I can't swim." We spent the rest of the evening drying out a wet Indian. No more hunting, saw no bears, and went back to camp at 10:00 p.m.

Al had seen two bears, both large, and got a shot at one but missed.

May 22, Al was going back up where he saw the bears. Robbie and I headed up the Iskut River at 4:00 p.m. We had gone about eight miles when we pulled the boat up on a large floodplain about three miles long and one mile wide. Fresh bear tracks were everywhere. We hunted this area about three hours. There was lots of driftwood and dog alder patches, but we saw no bears. We decided to go farther up the Iskut. There was a large sandbar in the middle of the Iskut, across from where we beached the boat. As we were pushing the boat into the river, I saw a large grizzly bear on the sandbar about 400 yards away. I shouted, "Robbie, Robbie, put me on the sandbar quick!" The motor caught immediately and we hit the sandbar with me standing in the bow one minute and sailing onto land the next. The sandbar was about 300 yards long and 25 yards wide. The river was about 50 yards wide on each side. I figured the bear had jumped into the river.

The current was quite swift. On the off side of the river, the bank was sheer and about four feet high. Just below where I stood was a place where the bank had caved in, making a ramp. I knew the bear had not gotten that far, if he was in the river. Where in the hell was he?

Out in the river, about 60 yards above me, was a small logjam I kept watching. All of a sudden he came paddling around the logjam. What should I do? You can't shoot a grizzly in the water, he will sink. I said, "Please Mr. Bear, come back ashore on the sandbar." But no, he went right on by, swimming with the current. There I stood, shell in chamber and safety off, and couldn't shoot. All of a sudden, the bear saw the caved-in bank. He poured on the power and made it across the current to that spot, where he climbed out. I had about three seconds to make up my mind whether I wanted this bear or not.

I have shot nine bears: two grizzly, two brown, one polar and four black. After the last eight-foot grizzly bear, I wasn't going to shoot any more unless it was very large. This was my fifth grizzly hunt; four times I had passed up nice grizzlies because they were not large enough. Would this one be it?

As he hit the top of the bank and started into the alders, I could see he was a big, big bear. This was it! One shot from my Winchester Model 70 in 30-06 (180 grain bullet) hit just back of the right front leg, going through into the left front shoulder. I saw him no more but followed his progress through the shaking alders. After about 15 yards, the alders shook in one place for a second or two and then were still.

We took the boat a half-mile upstream to where we could beach it, and then made our way back to the bear, rifles at the ready. He was very dead and very big. He squared at 9 feet 2 inches, with a score of 26-1/16 for the skull. He was aged at some 13-1/2 years old. He is mounted on all fours in my trophy room among the rest of my trophies.

My hunting partner Al also took a large bear. Al's would have made the book if he hadn't shot it in the head, blowing off the back of the skull.

As an interesting sidelight concerning my shooting of brown and grizzly bears, I note the following:

Date	Squared Hide	Type	Score
May 22, 1965	10 feet, 11 inches	brown	29
May 22, 1978	9 feet, 6 inches	brown	27-2/16
May 22, 1980	9 feet, 2 inches	grizzly	26-1/16

Well, October 1983 will see me on the Aleutian Peninsula hunting brown bear again.

GRIZZLY BEAR 26-4/16

Certificate of Merit

William G. Underhill

A few years ago, country singer Lefty Frizzel made the town of Saginaw, Michigan, famous with his song of that name. Then, as now, many of the men of the town enjoy big-game hunting. William G. Underhill, a family physican, is one of those people.

Underhill was hunting with Dave Goodwin, of Atlin, British Columbia, near the junction of Tatshenshini and O'Connor Rivers in mid-May 1970. They arrived on May 14th by floatplane to begin their hunt. After hunting for several days, they spotted the big bear. It was late in the day, and they got to within 80 yards of him. It was sunny and clear and Underhill had a good shot at the bear. He used his faithful 30-06 to bring him down.

A decade would pass before Underhill had his bear trophy measured. In fact, he was given a copy of the latest records book (1977 at that time) for Christmas of 1980. In reading through the book, he looked at the scores for grizzly. He remembered Dave Goodwin telling him, on a sheep hunt taken in 1978, that the bear he killed in May 1970 was the largest grizzly Goodwin had taken with a hunter since he became an outfitter.

Underhill made his own measurement of the skull, finding it to apparently be big enough for the records book. He then had it officially measured and found that indeed it did belong in the records book. A belated, but still very much appreciated, Christmas present for him.

Photos Courtesy of Robert K. Fisher and Javier Zubia

(Left) Robert K. Fisher was hunting near Owikeno Lake, B. C., when he took his grizzly bear in October 1981. It scores 25 points. (Right) Cinder River, Alaska, was the site of Javier Zubia's hunt for brown bear in October 1981. His bear scores 28-4/16 points.

Photo Courtesy of Leon A. Naccarato

Leon A. Naccarato holds the skull of his big brown bear shot in May 1980 near Bear Lake, Alaska. Naccarato's bear scores 28-11/16 points and was recognized with the First Award at the 18th. Awards, 1983.

ALASKA BROWN BEAR 28-11/16

First Award (tie)

Leon A. Naccarato

While hunting goats for eight days in 1970, out of Cordova, Alaska, I saw my first brown bears. The sow and cub were so far away that they looked like tiny spots. Even though I didn't get a good look at them, they made such an impression on me that I had a tough time sleeping that night. I went for the next ten years without seeing another brown bear, but the wait was well worthwhile.

Early in 1980, Ralph Young, George Douglass, and I planned a brown bear hunting trip. Ralph had been trapping the winter before around Port Heiden, Alaska. While trapping fox and other critters, he noticed considerable brown bear sign. This area seemed to be a good choice for our spring trip, so we decided to concentrate our hunt above Port Heiden.

Spring brown bear hunting opened on the 10th of May that year. By the 7th of May, the three of us had travelled from Anchorage to arrive at Naknek, Alaska, where Ralph owned a cabin. The weather turned out to be typical Alaska weather. Within a period of two hours, we had rain, a 35-mph wind, calm, and snow. We were eager to fly out, but we had to spend a couple of days waiting for the weather to calm down.

Finally, late one day we decided to chance it. Ralph figured he would have to make two, perhaps three, trips to get all three of us and our gear to camp. I went with him on the first trip, bringing along my gear, tent, and part of the supplies. After Ralph left to get the second load, I proceeded to set up camp. Soon the wind and rain began. Every man should have at least one experience of setting-up a tent by himself in a 30-mph wind, with rain dripping from his hat and running down his neck. The day wore into evening as I was trying to dry my clothes. I soon realized that I was a lone bear hunter, 400 miles from civilization. Needless to say, I was very happy when I heard the sound of an airplane engine.

The next morning the weather was so bad that we couldn't get out of camp. The wind and rain continued all that day and the next. We were getting edgy. The first day of brown bear hunting had arrived and we were stuck in camp. George decided to use the spotting scope to glass the surrounding area. But, after fighting the wind and trying to keep the scope dry, we withdrew to our dry tent like moles.

By morning, the weather changed for the better and we woke up early. Glassing the area was our first priority. After a half-hour of studying the terrain, Ralph thought he spotted a bear track that came down out of the mountains and across a big, flat-rolling hill area. We were ready for a hike to investigate, even though we knew it would be at least five miles across tundra and snow patches.

Ralph and I hiked for about two hours, when we came across a track. It wasn't a bear track, just an old moose track. We glassed the area and discovered a likely place for a bear den that was about two miles away. Since we had already come this far, a couple more miles couldn't hurt us. On the way over to the den, we came across some bear tracks. They looked fresh to us, so we started following them. The bear tracks came out of the rolling hills and headed across a large open flat. We followed the tracks for about 1-1/2 hours.

They led us along the top of a plateau and then dropped into a gully about 500 feet below. I was about 50 feet ahead of Ralph. I stopped at the edge of the gully and started glassing across to the flat and rolling hill area beyond. As I was slipping my gun off my shoulder to get a better look, I suddenly noticed something moving in the steep gully, about 90 feet below me in the brush. Realizing it was a bear, I threw the gun to my shoulder, aimed, and fired. I chambered another round and fired again. This time the bear looked up the hill at me, but kept walking into the brush.

My heart was thundering in my chest by the time Ralph ran up beside me. He began hollering at me to shoot the bear before it ate us. I chambered another round, took aim at its neck, and fired. My whole body was beginning to shake when Ralph yelled that I had hit him. He had seen hair fly. The bear looked back up the hill at me before stumbling and falling into the snow. Everything had happened so fast!

I sat down for a minute and savored the conquest of the hunt, while calming myself. Realizing that my trophy was a good one, I decided that the long wait since I had seen my first brown bear was indeed worthwhile.

Then, the hard work to get the bear skinned began. It was almost impossible for the two of us to roll the huge creature over in the snow. Skinning it took us over two hours. We knew that the bear was big, but we didn't realize that it might be a trophy bear until we returned to Naknek and spread the hide on the cabin floor. After being skinned and salted for days, it still squared 10 feet 7 inches!

ALASKA BROWN BEAR 28-11/16

First Award (Tie)

James S. Fogel

Dead Man Bay, Alaska, is famed as habitat for big brown bears. Over the years, some huge specimens have come from there. Fogel knew it would be a good place for his hunt.

Fogel left his home at Eagle River, Alaska, arriving at Dead Man Bay on April 26, 1982. As most folks travel in Alaska, Fogel used a floatplane to get to his hunting site. He had brought along an inflatable boat with an outboard motor to allow easy access to good locations in the bay.

As often happens, Fogel encountered several days of bad weather. The weather finally broke with a sunny and clear day on May 2nd. Fogel hunted most of day, finally spotting his trophy late in the afternoon. Getting to within 150 yards, he used his Ruger Model 77 in 338 caliber to bring down his prize.

Later examination by the state fish and game biologist indicated that the bear was 15 years old. The huge skull was carefully cleaned and dried for the prescribed 60 days. When measured, it easily exceeded the minimum entry score and placed in the top part of its category for the entry period.

Photograph by Wash. Dept. of Game

Lester H. Miller and his huge Columbia blacktail deer. Miller shot his buck in October 1953 in Lewis Co., Washington, but it wasn't scored until 1980. It was recognized as the new world's record at a score of 182-2/8 points at the 18th. Awards, 1983, where it also received the Certificate of Merit Award.

TABULATIONS OF RECORDED TROPHIES

18TH AWARDS ENTRY PERIOD
1980 - 1982

The trophy data shown herein have been taken from score charts in the Records Archives of the Boone and Crockett Club for the 18th Awards entry period, 1980-1982. Trophies listed are those that meet minimum score and other stated requirements of trophy entry for the period. The final scores and rank shown are official, except for trophies shown with an asterisk. The asterisk is assigned to trophies whose entry scores are subject to certification by an Awards Panel of Judges. The asterisk can be removed by the submitting of two additional, independent scorings by Official Measurers of the Boone and Crockett Club. The Records Committee of the club will review the three scorings available (original, plus two additional) and determine which, if any, will be accepted in lieu of the judges panel measurement. When the score has been accepted as final by the Records Committee, the asterisk will be removed in future editions of the records book, *Records of North American Big Game*, and other publications.

The Scientific and vernacular names, and the sequence of presentation, follows that suggested in the Revised Checklist of North American Mammals North of Mexico, 1979 (J. Knox Jones, *et al*; Texas Tech University, 14 December 1979.)

TROPHY BOUNDARIES

Many of the categories recognized in the records keeping are based upon subspecies differences. In nature, subspecies freely interbreed where their ranges overlap, thus necessitating the setting of geographic boundaries to keep them separate for records keeping purposes.

Geographic boundaries are described for a number of categories. These include: brown and grizzly bear; American and Roosevelt's elk; mule and Columbia blacktail deer; whitetail and Coues' deer; moose; and caribou. Pertinent information is included in the trophy data listings that follow, but the complete, detailed description for each is to be found in the latest edition (8th., 1981) of the records book, *Records of North American Big Game*.

In addition to category specific boundaries, all trophies must be from North America, north of the south border of Mexico, to be eligible. For pelagic trophies, such as walrus and polar bear, they must be from the U.S. side of the International Date Line to be eligible.

Trophy boundaries are set by the Boone and Crockett Club's Records of North American Big Game Committee, working with the latest and best available information from scientific researchers, guides, hunters, and other parties with serious interest in our big game resources. In general, boundaries are set so that it is highly unlikely that specimens of the larger category can be taken within the boundary set for the smaller category, thus upsetting the rankings of the smaller category. Trophy boundaries are revised as necessary to maintain this separation of the categories.

Black Bear

Ursus americanus americanus and related subspecies

Minimum Score 21   **World's Record 23 10/16**

Score	Greatest Length of Skull Without Lower Jaw	Greatest Width of Skull	Sex	Locality Killed	By Whom Killed	Owner	Date Killed	Rank
22 2/16	14 6/16	8 6/16	M	Porcupine Plains, Sask.	Calvin Parsons	Calvin Parsons	SE 1977	1
22 2/16	13 13/16	8 6/16	M	Arran, Sask.	Harry Kushniryk	Harry Kushniryk	AP 1981	2
22*	13 11/16	8 6/16	M	McKenzie Inlet, Alaska	Fred J. Hoppe	Fred J. Hoppe	MY 1981	3
21 14/16	13 9/16	8 6/16	M	Lincoln Co., Wisc.	Robert P. Faufau	Robert P. Faufau	SE 1981	4
21 10/16	13 5/16	8 6/16	M	Ouray Co., Colo.	Thomas C. Middleton	Thomas C. Middleton	OT 1978	5
21 9/16	12 4/16	8 10/16	M	Harrison Hot Springs, B. C.	Domenico Abbinante	Domenico Abbinante	JN 1982	6
21 9/16	13 5/16	8 6/16	M	Garfield Co., Colo.	Robert W. Jackson	Robert W. Jackson	JL 1980	6
21 7/16	13 5/16	8 3/16	M	Iron Co., Wisc.	Gary G. Johnson	Gary G. Johnson	SE 1982	8
21 7/16	13 5/16	8 3/16	M	Pierceland, Sask.	Bryce Burgess	Bryce Burgess	MY 1980	8
21 7/16	13 12/16	7 11/16	M	Sevier Co., Utah	Milton LaVal Robb	Milton LaVal Robb	JN 1980	8
21 5/16	12 7/16	8 5/16	M	Pitken Co., Colo.	Chris Green	Chris Green	JL 1980	11
21 4/16	13 1/16	7 9/16	M	Langlade Co., Wisc.	Michael Steliga	Michael Steliga	SE 1981	12
21 4/16	13 5/16	7 11/16	M	Gila Co., Ariz.	Larry S. Behrends	Larry S. Behrends	MY 1976	12
21 3/16	13 5/16	7 13/16	M	Tehama Co., Calif.	Jim Cox	Jim Cox	DC 1980	14
21 3/16	13 6/16	8 6/16	M	Khyex River, B. C.	Edward Dickens	Edward Dickens	MY 1982	14
21 3/16	13 7/16	7 9/16	M	Pinal Co., Ariz.	Bruce R. Gifford	Bruce R. Gifford	SE 1980	14
21 2/16	12 7/16	8 4/16	M	Carbon Co., Wyo.	Hugh D. Beavers, Jr.	Hugh D. Beavers, Jr.	JN 1981	17
21 2/16	13 5/16	8	M	Clinton Co., Pa.	Orwin W. Srock	Orwin W. Srock	NO 1981	17
21 1/16	12 13/16	8 6/16	M	Madison Co., Mont.	Gerald D. Morgan	Gerald D. Morgan	AG 1974	20
21 1/16	13 5/16	8	M	Preeceville, Sask.	David S. Hodgin	David S. Hodgin	MY 1982	21
21 1/16	12 15/16	8 2/16	M	Teller Co., Colo.	Samuel T. Harrelson, Jr.	Samuel T. Harrelson, Jr.	JN 1982	21
21 1/16	13 5/16	8	M	Spirit River, Alta.	John Dobish	John Dobish	MY 1982	21
21	12 13/16	8 5/16	M	Greenlee Co., Ariz.	Michael W. Goodyear	Michael W. Goodyear	SE 1979	24
21	13 5/16	7 11/16	M	Hamilton Co., N. Y.	Marshall E. Conklin	Marshall E. Conklin	SE 1981	24
21	12 12/16	8 6/16	M	Bradford Co., Pa.	Ray B. Moyer	Ray B. Moyer	NO 1981	24
21	13 5/16	7 11/16	M	Coconino Co., Ariz.	Michael P. Whelan	Michael P. Whelan	SE 1981	24
21	12 5/16	8 5/16	M	Fremont Co., Wyo.	Timothy B. Hill	Timothy B. Hill	OT 1981	24
21	13 5/16	7 13/16	M	Langlade Co., Wisc.	Michael Steliga	Michael Steliga	SE 1982	24

*Final Score subject to revision by additional verifying measurements.

Grizzly Bear
Ursus arctos horribilis

Minimum Score 24   **World's Record 27 5/16**

Score	Greatest Length of Skull Without Lower Jaw	Greatest Width of Skull	Sex	Locality Killed	By Whom Killed	Owner	Date Killed	Rank
26 13/16	16 1/16	10 3/16	M	Wakeman River, B. C.	Harry Leggett, Jr.	Harry Leggett, Jr.	OT 1980	1
26 6/16*	16 14/16	9 8/16	M	Seaskinnish Creek, B. C.	Paddy H. S. Wong	Fred Y. C. Wong	SE 1982	2
26 6/16	16 7/16	9 15/16	M	Tashenshini River, B. C.	William G. Underhill	William G. Underhill	MY 1970	3
26 6/16*	16 5/16	9 13/16	M	Wells Creek, Alaska	Wayman H. Hall, Jr.	Wayman H. Hall, Jr.	OT 1978	4
25 13/16	16	9 15/16	M	Iskut River, B. C.	Fritz A. Nachant	Fritz A. Nachant	MY 1980	5
25 14/16	16 7/16	9 12/16	M	Muskeg River, Alta.	Dale B. Kolberg	Dale B. Kolberg	MY 1981	6
25 14/16	16	9 14/16	M	Christmas Mt., Alaska	Mark E. Gilson	Mark E. Gilson	SE 1980	6
25 3/16	16 2/16	9 14/16	M	Kwatna River, B. C.	Robert C. Riggs	Robert C. Riggs	MY 1981	8
25 1/16	15 5/16	10	M	Meziadin Lake, B. C.	Jae Dea Jensen & R. Sam Curtis	Jae Dea Jensen	OT 1979	9
25 6/16	16 6/16	9	M	King Salmon Creek, B. C.	John K. Fritze	John K. Fritze	MY 1980	10
25 5/16	15 7/16	9 9/16	M	Kitlope River, B. C.	Darryl W. Hodson	Darryl W. Hodson	MY 1975	11
25 5/16	15 7/16	9 9/16	M	Toad River, B. C.	Paul E. Robey	Paul E. Robey	MY 1981	11
25 5/16	16 2/16	9 9/16	M	Andreafsky River, Alaska	John C. Bruno	John C. Bruno	MY 1981	11
25 5/16	15 5/16	10 3/16	M	Lakelse River, B. C.	William J. Harvey, Jr.	William J. Harvey, Jr.	JN 1979	11
25 5/16	15 5/16	10 5/16	M	Kuskokwim River, Alaska	Michael T. Carlucci	Michael T. Carlucci	MY 1981	15
25 5/16	16 5/16	9 6/16	M	Scoop Lake, B. C.	Darrell A. Farr	Dwight E. Farr	OT 1981	16
25 5/16	16 6/16	9 5/16	M	Skowquiltz River, B. C.	Robert C. McEntee	Robert C. McEntee	MY 1981	16
25 5/16	15 5/16	9 14/16	M	Andreafsky River, Alaska	James P. Barkman	James P. Barkman	MY 1980	18
25 5/16	15 5/16	9 12/16	M	Beaver Creek, Alaska	Picked Up	Abram Walter	PU 1979	19
25	14 7/16	10 5/16	M	Fortymile River, Alaska	James B. DeMoss	James B. DeMoss	MY 1980	20
25	16 5/16	8 11/16	M	Owikeno Lake, B. C.	Robert K. Fisher	Robert K. Fisher	OT 1981	20
24 13/16	15 5/16	9 9/16	M	Tonzona River, Alaska	Wayne J. Pensenstadler	Wayne J. Pensenstadler	SE 1982	22
24 14/16	15 13/16	9 5/16	M	Andreafsky River, Alaska	James W. Latreille	James W. Latreille	MY 1980	23
24 14/16	15 5/16	9 11/16	M	Klutina River, Alaska	Robert M. Decker	Robert M. Decker	OT 1979	23
24 14/16	15 5/16	9 5/16	M	Tatla Lake, B. C.	Donald L. Gardner	Donald L. Gardner	MY 1980	23
24 3/16	15	9 12/16	M	Turnagain River, B. C.	Arthur E. Crawford	Arthur E. Crawford	SE 1980	26
24 11/16	15 5/16	9 5/16	M	Toad River, B. C.	Bruce H. Morrill	Bruce H. Morrill	OT 1980	27
24 11/16	15	9 11/16	M	Toklat River, Alaska	Timothy A. Sanderson	Timothy A. Sanderson	SE 1976	27
24 6/16	15 5/16	9 5/16	M	Toklat River, Alaska	Howard W. Neice	Howard W. Neice	MY 1981	29
24 6/16	15 13/16	8 13/16	M	Chuckwalla River, B. C.	George B. Morris	George B. Morris	OT 1979	30
24 6/16	15 5/16	8 11/16	M	Kelly Creek, B. C.	Rick H. Jackson	Rick H. Jackson	SE 1980	31

24⁵/₁₆	15⁵/₁₆	9⁵/₁₆	M	Murray River, B. C.	Carl Kortmeyer	Carl Kortmeyer	OT 1980	32
24⁵/₁₆	15⁵/₁₆	8¹⁵/₁₆	M	Cranberry River, B. C.	Fred Y. C. Wong	Albert Wong	OT 1982	33
24⁵/₁₆	14¹³/₁₆	9⁵/₁₆	M	Selwyn Creek, Yukon	Rod G. Hardie	Rod G. Hardie	MY 1979	33
24⁵/₁₆	15⁵/₁₆	8¹³/₁₆	M	Big River, Alaska	Dale G. Moffat	Dale G. Moffat	MY 1977	35
24⁵/₁₆	15⁵/₁₆	9⁵/₁₆	M	Chatanika River, Alaska	Robert L. Nelson	Robert L. Nelson	AP 1981	36
24¹/₁₆	15	9⁵/₁₆	M	King Salmon River, B. C.	Phil Forte	Phil Forte	MY 1981	37
24	14¹²/₁₆	9⁵/₁₆	M	Andreafsky River, Alaska	Bruce K. Kent	Bruce K. Kent	MY 1980	38

*Final Score subject to revision by additional verifying measurements.

Alaska Brown Bear

Ursus arctos middendorffi and certain related subspecies

Minimum Score 28 **World's Record 30 12/16**

Score	Greatest Length of Skull Without Lower Jaw	Greatest Width of Skull	Sex	Locality Killed	By Whom Killed	Owner	Date Killed	Rank
30 12/16 *	18 5/16	12 7/16	M	Afognak Island, Alaska	Picked Up	Almin G. Thompson	PR 1970	1
28 13/16 *	17 7/16	11 6/16	M	Kiliuda Bay, Alaska	Dean J. Walden	Dean J. Walden	MY 1980	2
28 11/16	18 5/16	10 6/16	M	Bear Lake, Alaska	Leon A. Naccarato	Leon A. Naccarato	MY 1980	3
28 11/16	17 5/16	11 6/16	M	Deadman Bay, Alaska	James S. Fogel	James S. Fogel	MY 1982	3
28 10/16 *	17 7/16	11 3/16	M	Port Heiden, Alaska	Russ McLennan	Russ McLennan	MY 1980	5
28 10/16 *	17	11 6/16	M	Olga Bay, Alaska	Doug Latimer	Doug Latimer	AP 1980	5
28 5/16	18	10 5/16	M	Foot Bay, Alaska	Larry A. McComb	Larry A. McComb	MY 1982	7
28 5/16	17 3/16	11 2/16	M	Dog Salmon Creek, Alaska	John Della Valle	John Della Valle	OT 1981	7
28 3/16	17 3/16	11	M	Olga Bay, Alaska	Allan E. Bergland	Allan E. Bergland	AP 1981	9
28 3/16	17 13/16	10 6/16	M	Cinder River, Alaska	Javier Zubia	Javier Zubia	OT 1981	9
28 2/16	17 5/16	10 14/16	M	Cathedral Valley, Alaska	J. M. Norton	J. M. Norton	MY 1982	11
28	16 9/16	11 6/16	M	Ugak Bay, Alaska	Arnie Gutenkauf	Arnie Gutenkauf	MY 1981	12

*Final Score subject to revision by additional verifying measurements.

Cougar or Mountain Lion

Felis concolor hippolestes and related subspecies

Minimum Score 15   World's Record 16$^{4}/_{16}$

Score	Greatest Length of Skull Without Lower Jaw	Greatest Width of Skull	Sex	Locality Killed	By Whom Killed	Owner	Date Killed	Rank
16$^{4}/_{16}$	9$^{6}/_{16}$	6$^{11}/_{16}$	M	Tatlayoko Lake, B. C.	Douglas E. Schuk	Charles M. Travers	FE 1979	1
15$^{13}/_{16}$	8$^{13}/_{16}$	6$^{15}/_{16}$	M	Gold Creek, B. C.	Donovan W. Ellis	Donovan W. Ellis	DC 1981	2
15$^{13}/_{16}$*	9$^{6}/_{16}$	6$^{6}/_{16}$	M	Sandoval Co., N. M.	Thomas J. David	Thomas J. David	JA 1980	2
15$^{12}/_{16}$	9$^{6}/_{16}$	6$^{6}/_{16}$	M	Mesa Co., Colo.	Jack Harrison	Jack Harrison	JA 1980	4
15$^{12}/_{16}$*	8$^{13}/_{16}$	6$^{11}/_{16}$	M	Taos Co., N. M.	George P. Mann	George P. Mann	FE 1981	4
15$^{11}/_{16}$	9	6$^{9}/_{16}$	M	Wallowa Co., Oreg.	Duane E. Neuschwander	Duane E. Neuschwander	DC 1980	6
15$^{10}/_{16}$	9$^{5}/_{16}$	6$^{3}/_{16}$	M	Colfax Co., N. M.	Ronald G. Troyer	Ronald G. Troyer	FE 1982	7
15$^{10}/_{16}$	8$^{14}/_{16}$	6$^{8}/_{16}$	M	Baker Co., Oreg.	Joe J. Lay	Joe J. Lay	DC 1981	7
15$^{9}/_{16}$	8$^{13}/_{16}$	6$^{8}/_{16}$	M	Rio Arriba Co., N. M.	Anderson Bakewell	Anderson Bakewell	MY 1978	7
15$^{8}/_{16}$	8$^{13}/_{16}$	6$^{8}/_{16}$	M	Ferry Co., Wash.	Richard A. Bonander	Richard A. Bonander	DC 1981	10
15$^{8}/_{16}$	8$^{13}/_{16}$	6$^{8}/_{16}$	M	Stevens Co., Wash.	William K. Bean	William K. Bean	DC 1981	10
15$^{8}/_{16}$	8$^{13}/_{16}$	6$^{4}/_{16}$	M	Mt. Evans, B. C.	Larry N. Dent	Larry N. Dent	FE 1980	10
15$^{8}/_{16}$	8$^{11}/_{16}$	6$^{6}/_{16}$	M	Stevens Co., Wash.	Fritz G. Nagel	Fritz G. Nagel	DC 1981	10
15$^{5}/_{16}$	9	6$^{9}/_{16}$	M	Graveyard Creek, B. C.	Rod G. Hardie	Rod G. Hardie	JA 1972	13
15$^{5}/_{16}$	8$^{14}/_{16}$	6$^{6}/_{16}$	M	Adams Co., Idaho	Warren J. Mason	Warren J. Mason	JA 1982	13
15$^{5}/_{16}$	9$^{5}/_{16}$	6$^{1}/_{16}$	M	Colfax Co., N. M.	Philip H. Whitley	Philip H. Whitley	DC 1980	13
15$^{5}/_{16}$	8$^{2}/_{16}$	6$^{8}/_{16}$	M	Idaho Co., Idaho	Lawrence L. Seiler	Lawrence L. Seiler	JA 1977	13
15$^{2}/_{16}$	8$^{13}/_{16}$	6$^{2}/_{16}$	M	Pimainus Hills, B. C.	Norman W. Dougan	Norman W. Dougan	DC 1978	18
15$^{2}/_{16}$	8$^{13}/_{16}$	6$^{6}/_{16}$	M	Wallowa Co., Oreg.	Rollie Mattson	Rollie Mattson	DC 1978	18
15$^{2}/_{16}$	8$^{14}/_{16}$	6$^{3}/_{16}$	M	Mill Creek, Alta.	Richard C. Davidson	Richard C. Davidson	JA 1980	18
15$^{2}/_{16}$	8$^{13}/_{16}$	6$^{5}/_{16}$	M	Nez Perce Co., Idaho	Pete M. Baughman, Jr.	Pete M. Baughman, Jr.	NO 1979	18
15$^{2}/_{16}$	8$^{13}/_{16}$	6$^{3}/_{16}$	M	Rio Arriba Co., N. M.	Joseph Strasser, Jr.	Joseph Strasser, Jr.	FE 1980	18
15	8$^{11}/_{16}$	6$^{5}/_{16}$	M	San Miguel Co., Colo.	James N. McHolme	James N. McHolme	JA 1981	23
15	8$^{14}/_{16}$	6$^{2}/_{16}$	M	Madison Co., Mont.	George A. Dieruf	George A. Dieruf	DC 1980	23
15	8$^{13}/_{16}$	6$^{5}/_{16}$	M	Stevens Co., Wash.	Roger A. Rasching	Roger A. Rasching	DC 1979	23
15	9	6	M	Washington Co., Utah	J. Phil Goodson	J. Phil Goodson	NO 1980	23

*Final Score subject to revision by additional verifying measurements.

Pacific Walrus

Minimum Score 100 — ***Odobenus rosmarus divergens*** — **World's Record 145 6/8**

Score	Entire Length of Loose Tusk R.	Entire Length of Loose Tusk L.	Circumference of Base R.	Circumference of Base L.	Circumference at Third Quarter R.	Circumference at Third Quarter L.	Sex	Locality Killed	By Whom Killed	Owner	Date Killed	Rank
136 4/8*	32 6/8	32 4/8	9 5/8	9 3/8	7 4/8	7 2/8	M	Port Moller, Alaska	Picked Up	Larry R. Rivers	PU 1981	1
127 4/8*	32 2/8	30 3/8	9	8 6/8	6 6/8	6 6/8	M	Port Heiden, Alaska	Picked Up	Larry R. Rivers	PU 1981	2
125*	30 7/8	30 6/8	9 1/8	9 4/8	5 7/8	5 7/8	M	Gambell, Alaska	Charles McLaughlin	Charles McLaughlin	MY 1978	3
124 4/8*	31 2/8	30 4/8	8 3/8	8 3/8	6 3/8	6 2/8	M	Hagemeister Island, Alaska	Picked Up	Lloyd D. Friend	PU 1979	4
118 4/8	31 4/8	32	7 4/8	7 4/8	5 1/8	5 2/8	M	St. Lawrence Island, Alaska	Clifford Patz	Clifford Patz	MY 1979	5
109 6/8	28 1/8	28 2/8	7 3/8	7 4/8	5	5	M	Point Franklin, Alaska	Michael R. Bogan	Michael R. Bogan	JL 1978	6
104 4/8	26 4/8	26 4/8	7 4/8	7 7/8	4 7/8	5	M	Savoonga, Alaska	Andrew A. Samuels, Jr.	Andrew A. Samuels, Jr.	JN 1979	7
102	24 6/8	25	7 4/8	7 5/8	4 5/8	4 5/8	M	Savoonga, Alaska	Robert J. Bartlett	Robert J. Bartlett	MY 1979	8

*Final Score subject to revision by additional verifying measurements

Wapiti or American Elk

Minimum Score 375 — ***Cervus elaphus nelsoni* and related subspecies** — **World's Record 442 3/8**

Score	Length of Main Beam R.	Length of Main Beam L.	Inside Spread	Circumference at Smallest Place Between First and Second Points R.	Circumference at Smallest Place Between First and Second Points L.	Number of Points R.	Number of Points L.	Locality Killed	By Whom Killed	Owner	Date Killed	Rank
414 6/8*	55 3/8	58 3/8	53 3/8	13 5/8	13	9	7	Gunnison Co., Colo.	J. J. Carpenter	Hugh Carpenter	1900	1
399 3/8*	58 3/8	58	49 3/8	9 2/8	9 1/8	6	6	Coconino Co., Ariz.	Terry J. Rice	Terry J. Rice	NO 1979	2
397 7/8	52	55 1/8	52 1/8	8 1/8	7 6/8	7	7	Sublette Co., Wyo.	Ray Daugherty	Aldon L. Hale	OT 1950	3
394 2/8*	56 4/8	55 4/8	39 6/8	9 6/8	9 4/8	7	7	Grant Co., Oreg.	Drake J. Davis	Drake J. Davis	NO 1981	4
391 4/8*	57 5/8	57 3/8	42 4/8	10 3/8	10 3/8	6	7	Ouray Co., Colo.	Eugene D. Guilaroff	Eugene D. Guilaroff	OT 1973	5
390 2/8	55	55 4/8	49 2/8	8 6/8	8 6/8	7	7	Hood River Co., Oreg.	Bill Tensen	Bill Tensen	SE 1980	6
389 6/8*	52 7/8	55 1/8	44 4/8	9 7/8	9 2/8	6	6	Meagher Co., Mont.	David G. Snyder	David G. Snyder	SE 1981	7
385 1/8	46	48 2/8	44 3/8	7 6/8	8 2/8	6	6	Lincoln Co., Wyo.	Ken Clark	Ken Clark	NO 1979	8
384 2/8	58 1/8	60 6/8	49 3/8	10	8 3/8	6	7	Apache Co., Ariz.	Roy W. Baker	Roy W. Baker	SE 1980	9
383 2/8	55 5/8	53 1/8	45	10 3/8	10 5/8	6	7	Coconino Co., Ariz.	Jay E. Elmer	Jay E. Elmer	SE 1979	10
381 6/8	55 2/8	57 1/8	41	9 6/8	9 6/8	7	7	Red Deer River, Alta.	Allan E. Brown	Allan E. Brown	NO 1980	11
381 2/8	57	55 4/8	44 2/8	9	8 6/8	6	6	Kittitas Co., Wash.	Clinton W. Morrow	Clinton W. Morrow	NO 1957	12
378 6/8	51 7/8	50 6/8	39 7/8	7 7/8	8 6/8	7	9	Sanders Co., Mont.	John Fitchett	John Fitchett	NO 1980	13
377 5/8	53 7/8	53 3/8	51 7/8	9	8 1/8	7	6	Beaverhead Co., Mont.	Edmund J. Giebel	Edmund J. Giebel	OT 1981	14
376 1/8	58 3/8	56 4/8	42 1/8	8 4/8	8 2/8	6	6	Lincoln Co., N. M.	Jim Carter	Jim Carter	OT 1981	15
375 6/8	55 1/8	54 4/8	39 4/8	8 7/8	8 2/8	6	6	North Fall Creek, Wyo.	Picked Up	Bob F. Penny	PU 1981	16
375 5/8	54 3/8	54 1/8	43 7/8	8 2/8	8 3/8	7	6	Sanders Co., Mont.	Tony B. Cox	Tony B. Cox	NO 1980	17
375 2/8	56	55	38	8 4/8	8 4/8	6	6	Albany Co., Wyo.	Don Stewart	Don Stewart	SE 1981	18

*Final Score subject to revision by additional verifying measurements

Roosevelt's Elk

Minimum Score 290 — *Cervus elaphus roosevelti* — **World's Record 356**

The Roosevelt's elk category was established on 1 January 1980. Roosevelt's elk includes trophies from: west of Highway I-5 in Oregon and Washington; the Mt. St. Helen's herd of western Skamania County, Washington; Del Morte and Humboldt Counties, California; Afognak and Raspberry Islands, Alaska; and, Vancouver Island, B.C.

Score	Length of Main Beam R.	Length of Main Beam L.	Inside Spread	Circumference at Smallest Place Between First and Second Points R.	Circumference at Smallest Place Between First and Second Points L.	Number of Points R.	Number of Points L.	Locality Killed	By Whom Killed	Owner	Date Killed	Rank
356	50 3/8	53	37 4/8	9	8 5/8	7	7	Clatsop Co., Oreg.	Pravomil Raichl	Pravomil Raichl	NO 1959	1
355 6/8*	51 4/8	51 4/8	42 2/8	9 6/8	10 2/8	7	7	Clatsop Co., Oreg.	David A. Schoenborn	Larrys Sports Center	NO 1939	2
353 5/8*	54	54 3/8	40 1/8	9 2/8	8 5/8	7	9	Vancouver Island, B. C.	Lawrence A. Ondzik	Alf Spineto	OT 1981	3
352 6/8	43	45 5/8	35 4/8	9 6/8	9 5/8	7	8	Columbia Co., Oreg.	Floyd M. Lindberg	Floyd M. Lindberg	NO 1962	4
351 6/8*	55 4/8	53 4/8	42	9 5/8	8 7/8	8	8	Tillamook Co., Oreg.	Albert Hoffarber	Ray Hoffarber	SE 1940	5
344 6/8*	51 5/8	51 3/8	40 5/8	11 1/8	11 1/8	6	7	Columbia Co., Oreg.	Unknown	Harold E. Stepp	1962	6
344 2/8	46	44 4/8	37 6/8	8 7/8	8 7/8	7	7	Jefferson Co., Wash.	Dave D. Godfrey	Dave D. Godfrey	NO 1966	7
342 6/8*	52	50 2/8	41 2/8	10	10	6	6	Kelsey Bay, B. C.	David Webber	David Webber	OT 1981	8
340 4/8	49 2/8	47 5/8	40	8 4/8	8 5/8	7	7	Jefferson Co., Wash.	Carroll E. Koenke	Carroll E. Koenke	NO 1966	9
336 3/8*	47 2/8	49 6/8	43 1/8	8 2/8	7 5/8	8	7	Clallam Co., Wash.	C. F. & C. H. Bernhardt	C. F. & C. H. Bernhardt	NO 1979	10
334 4/8*	46 5/8	46	38 4/8	7 2/8	7 7/8	8	7	Columbia Co., Oreg.	Harry R. Olsen	Harry R. Olsen	NO 1970	11
333 1/8	51 2/8	51 7/8	42 1/8	10 1/8	10 3/8	7	7	Clatsop Co., Oreg.	Picked Up	Andy Mendenhall, Jr.	PU 1978	12
332 5/8	45 1/8	45 2/8	33 5/8	10 3/8	10	7	8	Columbia Co., Oreg.	Derl Roberts	Derl Roberts	NO 1965	13
332 1/8	46 6/8	46 6/8	40 3/8	8 7/8	9 1/8	7	6	Oregon Coast Range	Unknown	Richard Leach	PR 1981	14
329 2/8	46 1/8	45	36	9 3/8	9	6	8	Columbia Co., Oreg.	Bud Holmes	James C. Oroth	NO 1962	15
328 3/8	48 7/8	50 1/8	39 3/8	8 5/8	8 2/8	6	6	Tillamook Co., Oreg.	Gary H. Purdy	Gary H. Purdy	NO 1969	16
326 2/8	46 4/8	46 4/8	38 4/8	8 7/8	8 5/8	7	7	Vancouver Island, B. C.	Wayne H. Zaccarelli	Wayne H. Zaccarelli	OT 1981	17
324 7/8	47 2/8	46 4/8	44 2/8	9 1/8	9 1/8	8	7	Columbia Co., Oreg.	Al Glenn	Al Glenn	NO 1955	18
323	50	49	43 6/8	9	9 6/8	8	7	Columbia Co., Oreg.	Edgar J. Rea	Edgar J. Rea	NO 1973	19
320 7/8	45 5/8	47	37 7/8	7 2/8	7 1/8	7	7	Clatsop Co., Oreg.	Clarence V. Jurhs	Clarence V. Jurhs	OT 1958	20
315 6/8	43 2/8	41	41 2/8	10 3/8	10 3/8	7	7	Clatsop Co., Oreg.	Reed Holding	Reed Holding	OT 1939	21
315 3/8	47 3/8	46 5/8	43 1/8	10 3/8	10 1/8	6	6	Jefferson Co., Wash.	Hans Norbisrath	Hans Norbisrath	NO 1966	22
314 7/8	43 1/8	43 5/8	47 1/8	8 5/8	8 4/8	7	7	Columbia Co., Oreg.	Harry R. Olsen	Harry R. Olsen	NO 1961	23
314 4/8	48 2/8	47 7/8	42	9 4/8	9	6	6	Columbia Co., Oreg.	William E. Curtis	Duane M. Bernard	1965	24
314 2/8	47 6/8	44 5/8	38 1/8	8 7/8	9 2/8	8	7	Columbia Co., Oreg.	William E. Curtis	William E. Curtis	NO 1952	25
313 5/8	52 1/8	49 2/8	36 3/8	9 5/8	9 3/8	6	6	Coos Co., Oreg.	Robert Dean Dunson	Robert Dean Dunson	AG 1982	26

Score							Location	Hunter	Owner	Date	Rank
312 1/8	45 7/8	46 3/8	42 3/8	8	7	7	Clatsop Co., Oreg.	Robert L. Brown	Robert L. Brown	NO 1966	27
310	44 7/8	44 7/8	34	10 3/8	7	7	Jefferson Co., Wash.	Howard L. Hill	Michael R. Raffaell	1969	28
307 7/8	41 3/8	41 1/8	37 3/8	9	6	7	Columbia Co., Oreg.	Max Oblack	Max Oblack	NO 1967	29
305 7/8	50 1/8	50 3/8	38 5/8	7 7/8	8	6	Polk Co., Oreg.	James E. Wallen	James E. Wallen	SE 1980	30
304 7/8	49	41 7/8	39 7/8	9 7/8	6	7	Clatsop Co., Oreg.	William D. Mellinger	William D. Mellinger	NO 1958	31
304 3/8	43	43 7/8	36 7/8	8 7/8	6	8	Clatsop Co., Oreg.	Pravomil Raichl	Pravomil Raichl	NO 1963	32
303 5/8	46 7/8	46 5/8	42 3/8	8	8	8	Columbia Co., Oreg.	Picked Up	Harold E. Stepp	PU 1962	33
303 1/8	47	47 7/8	43 3/8	7 7/8	7	6	Humboldt Co., Calif.	Michael L. Johnson	Michael L. Johnson	NO 1976	34
302 7/8	50	50	36 7/8	7 7/8	6	6	Jefferson Co., Wash.	Gary Talley	Gary Talley	NO 1981	35
300 7/8	46 7/8	44	34 7/8	8 7/8	6	7	Jefferson Co., Wash.	C. F. & C. H. Bernhardt	C. F. & C. H. Bernhardt	NO 1973	36
299	43	40 7/8	37 7/8	9	6	6	Columbia Co., Oreg.	Harry R. Olsen	Harry R. Olsen	NO 1963	37
298 7/8	41 7/8	42 7/8	33 7/8	9 7/8	7	6	Grays Harbor Co., Wash.	Robert Lentz	Robert Lentz	NO 1948	38
296	47 7/8	47 7/8	42 7/8	8 7/8	7	5	Jefferson Co., Wash.	C. F. & C. H. Bernhardt	C. F. & C. H. Bernhardt	NO 1972	39
294 7/8	39 7/8	41 7/8	41	8	6	6	Columbia Co., Oreg.	Reed Holding	Reed Holding	NO 1950	40
294 1/8	45 7/8	45 7/8	34 7/8	8 7/8	6	6	Clatsop Co., Oreg.	Picked Up	Robert L. Brown	PU 1965	40
293 1/8	43 7/8	43 7/8	36 7/8	7 7/8	6	6	Tillamook Co., Oreg.	Steven F. Kellow	Steven F. Kellow	NO 1979	42
291 1/8	43 7/8	43 7/8	35 7/8	6 7/8	6	6	Clatsop Co., Oreg.	Picked Up	Robert L. Brown	PU 1979	43
290 7/8	45 7/8	44 7/8	37 7/8	9 7/8	6	6	Coos Co., Oreg.	Gerald W. Hurst	Gerald W. Hurst	NO 1979	44

*Final Score subject to revision by additional verifying measurements

Mule Deer *(Typical Antlers)*

Odocoileus hemionus hemionus and certain related subspecies

Minimum Score 195 — World's Record 225 6/8

Score	Length of Main Beam R.	Length of Main Beam L.	Inside Spread	Circumference at Smallest Place Between Burr and First Point R.	Circumference at Smallest Place Between Burr and First Point L.	Number of Points R.	Number of Points L.	Locality Killed	By Whom Killed	Owner	Date Killed	Rank
212	29	27	21 4/8	5 4/8	5 4/8	5	5	Grand Co., Colo.	Wesley Bruce Brock	Wesley Bruce Brock	OT 1963	1
210 6/8*	28 2/8	29 1/8	24 4/8	5	5	5	5	Idaho Co., Idaho	Urban H. Riener	Urban H. Riener	OT 1979	2
209*	27	27 4/8	27 3/8	5 2/8	5	5	6	Lincoln Co., Wyo.	Kirt I. Darner	Kirt I. Darner	OT 1979	3
208*	27 5/8	29 1/8	28 4/8	4 7/8	4 6/8	5	5	Rich Co., Utah	Dee Hildt	Dee Hildt	OT 1968	4
205 6/8	24 3/8	24 3/8	23 4/8	5 4/8	5 4/8	5	5	Eagle Co., Colo.	Mark A. McCormick	Mark A. McCormick	NO 1981	5
204 6/8*	26 2/8	26 2/8	24 6/8	4 7/8	4 6/8	5	5	Elko Co., Nev.	Donnie L. Thompson	Donnie L. Thompson	OT 1982	6
202 6/8	28 2/8	29 2/8	25 4/8	5 3/8	5 2/8	5	5	Rio Arriba Co., N. M.	James F. Leveritt, Jr.	James F. Leveritt, Jr.	NO 1980	7
202 3/8	26 3/8	25 5/8	24 5/8	5 6/8	5 6/8	8	7	Baker Co., Oreg.	Brett N. Hayes	Brett N. Hayes	OT 1982	8
201 4/8	27	26	26	5	5	5	5	Garfield Co., Colo.	Unknown	Ronald E. McKinney	OT 1954	9
200 7/8	28	26 5/8	30 5/8	5 4/8	5 2/8	6	5	Adams Co., Idaho	Roy Eastlick	Roy Eastlick	OT 1975	10
200	25 7/8	25 4/8	21 7/8	5 5/8	5 5/8	5	7	Hot Springs Co., Wyo.	Basil C. Bradbury	Basil C. Bradbury	NO 1977	11
199 7/8	26 6/8	25 6/8	28 4/8	5 2/8	5	6	6	Eagle Co., Colo.	Richard C. Bergquist	Richard C. Bergquist	OT 1981	12
199 6/8	25 1/8	25 3/8	25	5 1/8	5 1/8	5	5	Grant Co., Oreg.	Steve M. Stevenson	Steve M. Stevenson	OT 1982	13
199 5/8	27 5/8	26	21 5/8	5 5/8	5 6/8	5	5	Princeton, B. C.	Buddy D. Baker	Buddy D. Baker	NO 1979	14
199 4/8	26 7/8	27 3/8	25 6/8	5 6/8	5 6/8	4	4	Medicine Hat, Alta.	Duncan Baldie	Duncan Baldie & Kerry W. McKenzie	NO 1981	15
199 4/8	25 5/8	26 4/8	23 6/8	4 7/8	5	5	6	Sunpete Co., Utah	Kevin P. Price	Kevin P. Price	OT 1973	15
199	26 7/8	28 6/8	27 6/8	5 1/8	5 1/8	5	6	Bear Lake Co., Idaho	Frank Bidart	Frank Bidart	OT 1965	17
198 7/8	27	26 2/8	27 2/8	5 5/8	5 4/8	5	6	Laramie Co., Wyo.	David L. Shannon	David L. Shannon	OT 1981	18
197 4/8	22 1/8	24	24	5 6/8	5 5/8	6	5	Gunnison Co., Colo.	Thomas Gray, Jr.	Thomas Gray, Jr.	NO 1980	19
197 3/8	26	26 2/8	23 2/8	5 6/8	5 5/8	6	6	Gunnison Co., Colo.	Mark L. Hanna	Mark L. Hanna	NO 1980	20
197 2/8	26 5/8	25 7/8	26 4/8	5 2/8	5 3/8	5	6	Blaine Co., Idaho	Bart Hofmann	Bart Hofmann	OT 1980	21
197	25 3/8	27	22 3/8	5	4 7/8	5	6	Utah Co., Utah	L. Doug Carlton	L. Doug Carlton	OT 1982	22
197	25 2/8	24 1/8	25	4 7/8	4 6/8	5	5	Camas Co., Idaho	Bret C. Silver	Bret C. Silver	NO 1980	22
196 6/8	26 5/8	25 5/8	28	4 6/8	4 7/8	5	5	Wallowa Co., Oreg.	Dan L. Grober	Dan L. Grober	OT 1980	24
196 4/8	25 5/8	25 3/8	25 6/8	5 2/8	5	5	5	Johnson Co., Wyo.	Unknown	Toby J. Johnson	1940	25
196 2/8	23	24	25	4 6/8	4 4/8	7	5	Elko Co., Nev.	John C. Burman	John C. Burman	OT 1980	26
196	27 5/8	26 6/8	23 3/8	5 3/8	5 2/8	7	6	Kaibab Natl. For., Ariz.	Graves Peeler	John E. Conner Museum	PR 1930	27
195 6/8	25 3/8	24 3/8	24 6/8	4 5/8	4 5/8	5	5	Teton Co., Wyo..	Joel M. Leatham	Joel M. Leatham	NO 1979	28
195 5/8	25 3/8	25 4/8	21 3/8	5 2/8	5	5	6	Grand Co., Colo.	C. Jay Stout	C. Jay Stout	NO 1981	29
195 4/8	25 2/8	27 1/8	22 7/8	5 6/8	5 4/8	6	6	Flathead Co., Mont.	Sharon M. Gaughan	Sharon M. Gaughan	NO 1980	30
195 2/8	26 4/8	25 5/8	26 4/8	4 2/8	4 2/8	5	5	Antelope Lake, Sask.	Doug Westergaard	Doug Westergaard	NO 1977	31

Mule Deer *(Non-Typical Antlers)*

Minimum Score 240 — ***Odocoileus hemionus hemionus*** **and certain related subspecies** — **World's Record 355 2/8**

Score	Length of Main Beam R.	Length of Main Beam L.	Inside Spread	Circumference at Smallest Place Between Burr and First Point R.	Circumference at Smallest Place Between Burr and First Point L.	Number of Points R.	Number of Points L.	Locality Killed	By Whom Killed	Owner	Date Killed	Rank
311 6/8	26 7/8	24 7/8	24 1/8	6 1/8	6 5/8	22	21	Kaibab, Ariz.	Vernor Wilson	Heritage Gun Room	NO 1941	1
297 3/8*	26 1/8	26 3/8	26 5/8	6 4/8	6 6/8	17	15	Larimer Co., Colo.	Jack Autrey	Warren C. Autrey	1941	2
280 4/8	27	26 6/8	23 4/8	6	6	15	14	Gem Co., Idaho	Ronald S. Holbrook	Ronald S. Holbrook	OT 1982	3
272 4/8	28 3/8	27 2/8	21 2/8	6 3/8	6 2/8	19	17	Eagle Co., Colo.	Eddie Stephenson, Jr.	Eddie Stephenson, Jr.	NO 1978	4
266 4/8*	26 4/8	25 4/8	22 7/8	5 5/8	5 6/8	15	13	Ouray Co., Colo.	Eugene D. Guilaroff	Eugene D. Guilaroff	OT 1971	5
264 2/8	24 4/8	26 2/8	21	5 3/8	5 3/8	7	13	Southern Utah	Unknown	Earl Mecham	1932	6
259 7/8	28 4/8	27 4/8	29 4/8	5 7/8	5 5/8	12	15	Catron Co., N. M.	Jeff K. Gunnell	Jeff K. Gunnell	NO 1981	7
259 3/8	26 5/8	26 2/8	29 3/8	5 2/8	4 7/8	17	12	Mont.	Unknown	Nick M. Messmer	PR 1943	8
258 4/8	25 4/8	26 6/8	24 4/8	5 6/8	5 4/8	11	9	Grand Co., Utah	Vernon K. Heller	Vernon K. Heller	OT 1926	9
257 5/8	25 7/8	26 5/8	25 1/8	5 6/8	5 5/8	12	11	Kaibab Natl. For., Ariz.	Graves Peeler	John E. Connor Museum	1947	10
257 5/8	27 2/8	29	28 7/8	5 5/8	5 5/8	15	14	Kaibab Natl. For., Ariz.	Graves Peeler	John E. Connor Museum	1946	10
256	26 7/8	26 5/8	22 6/8	9 4/8	6 5/8	16	9	Gem Co., Idaho	Jay P. Baker	Jay P. Baker	OT 1981	12
254 3/8	25	25 7/8	26 5/8	4 7/8	5	7	9	Eagle Co., Colo.	Dennis Martinson	Dennis Martinson	OT 1980	13
252 6/8	20 1/8	22 1/8	22 6/8	5 2/8	5 3/8	15	22	Utah Co., Utah	Paul H. Mitchell	Paul H. Mitchell	OT 1953	14
250 1/8	26	26	24	5 4/8	5 6/8	15	11	Montezuma Co., Colo.	Jack E. Reed	Jack E. Reed	NO 1981	15
250	25	27 1/8	21 4/8	6 5/8	6 4/8	14	14	Mohave Co., Ariz.	Douglas C. Mallory	Douglas C. Mallory	OT 1980	16
249 2/8	27	27 4/8	27 5/8	6 1/8	6 2/8	7	11	Adams Co., Idaho	Howard E. Paradis	Howard E. Paradis	OT 1966	17
248 7/8	26 5/8	26 2/8	28 1/8	4 6/8	5	10	12	Petroleum Co., Mont.	Lawrence T. Keenan	Lawrence T. Keenan	NO 1979	18
247 3/8	28 6/8	28 1/8	25 2/8	5	5	10	9	Eagle Co., Colo.	Earl M. Johnson	Earl M. Johnson	OT 1966	19
244 7/8	25 6/8	26 4/8	22 1/8	4 7/8	4 7/8	11	9	Lincoln Co., Wyo.	Brian H. Suter	Brian H. Suter	SE 1981	20
243 4/8	23 6/8	22 7/8	21	5 4/8	5 5/8	10	13	Clear Creek Co., Colo.	Louis I. Kingsley	Louis I. Kingsley	OT 1981	21
242	22 6/8	23 5/8	18 6/8	5 4/8	5 7/8	12	14	Garfield Co., Colo.	Daniel J. Stanek	Daniel J. Stanek	NO 1981	22
240 5/8	26 2/8	26 6/8	28 1/8	5 4/8	5 4/8	10	8	Klamath Co., Oreg.	Corinne Fields	Corinne Fields	OT 1946	23
240 4/8	23 6/8	22	22 6/8	5 1/8	5 4/8	10	11	Eagle Co., Colo.	James Patrick Hale	James Patrick Hale	NO 1979	24

*Final Score subject to revision by additional verifying measurements

Columbia Blacktail Deer

Minimum Score 130 | ***Odocoileus hemionus columbianus* and *Odocoileus hemionus sitkensis*** | **World's Record 182 2/8**

Score	Length of Main Beam R.	Length of Main Beam L.	Inside Spread	Circumference at Smallest Place Between Burr and First Point R.	Circumference at Smallest Place Between Burr and First Point L.	Number of Points R.	Number of Points L.	Locality Killed	By Whom Killed	Owner	Date Killed	Rank
182 2/8	24 2/8	24 5/8	20 2/8	5 2/8	5 2/8	5	5	Lewis Co., Wash.	Lester H. Miller	Lester H. Miller	OT 1953	1
170 6/8*	24 6/8	24 7/8	19 5/8	5	5	5	6	Marion Co., Oreg.	Robert L. Brown	Robert L. Brown	NO 1980	2
162 6/8*	24 1/8	25 4/8	18 4/8	5 4/8	5 4/8	7	8	Clackamas Co., Oreg.	Curtis A. Lee	Steve Crossley	OT 1981	3
161 2/8*	24	23 3/8	19 2/8	4 5/8	4 5/8	5	5	Clackamas Co., Oreg.	Darrell Stewart	Darrell Stewart	NO 1977	4
152 5/8*	23 6/8	22 7/8	18 5/8	5	5 2/8	5	4	Trinity Co., Calif.	Larry Brown	Larry Brown	OT 1979	5
152 4/8	23	23	20	4	4	6	7	Tehama Co., Calif.	Don Strickler	Don Strickler	OT 1979	6
152	20 6/8	21 7/8	15 2/8	4 6/8	4 7/8	6	6	Clackamas Co., Oreg.	Larry W. Peterson	Larry W. Peterson	OT 1980	7
150 6/8	22	21 4/8	17	4 2/8	4 2/8	5	5	Siskiyou Co., Calif.	Raymond Whittaker	Raymond Whittaker	OT 1978	8
150 1/8	22 7/8	23 1/8	19 3/8	4 6/8	4 7/8	5	6	Clackamas Co., Oreg.	E. Clint Kuntz	E. Clint Kuntz	NO 1981	9
149 5/8	22 7/8	22 4/8	17 1/8	4 3/8	4 5/8	5	5	Clackamas Co., Oreg.	Ray W. Bunnell	Ray W. Bunnell	NO 1970	10
149 3/8	22 3/8	21 2/8	20 3/8	5 2/8	5 4/8	5	5	Trinity Co., Calif.	Lyle L. Johnson	Lyle L. Johnson	OT 1979	11
148 7/8	22 1/8	21 3/8	18	4 7/8	4 7/8	6	5	Humboldt Co., Calif.	F. Joe Parker	F. Joe Parker	OT 1946	12
148 4/8	22 5/8	22 1/8	16 5/8	4 4/8	4 4/8	6	5	Skamania Co., Wash.	Alan Dean Borroz	Alan Dean Borroz	NO 1978	13
147 7/8	22 1/8	22 2/8	18 5/8	4 2/8	4 3/8	6	6	Humboldt Co., Calif.	Melvin H. Kadle	Melvin H. Kadle	OT 1979	14
147 1/8	21 2/8	21	16 7/8	4 3/8	4 3/8	5	6	Trinity Co., Calif.	Craig L. Brown	Craig & Joy Brown	OT 1980	15
146 3/8	21	20 7/8	16 5/8	4 7/8	4 5/8	5	5	Humboldt Co., Calif.	Gerald Wescott	Gerald Wescott	OT 1980	16
145 7/8	22	23 5/8	16 3/8	4 5/8	4 7/8	5	5	Napa Co., Calif.	C. H. N. Dailey	Tony Stoer	AG 1948	17
145 4/8	21 1/8	20	16 2/8	4 7/8	4 7/8	5	5	Douglas Co., Oreg.	Daniel J. Fisher	Daniel J. Fisher	NO 1973	18
145 2/8	22 4/8	22 5/8	21	5 3/8	5 1/8	7	9	Tehama Co., Calif.	Clint Heiber	Clint Heiber	OT 1979	19
144 7/8	19 2/8	19 2/8	19 2/8	4 5/8	4 4/8	5	5	Douglas Co., Oreg.	Larry E. Waller	Larry E. Waller	NO 1980	20
144 7/8	20 6/8	20 4/8	13 3/8	4	4 1/8	5	5	Clatsop Co., Oreg.	Pravomil Raichl	Pravomil Raichl	OT 1959	20
144 4/8	21	21 7/8	17	3 7/8	3 6/8	4	4	Snohomish Co., Wash.	Roy Shogren	Roy Shogren	NO 1979	22
144 2/8	21	22 4/8	20 4/8	4 4/8	4 4/8	5	5	Mendocino Co., Calif.	Frank Kester	Frank Kester	OT 1981	23
144 2/8	21 6/8	21 3/8	15 6/8	4 6/8	4 6/8	6	5	Marion Co., Oreg.	Arthur L. Schmidt	Arthur L. Schmidt	OT 1978	23
144	21 2/8	21 5/8	17	4 7/8	5 1/8	5	5	Linn Co., Oreg.	Ed A. Taylor	Ed A. Taylor	OT 1981	25
143 6/8	20 5/8	20 2/8	19 7/8	5 2/8	5 2/8	6	6	Tehama Co., Calif.	Clint Heiber	Clint Heiber	OT 1978	26
142 5/8	21 4/8	20 3/8	19 7/8	4 4/8	4 3/8	4	4	Trinity Co., Calif.	Larry Brown	Larry Brown	OT 1979	27
142 5/8	23 1/8	22 1/8	20 1/8	4 6/8	4 7/8	7	6	Tehama Co., Calif.	Kenneth R. Hall	Kenneth R. Hall	OT 1979	27
142 4/8	21 6/8	22	16 6/8	4 3/8	4 3/8	6	5	Clackamas Co., Oreg.	Henry A. Charriere	Henry A. Charriere	NO 1970	29
142 4/8	22 4/8	22 7/8	21	4 3/8	3 7/8	4	3	Jackson Co., Oreg.	Donald G. Spence	Donald G. Spence	NO 1980	29

141 7/8	21 4/8	21 2/8	17 7/8	4 7/8	5	5	5	Trinity Co., Calif.	Pedro H. Henrich	Pedro H. Henrich	OT 1977	31
141 4/8	22	22 5/8	15 4/8	5 2/8	5 1/8	5	5	Pierce Co., Wash.	Ron Dick	Ron Dick	OT 1965	32
141 3/8	22 1/8	21 5/8	18 7/8	4 7/8	4 5/8	5	4	Trinity Co., Calif.	Larry Brown	Larry Brown	OT 1980	33
141 1/8	22 2/8	22 4/8	17 7/8	4 6/8	4 6/8	5	5	Pierce Co., Wash.	Jerry E. Burke	Jerry E. Burke	NO 1980	34
140 6/8	23	22 4/8	20	5 4/8	5 4/8	5	5	Mendocino Co., Calif.	Jerry D. Smith	Jerry D. Smith	AG 1978	35
140 4/8	19 4/8	20	17 2/8	4 4/8	4 4/8	5	5	Trinity Co., Calif.	Loran G. August	Larry Brown	SE 1980	36
140 3/8	20 1/8	20 5/8	16 5/8	3 7/8	4 3/8	4	5	Humboldt Co., Calif.	George S. Johnson	Roy F. Johnson	OT 1934	37
140	22	21 3/8	17 6/8	4 1/8	4 1/8	5	5	Humboldt Co., Calif.	Carl A. Anderson	Carl A. Anderson	OT 1980	38
140	21 5/8	22 1/8	19	3 7/8	4 2/8	4	5	Trinity Co., Calif.	William J. Olson	William J. Olson	OT 1981	38
139 7/8	22 1/8	20 7/8	21 3/8	5 1/8	5	4	5	Trinity Co., Calif.	Craig L. Brown	Craig & Joy Brown	OT 1981	40
139 7/8	19	18 6/8	15 5/8	4	4	4	5	Siskiyou Co., Calif.	Roy Eastlick	Roy Eastlick	OT 1954	40
139 3/8	20 7/8	20 6/8	19 5/8	4 6/8	4 5/8	5	5	Marion Co., Oreg.	Richard A. Hart	Richard A. Hart	OT 1982	42
139 2/8	22 5/8	21 1/8	18 6/8	3 3/8	3 5/8	4	6	Trinity Co., Calif.	Gary L. Mayberry	Gary L. Mayberry	SE 1968	43
138 1/8	18 5/8	20 3/8	17 1/8	4 2/8	4 3/8	5	5	Columbia Co., Oreg.	Virginia L. Brown	Steve Crossley	OT 1981	44
138	19 3/8	20 1/8	15	4 1/8	4 2/8	5	5	Marion Co., Oreg.	Frank C. Bersin	Frank C. Bersin	OT 1977	45
137 1/8	20 4/8	20 1/8	15 5/8	4 5/8	4 6/8	5	5	Tillamook Co., Oreg.	Iola M. Pfaff	Iola M. Pfaff	OT 1940	46
137	20	19 5/8	15 6/8	4 6/8	4 6/8	5	5	Polk Co., Oreg.	Ralph Cooper	Ralph Cooper	NO 1978	47
136 5/8	21 6/8	21 6/8	15 7/8	4 1/8	4	5	5	Marion Co., Oreg.	Ronald A. Bersin	Ronald A. Bersin	NO 1978	48
135 6/8	21 2/8	20 4/8	18	4 4/8	4	4	4	Linn Co., Oreg.	Gene Collier	Gene Collier	OT 1966	49
135 4/8	20 4/8	20 1/8	16 6/8	3 6/8	3 7/8	5	5	Lewis Co., Wash.	Oren Layton	Oren Layton	OT 1977	50
135	19 1/8	19 4/8	15 4/8	4 3/8	4 3/8	5	5	Clackamas Co., Oreg.	Ray W. Bunnell	Ray W. Bunnell	NO 1978	51
135	20	19 7/8	16 2/8	4 1/8	4 1/8	5	5	Whatcom Co., Wash.	Dennis R. Beebe	Dennis R. Beebe	NO 1981	51
134 7/8	19 6/8	20 5/8	14 5/8	4 1/8	4 1/8	5	5	Mendocino Co., Calif.	Jesse P. Foster, Jr.	Jesse P. Foster, Jr.	SE 1964	53
134 6/8	19 4/8	20	16 3/8	4 4/8	4 4/8	5	6	Trinity Co., Calif.	Donald E. Stevens	Donald E. Stevens	SE 1979	54
134 1/8	20 4/8	20 4/8	14 5/8	4 2/8	4 2/8	5	5	King Co., Wash.	Greg E. Connell	Greg E. Connell	NO 1979	55
134 1/8	18 2/8	18 2/8	14 7/8	4	4	6	5	Trinity Co., Calif.	David Deininger	David Deininger	OT 1980	55
133 6/8	21 2/8	21 5/8	17 2/8	4 3/8	4 3/8	5	4	Mendocino Co., Calif.	Marvin DeAngelis	Marvin DeAngelis	SE 1978	57
133 5/8	19	19 5/8	15 7/8	4 1/8	4 2/8	5	6	Clackamas Co., Oreg.	Richard K. Hughes	Richard K. Hughes	OT 1981	58
133 4/8	19 4/8	20 3/8	17 2/8	4	4	5	5	Coos Co., Oreg.	Toby J. Johnson	Toby J. Johnson	OT 1981	59
133 4/8	18 7/8	19 3/8	18	3 7/8	4	6	6	Josephine Co., Oreg.	Randy L. Hansen	Randy L. Hansen	NO 1981	59
133 2/8	20 2/8	20 7/8	17	4 2/8	4 2/8	5	5	Trinity Co., Calif.	Ralph L. Perry	Ralph L. Perry	SE 1980	61
132 7/8	21 6/8	23 3/8	19 4/8	4 5/8	4 4/8	6	5	Tehama Co., Calif.	Joe McBrayer	Joe McBrayer	SE 1981	62
132 7/8	18 4/8	19 4/8	18 1/8	4 7/8	4 6/8	5	5	Clackamas Co., Oreg.	Kerry L. Schoenborn	Kerry L. Schoenborn	OT 1978	62
132 3/8	22 2/8	22	19	5 1/8	4 5/8	5	4	Trinity Co., Calif.	David L. Matley	David L. Matley	OT 1981	64
132 1/8	21 1/8	20 4/8	13 1/8	4 3/8	4 5/8	5	5	Lewis Co., Wash.	George W. Rodrick, III	George W. Rodrick, III	OT 1980	65
132 1/8	20	19 4/8	18 1/8	4	4	5	5	Trinity Co., Calif.	Ronald L. Schneider	Ronald L. Schneider	OT 1979	65
131 6/8	20 2/8	20	18 2/8	3 6/8	4	5	5	Trinity Co., Calif.	Kenneth L. Cogle, Jr.	Kenneth L. Cogle, Jr.	OT 1981	67
131 6/8	18 5/8	19 3/8	13 6/8	5 1/8	4 6/8	6	5	Trinity Co., Calif.	Melvin M. Clair	Melvin M. Clair	SE 1979	67
131 5/8	19 1/8	18 5/8	14 4/8	4 2/8	4 2/8	5	5	Humboldt Co., Calif.	Larry Wilson	Larry Wilson	SE 1978	69
131 2/8	21 1/8	20 7/8	13 5/8	4 6/8	4 6/8	7	6	Skamania Co., Wash.	Thomas E. Krebs	Thomas E. Krebs	NO 1977	70
131	18 2/8	18 4/8	18 4/8	4 1/8	4 2/8	5	5	Siskiyou Co., Calif.	Raymond Whittaker	Raymond Whittaker	OT 1981	71

*Final Score subject to revision by additional verifying measurements

Whitetail Deer *(Typical Antlers)*

Minimum Score 170 | ***Odocoileus virginianus virginianus* and certain related subspecies** | **World's Record 206 1/8**

Score	Length of Main Beam R.	Length of Main Beam L.	Inside Spread	Circumference at Smallest Place Between Burr and First Point R.	Circumference at Smallest Place Between Burr and First Point L.	Number of Points R.	Number of Points L.	Locality Killed	By Whom Killed	Owner	Date Killed	Rank
196 4/8*	25	25 4/8	21 6/8	4 2/8	4 3/8	6	6	Antelope Co., Neb.	John R. Harvey	Walter Schreiner	NO 1963	1
191 7/8*	27 5/8	26 5/8	19 3/8	4 6/8	4 7/8	6	6	Waukesha Co., Wisc.	Kenneth Lange	Kenneth Lange	NO 1979	2
190 6/8*	27 7/8	27 5/8	22 4/8	5 3/8	5 6/8	5	5	Pelly, Sask.	James R. Strelioff	James R. Strelioff	NO 1980	3
187 5/8*	29 6/8	28 4/8	21 1/8	5 5/8	5 5/8	5	5	Somerset Co., Maine	M. Dana Goodwin	M. Dana Goodwin	NO 1981	4
186 2/8	25 2/8	25 6/8	21	4 6/8	4 6/8	6	6	La Salle Co., Texas	Herman C. Schliesing	Herman C. Schliesing	DC 1967	5
184 4/8	23 4/8	23 4/8	17	4 6/8	4 6/8	6	6	Fayette Co., Tenn.	Benny M. Johnson	Benny M. Johnson	DC 1979	6
184 3/8	27	26	18 3/8	5 5/8	5 6/8	7	10	Johnson Co., Iowa	Duane E. Papke	Duane E. Papke	DC 1981	7
184 2/8	27	26	27 4/8	6	6 1/8	6	5	Muskingum Co., Ohio	Dale Hartberger	Dale Hartberger	DC 1981	8
184 2/8	28 2/8	27 6/8	24	5	5 1/8	5	6	Franklin Parish, La.	H. B. Womble	Carey B. McCoy	1914	8
183 7/8	28	27 1/8	19 6/8	5	4 7/8	7	5	Forest Co., Wisc.	James M. Thayer	James M. Thayer	NO 1980	10
183 2/8	26 7/8	26 7/8	16	5	5	7	7	Ashland Co., Wisc.	Unknown	Martin Bonack	1900	11
182 7/8	27 4/8	28 2/8	19 3/8	5 5/8	5 5/8	6	5	Hale Co., Ala.	James Cecil Bailey	James Cecil Bailey	JA 1974	12
182 6/8	28 2/8	28	22 6/8	4 6/8	4 6/8	6	5	Vilas Co., Wisc.	George Sparks	MacsTaxidermy	NO 1942	13
181 5/8	27 6/8	27 6/8	21 5/8	5 2/8	5 2/8	6	6	Ionia Co., Mich.	Lester Bowen	Richard Bowen	NO 1947	14
181 5/8	25 6/8	25 7/8	19 7/8	5 4/8	5 4/8	6	7	Wilkinson Co., Miss.	Ronnie P. Whitaker	Ronnie P. Whitaker	JA 1981	14
181 4/8	29	28 5/8	23 5/8	4 6/8	4 5/8	7	5	Oxford Co., Maine	Dean W. Peaco	Dean W. Peaco	NO 1953	16
181 3/8	26	25	17 5/8	4 5/8	4 5/8	6	6	Winona Co., Minn.	Kenneth W. Schreiber	Kenneth W. Schreiber	OT 1980	17
181	27 7/8	27	20 3/8	5 2/8	5 1/8	8	7	Gallatin Co., Ky.	Kenneth D. Hoffman	Kenneth D. Hoffman	NO 1979	18
181	28 3/8	28 4/8	20	4 4/8	4 4/8	5	5	Wood Co., Wisc.	James D. Wyman	James D. Wyman	NO 1977	18
180 7/8	25 7/8	25 3/8	17 7/8	5 1/8	5 1/8	6	7	Castor, Alta.	Norman D. Stienwand	Norman D. Stienwand	NO 1981	20
180 4/8	29 2/8	28 4/8	20 6/8	4 7/8	4 6/8	6	5	Iron Co., Mich.	John Schmidt	Bob Schmidt	NO 1927	21
180 3/8	30	29 5/8	22 3/8	4 5/8	4 5/8	6	8	Meeker Co., Minn.	Stanley M. Messner	Stanley M. Messner	NO 1981	22
180 2/8	26 3/8	26 3/8	18 2/8	4 5/8	4 5/8	6	6	Eau Claire Co., Wisc.	Dennis B. Bryan	Dennis B. Bryan	NO 1979	23
180 1/8	26 4/8	26 5/8	20 1/8	4 4/8	4 5/8	6	6	Phelps Co., Mo.	William A. Hagenhoff	William A. Hagenhoff	NO 1973	24
179 6/8	26 3/8	26 2/8	19 6/8	4 6/8	4 5/8	6	6	Jim Hogg Co., Texas	William Bruce Van Fleet	William Bruce Van Fleet	DC 1979	25
179 4/8	27 3/8	28 4/8	20 1/8	5 3/8	5 5/8	6	5	Pawnee Co., Neb.	Kenneth C. Mort	Kenneth C. Mort	NO 1975	26
179 2/8	26 7/8	28	16	4 4/8	4 3/8	6	5	Ashland Co., Wisc.	Jack D. Hultman	Jack D. Hultman	NO 1981	27
179	28 4/8	28 5/8	20 6/8	4 5/8	4 7/8	5	5	Dooley Co., Ga.	Shannon Akin	Shannon Akin	DC 1981	28
179	25	23 7/8	18 2/8	5 2/8	5 3/8	5	6	Chippewa Co., Wisc.	John F. Kukuska	John F. Kukuska	NO 1931	28
178 6/8	27	24 4/8	22 1/8	5 7/8	5 7/8	7	7	Breton, Alta.	George Clark	George Clark	NO 1981	30

178 5/8	25 4/8	25 5/8	22 7/8	4 4/8	4 4/8	5	5	Itasca Co., Minn.	Gino P. Maccario	Gino P. Maccario	NO 1980	31
178 4/8	27 3/8	27 3/8	18 6/8	4 7/8	4 5/8	6	6	Cumberland Co., Maine	Patrick D. Wescott	Patrick D. Wescott	NO 1980	32
178 4/8	24 2/8	25 2/8	18 1/8	5 5/8	5 5/8	5	6	St. Clair Co., Ill.	Emil W. Kromat	Emil W. Kromat	NO 1981	32
178 3/8	27 2/8	26 4/8	18 5/8	4 6/8	4 6/8	6	6	Goochland Co., Va.	Edward W. Fielder	Edward W. Fielder	DC 1981	34
178	27 5/8	27 2/8	20	5 1/8	5 2/8	7	7	Price Co., Wisc.	John E. Martinson	John E. Martinson	NO 1981	35
177 6/8	26 4/8	26 4/8	18 2/8	5	5 1/8	9	7	Shaunavon, Sask.	Stan J. Crawford	Stan J. Crawford	NO 1979	36
177 3/8	26	26	20 2/8	5 3/8	5 2/8	6	5	Rusk Co., Wisc.	David A. Reichel	David A. Reichel	NO 1981	37
177 2/8	25 3/8	24 3/8	21 5/8	4 1/8	4 1/8	8	9	Golden Valley Co., N. D.	Allen Goltz	Allen Goltz	NO 1964	38
177	28 1/8	28	17 2/8	4 6/8	4 6/8	6	7	Bayfield Co., Wisc.	Elof E. Sjostrom	Mrs. Elof E. Sjostrom	NO 1932	39
176 6/8	26 3/8	25	19	5 3/8	5 4/8	5	6	Langlade Co., Wisc.	Jack Ryan	LaVern Emerich	NO 1950	40
176 4/8	23 5/8	23 5/8	17 4/8	5 4/8	5 3/8	5	5	St. Louis Co., Minn.	Michael J. Nielsen	Michael J. Nielsen	NO 1962	41
176 3/8	25	25 1/8	17 5/8	4 5/8	5 1/8	6	5	Stockton, Man.	Robert R. Blain	Robert R. Blain	NO 1977	42
176 2/8	25 6/8	25 7/8	20 3/8	5 4/8	5 4/8	7	6	Rappahannock Co., Va.	George W. Beahm	George W. Beahm	NO 1959	43
176 2/8	28	26 4/8	21	5 4/8	5 4/8	8	7	Macon Co., Ga.	Charles M. Wilson	Charles M. Wilson	NO 1981	43
176	24 5/8	25 6/8	21 6/8	4 7/8	4 7/8	5	5	Russell Co., Kan.	Don Mai	Don Mai	DC 1981	45
175 6/8	27 2/8	26 7/8	22 6/8	5 4/8	5	7	6	Webb Co., Texas	Norman Frede	Norman Frede	DC 1978	46
175 6/8	26 2/8	26 5/8	22 4/8	5 1/8	5	5	6	Pope Co., Ill.	Picked Up	James W. Seets	PR 1982	46
175 6/8	25 4/8	26 4/8	20	5 3/8	5 2/8	6	6	Dimmit Co., Texas	George E. Light, III	George E. Light, III	DC 1979	46
175 5/8	26	27 4/8	18 1/8	4 4/8	4 4/8	5	6	Allegany Co., N. Y.	William L. Damon	William L. Damon	NO 1981	49
175 3/8	29 6/8	28	22 3/8	4 6/8	4 4/8	6	5	Todd Co., Ky.	Gary W. Crafton	Gary W. Crafton	NO 1981	50
175 2/8	28 1/8	28 6/8	17 6/8	5 2/8	5 2/8	5	6	Val Marie, Sask.	Leon Perrault	Leon Perrault	NO 1977	51
175 1/8	25 4/8	24 5/8	19 7/8	5 2/8	5 1/8	6	5	Shaunavon, Sask.	Richard Klink	Richard Klink	NO 1981	52
175 1/8	26 2/8	27 2/8	19 5/8	4 4/8	4 7/8	5	5	Alger Co., Mich.	Warren Beebe	Donald J. Docking	NO 1936	52
175	23 2/8	24	19 6/8	5 1/8	5 2/8	5	5	Harrison Co., Mo.	Carl J. Graham	Carl J. Graham	NO 1973	54
174 5/8	26	26 2/8	21 1/8	5 3/8	5 3/8	5	6	Baldonnel, B. C.	D. Ian Williams	D. Ian Williams	NO 1978	55
174 4/8	26 3/8	26 2/8	19 1/8	5 2/8	5 6/8	5	7	Charlotte Co., Va.	Jerry C. Claybrook	Jerry C. Claybrook	DC 1977	56
174 4/8	27 4/8	27 3/8	21	4 2/8	4	6	6	Knox Co., Maine	Robert E. Young	Robert E. Young	NO 1979	56
174 1/8	26 4/8	26 3/8	20	5 1/8	5	6	6	Anarchist Mt., B. C.	George Urban	George Urban	SE 1980	58
173 6/8	26 6/8	26 6/8	19 1/8	4 7/8	4 7/8	5	7	Minburn, Alta.	Joseph R. McGillis	Joseph R. McGillis	OT 1981	59
173 6/8	25 6/8	25 6/8	19 6/8	4 1/8	4 4/8	5	5	Pulaski Co., Ill.	Rose Marie Blanchard	Rose Marie Blanchard	NO 1973	59
173 6/8	25 6/8	25 6/8	18 4/8	4 3/8	4 3/8	6	6	Livingston Co., Mich.	Terry J. Kemp	Terry J. Kemp	NO 1979	59
173 6/8	25 1/8	25 5/8	18 6/8	5 3/8	5 4/8	7	6	Knox Co., Neb.	Paul H. Klawitter	Paul H. Klawitter	NO 1970	59
173 5/8	26 6/8	26 6/8	17 5/8	4 4/8	4 4/8	5	5	Sawyer Co., Wisc.	Maurice Peterson	MacsTaxidermy	DC 1940	63
173 4/8	30 5/8	29 6/8	20 7/8	5 2/8	5 3/8	7	5	Todd Co., Ky.	Troy L. Harris	Troy L. Harris	NO 1965	64
173 4/8	26	26	21	5 3/8	5 1/8	5	5	Vilas Co., Wisc.	Unknown	Donald Krueger	NO 1967	64
173 3/8	28	28 4/8	20 5/8	5 2/8	5 2/8	9	8	Allen Co., Ky.	Terry Wayne Sims	Terry Wayne Sims	NO 1979	66
173 2/8	26 7/8	28 5/8	23 5/8	4 4/8	4 4/8	6	6	Warren Co., Mo.	Jerome E. Ley	Jerome E. Ley	NO 1980	67
173 1/8	26 5/8	27 6/8	19 5/8	4 4/8	4 5/8	7	6	Shelby Co., Mo.	William A. Light, Jr.	William A. Light, Jr.	NO 1981	68
173	26	26	21	4 5/8	4 6/8	6	6	Somerset Co., Maine	Charles A. Moulton	Charles A. Moulton	NO 1981	69
173	27 1/8	27 2/8	21 6/8	4 5/8	4 5/8	5	6	Cook Co., Minn.	Wesley A. Nelson	Wesley A. Nelson	NO 1980	69
173	25 2/8	24 2/8	21 7/8	4 5/8	4 6/8	9	6	Hidalgo Co., Texas	William L. Turk	William L. Turk	DC 1979	69
172 7/8	24 6/8	24 3/8	20 1/8	5 4/8	5 3/8	5	5	Ashland Co., Wisc.	Einar Sein	Rick Iacono	NO 1965	72
172 7/8	26 4/8	26 1/8	16 7/8	4 2/8	4 1/8	6	6	Olmsted Co., Minn.	Wesley W. Holtz	Wesley W. Holtz	NO 1966	72
172 6/8	25 1/8	24 3/8	22 2/8	4 7/8	5 2/8	5	6	Allamakee Co., Iowa	Picked up	Tom Kernat, Sr.	PU 1976	74

Whitetail Deer *(Typical Antlers)—Continued*

Odocoileus virginianus virginianus and certain related subspecies

Score	Length of Main Beam R.	Length of Main Beam L.	Inside Spread	Circumference at Smallest Place Between Burr and First Point R.	Circumference at Smallest Place Between Burr and First Point L.	Number of Points R.	Number of Points L.	Locality Killed	By Whom Killed	Owner	Date Killed	Rank
172 6/8	24 3/8	23 4/8	16 5/8	5	5	7	6	Edgerton, Alta.	Richard T. Abbott	Richard T. Abbott	NO 1980	74
172 5/8	26 7/8	25 5/8	18 4/8	5 4/8	5 3/8	6	5	Cass Co., Mich.	Ben R. Williams	Ben R. Williams	NO 1971	76
172 5/8	26 6/8	25	17 2/8	4 5/8	4 7/8	9	6	Knox Co., Maine	Willis A. Moody, Jr.	Willis A. Moody, Jr.	NO 1974	76
172 5/8	26 3/8	26 4/8	21 3/8	4 7/8	4 7/8	5	7	Highland Co., Ohio	Wilbur D. Rhoads	Wilbur D. Rhoads	NO 1979	76
172 4/8	26 7/8	25 2/8	19	4 6/8	4 5/8	5	5	Randolph Co., Ga.	Robert D. Bell	Robert D. Bell	NO 1979	79
172 2/8	25 6/8	24 2/8	20	4 5/8	4 5/8	6	8	Perkins Co., S. D.	Randy G. Swenson	Randy G. Swenson	NO 1979	80
172 1/8	27 2/8	26 5/8	18 6/8	4 6/8	4 6/8	6	5	Queen Annes Co., Md.	James Robert Spies, Jr.	James Robert Spies, Jr.	NO 1976	81
172 1/8	26 3/8	26 4/8	21 5/8	5 1/8	5 3/8	5	5	Pickens Co., Ala.	Walter Jaynes	Walter Jaynes	DC 1968	81
172 1/8	25 3/8	24 7/8	18 3/8	4 6/8	4 5/8	5	5	Grant Co., Minn.	Gary P. Kollman	Gary P. Kollman	NO 1980	81
172 1/8	25 1/8	25 5/8	16 4/8	4 7/8	4 7/8	6	6	Winona Co., Minn.	Robert J. Cordie	Robert J. Cordie	NO 1979	81
172	25 1/8	26	19 3/8	5 2/8	4 7/8	7	5	Furnas Co., Neb.	Marvin A. Briegel	Marvin A. Briegel	NO 1980	85
172	26	25 6/8	22 3/8	4 4/8	4 3/8	6	7	Muskingkum Co., Ohio	David R. Hatfield	David R. Hatfield	NO 1980	85
171 7/8	27 6/8	27 2/8	20 1/8	5	5	5	5	Madison Parish, La.	M. L. Arnold	David D. Arnold	DC 1941	87
171 7/8	25 2/8	26 1/8	21 1/8	4 2/8	4 4/8	5	5	Oxford Co., Maine	Picked Up	Francis Ontengco	PU 1980	87
171 7/8	25 5/8	24 5/8	25 6/8	5 1/8	5 4/8	5	6	Perry Co., Ohio	Bill Pargeon	Bill Pargeon	NO 1976	87
171 5/8	22 1/8	23	19	5 2/8	5 4/8	5	6	Tensas Parish, La.	Jim Keahey	Gerald P. Begnaud, Jr.	1960	90
171 3/8	26	24 4/8	15 1/8	4 3/8	4	5	6	La Salle Co., Texas	Charles D. Johnson	Charles D. Johnson	DC 1964	91
171 1/8	23 4/8	23 4/8	18 3/8	7 2/8	6 3/8	5	5	Bayfield Co., Wisc.	James A. Peters	James A. Peters	NO 1979	92
171	27 1/8	26 3/8	19 4/8	4 4/8	4 4/8	5	5	Hampshire Co., W. Va.	Conda L. Shanholtz	Conda L. Shanholtz	DC 1958	93
170 7/8	26 4/8	25 7/8	17 6/8	5	5	7	6	Frio Co., Texas	Lex Stewart	Lex Stewart	DC 1930	94
170 7/8	27 2/8	26 5/8	22 2/8	5 2/8	5 2/8	8	6	Warren Co., Iowa	Gary L. Johnson	Gary L. Johnson	DC 1981	94
170 7/8	27	26 5/8	23 1/8	4 7/8	5	8	6	Steuben Co., N. Y.	Duane L. Horton	Duane L. Horton	NO 1976	94
170 6/8	23 7/8	23 4/8	19 2/8	4 6/8	4 6/8	5	5	Winn Parish, La.	William Charles Erwin	William Charles Erwin	NO 1980	97
170 5/8	21 5/8	21 7/8	15 3/8	4 5/8	4 5/8	6	6	Allegan Co., Mich.	William Caywood	William Caywood	NO 1948	98
170 5/8	26 7/8	25 4/8	18 2/8	5 4/8	5 2/8	5	7	Atchison Co., Mo.	Roy E. Munsey	Roy E. Munsey	NO 1980	98
170 5/8	24 3/8	26 4/8	17 3/8	5 1/8	4 7/8	5	5	St. Marys Co., Md.	Brian M. Boteler	Brian M. Boteler	DC 1980	98
170 4/8	27	27 4/8	23 4/8	4 2/8	4 2/8	5	6	Webb Co., Texas	R. W. Mann	R. W. Mann	DC 1979	101
170 4/8	29 6/8	29 2/8	21 2/8	4 6/8	4 4/8	7	8	Sherburne Co., Minn.	Curtis G. Nelson	Curtis G. Nelson	NO 1981	101
170 3/8	23 6/8	24 3/8	15 7/8	4 4/8	4 4/8	5	6	Wilcox Co., Ga.	Scott H. Urguhart	Scott H. Urguhart	NO 1981	103
170 3/8	27 4/8	25 4/8	21 1/8	6 7/8	6 4/8	4	4	Franklin Co., Kan.	Judy E. Wiederholt	Fran E. Wiederholt	DC 1981	103

170 2/8	25 5/8	26 2/8	18 5/8	4 7/8	5	5	5	Newago Co., Mich.	Dennis Carlson	NO 1978	103
170 1/8	27 1/8	27 3/8	21	5 3/8	5 5/8	4	4	Lee Co., Ala.	George P. Mann	NO 1980	106
170 1/8	20 6/8	21 3/8	16 5/8	4 4/8	4 4/8	6	5	Smoky River, Alta.	Bernie Reiswig	SE 1980	107
170 1/8	22 3/8	24 3/8	16 3/8	4 7/8	4 7/8	7	6	Morehouse Parish, La.	Johnnie Kovac, Jr.	DC 1979	107
170 1/8	22 4/8	25 3/8	20 3/8	4 4/8	4 4/8	6	6	Logan Co., Ill.	Gary L. Humbert	NO 1979	107
170 1/8	24 5/8	25 5/8	19	5 3/8	4 5/8	7	5	Warren Co., Iowa	Arnold J. Hoch	DC 1975	107

*Final Score subject to revision by additional verifying measurements

Whitetail Deer *(Non-Typical Antlers)*

Minimum Score 195 | ***Odocoileus virginianus virginianus* and certain related subspecies** | **World's Record 333 7/8**

Score	Length of Main Beam R.	Length of Main Beam L.	Inside Spread	Circumference at Smallest Place Between Burr and First Point R.	Circumference at Smallest Place Between Burr and First Point L.	Number of Points R.	Number of Points L.	Locality Killed	By Whom Killed	Owner	Date Killed	Rank
333 7/8	24 1/8	23 3/8	23 3/8	5 1/8	5 1/8	19	25	St. Louis Co., Mo.	Picked Up	Missouri Dept. of Conservation	PU 1981	1
248 5/8	25	24	20 5/8	5 1/8	5 2/8	16	12	Snowy Mts., Mont.	Unknown	McLean Bowman	PR 1980	2
248 1/8*	31 1/8	32 1/8	22 6/8	5 2/8	5 4/8	15	15	Penobscot Co., Maine	Unknown	James L. Mason, Sr.	1945	3
242 3/8*	27 1/8	30 5/8	18 1/8	5 1/8	5	12	9	Mahoning Co., Ohio	David L. Klemm	Dick Idol Safaries	DC 1980	4
237 5/8*	25 2/8	25 1/8	18 2/8	5 1/8	5	15	12	Sawyer Co., Wisc.	David D. Sprangers	David D. Sprangers	NO 1980	5
236 3/8	25 7/8	23 6/8	20 3/8	5 4/8	5 4/8	14	16	Union Co., Ky.	Wilbur E. Buchanan	Wilbur E. Buchanan	NO 1970	6
236	22 3/8	24 6/8	19 5/8	5 4/8	5 1/8	11	12	Winona Co., Minn.	Francis A. Pries	Francis A. Pries	NO 1964	7
233 2/8	26 7/8	26 2/8	24 6/8	4 3/8	4 5/8	9	9	Acadia Valley, Alta.	James J. Niwa	James J. Niwa	NO 1973	8
233	26	27 4/8	20 4/8	5 7/8	6	14	11	Burnett Co., Wisc.	Victor Rammer	Jerry C. Ganske	NO 1949	9
231 5/8	28 1/8	26 5/8	19 2/8	5 1/8	5 1/8	11	11	Dane Co., Wisc.	Dennis D. Shanks	Dennis D. Shanks	OT 1979	10
226 4/8	21 3/8	22 2/8	19 2/8	4 6/8	4 5/8	13	11	Muskingum Co., Ohio	Rex Allen Thompson	Rex Allen Thompson	NO 1981	11
225 2/8	29 1/8	29 2/8	23 4/8	6 2/8	6 1/8	9	8	St. Louis Co., Minn.	Elmer H. Sellin	Elmer H. Sellin	NO 1938	12
224 5/8	24 6/8	27 1/8	25 1/8	5 7/8	5 4/8	15	7	Perry Co., Ala.	Robert Eugene Royster	Robert Eugene Royster	DC 1976	13
224 2/8	23 2/8	23 2/8	22	5 3/8	5 2/8	18	15	Pine Co., Minn.	Greg S. Blom	Greg S. Blom	NO 1980	14
222 5/8	27	25 5/8	19 2/8	5 3/8	5 7/8	9	12	Mair, Sask.	R. A. McGill	Mr. & Mrs. Murray Melom	1952	15
220 2/8	25	26 4/8	19 1/8	5 4/8	5 4/8	11	12	Union Co., Iowa	George Foster	George Foster	DC 1968	16
219 2/8	24 6/8	24 6/8	21 6/8	5 4/8	5 4/8	9	11	Aroostook Co., Maine	Harold C. Kitchin	Harold C. Kitchin	NO 1973	17
219 2/8	26	30 5/8	19 2/8	6 2/8	6 2/8	13	11	Buffalo Co., Wisc.	Glenn Lehman	Glenn Lehman	NO 1958	17
218 5/8	26 2/8	25 6/8	18 4/8	4 4/8	4 4/8	9	11	Chariton Co., Mo.	Stanley McSparren	Stanley McSparren	NO 1979	19
218 4/8	27	26 3/8	18 7/8	5 2/8	5 3/8	12	12	Sawyer Co., Wisc.	Walter Kittleson	Walter Kittleson	NO 1920	20
218 3/8	24 7/8	25 5/8	23 2/8	5 2/8	5 2/8	10	11	Keweenaw Co., Mich.	Bernard J. Murn	Bernard J. Murn	NO 1980	21
217 3/8	27	28 5/8	18 3/8	5 2/8	5 4/8	12	15	Meeker Co., Minn.	Steven R. Turek	Steven R. Turek	OT 1982	22
216 5/8	23	25 4/8	25 7/8	5 7/8	5 6/8	11	11	Isle of Wight Co., Va.	Peter Frank Crocker, Jr.	Peter Frank Crocker, Jr.	JA 1963	23
215	28 6/8	27 2/8	14 6/8	6	6	12	15	Hardin Co., Ky.	Michael F. Meredith	Michael F. Meredith	NO 1980	24
212 7/8	27 1/8	26 5/8	27 7/8	6	5 2/8	9	6	Schuyler Co., Ill.	Donald E. Ziegenbein	Donald E. Ziegenbein	NO 1981	25
212 3/8	23 2/8	23 4/8	18 4/8	5	4 7/8	10	10	Rosebud Co., Mont.	Picked Up	Art F. Hayes, III	PU 1979	26
211 6/8	22 3/8	25 5/8	21	5	5	10	11	Cottonwood Co., Minn.	James A. Sykora	James A. Sykora	NO 1981	27
211 5/8	28 2/8	28 4/8	23	5 7/8	6	11	11	Glaslyn, Sask.	Carl R. Frohaug	Carl R. Frohaug	NO 1981	28

210 6/8	23 6/8	25 4/8	22	5	5	11	8	Coahuila, Mexico	Picked Up	Jim Jacob	PU 1981	29
210 2/8	26 4/8	25 2/8	21 4/8	5 3/8	5 3/8	8	9	Columbiana Co., Ohio	Harold L. Hawkins	Harold L. Hawkins	DC 1981	30
209 7/8	25 6/8	25 4/8	18 1/8	4 5/8	4 5/8	10	15	Pine Co., Minn.	Scott A. Miller	Scott A. Miller	NO 1980	31
209 6/8	24 6/8	24 2/8	20 7/8	5 6/8	5 3/8	10	11	Franklin Co., Miss.	Ronnie Strickland	Ronnie Strickland	NO 1981	32
209 5/8	24 4/8	25 3/8	22 4/8	4 6/8	5	10	11	Butler Co., Ky.	Dean A. Hannold	Dean A. Hannold	NO 1979	33
208 6/8	26 3/8	27 4/8	21 7/8	5 3/8	5 4/8	9	8	Unknown	Unknown	David A. Boys	PR 1982	34
207 7/8	26 5/8	26	24 2/8	5 3/8	5 2/8	7	9	Monitor, Alta.	Raymond Worobo	Raymond Worobo	NO 1979	35
207 6/8	27	27 5/8	25 4/8	6 6/8	6 4/8	9	9	Aroostook Co., Maine	Alfred Wardwell	Alfred Wardwell	NO 1945	36
207 3/8	28 7/8	29 1/8	18 5/8	6 5/8	6 2/8	10	10	Lincoln Co., Mo.	Melvin Zumwalt	Melvin Zumwalt	NO 1955	37
206 6/8	25 6/8	23 3/8	23 7/8	5 4/8	5 5/8	12	9	Somerset Co., Maine	Mark T. Lary	Mark T. Lary	NO 1979	38
206 4/8	22 1/8	22 2/8	19 4/8	5	5	10	13	Brooks Co., Texas	John E. Wilson	James Martin Hancock, Jr.	DC 1947	39
205 5/8	25 4/8	26 1/8	22 5/8	5	5	10	12	Midway, B. C.	Gordon Kamigochi	Gordon Kamigochi	NO 1980	40
205 4/8	25	25 6/8	19 4/8	6 1/8	5 6/8	11	7	Adams Co., Ill.	Eldon K. Dagley	Eldon K. Dagley	DC 1981	41
205 3/8	22 4/8	23 2/8	17	6	6	10	12	Todd Co., Minn.	Mark A. Miksche	Mark A. Miksche	NO 1979	42
204	26 1/8	25 5/8	18 6/8	5 3/8	5 2/8	13	10	Grant Co., Minn.	Douglas S. Olson	Douglas S. Olson	NO 1977	43
203 6/8	25	26 2/8	17 6/8	4 4/8	4 4/8	9	8	McCurtain Co., Okla.	Gary L. Birge	Gary L. Birge	NO 1981	44
203 5/8	23 2/8	25 2/8	17 3/8	6	5 6/8	10	9	Grand Forks Co., N. D.	Thomas G. Bernotas	Thomas G. Bernotas	NO 1975	45
203 3/8	26 2/8	26 1/8	17 6/8	5 4/8	5 4/8	8	10	Olmsted Co., Minn.	Daniel J. Bernard	Daniel J. Bernard	NO 1967	46
202 7/8	25 1/8	24 2/8	23 7/8	5	5	7	10	Marinette Co., Wisc.	Theodore Maes	Theodore Maes	NO 1932	47
202	28 6/8	27 3/8	15 5/8	5 6/8	6	12	11	Nodaway Co., Mo.	Richard L. Stewart	Richard L. Stewart	NO 1972	48
202	26 7/8	27	23 4/8	5 2/8	5 2/8	13	10	Powell Co., Ky.	Hershel Ingram	Hershel Ingram	NO 1980	48
201 5/8	25 1/8	24 7/8	19 7/8	6 3/8	6 1/8	7	8	Baraga Co., Mich.	Dennis D. Bess	Dennis D. Bess	NO 1981	50
201 3/8	26 3/8	25 7/8	18 4/8	5 2/8	5 1/8	10	8	St. Louis Co., Minn.	Andrew G. Groen	Andrew G. Groen	NO 1958	51
201 3/8	24 7/8	25 1/8	19	5 2/8	5 3/8	12	10	Queen Annes Co., Md.	Franklin E. Jewell	Franklin E. Jewell	NO 1978	51
201 2/8	28 3/8	28 5/8	23 1/8	4 6/8	4 7/8	11	10	Coshocton Co., Ohio	Lou L. Rogers	Lou L. Rogers	NO 1979	53
200 6/8	24 1/8	24 3/8	17 6/8	5	5	11	9	Juneau Co., Wisc.	Anchor Nelson	J. D. Andrews	1946	54
200 3/8	25 4/8	27	19 1/8	6 4/8	5 4/8	10	10	Tuscarawas Co., Ohio	Michael D. Korns, Sr.	Michael D. Korns, Sr.	DC 1978	55
199 6/8	23 2/8	24	17 4/8	5 1/8	5 3/8	8	9	Rochester, Alta.	James Weismantel	James Weismantel	NO 1979	56
198 7/8	26 7/8	25 6/8	21 4/8	5 4/8	5 2/8	10	7	Chippewa Co., Minn.	Ray N. Strand	Ray N. Strand	NO 1976	57
198 4/8	26 2/8	24 2/8	21 5/8	4 7/8	4 6/8	7	8	Lincoln Co., Minn.	Dennis G. Geiken	Dennis G. Geiken	NO 1980	58
198 4/8	26 4/8	22 5/8	18 7/8	5 6/8	5 5/8	9	10	Clay Co., Minn.	F. W. Kolle	Kolle Farms, Inc.	NO 1946	58
197 4/8	25 7/8	25 6/8	20 1/8	6 1/8	6 1/8	11	10	Garfield Co., Okla.	Derald D. Crissop	Derald D. Crissop	NO 1980	60
197	24 2/8	26 4/8	25 3/8	5	5 1/8	8	9	Kootenai Co., Idaho	David L. Whatcott & Randy C. Carlson	David L. Whatcott & Randy C. Carlson	NO 1980	61
196 6/8	22 2/8	22 5/8	17 5/8	5	5	8	8	Vilas Co., Wisc.	Joe Wilfer	Rick Iacono	NO 1934	62
196 5/8	21 2/8	20 5/8	19 4/8	4 7/8	4 7/8	10	12	Wilkinson Co., Miss.	Robert D. Sullivan	Robert D. Sullivan	JA 1982	63
196 2/8	27	25 1/8	27	6	6	7	14	Dorchester Co., Md.	Kevin R. Coulbourne	Kevin R. Coulbourne	DC 1979	64
195 5/8	23 7/8	24 2/8	13	5	5 2/8	14	10	Adams Co., Miss.	Kathleen McGehee	Kathleen McGehee	DC 1981	65
195 5/8	25 4/8	25 6/8	19 1/8	5	5 2/8	8	8	Duffield, Alta.	Robert A. Schaefer	Robert A. Schaefer	NO 1980	65
195 4/8	21 3/8	22 4/8	17 2/8	5	5	10	8	Carlisle Co., Ky.	William H. Deane, IV	William H. Deane, IV	NO 1979	67
195 3/8	25 2/8	26 3/8	0	5 3/8	5 2/8	11	8	Grassland, Alta.	Frederick Neuhmann	Frederick Neuhmann	OT 1980	68
195 3/8	20 1/8	22 4/8	16 2/8	7 3/8	7 5/8	10	12	Beltrami Co., Minn.	John G. Binsfeld	John G. Binsfeld	NO 1980	68
195 2/8	25 3/8	25 5/8	22 2/8	5 3/8	5 3/8	12	13	Stevens Co., Wash.	Floyd E. Newell	Floyd E. Newell	NO 1981	70

*Final Score subject to revision by additional verifying measurements

Coues' Whitetail Deer *(Typical Antlers)*

Minimum Score 110 | ***Odocoileus virginianus couesi*** | **World's Record 143**

Score	Length of Main Beam R.	Length of Main Beam L.	Inside Spread	Circumference at Smallest Place Between Burr and First Point R.	Circumference at Smallest Place Between Burr and First Point L.	Number of Points R.	Number of Points L.	Locality Killed	By Whom Killed	Owner	Date Killed	Rank
130 4/8	20 6/8	20 6/8	15 6/8	4 6/8	4 5/8	8	6	Pima Co., Ariz.	Kim J. Poulin	Kim J. Poulin	NO 1981	1
115*	18	18 1/8	16 4/8	4	4	5	5	Pima Co., Ariz.	Glen Alan Elmer	Glen Alan Elmer	DC 1980	2
113 6/8*	18	17 7/8	14 6/8	4	4	4	4	Pima Co., Ariz.	Richard N. Huber	Richard N. Huber	NO 1979	3
113 6/8*	18 4/8	18	13 2/8	3 6/8	4	5	5	Pima Co., Ariz.	Andy A. Ramirez	Andy A. Ramirez	NO 1979	3
112 2/8	18	17 6/8	17	4	3 7/8	5	5	Maricopa Co., Ariz.	Gary D. Nichols	Gary D. Nichols	NO 1980	5
111 6/8	17 1/8	16 5/8	14	3 7/8	3 7/8	4	4	Pima Co., Ariz.	George V. Borquez	George V. Borquez	NO 1979	6
110 3/8	17 6/8	18 6/8	15 7/8	3 6/8	3 4/8	4	5	Hidalgo Co., N. M.	Ronald M. Gerdes	Ronald M. Gerdes	NO 1979	7
110 2/8	16	15 4/8	15 4/8	3 6/8	4	5	4	Hidalgo Co., N. M.	Jay M. Gates, III	Jay M. Gates, III	NO 1981	8
110 1/8	16 4/8	17	12 3/8	4 7/8	4 4/8	4	4	Pima Co., Ariz.	Andy C. Strebe	Andy C. Strebe	NO 1981	9

*Final Score subject to revision by additional verifying measurements

Coues' Whitetail Deer *(Non-Typical Antlers)*

Minimum Score 120 — ***Odocoileus virginianus couesi*** — **World's Record 151 4/8**

Score	Length of Main Beam R.	Length of Main Beam L.	Inside Spread	Circumference at Smallest Place Between Burr and First Point R.	Circumference at Smallest Place Between Burr and First Point L.	Number of Points R.	Number of Points L.	Locality Killed	By Whom Killed	Owner	Date Killed	Rank
135 4/8*	18 4/8	18 5/8	14 2/8	4 4/8	4 3/8	7	7	Cochise Co., Ariz.	Todd A. Doser	Todd A. Doser	NO 1979	1
126 1/8*	14 7/8	15 2/8	11 2/8	4 5/8	4 6/8	8	6	Pima Co., Ariz.	William F. Crull	William F. Crull	NO 1979	2
120 7/8	16 7/8	17	13 3/8	4 6/8	4 4/8	6	6	Pima Co., Ariz.	Carl E. Fasel	Carl E. Fasel	NO 1981	3
120 1/8*	18 5/8	19	13 6/8	4 1/8	4	8	6	Santa Cruz Co., Ariz.	Gerald M. Kluzik	Gerald M. Kluzik	NO 1981	4

*Final Score subject to revision by additional verifying measurements

Canada Moose

Minimum Score 195 ***Alces alces americana* and *Alces alces andersoni*** **World's Record 242**

Three categories of moose are recognized for records keeping, with boundaries based on geographic lines. Canada moose includes trophies from Newfoundland and Canada (except for the Yukon and Northwest Territories), Minnesota, and Maine.

Score	Greatest Spread	Length of Palm R.	Length of Palm L.	Width of Palm R.	Width of Palm L.	Circumference of Beam at Smallest Place R.	Circumference of Beam at Smallest Place L.	Number of Normal Points R.	Number of Normal Points L.	Locality Killed	By Whom Killed	Owner	Date Killed	Rank
242	63	44 5/8	45	21 6/8	23	8 1/8	9 2/8	15	16	Grayling River, B. C.	Michael E. Laub	Michael E. Laub	OT 1980	1
240 2/8	66 6/8	46 3/8	45 4/8	19	18 6/8	7 4/8	7 7/8	15	15	Teslin River, B. C.	Albertoni Ferruccio	Albertoni Ferruccio	SE 1982	2
216 1/8	58 1/8	41 4/8	42 4/8	18 4/8	19 4/8	7	7 2/8	17	12	Dease Lake, B. C.	George A. Sinclair	George A. Sinclair	SE 1981	3
209 6/8*	64 6/8	39 4/8	44	12	13 5/8	7	7 2/8	14	14	Oba Lake, Ont.	Bruce McPherson	Bruce McPherson	OT 1963	4
207 4/8	60 4/8	38 4/8	40 3/8	16 4/8	15 4/8	7 4/8	7 6/8	12	16	Sulphur Creek, Alta.	Willard L. Gamin	Willard L. Gamin	OT 1980	5
207 4/8	51 2/8	43 3/8	43	14 1/8	14 4/8	7	7	14	15	Prophet River, B. C.	Arvin Harrell	Arvin Harrell	SE 1981	5
206 1/8	59 1/8	42 4/8	42 4/8	14 3/8	15 3/8	7 1/8	7 1/8	12	11	Klappan River, B. C.	Bert Varkonyi	Joe & Nini Varkonyi	SE 1979	7
203 1/8	56 1/8	37 4/8	37 6/8	14 2/8	15	7 6/8	7 6/8	15	14	Scoop Lake, B. C.	Dwight E. Farr, Jr.	Dwight E. Farr, Jr.	SE 1980	8
202 7/8	56 1/8	41 6/8	46 1/8	18 6/8	13 6/8	8 1/8	7 7/8	13	10	Frog River, B. C.	Malcom Dan Dinges, Jr.	Malcom Dan Dinges, Jr.	SE 1980	9
202 7/8	57 1/8	43 4/8	46 3/8	15	11 5/8	8 1/8	7 6/8	10	11	Lower Manitou Lake, Ont.	Donald R. Anderson	Donald R. Anderson	OT 1979	9
202 4/8	62 4/8	43 6/8	40 2/8	13 4/8	14	7 2/8	7 3/8	9	10	Stewart Lake, B. C.	Keith Wilson	Keith Wilson	DC 1980	11
202 1/8	66 7/8	43 3/8	39 3/8	13 1/8	13 4/8	7 1/8	7 5/8	9	8	Kawdy Mt., B. C.	Herman Kirn	Herman Kirn	AG 1981	12
202 1/8	51 5/8	44 2/8	42 6/8	13 5/8	14	7	6 7/8	14	12	Graham River, B. C.	Thomas H. Morrison	Thomas H. Morrison	OT 1981	12
201 2/8	54	39 1/8	39 6/8	15	14 6/8	6 6/8	7	13	14	Fox River, B. C.	Toby J. Johnson	Toby J. Johnson	SE 1980	14
201 1/8	57 5/8	38 3/8	40 3/8	11 6/8	14 5/8	8 5/8	8 6/8	13	13	Piscataquis Co., Maine	Walter V. Scott	Walter V. Scott	SE 1980	15
201	54 4/8	43 4/8	42	14	13 1/8	8 5/8	8 1/8	10	12	Toad River, B. C.	Steven Ronshausen	Steven Ronshausen	OT 1981	16
200 1/8	52 3/8	43 5/8	43 4/8	12 4/8	11	8	7 7/8	11	12	Iskut, B. C.	Larry Zilinski	Larry Zilinski	SE 1979	17
200	59	43	42 2/8	14 5/8	12 6/8	7	7	9	11	Cold Fish Lake, B. C.	G. Kenneth Whitehead	G. Kenneth Whitehead	SE 1964	18
199 6/8	60 6/8	37 3/8	41	13	12 7/8	8 2/8	8 6/8	11	11	Lake Co., Minn.	L. D. Holtegaard	L. D. Holtegaard, R. Smith, B. Nessler, & P. Nietz	OT 1981	19
199	53 4/8	41 3/8	41 1/8	14 1/8	13 3/8	7 2/8	7 2/8	15	11	Trout Lake, B. C.	William R. Lee	William R. Lee	SE 1982	20
198 7/8	53 3/8	41 5/8	40	15	12	8 2/8	7 6/8	13	13	Coconino Creek, B. C.	Allan C. Endersby	Allan C. Endersby	OT 1980	21
198	54 2/8	39 4/8	42 6/8	16 2/8	17	7 1/8	7 2/8	11	9	Pink Mt., B. C.	Wallace E. Anderson	Wallace E. Anderson	SE 1982	22
197 4/8	50 6/8	43 4/8	41 4/8	13 4/8	13 3/8	7 4/8	7 4/8	11	11	Kelly Creek, B. C.	Leonard O. Farlow	Leonard O. Farlow	SE 1980	23

196 5/8	53 7/8	38 2/8	36 7/8	16 7/8	16 4/8	7	7	14	12	Lake Co., Minn.	Brian S. Agnoli	Brian S. Agnoli	OT 1981	24
196 5/8	62 5/8	41 4/8	39 3/8	11 5/8	11 7/8	7	7	11	9	Adsit Creek, B. C.	Loren D. Bliss	Loren D. Bliss	OT 1980	24
196	53 6/8	39 2/8	40 3/8	13 1/8	15 5/8	6 6/8	6 7/8	12	12	Wollaston Lake, Sask.	Daryl V. Johannesen	Daryl V. Johannesen	SE 1982	26
196	54 6/8	43 7/8	40 4/8	10 5/8	12 2/8	7	7	13	14	Tatuk Lake, B. C.	Erling E. Gull	Erling E. Gull	NO 1980	26
195 2/8	54	37 4/8	39	13	14 4/8	7 1/8	7 3/8	13	13	Turnagain River, B. C.	Donald E. Franklin	Donald E. Franklin	SE 1977	28
195 2/8	54 4/8	35	42	15 2/8	15 6/8	7 1/8	7 2/8	13	17	Piscataquis Co., Maine	W. H. Gagnon, Jr.	W. H. Gagnon, Jr. & R. R. Gagnon	SE 1980	28
195 1/8	56 1/8	36	36 5/8	15 3/8	16	7 1/8	7 1/8	11	14	Muskwa River, B. C.	Buck Heide	Buck Heide	OT 1979	30
195	54 6/8	38	37 2/8	15	14 6/8	7 3/8	7 1/8	11	11	Piscataquis Co., Maine	Keith B. Gould	Keith B. Gould	SE 1980	31
195	54 2/8	39	38 2/8	14	14 3/8	7 1/8	7 3/8	11	11	Lake Co., Minn.	Lewis N. Hostrawser	Lewis N. Hostrawser	SE 1981	31

*Final Score subject to revision by additional verifying measurements

Alaska-Yukon Moose
Alces alces gigas

Minimum Score 224   **World's Record 255**

Alaska-Yukon moose includes trophies from Alaska, the Yukon Territory, and the Northwest Territories.

Score	Greatest Spread	Length of Palm R.	Length of Palm L.	Width of Palm R.	Width of Palm L.	Circumference of Beam at Smallest Place R.	Circumference of Beam at Smallest Place L.	Number of Normal Points R.	Number of Normal Points L.	Locality Killed	By Whom Killed	Owner	Date Killed	Rank
254 4/8*	71 3/8	51 3/8	53 3/8	21 1/8	17 3/8	9 3/8	9 3/8	13	13	Alagnak River, Alaska	Robert L. Marvin	Robert L. Marvin	SE 1981	1
243 1/8	67 3/8	52	53 3/8	16 3/8	16 3/8	8	8 3/8	12	13	Talkeetna Mts., Alaska	Duane E. Stroupe	Duane E. Stroupe	SE 1982	2
242	68	48 3/8	49 3/8	19 3/8	19 3/8	7 3/8	7 3/8	14	16	Grass Lakes, Yukon	Melvin R. Spohn	Melvin R. Spohn	SE 1981	3
240 3/8*	70 3/8	43 3/8	43 3/8	17 3/8	19 3/8	7 3/8	7 3/8	17	17	Yukon River, Alaska	Unknown	G. Kenneth Whitehead	PR 1899	4
239 3/8	62 3/8	47 3/8	50 3/8	16 3/8	17 3/8	8 3/8	8 3/8	16	18	Clear Creek, Alaska	Douglas A. Hulme	Douglas A. Hulme	SE 1980	5
236 3/8	68 3/8	50	49 3/8	16 3/8	17 3/8	8 3/8	8 3/8	13	9	Alaska Range, Alaska	Dennis R. Johnson	Dennis R. Johnson	SE 1980	6
234 3/8	71 3/8	47 3/8	49 3/8	14 3/8	15 3/8	8 3/8	8 3/8	11	11	Council, Alaska	Arden L. Peterson	Arden L. Peterson	SE 1979	7
230	73	44 3/8	44 3/8	14 3/8	14 3/8	7 3/8	7 3/8	12	12	Miner River, Yukon	Gary L. Knepp	Gary L. Knepp	OT 1979	8
228 3/8	68 3/8	45	47 3/8	15 3/8	16	7 3/8	8 3/8	12	16	Brooks Range, Alaska	Robert L. Nelson	Robert L. Nelson	SE 1981	9
227 3/8	70 3/8	41 3/8	41 3/8	14 3/8	15 3/8	7 3/8	7 3/8	14	15	Aniak River, Alaska	Donn W. Ulrich	Donn W. Ulrich	SE 1980	10
226 3/8	70 3/8	45 3/8	41 3/8	18	17 3/8	7 3/8	7 3/8	12	12	Alaska Pen., Alaska	Gerald F. McNamara	MacsTaxidermy	SE 1979	11
226 3/8	68 3/8	44 3/8	46 3/8	13 3/8	13 3/8	8	7 3/8	14	13	Talkeetna Mts., Alaska	Wolfgang Porsche	Wolfgang Porsche	SE 1981	12
226 3/8	61 3/8	44	44 3/8	16 3/8	17	8 3/8	8 3/8	15	14	Talkeetna Mts., Alaska	Lino Fred Vannelli	Lino Fred Vannelli	SE 1979	12
225 3/8	67 3/8	43 3/8	42	15 3/8	16	8 3/8	8 3/8	13	13	Glennallen, Alaska	Eugene E. Wheeler	Eugene E. Wheeler	SE 1981	14
225 3/8	66 3/8	44	49 3/8	15 3/8	13 3/8	8 3/8	8 3/8	14	14	Chandalar River, Alaska	William O. Dudley	William O. Dudley	SE 1980	15
225	70	44	44 3/8	13 3/8	15 3/8	8 3/8	10 3/8	12	14	Talkeetna, Mts., Alaska	Eberhart Herzog	Eberhart Herzog	SE 1981	16

*Final Score subject to revision by additional verifying measurements

Wyoming or Shiras Moose

Minimum Score 155

Alces alces shirasi

World's Record 205 4/8

Wyoming (Shiras) moose includes trophies taken in Utah, Idaho, Montana, Wyoming, and Washington.

Score	Greatest Spread	Length of Palm R.	Length of Palm L.	Width of Palm R.	Width of Palm L.	Circumference of Beam at Smallest Place R.	Circumference of Beam at Smallest Place L.	Number of Normal Points R.	Number of Normal Points L.	Locality Killed	By Whom Killed	Owner	Date Killed	Rank
200 3/8	55 7/8	38 4/8	36 6/8	13 1/8	13 4/8	7	6 3/8	16	17	Lincoln Co., Wyo.	Aldon L. Hale	Aldon L. Hale	SE 1981	1
180 2/8	51 2/8	35 1/8	34 3/8	13 5/8	14 4/8	6 4/8	6 5/8	11	10	Weber Co., Utah	Robert S. Mastronardi	Robert S. Mastronardi	OT 1981	2
179 2/8*	48 6/8	34 1/8	36 4/8	12 1/8	14 6/8	7	7 1/8	12	12	Gallatin Co., Mont.	L. C. Hulslander	L. C. Hulslander & K. Bennet	OT 1981	3
176 7/8*	47 5/8	34 1/8	33	13 7/8	13 1/8	7	7 1/8	12	11	Teton Co., Wyo.	J. Bryan Midgley	J. Bryan Midgley	SE 1979	4
174 3/8*	58 1/8	32 4/8	29 3/8	12 5/8	12 5/8	6 2/8	6 1/8	13	10	Idaho Co., Idaho	Paul L. White	Paul L. White	SE 1981	5
174 2/8	46	32 2/8	32 1/8	14 3/8	13 3/8	6 5/8	6 5/8	12	14	Teton Co., Wyo.	John R. Harju	John R. Harju	SE 1980	6
172	46 2/8	35 7/8	38 5/8	9 3/8	10	6 5/8	6 5/8	11	12	Teton Co., Wyo.	Holland C. McHenry	Holland C. McHenry	DC 1980	7
171 7/8	58 3/8	30	33 5/8	9 5/8	9 5/8	6 1/8	6 1/8	11	13	Weber Co., Utah	Kent G. Yearsley	Kent G. Yearsley	OT 1981	8
171 2/8	50	34 4/8	37 5/8	10 6/8	10 3/8	6 6/8	6 6/8	9	9	Silver Bow Co., Mont.	Martin E. Carlson	Martin E. Carlson	OT 1980	9
167 6/8	44	33 7/8	37	12 7/8	11 6/8	6 2/8	6 2/8	10	12	Beaverhead Co., Mont.	Peter A. Parini	Peter A. Parini	NO 1981	10
166 7/8	51 1/8	33 5/8	33 7/8	9 7/8	10	6 3/8	6 3/8	10	8	Gallatin Co., Mont.	Rodney R. Richardson	Rodney R. Richardson	NO 1979	11
161 5/8	51 3/8	30 5/8	32 2/8	10 3/8	9 4/8	6	6 1/8	9	10	Cache Co., Utah	Kenneth Hamilton	Kenneth Hamilton	SE 1980	12
161 4/8	40 4/8	36 1/8	30 4/8	12 7/8	11 7/8	6 3/8	6 1/8	12	12	Bonneville Co., Idaho	Joe M. Coelho, III	Joe M. Coelho, III	SE 1982	13
161 4/8	40 2/8	34 3/8	34 6/8	12 7/8	12 6/8	6 4/8	6 4/8	9	8	Teton Co., Wyo.	Lynn C. Hill	Oliver Hill	OT 1979	13
160 4/8	43 2/8	31 7/8	31 2/8	11 2/8	11	7 4/8	7 3/8	10	9	Beaverhead Co., Mont.	Morton L. Arkava	Morton L. Arkava	NO 1980	15
160 3/8	50 1/8	29 4/8	29 4/8	10 2/8	10 1/8	5 4/8	5 4/8	10	10	Teton Co., Wyo.	Joy Lee Gage	Joy Lee Gage	SE 1981	16
159 2/8	52 4/8	31 4/8	31	7 6/8	9 4/8	6 5/8	6 6/8	8	8	Lincoln Co., Wyo.	Orlando J. Bernardi	Orlando J. Bernardi	NO 1979	17
158 5/8	40 1/8	30 7/8	30 5/8	10 5/8	10 5/8	6 1/8	6	12	13	Lincoln Co., Wyo.	Caroline Nare	Caroline Nare	OT 1979	18
156 7/8	43 5/8	34 4/8	33 4/8	9 5/8	13 2/8	6	6	8	13	Flathead Co., Mont.	Jim M. Milligan	Jim M. Milligan	OT 1982	19
156 2/8	46 6/8	31 4/8	30 5/8	8	9 5/8	6 1/8	6 1/8	10	10	Summit Co., Utah	John G. Allred	John G. Allred	NO 1980	20
155 5/8	41 5/8	30	31 4/8	11 3/8	11 3/8	5 5/8	6	10	11	Lincoln Co., Mont.	Robert D. Nolin	Robert D. Nolin	SE 1979	21

*Final Score subject to revision by additional verifying measurements

Mountain Caribou

Minimum Score 390 | ***Rangifer tarandus caribou*** | **World's Record 452**

Four categories of caribou are recognized for records keeping, with boundaries based on geographic lines. Mountain caribou includes trophies from British Columbia, Alberta, southern Yukon, and the Mackenzie Mountains of the Northwest Territories.

Score	Length of Main Beam		Inside Spread	Circumference at Smallest Place Between Brow and Bez Points		Length of Brow Points		Width of Brow Points		Number of Points		Locality Killed	By Whom Killed	Owner	Date Killed	Rank
	R.	L.		R.	L.	R.	L.	R.	L.	R.	L.					
419 3/8	51 2/8	49 5/8	40 7/8	7 2/8	7 1/8	18 1/8	20 5/8	2 4/8	13	15	13	Mount Mye, Yukon	Clark A. Johnson	Clark A. Johnson	AG 1981	1
413 2/8	41	44 1/8	40 3/8	8 7/8	7 6/8	15 6/8	13 6/8	6 7/8	9 6/8	19	20	Nisutlin Lake, Yukon	James V. Bosco, Sr.	James V. Bosco, Jr.	1935	2
413 2/8	43	46 7/8	25 7/8	7 5/8	6 4/8	17 1/8	19 6/8	4 6/8	14 4/8	22	26	Livingstone, Yukon	Mike J. Chirpich	Mike J. Chirpich	AG 1977	2
411 4/8*	45 4/8	45 2/8	37 4/8	7 2/8	7 1/8	15 5/8	20	1 3/8	13 3/8	17	21	Watson Lake, Yukon	Gary Lundstrom	Gary Lundstrom	AG 1980	4
410 1/8*	52 4/8	53 7/8	39	6 6/8	7 6/8	19 5/8	18 1/8	16	10 1/8	22	21	Ram River, N. W. T.	Michael N. Anderson	Michael N. Anderson	AG 1979	5
407	51 4/8	54	42 1/8	7 1/8	6 5/8	6	19 6/8	7/8	10 6/8	14	18	Norman Wells, N. W. T.	Thomas P. Warner	Thomas P. Warner	SE 1980	6
406	54	53	42 1/8	7	6 5/8	16 4/8	17 6/8	5 7/8	11	17	18	Dawson Range, Yukon	John M. Domingos	John M. Domingos	AG 1980	7
404 3/8	44	44	36	6 5/8	6 2/8	16 4/8	15	12	6 1/8	22	23	June Lake, N. W. T.	Myron A. Peterson	Myron A. Peterson	AG 1980	8
393 1/8	54 4/8	54 2/8	33 7/8	6 4/8	6 2/8	11 4/8	20 4/8	1	10	13	18	Grass Lakes, Yukon	Melvin R. Spohn	Melvin R. Spohn	SE 1981	9
392 3/8	47 7/8	45 4/8	32 4/8	6 3/8	6 6/8	16 6/8	17 2/8	9 3/8	6	15	12	Logan Mts., Yukon	Gordon Graham	Gordon Graham	SE 1978	10

*Final Score subject to revision by additional verifying measurements

Woodland Caribou

Rangifer tarandus caribou

Minimum Score 295 **World's Record 419 5/8**

Woodland caribou includes trophies from Nova Scotia, New Brunswick, and Newfoundland.

Score	Length of Main Beam R.	Length of Main Beam L.	Inside Spread	Circumference at Smallest Place Between Brow and Bez Points R.	Circumference at Smallest Place Between Brow and Bez Points L.	Length of Brow Points R.	Length of Brow Points L.	Width of Brow Points R.	Width of Brow Points L.	Number of Points R.	Number of Points L.	Locality Killed	By Whom Killed	Owner	Date Killed	Rank
329 4/8	37 6/8	38 6/8	26 2/8	5	5 1/8	15 2/8	16	11 5/8	7 7/8	17	16	Robinsons River, Nfld.	Timothy E. Fiedler	Timothy E. Fiedler	OT 1980	1
325 4/8*	42 4/8	41	36 1/8	5 4/8	5 2/8	17	17 5/8	10 7/8	10 7/8	11	12	Caribou Lake, Nfld.	Lyle M. Paro	Lyle M. Paro	OT 1981	2
322 2/8	40	40 4/8	25	5 6/8	5 6/8	15	14 7/8	13 5/8	14	15	16	Lloyds River, Nfld.	Richard P. Navas	Richard P. Navas	SE 1980	3
322 1/8*	42 4/8	41 6/8	34 2/8	5 7/8	5 6/8	14 4/8	14 1/8	4 4/8	11	13	15	Cappahayden, Nfld.	Thomas E. Best, Jr. & Harry A. Chafe	Thomas E. Best, Jr.	SE 1982	4
314 7/8	42 4/8	42 4/8	34 2/8	5 2/8	5 2/8	14 6/8	14 7/8	9 6/8	3 4/8	16	12	Long Range Mts., Nfld.	James J. McBride	James J. McBride	OT 1982	5
313 3/8	33 3/8	32 2/8	29 5/8	5 7/8	5 5/8	12 3/8	10 5/8	11 2/8	9	20	17	Buchans Plateau, Nfld.	Robert R. Kampstra	Robert R. Kampstra	SE 1980	6
309	46 3/8	43 7/8	38 7/8	5 5/8	5 6/8	3 1/8	13	1/8	9 1/8	13	13	Alex Lake, Nfld.	James E. Conklin	James E. Conklin	OT 1981	7
305 1/8	37 4/8	36 5/8	28 2/8	5 2/8	5	11 5/8	13 5/8	10 2/8	11 7/8	17	19	Buchans Plateau, Nfld.	Raymond M. Cappelli	Raymond M. Cappelli	OT 1981	8
300 1/8	38 7/8	36 7/8	34 6/8	5	5 2/8	16	16 3/8	2 4/8	13 6/8	12	13	Buchans Plateau, Nfld.	Ernest J. Morgan	Ernest J. Morgan	SE 1979	9
298	42 4/8	39 6/8	35	5 3/8	5 2/8	17	15 7/8	7 2/8	11 3/8	9	10	Buchans Plateau, Nfld.	Stewart N. Shaft	Stewart N. Shaft	OT 1982	10

*Final Score subject to revision by additional verifying measurements

Barren Ground Caribou

Minimum Score 400 ***Rangifer tarandus granti*** **and** ***Rangifer tarandus groenlandicus*** **World's Record 463 5/8**

Barren ground caribou includes trophies from Alaska, northern Yukon Territory, the Northwest Territories (except the Mackenzie Mountains), Saskatchewan, Manitoba, and Ontario.

Score	Length of Main Beam R.	Length of Main Beam L.	Inside Spread	Circumference at Smallest Place Between Brow and Bez Points R.	Circumference at Smallest Place Between Brow and Bez Points L.	Length of Brow Points R.	Length of Brow Points L.	Width of Brow Points R.	Width of Brow Points L.	Number of Points R.	Number of Points L.	Locality Killed	By Whom Killed	Owner	Date Killed	Rank
453 5/8*	49 1/8	49 3/8	50 2/8	6 1/8	6 2/8	20 3/8	23	2 2/8	13 5/8	13	16	Meshik River, Alaska	Robert D. Jones	Robert D. Jones	OT 1980	1
451 4/8	51 3/8	52 6/8	47 7/8	6 3/8	6 3/8	20	8 1/8	14 5/8	1/8	22	13	Wood River, Alaska	Q. Odell Robinson	Q. Odell Robinson	SE 1980	2
449 1/8	45 3/8	43 5/8	42 5/8	5 6/8	5 7/8	20 6/8	23 2/8	1/8	16 5/8	18	24	Alaska Pen., Alaska	Eddie L. House	Eddie L. House	OT 1979	3
440 2/8	55 3/8	55 1/8	40 4/8	5 6/8	6 1/8	20 4/8	18 2/8	10 4/8	11	18	17	Kenai, Alaska	Picked Up	Marcia L. King	PU 1972	4
438 4/8	52 4/8	51 6/8	41 5/8	6 3/8	6 3/8	17 4/8	15 2/8	8 1/8	7 6/8	21	19	Maclaren River, Alaska	Donald W. Bunselmeier	Donald W. Bunselmeier	SE 1981	5
438	53 7/8	49	47	5 2/8	5 1/8	19 4/8	14	14 4/8	7 4/8	20	18	Lower Ugashik Lake, Alaska	Bert A. McLay	Bert A. McLay	SE 1981	6
433 1/8	50 2/8	48 4/8	39 1/8	9	12 4/8	14 2/8	15 1/8	1/8	8 4/8	16	21	Healy River, Alaska	Anitra Talerico	Frank Talerico	SE 1982	7
431 7/8	48	53 5/8	37 6/8	5 6/8	6	17 4/8	17 2/8	11 3/8	11	18	21	Nondalton, Alaska	Gordon S. Swift	Gordon S. Swift	AG 1981	8
426	53 5/8	52 5/8	42 1/8	6 5/8	6 7/8	19 1/8	19 3/8	8 4/8	11 1/8	22	20	Fog Lakes, Alaska	Larry F. Grout	Larry F. Grout	SE 1981	9
425 5/8	48 1/8	47 5/8	46 7/8	5 5/8	5 4/8	20 5/8	19	4 3/8	14 6/8	17	21	Becharof Lake, Alaska	Lavon L. Chittick	Lavon L. Chittick	SE 1981	10
424 7/8	58 3/8	54 5/8	45 4/8	6 4/8	6 4/8	3 7/8	25 2/8	1/8	18 5/8	14	17	Ugashik Lake, Alaska	Robert C. Jones	Robert C. Jones	OT 1981	11
424 7/8	53 3/8	53 5/8	36 7/8	6 7/8	6 4/8	21 1/8	2 3/8	16 1/8	1/8	18	20	Alaska Range, Alaska	Dennis R. Johnson	Dennis R. Johnson	SE 1980	11
424 2/8	57 2/8	58 2/8	40 2/8	5 3/8	5 4/8	15 5/8	19 1/8	10 4/8	15 6/8	17	19	King Salmon, Alaska	Samuel C. Johnson	Samuel C. Johnson	OT 1978	13
423 6/8	55	54 7/8	47	5 6/8	5 6/8	17 2/8	10 7/8	11 3/8	3 2/8	25	17	Cinder River, Alaska	Gary F. Romaniw	Gary F. Romaniw	SE 1981	14
423	43 5/8	43 7/8	40	5 6/8	7 2/8	6 7/8	16 7/8	3	11	14	15	Port Heiden, Alaska	Robert D. Jones	Robert D. Jones	OT 1981	15
422 1/8	57 3/8	59 3/8	54 4/8	6 1/8	5 7/8	22 2/8	1 4/8	17 4/8	1/8	21	14	King Salmon, Alaska	Jerry R. Jones	Jerry R. Jones	OT 1981	16
421 2/8	57 2/8	57	43 4/8	6	7	11 6/8	12 7/8	8 3/8	11 4/8	19	22	Cantwell, Alaska	Richard L. Miller	Richard L. Miller	SE 1979	17
420 6/8	45 6/8	47 6/8	36 4/8	6	6 3/8	16		10 2/8		27	21	Becharof Lake, Alaska	Glenn E. Anderson	Glenn E. Anderson	SE 1982	18
418 4/8	54 5/8	55	38 6/8	7 3/8	7 2/8	2 3/8	18	1/8	13 4/8	17	19	Ivishak River, Alaska	William O. Dudley	William O. Dudley	SE 1979	19
418 1/8	57 5/8	55 3/8	41 5/8	6	5 6/8	22	19	9 7/8	5 1/8	17	11	Becharof Lake, Alaska	William M. Beyl	William M. Beyl	SE 1981	20
418	54 6/8	53 6/8	47 3/8	7 5/8	7 6/8	17	20 4/8	1/8	14 4/8	12	17	Kenai, Alaska	Gary L. Zerbe	Gary L. Zerbe	SE 1981	21
416 3/8	49 2/8	49 1/8	43 3/8	6 4/8	6 6/8	13 3/8	16 7/8	1 1/8	9 1/8	17	19	Port Heiden, Alaska	Charlie Martin	Charlie Martin	SE1981	22

Score										Locality	Hunter	By Whom Killed	Date Killed	Rank
41 5/8	51%	52%	40%	6%	6%	18%	12%	12%	14	Alaska Pen., Alaska	Richard A. Bengraff	Richard A. Bengraff	OT 1981	23
41 5/8	49%	48	33	6	6%	21%	17%	8%	13%	16	Watana Lake, Alaska	Kurt K. Knutson	Kurt K. Knutson	SE 1981	24
41 5/8	58%	60%	60%	5%	5%	3%	17%	10%	%	15	Becharof Lake, Alaska	Max E. Chittick	Max E. Chittick	SE 1980	25
41 5/8	59	57%	51%	6%	6%		17%		11%	18	Becharof Lake, Alaska	L. Keith Mortensen	L. Keith Mortensen	OT 1980	26
41 4/8	50%	53	37	7%	6%	14%	16%	10%	13%	29	Miner River, Yukon	Gary L. Selig	Gary L. Selig	OT 1979	27
41 0/8	64%	65%	53%	6	6%	16%		8%		12	Becharof Lake, Alaska	Gordon G. Chittick	Gordon G. Chittick	SE 1981	28
41 0/8	58%	53%	46%	6%	5%	13	21	%	12%	20	Becharof Lake, Alaska	Lavon L. Chittick	Lavon L. Chittick	SE 1981	29
41 0/8	48%	49%	36%	5%	5%	17%	17%	15%	10%	19	Lake Clark, Alaska	Donald J. Hotter, III	Donald J. Hotter, III	AG 1979	29
41 0/8	55%	57%	55%	5%	5%	20%	14%	13%	6	26	King Salmon, Alaska	Richard J. Gutherie	Richard J. Gutherie	OT 1979	31
40 8/8	52%	53%	34	8%	7%	17%	17%	12%	4%	18	David River, Alaska	W. K. Leech	W. K. Leech	SE 1979	32
40 7/8	50%	49%	44%	5%	6	6	20%	%	14%	13	Becharof Lake, Alaska	Max E. Chittick	Max E. Chittick	SE 1981	33
40 7/8	56%	56%	43%	6	5%	19%	12%	16	1	30	Ugashik Lakes, Alaska	Gary J. Gray	Gary J. Gray	SE 1981	34
40 7/8	62%	58%	45%	5%	6	8%	15%	%	12%	12	Kanuti River, Alaska	Leslie A. Olson	Leslie A. Olson	NO 1981	35
40 7/8	49%	44%	34%	7	6%	16%	8%	11		22	Lake Clark, Alaska	Arthur L. Patterson	Arthur L. Patterson	SE 1978	35
40 6/8	48%	52%	32%	5	5%	15%	23%	%	18%	15	King Salmon, Alaska	Joe B. Reynolds	Joe B. Reynolds	SE 1981	37
40 6/8	65%	59%	57%	6	6%	1%	17%	%	12	17	Becharof Lake, Alaska	Gordon G. Chittick	Gordon G. Chittick	SE 1980	38
40 6/8	58	53%	46%	6%	6%	16%	15%	12	%	13	Kenai, Alaska	Ernest A. Stirman	Ernest A. Stirman	SE 1981	39
40 4/8	42%	46%	33%	7%	6%	16%	15%	10%	10%	21	Lake Clark, Alaska	Doug Butler	Doug Butler	SE 1980	40
40 4/8	54%	54%	38%	5%	5%	23	15%	9%	11	22	Cathedral Valley, Alaska	Victor Koenig	Victor Koenig	SE 1981	40
40 4/8	49%	51%	37%	5%	5%	14%	18%	%	12%	19	Black River, Alaska	Alfred Eugene Wochner	Alfred Eugene Wochner	AG 1981	42
40 3/8	38%	41%	37%	7%	6%	15	13%	7	5%	22	Holitna River, Alaska	Tony Weiss	Tony Weiss	AG 1979	43
40 3/8	60%	60%	59%	5%	5%	27%	21%	15%	%	13	Becharof Lake, Alaska	Max E. Chittick	Max E. Chittick	SE 1979	44
40 3/8	49%	49%	37%	5%	5%	20%	8%	16	%	27	Pear Lake, Alaska	William M. Sowers	William M. Sowers	AG 1981	45
40 3	56%	54%	39%	7	7	18%	4%	14	%	20	Wood River, Alaska	Norman L. Akau, Jr.	Norman L. Akau, Jr.	SE 1980	46
40 2/8	52	50%	43%	5	4%	15%	16	8%	7%	22	Ugashik Lakes, Alaska	Vincent T. Ciaburri	Vincent T. Ciaburri	SE 1977	47
40 2/8	53%	53%	44%	6%	5%	17%	18	9%	2%	16	White Fish Lake, Alaska	Carol Ann Rollings	Carol Ann Rollings	SE 1981	48
40 0/8	60	60%	50	7%	9%		24%		17	14	King Salmon, Alaska	Richard O. Burns, III	Richard O. Burns, III	SE 1982	49

*Final Score subject to revision by additional verifying measurements.

Quebec-Labrador Caribou

Minimum Score 375

Rangifer tarandus from Quebec and Labrador

World's Record 474 6/8

Score	Length of Main Beam R.	Length of Main Beam L.	Inside Spread	Circumference at Smallest Place Between Brow and Bez Points R.	Circumference at Smallest Place Between Brow and Bez Points L.	Length of Brow Points R.	Length of Brow Points L.	Width of Brow Points R.	Width of Brow Points L.	Number of Points R.	Number of Points L.	Locality Killed	By Whom Killed	Owner	Date Killed	Rank
429 2/8	51 6/8	50 1/8	48 3/8	5 6/8	5 4/8	18 1/8	18 5/8	13 1/8	14 6/8	21	21	Mistinibi Lake, Que.	Charles E. Wilson, Jr.	Charles E. Wilson, Jr.	SE 1980	1
421 4/8	52 7/8	54 4/8	53 5/8	5 7/8	5 3/8	17 2/8	5 6/8	12 3/8	1/8	20	16	George River, Que.	Maurice Southmayd	Maurice Southmayd	SE 1979	2
419 3/8*	59 5/8	59 2/8	52 4/8	6 1/8	6	17 6/8	3 4/8	15 5/8	5/8	22	16	De Paw River, Que.	William R. Branson	William R. Branson	SE 1979	3
417*	60 1/8	56 2/8	50 4/8	6 3/8	6 2/8	24 5/8	19 2/8	18 1/8	1 3/8	21	15	Mistinibi Lake, Que.	Howard M. Barnett	Howard M. Barnett	SE 1980	4
416 1/8*	49 2/8	50 3/8	42 1/8	5 4/8	5 6/8	15 4/8	15 3/8	12 7/8	13	27	20	Tunulik Lake, Que.	Robert F. Cook	Robert F. Cook	SE 1979	5
415 5/8	54 6/8	52 4/8	46	5	5 2/8	17 3/8	18 2/8	8 3/8	16 6/8	15	21	George River, Que.	George E. Poleshock	George E. Poleshock	SE 1980	6
414 7/8	62 4/8	66	43 6/8	5 1/8	5 6/8	2 3/8	21 5/8	1/8	16 6/8	16	22	Schefferville, Que.	Peggy A. Vallery	Peggy A. Vallery	SE 1980	7
411 1/8	61 4/8	63 4/8	48	5 7/8	6	16 7/8	3 2/8	17 7/8	1/8	18	18	Mistinibi Lake, Que.	David H. Crum	David H. Crum	SE 1980	8
409 6/8	51 2/8	50 6/8	51 1/8	5 1/8	5 2/8	14	16 2/8	8 7/8	11	18	20	Mistinibi Lake, Que.	George H. Fearons	George H. Fearons	SE 1982	9
408 6/8	44 5/8	42 4/8	46 4/8	6 1/8	5 7/8	13 4/8	13 4/8	14 5/8	13 7/8	25	24	George River, Que.	Gail W. Holderman	Gail W. Holderman	SE 1979	10
408 4/8	57 2/8	47 6/8	45	5 3/8	5 3/8	21 6/8	20 7/8	15 4/8	1 7/8	19	14	Mistinibi Lake, Que.	Lee Frudden	Lee Frudden	SE 1980	11
407 7/8	54 6/8	56 3/8	42 1/8	6	6 3/8	17 6/8	15 2/8	11 4/8	10	19	17	Tunulik Lake, Que.	Robert L. Sprinkle, Jr.	Robert L. Sprinkle, Jr.	SE 1979	12
405 4/8	55	56 1/8	51 3/8	5 4/8	5 7/8	18 4/8	17 5/8	12 2/8	11 2/8	19	19	Tunulik River, Que.	Jerry Ippolito	Jerry Ippolito	SE 1980	13
405 2/8	52	53	44 6/8	5 6/8	6	16 6/8	22	12 4/8	17 6/8	19	23	De Pas River, Que.	Herbert J. Englemann	Herbert J. Englemann	SE 1979	14
404 6/8	46 4/8	46	40 4/8	6 4/8	6 1/8	20 3/8	20 4/8	15 3/8	19 2/8	19	14	Ungava Bay, Que.	Daniel W. Inserra	Daniel W. Inserra	SE 1979	15
404 5/8	53 4/8	57 6/8	42 6/8	5 2/8	5 2/8	17 3/8	18 2/8	10 2/8	9 6/8	13	15	Camp Tuktu, Que.	Robert E. Prittinen	Robert E. Prittinen	SE 1980	16
402 2/8	60 2/8	57 3/8	48 3/8	4 6/8	5	16 6/8	15 3/8	11 6/8	8 2/8	19	16	George River, Que.	Paul B. Brunner	Paul B. Brunner	SE 1980	17
401 2/8	57	58 3/8	48 1/8	5 1/8	5	18 6/8	16 4/8	9 6/8	8 7/8	17	15	Indian River, Que.	Bruce Hartel	Bruce Hartel	SE 1981	18
401	46 1/8	48 2/8	50 7/8	5 4/8	5	17 1/8	16 7/8	9 2/8	13 3/8	20	18	Schefferville, Que.	L. C. Harold	L. C. Harold	SE 1982	19
400 5/8	46	46 1/8	46 1/8	6	6	15 2/8	14 4/8	11 3/8	13 3/8	21	18	Mistinibi Lake, Que.	Dennis E. Moos	Dennis E. Moos	SE 1980	20
399 3/8	57 7/8	59 3/8	45 3/8	6	6 2/8	17 4/8	17 1/8	14 4/8	1/8	15	14	Dihourse Lake, Que.	George E. Rommler	George E. Rommler	SE 1980	21
398 6/8	52 4/8	51 1/8	48 3/8	5 4/8	5 3/8	13 4/8	15 6/8	3 5/8	9 4/8	16	14	George River, Que.	Bob Bates	Bob Bates	SE 1980	22
398 4/8	52 7/8	51 6/8	45	6	6	16 4/8	16 5/8	12 2/8	11 3/8	14	14	Tunulik River, Que.	Jack S. Schwabland	Jack S. Schwabland	SE 1980	23
397	54 2/8	54 2/8	40	5 1/8	5 1/8	14	15 1/8	14 1/8	15 4/8	19	22	Ungava Bay, Que.	Charles T. Sheley	Charles T. Sheley	SE 1979	24
396 2/8	54 1/8	55 2/8	48 5/8	6 4/8	7 3/8	17 5/8	11 4/8	13 4/8	6 2/8	19	14	George River, Que.	John E. Clark	John E. Clark	SE 1980	25
395 5/8	55 2/8	58 3/8	51	5 5/8	5 6/8	1	18 7/8	1/8	14 3/8	15	22	Ungava Bay, Que.	Bruce S. Markham	Bruce S. Markham	SE 1979	26
394 4/8	51 4/8	48 4/8	42 7/8	5 1/8	4 6/8	19 4/8	17 7/8	2 6/8	11 4/8	17	15	De Pas River, Que.	William A. O'Connor	William A. O'Connor	SE 1980	27

394 2/8	49 1/8	50 6/8	41	5 6/8	5 7/8	18 5/8	1 1/8	12	1	13	16	Mistinibi Lake, Que.	Paul E. Robey	Paul E. Robey	SE 1981	28
392 5/8	55	53 4/8	45 6/8	5 1/8	5 2/8	18 5/8	7 2/8	15 3/8	1/8	20	20	Schefferville, Que.	Robert Henn	Robert Henn	SE 1979	29
392 1/8	56 6/8	55 2/8	40 5/8	4 6/8	4 6/8	3 5/8	20 4/8	1/8	15 6/8	15	23	Tunulik River, Que.	Salvatore A. Gusmano	Salvatore A. Gusmano	SE 1981	30
391 4/8	60 4/8	57	54 7/8	5 3/8	5 6/8	15	19 3/8	2 4/8	13 6/8	13	15	Tunulik River, Que.	Kenneth J. Gerstung	Kenneth J. Gerstung	SE 1979	31
390 5/8	54	54 6/8	47 4/8	6 7/8	6 4/8	8	20	1/8	13 4/8	15	17	Mistinibi Lake, Que.	Thomas J. Merkley	Thomas J. Merkley	SE 1979	32
390 4/8	54	55 2/8	42 1/8	5 5/8	5 5/8	18 4/8	14 6/8	12	6 5/8	14	14	George River, Que.	James E. Prevost	James E. Prevost	SE 1979	33
388 1/8	51 1/8	49 6/8	43 6/8	5 4/8	5 5/8	15 7/8	17 6/8	11 1/8	13 7/8	18	19	Mistinibi Lake, Que.	William A. S. Heuer	William A. S. Heuer	SE 1981	34
385 2/8	51	49 7/8	47 1/8	6	5 6/8		15 3/8		10	14	20	George River, Que.	James J. McBride	James J. McBride	SE 1982	35
384 4/8	53 4/8	52 1/8	46 6/8	6	5 7/8	17 3/8		12 7/8		18	15	Mistinibi Lake, Que.	Stewart N. Shaft	Stewart N. Shaft	SE 1979	36
380 4/8	58	60 2/8	44 4/8	5 5/8	5 4/8	16	22 4/8	12 4/8	8 4/8	15	17	Whale River, Que.	John A. Yeager	John A. Yeager	SE 1979	37
380 2/8	53 4/8	55	39 6/8	6 2/8	6 2/8	16 7/8	14 4/8	11 4/8	1/8	20	16	George River, Que.	Roger R. Card	Roger R. Card	SE 1980	38
380 2/8	62 4/8	65	55 5/8	5 6/8	5 6/8	8	15 4/8	1/8	11 2/8	10	11	George River, Que.	Randal L. Diehl	Randal L. Diehl	SE 1980	38
377 1/8	56 2/8	58 6/8	49 7/8	5 3/8	5 1/8	20 1/8		13 3/8		24	18	Mistinibi Lake, Que.	James H. Meckes, Jr.	James H. Meckes, Jr.	SE 1980	40
376 1/8	49 5/8	50 4/8	47 6/8	6 2/8	6 3/8	13 2/8	12 4/8	8 6/8	9 7/8	17	15	Schefferville, Que.	Charles Lanzarone	Charles Lanzarone	SE 1980	41

*Final Score subject to revision by additional verifying measurements.

Pronghorn

Minimum Score 82 — ***Antilocapra americana americana* and related subspecies** — **World's Record 93**

Score	Length of Horn R.	Length of Horn L.	Circumference of Base R.	Circumference of Base L.	Circumference at Third Quarter R.	Circumference at Third Quarter L.	Inside Spread	Tip to Tip Spread	Length of Prong R.	Length of Prong L.	Locality Killed	By Whom Killed	Owner	Date Killed	Rank
87 2/8*	16 6/8	16 6/8	7 5/8	7 5/8	2 6/8	2 6/8	12 6/8	9	5 4/8	6 1/8	Sweetwater Co., Wyo.	Stanley L. Ackerman	Stanley L. Ackerman	SE 1980	1
87*	16 7/8	16 4/8	7 5/8	7 5/8	2 2/8	2 3/8	14 5/8	10 5/8	6 2/8	6	Fremont Co., Wyo.	Ronald K. Morrison	Ronald K. Morrison	SE 1980	2
86 6/8	17	17 1/8	7	6 7/8	3 1/8	3 1/8	14	9 1/8	5 5/8	5 6/8	Humboldt Co., Nev.	Rebecca J. Hall	Rebecca J. Hall	AG 1981	3
86 6/8	17 3/8	17 1/8	7	6 6/8	2 6/8	2 7/8	10 2/8	6 5/8	5 4/8	5 2/8	Coconino Co., Ariz.	Ralph C. Stayner	Ralph C. Stayner	SE 1980	3
86 4/8	17 2/8	17 4/8	7 2/8	7 2/8	2 6/8	3	9	6 6/8	4 1/8	5 3/8	Sweetwater Co., Wyo.	Richard E. Hueckstaedt	Richard E. Hueckstaedt	SE 1982	5
86 4/8	17	16 7/8	7 4/8	7 6/8	2 6/8	2 5/8	11	6 7/8	6	5 6/8	Sweetwater Co., Wyo.	Rex A. Behrends	Rex A. Behrends	SE 1980	5
86 4/8	18	17 5/8	6 4/8	6 4/8	2 7/8	3	10 4/8	6 4/8	5 3/8	6	Navajo Co., Ariz.	John D. Higginbotham	John D. Higginbotham	SE 1979	5
86 2/8	16 5/8	17	7 5/8	7 2/8	2 7/8	3 2/8	14 3/8	8 1/8	5 2/8	5 1/8	El Paso Co., Colo.	Maurice Cutting	Maurice Cutting	SE 1981	8
86 2/8	17 4/8	17 1/8	7 5/8	6 6/8	2 5/8	2 4/8	7 5/8	5	6 1/8	6 3/8	Sweetwater Co., Wyo.	J. Robert Tigner	J. Robert Tigner	SE 1980	8
86	17	17 3/8	7 1/8	7 1/8	2 3/8	2 4/8	10 1/8	4 2/8	6 5/8	6 4/8	Sweetwater Co., Wyo.	F. A. Oliver	F. A. Oliver	SE 1981	10
85 6/8	16 1/8	16	7	7 1/8	2 5/8	2 6/8	11 2/8	8 7/8	6 2/8	6 1/8	Natrona Co., Wyo.	Terrie Lynne Morrison	Terrie Lynne Morrison	SE 1980	11
85 6/8	15 4/8	15 5/8	7 3/8	7 4/8	2 6/8	2 6/8	7 4/8	3	5 5/8	5 6/8	Carbon Co., Wyo.	James M. Jagusch	James M. Jagusch	SE 1981	11
85 6/8	15 7/8	16	6 7/8	6 7/8	2 7/8	2 7/8	9 4/8	4 3/8	5 4/8	5 5/8	Sweetwater Co., Wyo.	Mark E. Nedrow	Mark E. Nedrow	AG 1981	11
85 4/8	17 2/8	17 3/8	6 6/8	6 3/8	2 7/8	2 7/8	11 4/8	9 4/8	6 7/8	6 2/8	Mora Co., N. M.	Roger B. Heemeier	Roger B. Heemeier	AG 1982	14
85 4/8	16	16	6 7/8	7	2 5/8	2 6/8	7 3/8	3 3/8	6 5/8	6 4/8	Stillwater Co., Wyo.	Lee Frudden	Lee Frudden	SE 1982	14
85 4/8	16 4/8	17 1/8	7	6 7/8	2 6/8	3	13	9 3/8	5 5/8	5 7/8	Fremont Co., Wyo.	Jerry A. Martin	Jerry A. Martin	SE 1982	14
85 4/8	17 2/8	17 1/8	6 4/8	6 3/8	2 5/8	2 5/8	15 1/8	11 1/8	6 1/8	6	Washoe Co., Nev.	Maryanne Robinson	Melbourne & Maryanne Robinson	AG 1981	14
85 2/8	17 4/8	17 3/8	6 1/8	6 1/8	2 6/8	2 7/8	9 3/8	6 5/8	5 4/8	5 7/8	Natrona Co., Wyo.	Margery H. T. Torrey	Margery H. T. Torrey	SE 1981	18
85 2/8	16	15 5/8	6 4/8	6 5/8	2 6/8	2 7/8	12	8 4/8	6	6 2/8	Fremont Co., Wyo.	Richard A. Fruchey	Richard A. Fruchey	SE 1981	18
85 2/8	17 7/8	17 6/8	7 5/8	7 4/8	2 3/8	2 3/8	13 6/8	8 1/8	5 1/8	4 6/8	Lake Co., Oreg.	Rodger D. Bates	Rodger D. Bates	AG 1980	18
85 2/8	15 4/8	15 6/8	7 6/8	7 3/8	3 2/8	2 7/8	8	4 1/8	5 7/8	5 6/8	Baker Co., Oreg.	Eldon L. Buckner	Eldon L. Buckner	AG 1981	18

85	16 5/8	16 6/8	6 4/8	6 4/8	2 7/8	2 6/8	10 2/8	5 2/8	5 6/8	5 6/8	Lincoln Co., Wyo.	Ross M. Wilde	Ross M. Wilde	SE 1980	22
84 6/8	14 1/8	14 1/8	7 3/8	7 3/8	3 3/8	3 2/8	9 2/8	7 4/8	5	5 1/8	Fremont Co., Wyo.	James E. Egger	James E. Egger	SE 1981	23
84 6/8	16 6/8	16 5/8	6 1/8	6 1/8	2 5/8	2 6/8	9 7/8	5	6 3/8	6 1/8	Modoc Co., Calif.	Earnest Anacleto	Earnest Anacleto	AG 1980	23
84 6/8	16 4/8	16 4/8	6 2/8	6 2/8	3	3	13 6/8	11 4/8	4 4/8	4 4/8	Lincoln Co., N. M.	Pat McCarty	Pat McCarty	SE 1980	23
84 6/8	17 1/8	17 4/8	6 2/8	6 4/8	2 6/8	2 6/8	10	5	5 1/8	5 2/8	Washoe Co., Nev.	Lloyd B. Miller	Lloyd B. Miller	SE 1980	23
84 6/8	16 4/8	16 5/8	6 4/8	6 5/8	2 5/8	2 6/8	9 6/8	4 4/8	6 4/8	6 4/8	Yavapai Co., Ariz.	Randy Modisett	Randy Modisett	SE 1974	23
84 6/8	16 2/8	16 3/8	6 4/8	6 3/8	2 5/8	2 6/8	11 1/8	8 3/8	6 5/8	6 2/8	Baker Co., Oreg.	Martin Vavra	Martin Vavra	AG 1980	23
84 6/8	15 4/8	15 6/8	6 3/8	6 3/8	2 7/8	2 6/8	8 5/8	3 2/8	6 5/8	6 4/8	Natrona Co., Wyo.	W. Bruce Mouw	W. Bruce Mouw	AG 1980	23
84 4/8	15	15 3/8	7 5/8	7 2/8	2 6/8	2 6/8	6 5/8	4 6/8	6 6/8	5 6/8	Carbon Co., Wyo.	Stephen C. LeBlanc	Stephen C. LeBlanc	SE 1976	30
84 4/8	17 2/8	17	6 5/8	6 5/8	3	2 7/8	8 3/8	4 1/8	5 5/8	6	Sweetwater Co., Wyo.	Lee Frudden	Lee Frudden	SE 1981	30
84 2/8	15 5/8	16 1/8	6 2/8	6 2/8	2 7/8	3 1/8	9 1/8	5 2/8	6 2/8	6 7/8	Modoc Co., Calif.	Larry A. Owens, Sr.	Larry A. Owens, Sr.	SE 1981	32
84 2/8	17 2/8	17 4/8	6 3/8	6 2/8	2 6/8	2 6/8	14 6/8	10 4/8	6 1/8	6	Powder River Co., Mont.	Sam C. Borla	Sam C. Borla	OT 1982	32
84 2/8	16	15 6/8	6 6/8	6 6/8	2 4/8	2 4/8	10	5 2/8	5 5/8	5 6/8	Carbon Co., Wyo.	Ernest L. Tollini	Ernest L. Tollini	SE 1982	32
84 2/8	17	16 6/8	6 4/8	6 3/8	2 5/8	2 4/8	12 2/8	8 4/8	6	6 1/8	Coconino Co., Ariz.	Michael A. Cromer	Michael A. Cromer	OT 1982	32
84 2/8	15 5/8	15 6/8	7	6 7/8	2 4/8	2 4/8	6 4/8	2	6 6/8	6 6/8	Humboldt Co., Nev.	James R. Puryear	James R. Puryear	AG 1980	32
84 2/8	17	17 3/8	6 6/8	6 5/8	2 6/8	2 7/8	12 2/8	10 2/8	5 4/8	5 6/8	Sweetwater Co., Wyo.	John Victor Wilgus	John Victor Wilgus	SE 1980	32
84 2/8	15 4/8	15 2/8	7 4/8	7 4/8	2 5/8	2 5/8	12 3/8	8	6 2/8	6 2/8	Fremont Co., Wyo.	William D. Baldwin	William D. Baldwin	SE 1980	32
84 2/8	16 4/8	16 2/8	6 7/8	6 6/8	2 4/8	2 6/8	13 7/8	10 3/8	6	6	Malheur Co., Oreg.	Matt J. Brundridge	Matt J. Brundridge	AG 1982	32
84	14 7/8	14 5/8	7 6/8	7 3/8	3	3	11 1/8	10	6 3/8	6	Natrona Co., Wyo.	Bill E. Boatman	Bill E. Boatman	SE 1980	40
84	16	15 4/8	7	7	2 7/8	2 5/8	12 6/8	9 1/8	6 2/8	6 3/8	Carbon Co., Wyo.	Dudley R. Elmgren	Dudley R. Elmgren	SE 1982	40
84	16 7/8	16 4/8	6 6/8	6 6/8	2 5/8	2 4/8	10 6/8	6	6 1/8	6	Sweetwater Co., Wyo.	Lorio Verzasconi	Lorio Verzasconi	SE 1982	40
84	16	15 6/8	6 3/8	6 3/8	2 4/8	2 3/8	14 2/8	12 6/8	5	4 6/8	Blaine Co., Idaho	Charles R. Hisaw	Charles R. Hisaw	OT 1981	40
84	15 2/8	15 7/8	7 2/8	7 1/8	2 4/8	2 4/8	15 3/8	13 6/8	6 2/8	6 2/8	Fremont Co., Wyo.	Victor M. McCullough	Victor M. McCullough	SE 1981	40
84	16 1/8	16 4/8	6 7/8	6 6/8	2 5/8	2 7/8	11 2/8	5 7/8	6 4/8	5 6/8	Fremont Co., Wyo.	Joel E. Hensley	Joel E. Hensley	SE 1981	40
84	17 6/8	17 4/8	6 2/8	6 1/8	2 6/8	2 5/8	6	5 3/8	6	5 3/8	Washoe Co., Nev.	Jamie L. Kent	Jamie L. Kent	AG 1980	40
84	17 6/8	17 5/8	6 1/8	6 2/8	2 7/8	2 7/8	13 6/8	8 2/8	5	4 7/8	Yavapai Co., Ariz.	James O. Pierce	James O. Pierce	SE 1980	40
83 6/8	17 2/8	16 3/8	6 5/8	6 6/8	2 5/8	2 3/8	7 1/8	2 5/8	6 4/8	6 1/8	Natrona Co., Wyo.	Ronald Kim Morrison	Ronald Kim Morrison	SE 1982	48
83 6/8	16 6/8	17 4/8	6 4/8	6 3/8	2 5/8	2 6/8	11 6/8	7 7/8	6 3/8	6 1/8	Wamsutter, Wyo.	James A. White	James A. White	SE 1980	48
83 6/8	15	15 1/8	6 7/8	6 6/8	2 6/8	2 7/8	10 2/8	6 6/8	6 6/8	6 2/8	Big Horn Co., Mont.	Michael Ferri	Michael Ferri	OT 1982	48
83 6/8	16	16	6 4/8	6 4/8	3 2/8	3 3/8	13	9 6/8	5 6/8	5 4/8	Sheridan Co., Wyo.	John T. Yarrington	John T. Yarrington	SE 1951	48
83 6/8	14 7/8	15 2/8	6 2/8	6 3/8	2 6/8	3	6 5/8	3 1/8	5	4 5/8	Washoe Co., Nev.	Robert A. Colon	Robert A. Colon	SE 1982	48
83 4/8	16 6/8	16 6/8	6 4/8	6 4/8	2 5/8	2 4/8	11 4/8	5 6/8	5 4/8	5 4/8	Custer Co., Idaho	Wayne L. Coleman	Wayne L. Coleman	OT 1981	53
83 4/8	16 7/8	17	6 6/8	6 5/8	2 6/8	2 7/8	10 3/8	4 6/8	5	5 1/8	Harding Co., S. D.	John R. Simpson	John R. Simpson	OT 1981	53
83 4/8	16 4/8	16 6/8	6 4/8	6 3/8	2 3/8	2 3/8	10 1/8	2 7/8	6 4/8	6 2/8	Prairie Co., Mont.	L. H. Lindquist	L. H. Lindquist	OT 1982	53
83 4/8	17 4/8	17	6 5/8	7 4/8	2 6/8	2 5/8	9 4/8	4 6/8	5	5 2/8	Colfax Co., N. M.	James H. Hoffman	James H. Hoffman	AG 1982	53
83 4/8	14 6/8	14 7/8	6 3/8	6 3/8	2 3/8	2 2/8	9	3 5/8	7 3/8	7 4/8	Lake Co., Oreg.	Thomas A. Jones	Thomas A. Jones	AG 1980	53
83 3/8	15 3/8	15 3/8	7 2/8	7 2/8	2 4/8	2 4/8	16 2/8	13 4/8	6	5 7/8	Sweetwater Co., Wyo.	Richard D. Ullery	Richard D. Ullery	SE 1980	58

Pronghorn—*Continued*

Antilocapra americana americana and related subspecies

Score	Length of Horn R.	Length of Horn L.	Circumference of Base R.	Circumference of Base L.	Circumference at Third Quarter R.	Circumference at Third Quarter L.	Inside Spread	Tip to Tip Spread	Length of Prong R.	Length of Prong L.	Locality Killed	By Whom Killed	Owner	Date Killed	Rank
83 2/8	17 4/8	17 3/8	6 2/8	6 2/8	3	2 7/8	8	2 4/8	5 1/8	4 6/8	Campbell Co., Wyo.	Dwayne A. Anderson	Dwayne A. Anderson	OT 1982	59
83 2/8	15 1/8	15 2/8	6 7/8	6 4/8	2 6/8	2 6/8	9 5/8	6 7/8	6	5 7/8	Natrona Co., Wyo.	Andy Van Patten	Andy Van Patten	SE 1981	59
83 2/8	16 2/8	16 2/8	6 6/8	6 6/8	3	2 7/8	8 5/8	5 2/8	5 2/8	5 2/8	Musselshell Co., Mont.	Caroll M. Lumpkin, Jr.	Caroll M. Lumpkin, Jr.	OT 1980	59
83 2/8	17 2/8	16 4/8	6 4/8	6 4/8	3 1/8	2 4/8	7 2/8	2 2/8	5 3/8	6	Fremont Co., Wyo.	Benjamin T. Tonn	Benjamin T. Tonn	SE 1981	59
83 2/8	16 3/8	16 6/8	7 5/8	7 4/8	2 4/8	2 5/8	12 2/8	7 3/8	5 2/8	5 3/8	Harney Co., Oreg.	Gary L. Wilfert	Gary L. Wilfert	AG 1981	59
83 2/8	16	16	7	7	2 7/8	3	10 1/8	5 5/8	5	6 2/8	Natrona Co., Wyo.	Bill E. Boatman	Bill E. Boatman	SE 1981	59
83 2/8	17 1/8	17 2/8	6 2/8	6 2/8	2 6/8	2 5/8	16 1/8	13	4 6/8	4 7/8	Roosevelt Co., N. M.	Danny L. Tivis	Danny L. Tivis	SE 1979	59
83 2/8	17 5/8	17 7/8	6 5/8	6 4/8	2 6/8	2 6/8	15	9 1/8	4 2/8	4 7/8	Humboldt Co., Nev.	Robert E. Stopper	Robert E. Stopper	AG 1979	59
83 2/8	16 3/8	16 2/8	6 4/8	6 4/8	2 5/8	2 5/8	12 1/8	7 2/8	6	6 1/8	Beaverhead Co., Mont.	Scott Withers	Scott Withers	SE 1980	59
83 2/8	16 3/8	16 1/8	7 2/8	6 7/8	2 7/8	2 6/8	10 7/8	4 6/8	4 6/8	4	Socorro Co., N. M.	Charles M. McLaughlin	Charles M. McLaughlin	SE 1979	59
83	16 2/8	16 1/8	6 6/8	6 5/8	2 5/8	2 5/8	11 6/8	10 7/8	5 7/8	5 4/8	Harding Co., N. M.	Stephen C. LeBlanc	Stephen C. LeBlanc	SE 1977	69
83	15 4/8	15 4/8	6 3/8	6 3/8	3 1/8	3 1/8	7 7/8	4 7/8	5 2/8	5 4/8	Campbell Co., Wyo.	Richard S. Alford	Richard S. Alford	OT 1982	69
83	15 6/8	15 6/8	7 3/8	7 3/8	2 4/8	2 4/8	8 1/8	1 7/8	5 6/8	5 6/8	Sweetwater Co., Wyo.	Keith Penner	Keith Penner	AG 1980	69
83	15 7/8	15 5/8	6 4/8	6 4/8	2 6/8	2 5/8	10 1/8	8 5/8	5 7/8	5 7/8	Lake Co., Oreg.	Jerry J. Peacore	Jerry J. Peacore	AG 1980	69
83	16	16 2/8	7 5/8	7 5/8	2 3/8	2 5/8	14 5/8	10 5/8	5 3/8	5 4/8	Sweetwater Co., Wyo.	Glen W. Coates	Glen W. Coates	SE 1979	69
83	15 6/8	15 6/8	6 6/8	6 6/8	2 5/8	2 6/8	9	4 4/8	5 5/8	5 3/8	Albany Co., Wyo.	Mark T. Gleason	Mark T. Gleason	OT 1982	69
83	15 7/8	15 7/8	6 7/8	7	2 5/8	2 5/8	8 6/8	6 1/8	5 2/8	5 4/8	Washoe Co., Nev.	Richard J. Depaoli	Richard J. Depaoli	AG 1982	69
83	16 1/8	16 4/8	6 4/8	6 4/8	2 7/8	3	15	14 2/8	5 2/8	5 3/8	Washington Co., Colo.	Gina R. Cass	Gina R. Cass	SE 1979	69
83	16	16 3/8	5 5/8	5 5/8	3 1/8	3 2/8	8 1/8	1 2/8	4	4 2/8	Hudspeth Co., Texas	Charles E. Davis	Charles E. Davis	OT 1980	69
83	16 2/8	16 3/8	6 3/8	6 4/8	2 6/8	2 6/8	11 1/8	7 5/8	5 3/8	5 1/8	Custer Co., S. D.	Edward J. Schauer	Edward J. Schauer	OT 1979	69
82 6/8	16 1/8	16 1/8	7 4/8	7 3/8	2 4/8	2 4/8	8 7/8	2 1/8	5 2/8	5 2/8	Natrona Co., Wyo.	Bill E. Boatman	Bill E. Boatman	SE 1982	79
82 6/8	15 4/8	15 4/8	6 3/8	6 1/8	3 5/8	2 7/8	9 2/8	4 6/8	5	4 5/8	Carbon Co., Wyo.	Roger D. George	Roger D. George	SE 1975	79
82 6/8	15 3/8	15 4/8	6 6/8	6 6/8	2 6/8	2 6/8	12	9	5 6/8	6 1/8	Carter Co., Mont.	Lloyd R. Norvell	Lloyd R. Norvell	OT 1982	79
82 6/8	15 6/8	15 7/8	6 4/8	6 5/8	2 7/8	2 7/8	8	5 3/8	5 5/8	5 6/8	Hudspeth Co., Texas	L. A. Grelling	L. A. Grelling	OT 1980	79
82 6/8	15 6/8	15 3/8	6 5/8	6 5/8	2 6/8	2 6/8	10 5/8	8 2/8	6 5/8	6 1/8	Carbon Co., Wyo.	Robert J. Smith	Robert J. Smith	SE 1980	79
82 4/8	15 1/8	15 1/8	6 2/8	6 2/8	3	3	10 2/8	8 2/8	6	6 1/8	Socorro Co., N. M.	Clyde C. Brumley	Clyde C. Brumley	OT 1981	84
82 4/8	17	16 6/8	6 3/8	6 4/8	2 4/8	2 4/8	9 2/8	3 3/8	5 4/8	5 4/8	Sweetwater Co., Wyo.	Donald R. Williamson	Donald R. Williamson	AG 1981	84
82 4/8	14 7/8	14 6/8	6 7/8	7 2/8	2 6/8	2 5/8	9 7/8	6 6/8	6 3/8	6 4/8	Campbell Co., Wyo.	Larry L. Helgerson	Larry L. Helgerson	OT 1981	84

82 4/8	15 3/8	15 2/8	6 5/8	6 3/8	3	2 6/8	8 7/8	4 6/8	6 4/8	6 2/8	Moffat Co., Colo.	Charles W. Klaassens	Charles W. Klaassens	SE 1981	84
82 4/8	15 7/8	16 2/8	6 1/8	6 3/8	2 4/8	2 5/8	14 6/8	9 7/8	6 1/8	6 2/8	White Pine Co., Nev.	Tom I. Papagna, Jr.	Tom I. Papagna, Jr.	AG 1980	84
82 4/8	15 1/8	15 2/8	6 6/8	6 6/8	2 4/8	2 4/8	12 1/8	10 3/8	6 1/8	6 3/8	Carbon Co., Wyo.	Barry L. Alger	Barry L. Alger	SE 1980	84
82 4/8	15 4/8	15 5/8	6 6/8	6 4/8	2 5/8	2 5/8	9 4/8	4 5/8	5 3/8	5 3/8	Millard Co., Utah	William Randall Houston	William Randall Houston	SE 1979	84
82 4/8	16 6/8	16 6/8	6 3/8	6 3/8	3	3	10 6/8	5 4/8	5	5 4/8	Union Co., N. M.	John W. Saunders	John W. Saunders	AG 1982	84
82 2/8	16	15 6/8	6 2/8	6 1/8	3	3	13 2/8	10	6	5 4/8	Morgan Co., Colo.	Kenneth Lee Kelly	Kenneth Lee Kelly	SE 1977	92
82 2/8	17	16 6/8	6 5/8	6 4/8	2 6/8	2 4/8	8 4/8	5 6/8	4 7/8	4 7/8	Valley Co., Mont.	David D. Rittenhouse	David D. Rittenhouse	OT 1982	92
82 2/8	15 5/8	15 4/8	6 5/8	6 5/8	2 6/8	2 7/8	10 2/8	4 3/8	5 5/8	5 6/8	Butte Co., Idaho	Jon L. Wadkins	Jon L. Wadkins	OT 1981	92
82 2/8	15 1/8	15	6 6/8	6 7/8	2 5/8	2 6/8	9 5/8	7	6 4/8	6 2/8	Lake Co., Oreg.	Richard R. Delfs	Richard R. Delfs	AG 1981	92
82 2/8	14 5/8	14 7/8	6 5/8	6 6/8	2 4/8	2 4/8	9 5/8	6 2/8	6 5/8	6 2/8	Stillwater Co., Wyo.	Gregg R. Landrum	Gregg R. Landrum	SE 1982	92
82 2/8	17 3/8	17 4/8	6 2/8	6 3/8	2 3/8	2 4/8	14 5/8	11 7/8	5 3/8	5 4/8	Niobrara Co., Wyo.	W. L. McMillan	W. L. McMillan	OT 1981	92
82	14 1/8	14	7 2/8	7 1/8	2 5/8	2 5/8	10 6/8	7 5/8	6 2/8	6 1/8	Sweetwater Co., Wyo.	Brett A. Ward	Brett A. Ward	SE 1982	98
82	15 5/8	15 3/8	6 2/8	6 2/8	2 6/8	2 5/8	10 4/8	6 3/8	6 2/8	6 4/8	Fremont Co., Wyo.	Thomas O. Martens	Thomas O. Martens	SE 1982	98
82	16 1/8	16	7	6 7/8	2 6/8	2 5/8	9	2 1/8	5 2/8	4 6/8	Fremont Co., Wyo.	Steven E. Clingman	Steven E. Clingman	SE 1980	98
82	16 3/8	16 2/8	6 3/8	6 4/8	2 6/8	2 5/8	9 6/8	3 5/8	5 5/8	5 5/8	Coconino Co., Ariz.	Fred W. Fernow, Jr.	Fred W. Fernow, Jr.	AG 1981	98
82	15 3/8	15 2/8	6 7/8	6 7/8	2 6/8	2 5/8	15 5/8	14 5/8	5 5/8	5 7/8	Carbon Co., Wyo.	Jerry G. Hagen	Jerry G. Hagen	SE 1980	98
82	15 7/8	15 3/8	7 2/8	7 1/8	2 7/8	2 6/8	16 1/8	14 1/8	6 2/8	5 3/8	Natrona Co., Wyo.	Wade Dumont	Wade Dumont	SE 1981	98
82	16 6/8	16 5/8	6 3/8	6 2/8	2 2/8	2 2/8	15	11 5/8	5 5/8	5 2/8	Natrona Co., Wyo.	Theresa Fulfaro	Theresa Fulfaro	SE 1980	98
82	16 1/8	16 1/8	6 5/8	6 4/8	2 6/8	2 6/8	12 6/8	7 3/8	5 5/8	5 5/8	Lassen Co., Calif.	Robert D. Luna, Jr.	Robert D. Luna, Jr.	AG 1979	98
82	17	17	6 4/8	6 3/8	2 5/8	2 4/8	8 6/8	6 4/8	4 6/8	5 1/8	Brewster Co., Texas	Peggy F. Brady	Peggy F. Brady	SE 1979	98
82	15 6/8	15 6/8	7	7	2 6/8	2 6/8	8 4/8	2 6/8	5 2/8	5 2/8	Crook Co., Wyo.	Jay Dee Hacklin	Jay Dee Hacklin	OT 1982	98
82	16 2/8	16 1/8	6 6/8	6 6/8	2 5/8	2 5/8	12	8 3/8	5 2/8	5 1/8	Natrona Co., Wyo.	Joseph P. Prinzi	Joseph P. Prinzi	AG 1982	98

*Final Score subject to revision by additional verifying measurements.

Bison

Minimum Score 115 — ***Bison bison bison* and *Bison bison athabascae*** — **World's Record 136 4/8**

Beginning in 1977, hunter taken trophies from the lower 48 states are acceptable only for records, not awards, and only from states that recognize bison as wild and free-ranging and for which a hunting license and/or big game tag is required for hunting.

Score	Length of Horn R.	Length of Horn L.	Circumference of Base R.	Circumference of Base L.	Circumference at Third Quarter R.	Circumference at Third Quarter L.	Greatest Spread	Tip to Tip Spread	Sex	Locality Killed	By Whom Killed	Owner	Date Killed	Rank
127	18 7/8	19	15 4/8	15 6/8	6 7/8	7 1/8	26 3/8	23 5/8	M	Custer Co., S. D.	Henry E. McLemore	Henry E. McLemore	DC 1980	1
125	19 7/8	20	14 4/8	14 4/8	6 1/8	6	28	20 3/8	M	Man.	Unknown	James Fredrick	1928	2
121 2/8	18 1/8	18 4/8	15	15 1/8	5 5/8	6	28 4/8	21 4/8	M	Custer Co., S. D.	Robert L. Trupe	Robert L. Trupe	DC 1979	3
119 4/8	18	17 3/8	16 1/8	15 6/8	5 4/8	5 5/8	30 6/8	24 5/8	M	Coconino Co., Ariz.	Dorothy B. Gilliam	Dorothy B. Gilliam	NO 1980	4
118 6/8	17 7/8	17 5/8	15 6/8	16	5 4/8	5 5/8	30 4/8	24 7/8	M	Custer Co., S. D.	Joel J. Torgerson	Joel J. Torgerson	DC 1981	5
117	19 6/8	20 2/8	14 6/8	14 5/8	4 4/8	4 5/8	30 4/8	24 3/8	M	Donnelly Dome, Alaska	Debra S. Darland	Debra S. Darland	OT 1981	6
117	19 5/8	19 7/8	14	14 2/8	5	5	29 4/8	26 4/8	M	Farewell, Alaska	Kevin G. Meyer	Kevin G. Meyer	SE 1982	6
115 4/8	19 4/8	20	13 4/8	13 2/8	5	5 2/8	29 6/8	22 6/8	M	Chitna River, Alaska	Ronald A. Sturgeon	Ronald A. Sturgeon	SE 1979	8

* Final Score subject to revision by additional verifying measurements.

Rocky Mountain Goat

Oreamnos americanus americanus and related subspecies

Minimum Score 50 | **World's Record 56 6/8**

Score	Length of Horn R.	Length of Horn L.	Circumference of Base R.	Circumference of Base L.	Circumference at Third Quarter R.	Circumference at Third Quarter L.	Greatest Spread	Tip to Tip Spread	Sex	Locality Killed	By Whom Killed	Owner	Date Killed	Rank
54 6/8*	10 4/8	10	6 1/8	6 1/8	2 2/8	2 2/8	6 6/8	5 7/8	M	Cleveland Pen., Alaska	Lana L. DeLong	Roger DeLong	OT 1979	1
54 4/8*	10 3/8	10 4/8	5 4/8	5 4/8	2 3/8	2 3/8	8	8 1/8	M	McCarthy Creek, Alaska	George A. Morelock	George A. Morelock	SE 1981	2
53 4/8	10 6/8	10 3/8	6 2/8	6 2/8	2	2	7	5 2/8	M	Mt. Horetzky, B. C.	Jackie O. Arnold	Jackie O. Arnold	SE 1980	3
53 2/8	11 2/8	11 5/8	5 4/8	5 4/8	1 7/8	2	7	6 1/8	M	Halfmoon Lake, Alaska	Robert A. Hewitt	Robert A. Hewitt	OT 1980	4
52 6/8	10 4/8	10 2/8	5 6/8	5 7/8	2	2	8 2/8	7 4/8	M	Cassiar Mts., B. C.	H. Scott Whyel	H. Scott Whyel	AG 1981	5
52 2/8	10 4/8	10 4/8	5 6/8	5 6/8	2	2	7 3/8	7	M	Lewis & Clark Co., Mont.	Charles N. Johns	Charles N. Johns	NO 1981	6
52 2/8	10 2/8	10 4/8	6	6 1/8	1 6/8	1 7/8	7	6 2/8	M	Chelan Co., Wash.	Nat Steele	Nat Steele	SE 1980	6
52	10 4/8	10 6/8	6 2/8	6 2/8	1 6/8	1 7/8	6 3/8	5 7/8	M	Mt. Saint Elias, Alaska	Terry L. Friske	Terry L. Friske	OT 1980	8
52	12 1/8	11 6/8	5 3/8	5 3/8	1 7/8	1 7/8	8 1/8	7 5/8	M	Horn Cliffs, Alaska	Jack W. McKernan	Jack W. McKernan	NO 1981	8
51 6/8	9 7/8	10 5/8	5 4/8	5 4/8	2 1/8	2 2/8	6 4/8	5 5/8	M	Snohomish Co., Wash.	Michael J. Simon	John M. Mitchell	NO 1981	10
51 6/8	10 3/8	10 3/8	5 7/8	5 6/8	1 6/8	1 6/8	6 5/8	5 4/8	M	Kaza Lake, B. C.	John C. Priebe & William A. Bolles	John C. Priebe & William A. Bolles	OT 1980	10
51 6/8	10 2/8	10 1/8	6	5 7/8	2	2	7 7/8	7 2/8	M	Behm Canal, Alaska	Michael L. Ward	Michael L. Ward	OT 1980	10
51 6/8	10 3/8	10 4/8	5 6/8	5 7/8	2	2	6 6/8	5 4/8	M	Mt. Carthew, B. C.	Harry McCowan	Harry McCowan	AG 1980	10
51 4/8	10 1/8	10 1/8	5 7/8	5 6/8	1 7/8	1 7/8	7 4/8	6 5/8	M	Halfmoon Lake, Alaska	Kurt W. Kuehl	Kurt W. Kuehl	OT 1982	14
51 4/8	10 2/8	10 4/8	6 1/8	6 1/8	1 7/8	1 7/8	8 1/8	7 5/8	M	Mont.	Unknown	James Fredrick	PR 1981	14
51 4/8	9 7/8	9 7/8	6	6	2	2	8 5/8	8 1/8	M	Telegraph Creek, B. C.	Casey G. Terry	Casey G. Terry	AG 1979	14
51 2/8	10 4/8	10 2/8	5 5/8	5 5/8	2	2	7	8 1/8	M	Duti Lake, B. C.	T. J. Tucker	T. J. Tucker	SE 1981	17
51 2/8	9 6/8	9 6/8	6 1/8	6 1/8	1 6/8	1 6/8	8 2/8	7 5/8	M	Swan Lake, B. C.	John Dobish	John Dobish	AG 1981	17
51 2/8	10 6/8	10 7/8	5 6/8	5 5/8	1 6/8	1 6/8	7 3/8	6 5/8	M	Chilkat Mt., Alaska	Terry L. Friske	Terry L. Friske	OT 1980	17
51 2/8	10 6/8	10 6/8	5 4/8	5 3/8	2	2	8 3/8	7 7/8	M	Kittitas Co., Wash.	Michael W. Duby	Michael W. Duby	OT 1980	17
51	10 4/8	10 4/8	5 6/8	5 6/8	1 7/8	1 7/8	7 2/8	5 7/8	M	Tahtsa Lake, B. C.	Vernon J. Boose	Vernon J. Boose	SE 1981	21
51	10 3/8	10 6/8	5 7/8	6	1 6/8	1 7/8			M	Ravalli Co., Mont.	John K. Frederikson	John K. Frederikson	NO 1979	21
50 6/8	10 3/8	10 2/8	5 5/8	5 6/8	1 7/8	1 7/8	7 6/8	7 2/8	M	Johnston Lake, B. C.	Brian A. Halina	Brian A. Halina	OT 1979	23
50 4/8	10 4/8	10 4/8	5 5/8	5 5/8	1 6/8	1 6/8	6 7/8	5 7/8	M	Bingay Creek, B. C.	C. P. Podrasky	C. P. Podrasky	OT 1981	24
50	10 1/8	10 2/8	5 5/8	5 6/8	1 6/8	1 7/8	7 4/8	6 6/8	M	Skeena Mts., B. C.	Dee J. Burnett	Dee J. Burnett	SE 1982	25
50	9 6/8	9 7/8	5 6/8	5 5/8	1 7/8	1 7/8	6 4/8	6	M	Rudyerd Bay, Alaska	Gerry D. Downey	Gerry D. Downey	NO 1975	25

*Final Score subject to revision by additional verifying measurements.

Muskox

Minimum Score 90 — ***Ovibos moschatus moschatus* and certain related subspecies** — **World's Record 122**

Score	Length of Horn R.	Length of Horn L.	Width of Boss R.	Width of Boss L.	Circumference at Third Quarter R.	Circumference at Third Quarter L.	Tip to Tip Spread	Greatest Spread	Sex	Locality Killed	By Whom Killed	Owner	Date Killed	Rank
118 4/8*	24 5/8	26	15 3/8	15	4 7/8	5 2/8	23 4/8	27 3/8	M	Sachs Harbour, N. W. T.	Albert D. Seeno, Jr.	Albert D. Seeno, Jr.	MR 1982	1
114 6/8*	27 1/8	27 2/8	10 4/8	11	5 2/8	5 2/8	29 1/8	29 5/8	M	Victoria Island, N. W. T.	Jimmy Memogana	Terry Pellow	MR 1977	2
113 4/8*	30 5/8	28 7/8	9 2/8	9 4/8	5	3 7/8	26 2/8	27 1/8	M	Banks Island, N. W. T.	Norman F. Taylor	Norman F. Taylor	MR 1981	3
113 2/8*	26 6/8	26 7/8	9 7/8	10 1/8	4 7/8	5 1/8	26 1/8	28	M	Swan Lake, N. W. T.	Basil C. Bradbury	Basil C. Bradbury	MR 1982	4
110	26 2/8	26 6/8	8 6/8	9 1/8	4 6/8	5 4/8	26 4/8	28	M	Banks Island, N. W. T.	Billy Ellis, III	Billy Ellis, III	OT 1982	5
109 4/8	25	26 5/8	9 4/8	9 4/8	4 6/8	5 7/8	25 6/8	27	M	Banks Island, N. W. T.	James M. Domokos	James M. Domokos	MR 1981	6
108 6/8	26 7/8	27 2/8	9 2/8	8 7/8	4 5/8	4 6/8	21 7/8	24 5/8	M	Banks Island, N. W. T.	Toby J. Johnson	Toby J. Johnson	MR 1981	7
108 6/8	25 1/8	25 1/8	10 1/8	10	5	5	27 3/8	28 5/8	M	Banks Island, N. W. T.	William M. Wheless, III	William M. Wheless, III	OT 1980	7
108 4/8	27	26 3/8	9 2/8	9 4/8	4 5/8	4 6/8	23 6/8	25 5/8	M	Banks Island, N. W. T.	James W. Owens	James W. Owens	MR 1981	9
108 4/8	25 4/8	26 3/8	9 7/8	10 2/8	4 4/8	5 6/8	26 6/8	27 6/8	M	Banks Island, N. W. T.	Herman A. Bennett	Herman A. Bennett	MR 1982	9
108	30 1/8	30 4/8	7 4/8	7 4/8	4 2/8	5 6/8	23 4/8	25 3/8	M	Cape Mendenhall, Alaska	Donald E. Franklin	Donald E. Franklin	FE 1978	11
107 2/8	28 7/8	27 5/8	8 6/8	8 4/8	4 5/8	4 6/8	23 3/8	24 7/8	M	Banks Island, N. W. T.	Picked Up	Toby J. Johnson	PU 1981	12
107	26 1/8	24 7/8	9 7/8	10 1/8	5 5/8	4 2/8	22 7/8	24 6/8	M	Holman Island, N. W. T.	I. D. Shapiro	I. D. Shapiro	MR 1982	13
107	24 3/8	25	9	9 4/8	5 4/8	5 2/8	23 5/8	24 6/8	M	Delesse Lake, N. W. T.	Franco Mazzucchelli	Franco Mazzucchelli	MR 1981	13
104 6/8	24 1/8	25 5/8	9 3/8	9 2/8	4 2/8	5 1/8	22 4/8	25	M	Sachs Harbour, N. W. T.	Michel Laurent	Michel Laurent	MR 1982	15
104 2/8	25 4/8	25 4/8	9 2/8	9 3/8	4 6/8	4 4/8	21 7/8	26 1/8	M	Banks Island, N. W. T.	Lawrence T. Keenan	Lawrence T. Keenan	MR 1981	16
104	23 4/8	23 7/8	10 3/8	10 2/8	4 3/8	5 1/8	25 1/8	28 2/8	M	Sachs Harbour, N. W. T.	Paul Giesel	Paul Giesel	OT 1980	17
102 2/8	24 1/8	25 1/8	9 1/8	9	4 1/8	4 5/8	25 6/8	27 7/8	M	Victoria Island, N. W. T.	Robert J. Matyas	Robert J. Matyas	MR 1981	18
102 2/8	23 6/8	24	8	7 7/8	5 1/8	5	28 1/8	28 5/8	M	Nunivak Island, Alaska	Russell H. Underdahl	Russell H. Underdahl	FE 1979	18
101 6/8	24 5/8	25 5/8	8 1/8	8 1/8	4 3/8	4 7/8	27 4/8	27 7/8	M	Nunivak Island, Alaska	Patrick P. Wright	Patrick P. Wright	FE 1981	20
101 4/8	25 1/8	26 2/8	8 4/8	8 4/8	4 1/8	4 3/8	26 5/8	27 3/8	M	Nunivak Island, Alaska	Vernie T. Epperson	Vernie T. Epperson	MR 1982	21
101 2/8	25 4/8	25 3/8	7 4/8	7 6/8	4 6/8	4 4/8	26 3/8	26 4/8	M	Seemalik Butte, Alaska	Edward C. Luther	Edward C. Luther	FE 1982	22
101 2/8	25 1/8	25 5/8	7 2/8	7 3/8	5	5 2/8	25 1/8	26 3/8	M	Delesse Lake, N. W. T.	Massimo Bertoni	Massimo Bertoni	MR 1981	22

Score									Sex	Location	Hunter	Owner	Date	Rank
99 6/8	24 6/8	24	8 2/8	8 2/8	4 4/8	4 4/8	27 4/8	28 4/8	M	Nunivak Island, Alaska	Robert C. Jones	Robert C. Jones	AG 1980	24
97 2/8	24 4/8	25 2/8	8	7 2/8	4	4 4/8	27 2/8	28 2/8	M	Nash Harbor, Alaska	L. Irvin Barnhart	L. Irvin Barnhart	MR 1980	25
97	25 2/8	24 2/8	7 2/8	8 2/8	4 2/8	3 6/8	25 2/8	26 2/8	M	Sor Fiord, N. W. T.	Earl A. Shelsby, Jr.	Earl A. Shelsby, Jr.	MR 1981	26
96 2/8	23 6/8	25 2/8	8 2/8	8 2/8	3 6/8	4 2/8	27 2/8	28 2/8	M	Nunivak Island, Alaska	Stewart N. Shaft	Stewart N. Shaft	MR 1982	27
96 2/8	22 6/8	24	7 2/8	7 2/8	5 2/8	5 2/8	23 2/8	24 2/8	M	Sor Fiord, N. W. T.	Vincent T. Ciaburri	Vincent T. Ciaburri	MR 1982	27
95	24 2/8	25 2/8	7 2/8	7 2/8	4	4 2/8	25 2/8	26 2/8	M	Nunivak Island, Alaska	M. L. Warne	M. L. Warne	MR 1979	29
94 2/8	23 2/8	21 2/8	7 2/8	8 2/8	5 2/8	4 2/8	26 2/8	26 2/8	M	Nunivak Island, Alaska	Picked Up	Robert C. Jones	PU 1980	30
93 2/8	22 2/8	24 2/8	8 2/8	9	3 2/8	5	22 2/8	24 2/8	M	Banks Island, N. W. T.	James K. Montgomery	James K. Montgomery	MR 1980	31
92	22 2/8	25 2/8	8 2/8	8 2/8	3 2/8	4 2/8	23 2/8	24 1/8	M	Unknown	Picked Up	Doreen Vair	PR 1981	32

*Final Score subject to revision by additional verifying measurements.

Bighorn Sheep

Minimum Score 180 — ***Ovis canadensis canadensis*** **and certain related subspecies** — **World's Record 208 1/8**

Score	Length of Horn R.	Length of Horn L.	Circumference of Base R.	Circumference of Base L.	Circumference at Third Quarter R.	Circumference at Third Quarter L.	Greatest Spread	Tip to Tip Spread	Locality Killed	By Whom Killed	Owner	Date Killed	Rank
197 1/8	44 3/8	45 4/8	15 7/8	15 5/8	8 5/8	9 4/8	28 6/8	28 7/8	Sanders Co., Mont.	Armand H. Johnson	Armand H. Johnson	NO 1979	1
197*	42 6/8	44	15 4/8	15 6/8	10	10	24	20 7/8	Missoula Co., Mont.	Bonnie Atchison Ford	Bonnie Atchison Ford	OT 1982	2
188 7/8*	40 3/8	40 6/8	14 7/8	14 6/8	10 3/8	10 5/8	23 2/8	20 4/8	Canyon Creek, Alta.	Edith J. Nagy	Edith J. Nagy	AG 1981	3
188 2/8	45 4/8	44 2/8	13 6/8	13 6/8	9 4/8	9 7/8	23 4/8	22 7/8	Panther River, Alta.	Unknown	Harvey A. Trimble	1932	4
188 1/8	44 3/8	42 2/8	14 3/8	14 7/8	9 6/8	9 2/8	25 3/8	25 3/8	Lincoln Co., Mont.	Alfred E. Journey	Alfred E. Journey	NO 1980	5
187	37 4/8	38 4/8	16 3/8	16 5/8	9 4/8	9 7/8	25	22 4/8	Sanders Co., Mont.	Richard F. Lukes	Richard F. Lukes	NO 1980	6
187	40 4/8	38 6/8	16	15 7/8	9 4/8	8 6/8	15	22 7/8	Elbow River, B. C.	Ralph Cervo	Ralph Cervo	SE 1981	6
186 3/8	41	42 3/8	15 1/8	15 1/8	8 2/8	8 7/8	20 1/8	20 1/8	Simpson River, B. C.	James A. Walls	James A. Walls	OT 1981	8
186	39 4/8	39	14 6/8	14 6/8	10 6/8	10 6/8	21	21	Granite Co., Mont.	Dale W. Hoth	Dale W. Hoth	SE 1981	9
185 5/8	39 1/8	39 4/8	14 7/8	14 6/8	10 1/8	10 5/8	22 4/8	18	Black Diamond, Alta.	Picked Up	Gordon Lait	PU 1962	10
185 2/8	38 5/8	41 3/8	15 5/8	15 1/8	8 6/8	9 2/8	21 4/8	20 4/8	Teton Co., Mont.	Picked Up	Tim French	PU 1980	11
184 4/8	38 7/8	39 5/8	16	16 1/8	8 5/8	8 4/8	22 4/8	18 5/8	Custer Co., Idaho	Stanley V. Potts	Stanley V. Potts	SE 1981	12
184 3/8	39 6/8	39 7/8	14 1/8	14	11	11 6/8	22	21	Carbon Co., Mont.	Picked Up	Monte Berzel	PU 1977	13
184 1/8	40 2/8	38 1/8	15 2/8	15 3/8	9 6/8	8 6/8	23	22	Vaseux Lake, B. C.	Bob McDowell	Bob McDowell	SE 1960	14
184	37 5/8	39 5/8	16 4/8	16 3/8	8 2/8	8 7/8	21	20	Sanders Co., Mont.	Don Robinson	Don Robinson	NO 1980	15
183 5/8	36 7/8	37	16 1/8	16 1/8	9 6/8	9 5/8	24 7/8	24 7/8	Granite Co., Mont.	Sandy C. Antonich	Sandy C. Antonich	SE 1982	16
183 3/8	38 7/8	39 4/8	16 4/8	16 6/8	7 7/8	8 2/8	21	15 6/8	Sanders Co., Mont.	John P. Dilley	John P. Dilley	SE 1981	17
183	40 5/8	40 7/8	13 7/8	14 1/8	10 5/8	10 4/8	20 2/8	19 4/8	Ram River, Alta.	Robert G. Morgan	Robert G. Morgan	AG 1980	18
182 4/8	38 4/8	41 2/8	15 4/8	15 2/8	8 2/8	9	22 5/8	17 2/8	Mary Ann Creek, B. C.	Jack Bridgewater	Jack Bridgewater	SE 1981	19
182 4/8	35 7/8	36 3/8	16 2/8	16 2/8	9 7/8	9 7/8	22 4/8	19	Blind Canyon, Alta.	Alan W. Foster	Alan W. Foster	SE 1981	19
182 4/8	38 6/8	35 6/8	15 3/8	15 5/8	11 1/8	10 1/8	23 2/8	23 2/8	Wallowa Co., Oreg.	Randy Craddock	Randy Craddock	SE 1981	19
182 3/8	38 6/8	37 1/8	16	16	8 3/8	8 7/8	23 7/8	18 6/8	West Sulphur River, Alta.	Robert Highberg	Robert Highberg	AG 1980	22
182	39 1/8	41 7/8	15	15	8 3/8	7 6/8	23 5/8	23 3/8	Lewis & Clark Co., Mont.	Allan L. Davies	Allan L. Davies	NO 1981	23
181 7/8	38 3/8	39	15 2/8	15 1/8	9 4/8	9 4/8	21 1/8	19	Hinton, Alta.	Darla J. Smith	Ben Morris	SE 1980	24
181 7/8	39 5/8	40 6/8	15 1/8	14 7/8	8 4/8	8 6/8	21 1/8	21 1/8	Sundre, Alta.	Dennis George Overguard	Dennis George Overguard	OT 1980	24
181 4/8	37	39	16 2/8	16 3/8	8 4/8	8 3/8	24 3/8	24 3/8	Lewis & Clark Co., Mont.	Donel G. Hayes	Donel G. Hayes	NO 1980	26
181 3/8	37 5/8	37 4/8	15	15	10 5/8	10 5/8	19	15 3/8	Cardinal River, Alta.	Randy Babala	Randy Babala	OT 1980	27

181 3/8	39 3/8	41 1/8	15 1/8	15 1/8	8 1/8	7 7/8	21 1/8	20 7/8	Granite Co., Mont.	David D. Rittenhouse	David D. Rittenhouse	SE 1980	27
180 7/8	38 7/8	39 7/8	14	14	10 1/8	10 1/8	19 7/8	18	Park Co., Wyo.	Picked Up	Jay Thomas	PU 1979	29
180 5/8	37	37 7/8	14 7/8	15	10 1/8	10	22 7/8	18 7/8	Park Co., Wyo.	Dwight Lyman	Dwight Lyman	OT 1982	30
180 3/8	37 7/8	36 7/8	16	16	9 7/8	8 1/8	21	17 7/8	Junction Creek, Alta.	Spencer T. Nichols	Spencer T. Nichols	SE 1981	30
180 3/8	40 7/8	39 7/8	15 7/8	15 7/8	8 1/8	7 7/8	20	18 7/8	Lewis & Clark Co., Mont.	William J. McRae	William J. McRae	OT 1980	32
180 3/8	40 7/8	40 7/8	15 7/8	15 7/8	7 7/8	7 7/8	22 7/8	20 7/8	Luscar Mt., Alta.	Jerry L. Christian	Jerry L. Christian	OT 1979	33
180 5/8	35 7/8	38 7/8	15 7/8	15	10 7/8	9 7/8	22	17	Lake Louise, B. C.	Unknown	Martin Bonack	PR 1951	33
180 7/8	41 7/8	41 7/8	15	15	7	7 7/8	28 7/8	28 7/8	Deer Lodge Co., Mont.	Arden Holden	Arden Holden	OT 1979	35
180	40 7/8	37 7/8	15 7/8	15 7/8	8 7/8	8 7/8	22 7/8	22 7/8	Granite Co., Mont.	Jerry E. Gallagher	Jerry E. Gallagher	SE 1980	36

*Final Score subject to revision by additional verifying measurements.

Desert Sheep

Minimum Score 168 — ***Ovis canadensis nelsoni* and certain related subspecies** — **World's Record 205 1/8**

Score	Length of Horn R.	Length of Horn L.	Circumference of Base R.	Circumference of Base L.	Circumference at Third Quarter R.	Circumference at Third Quarter L.	Greatest Spread	Tip to Tip Spread	Locality Killed	By Whom Killed	Owner	Date Killed	Rank
192 5/8	41 6/8	42 3/8	15	15 1/8	10 6/8	10 4/8	25 4/8	25	Baja Calif., Mexico	Javier Lopez del Bosque	Javier Lopez del Bosque	NO 1979	1
191 2/8	38 4/8	40 4/8	16 2/8	16 2/8	10 3/8	10 7/8	21 6/8	17 2/8	Baja Calif., Mexico	Claude Bourguignon	Claude Bourguignon	FE 1982	2
187 7/8	39 6/8	39 5/8	15 6/8	15 7/8	9 4/8	9 4/8	21 4/8	16 6/8	Pima Co., Ariz.	Carl A. Mattias, Sr.	Carl A. Mattias, Sr.	JA 1982	3
186 6/8*	42 3/8	38 7/8	16 2/8	16 1/8	8 5/8	8 4/8	24 2/8	23 2/8	Baja Calif., Mexico	James N. McHolme	James N. McHolme	MR 1981	4
186 2/8	40 6/8	40 2/8	14 6/8	14 7/8	10	10	20 2/8	23	Baja Calif., Mexico	Robert P. Miller	Robert P. Miller	FE 1981	5
186	38 2/8	38 4/8	15 4/8	15 5/8	10 6/8	10 6/8	22 3/8	19 5/8	Yuma Co,. Ariz.	Gerry W. Nikolaus	Gerry W. Nikolaus	DC 1979	6
184	41 6/8	40 4/8	15 4/8	15 4/8	8 3/8	8 7/8	25 6/8	25 6/8	Baja Calif., Mexico	Thomas J. Brimhall	Thomas J. Brimhall	MR 1981	7
180	38 2/8	38 6/8	15 2/8	15 2/8	9	9 2/8	22	20 6/8	Clark Co., Nev.	John Virgil Zenz	John Virgil Zenz	NO 1980	8
179 7/8	37 6/8	37 5/8	16	16 1/8	8 4/8	9	24 3/8	24 3/8	Baja Calif., Mexico	Paul E. Robey	Paul E. Robey	NO 1979	9
179 2/8	36 7/8	36 7/8	14 7/8	14 7/8	9 7/8	9 6/8	20 4/8	20 4/8	Clark Co., Nev.	Andy S. Burnett	Andy S. Burnett	DC 1979	10
178 7/8	35 2/8	36 3/8	15 2/8	15 2/8	9 7/8	10 2/8	29 5/8	29 5/8	Mohave Co., Ariz.	Earle H. Smith	Earle H. Smith	DC 1981	11
178 6/8	37 2/8	36 6/8	15 7/8	15 7/8	8 4/8	8 3/8	21 4/8	21 4/8	Baja Calif., Mexico	Hobson L. Sanderson, Jr.	Hobson L. Sanderson, Jr.	FE 1981	12
178	35 4/8	38 2/8	16	16	8 2/8	8 2/8	24	24	Baja Calif., Mexico	James G. Lagiss	James G. Lagiss	MR 1980	13
177 3/8	37	37 5/8	16	16 2/8	8 4/8	8	19 4/8	16	Baja Calif., Mexico	Don McBride	Don McBride	FE 1980	14
177 3/8	34 6/8	36 3/8	15 1/8	15	10 4/8	11	19	19	Clark Co., Nev.	Ralph W. McClintock	Ralph W. McClintock	DC 1980	14
177 1/8	37 6/8	38 5/8	15 2/8	15 2/8	8 6/8	8 2/8	22 5/8	22 5/8	Baja Calif., Mexico	G. Dale Monson	G. Dale Monson	JA 1982	16
176 5/8	39	38 5/8	14 4/8	14 4/8	8 6/8	8 4/8	28 3/8	28 3/8	Clark Co., Nev.	Allan R. Sundell	Kent A. Sundell	NO 1979	17
176 2/8	38 2/8	36	15 3/8	15 3/8	8 4/8	8 4/8	21 6/8	19 4/8	Clark Co., Nev.	Christine J. Burrows	Christine J. Burrows	DC 1981	18
176 2/8	38 1/8	37 5/8	15	15 1/8	8 4/8	8 4/8	21 5/8	21 5/8	Yuma Co., Ariz.	Vicki L. Clark	Vicki L. Clark	DC 1980	18
175 7/8	39 5/8	38 6/8	14	14	8 6/8	9 2/8	22 5/8	22 5/8	Yuma Co., Ariz.	Fred W. Jerome	Fred W. Jerome	DC 1979	20
175 7/8	36 7/8	37	15 2/8	15 1/8	9 4/8	9 6/8	22 4/8	19	Pinal Co., Ariz.	Tracy L. Contreras	Tracy L. Contreras	DC 1980	20
175 1/8	36 2/8	36 1/8	15 1/8	15	9	9 5/8	23 7/8	23 7/8	Clark Co., Nev.	Lloyd G. Bare	Lloyd G. Bare	DC 1980	22
175 1/8	36 4/8	37 3/8	15 2/8	15 2/8	8 4/8	8 4/8	23 1/8	23 1/8	Clark Co., Nev.	Lenda Z. Azcarate	Lenda Z. Azcarate	NO 1979	22
174 7/8	35 1/8	35	15 7/8	15 6/8	8 7/8	8 6/8	23 5/8	23 1/8	Clark Co., Nev.	Herman H. Storey, Jr.	Herman H. Storey, Jr.	NO 1980	24
174 3/8	38 1/8	38 4/8	14 4/8	14 4/8	8	7 6/8	24 4/8	23 5/8	Clark Co., Nev.	Glenn & Kathy Seaberg	Kathy E. Seaberg	NO 1981	25
174 2/8	35 3/8	36 1/8	14 7/8	14 7/8	9 7/8	10	25 5/8	25 5/8	Mohave Co., Ariz.	Susan C. Nelson	Susan C. Nelson	DC 1979	26
173 5/8	37 1/8	36 6/8	15 1/8	15	8 6/8	8 6/8	23 4/8	23 4/8	Clark Co., Nev.	Buddy H. Fujii	Buddy H. Fujii	NO 1980	27
173 3/8	40 5/8	38	13 7/8	14 6/8	8 2/8	8 1/8			Baja Calif., Mexico	Tim C. Boyd	Tim C. Boyd	JA 1981	28
172 6/8	36	36 4/8	15 5/8	15 3/8	8 2/8	8 5/8	19 1/8	18 3/8	Pima Co., Ariz.	Paul H. Harrison	Paul H. Harrison	DC 1981	29
172 6/8	36 5/8	36 5/8	14	13 7/8	10 1/8	9 6/8	19 6/8	19 6/8	Yuma Co., Ariz.	Larry J. Landes	Larry J. Landes	DC 1981	29

172 3/8	35 1/8	34 6/8	15 2/8	15 1/8	9	9	23 1/8	23 1/8	Clark Co., Nev.	Ronald L. Giovanetti	Ronald L. Giovanetti	NO 1980	31
172 3/8	36 3/8	35 2/8	14 5/8	14 3/8	9 4/8	9 4/8	20 1/8	19 1/8	Baja Calif., Mexico	H. Varley Grantham	H. Varley Grantham	DC 1980	31
171 4/8	33 6/8	35	15	15 1/8	8 6/8	9 2/8	21 4/8	20 2/8	Maricopa Co., Ariz.	Unknown	Clarence House	PR 1979	33
171 3/8	38 1/8	37	14	14 2/8	9 3/8	8 6/8	24	23 5/8	Clark Co., Nev.	Daniel T. Magee	Daniel T. Magee	DC 1980	34
171 1/8	35 2/8	35 3/8	15	14 7/8	9 2/8	8 6/8	25 2/8	25 2/8	Clark Co., Nev.	Ray W. Diehl	Ray W. Diehl	NO 1979	35
170 7/8	36 5/8	37	15	15	8 2/8	8 2/8	21 4/8	21	Baja Calif., Mexico	Daniel B. Moore	Daniel B. Moore	DC 1979	36
170 4/8	36	34 6/8	15 7/8	16	7 5/8	7 6/8	18 7/8	18 7/8	Baja Calif., Mexico	Don Turner	Don Turner	DC 1980	37
170 3/8	35 5/8	35 6/8	14 4/8	14 1/8	8 4/8	9	23 6/8	23	Yuma Co., Ariz.	Gary V. Harmon	Gary V. Harmon	DC 1979	38
170 3/8	32 5/8	32 4/8	16	16	9 1/8	9 3/8	20 2/8	15 5/8	Hermosillo, Mexico	Michael Follett	Michael Follett	NO 1979	38
170 2/8	36	35 2/8	15 1/8	15 1/8	8 1/8	8 2/8	21 7/8	21 7/8	Baja Calif., Mexico	David C. Southard, Jr.	David C. Southard, Jr.	MR 1982	40
170 2/8	34 4/8	34 2/8	15	15	9 5/8	9 4/8	18 1/8	18	Baja Calif., Mexico	A. Verne Crowell	A. Verne Crowell	NO 1979	40
170 1/8	34 4/8	35 3/8	15 4/8	15 3/8	8 4/8	8 4/8	20 4/8	18 4/8	Clark Co., Nev.	William F. Zenz, Jr.	William F. Zenz, Jr.	NO 1980	42
169 5/8	34	33 7/8	15 1/8	15 1/8	8 7/8	8 6/8	20 7/8	18 4/8	Yuma Co., Ariz.	Brad J. Ullery	Brad J. Ullery	DC 1981	43
169 4/8	39	37 2/8	15 2/8	15	6 6/8	6 7/8	19 4/8	19 4/8	Baja Calif., Mexico	James A. Bush, Jr.	James A. Bush, Jr.	FE 1981	44
169 3/8	33 3/8	38 2/8	15	15	8	8	23	22	Pima Co., Ariz.	Don L. Mattausch	Don L. Mattausch	DC 1979	45
169 1/8	34 4/8	35 5/8	14	14	10	10 1/8	21 6/8	21 6/8	Clark Co., Nev.	Lee Matt Smith, Jr.	Lee Matt Smith, Jr.	NO 1979	46
169	34 3/8	35 3/8	15 3/8	15 1/8	7 7/8	8	14 2/8	21	Baja Calif., Mexico	Gordon L. Shuster	Gordon L. Shuster	FE 1980	47
169	35 2/8	35 2/8	13 6/8	13 6/8	10	10	20 5/8	18 2/8	Baja Calif., Mexico	Arthur L. Wehner	Arthur L. Wehner	DC 1980	47
168 7/8	33 4/8	33 7/8	14 7/8	14 7/8	9 3/8	9 2/8	20 6/8	20 6/8	Lincoln Co., Nev.	Melvin J. Lowe	Melvin J. Lowe	DC 1981	49
168 6/8	36 4/8	37 4/8	13 5/8	13 5/8	8 6/8	9 2/8	21 2/8	22 2/8	Yuma Co., Ariz.	Frances B. Boggess	Frances B. Boggess	DC 1980	50
168 5/8	35 5/8	34 6/8	14 3/8	14 3/8	8 7/8	9	18 3/8	18 2/8	Sonora, Mexico	Lionel Heinrich	Lionel Heinrich	FE 1982	51
168 4/8	37 2/8	37	15 2/8	15 1/8	7 2/8	7 1/8	23 4/8	23 4/8	Baja Calif., Mexico	Dan L. Duncan	Dan L. Duncan	NO 1979	52
168 1/8	34 6/8	35 3/8	14 6/8	14 4/8	8 5/8	8 7/8	22 2/8	22 2/8	Baja Calif., Mexico	C. R. Palmer	C. R. Palmer	DC 1979	53
168	37 2/8	35 2/8	14 6/8	14 6/8	6 6/8	6 5/8	26 3/8	26 3/8	Mohave Co., Ariz.	Tom H. Martin	Tom H. Martin	DC 1980	54

*Final Score subject to revision by additional verifying measurements.

Dall's Sheep

Ovis dalli dalli and *Ovis dalli kenaiensis*

Minimum Score 170 **World's Record 189 6/8**

Score	Length of Horn R.	Length of Horn L.	Circumference of Base R.	Circumference of Base L.	Circumference at Third Quarter R.	Circumference at Third Quarter L.	Greatest Spread	Tip to Tip Spread	Locality Killed	By Whom Killed	Owner	Date Killed	Rank
176 6/8	43 1/8	43 1/8	14 3/8	14 6/8	6 4/8	6 4/8	27	27	Chugach Mts., Alaska	Charles H. Rohrer	Charles H. Rohrer	AG 1982	1
175 6/8*	42	43 2/8	15 2/8	15	6	6	27 3/8	27 3/8	Mt. Ingram, Yukon	Steve Zimmerman	Steve Zimmerman	SE 1979	2
173 3/8*	44	43 7/8	14 4/8	14 4/8	5 3/8	5 3/8	30 2/8	30 2/8	Cache Lake, N. W. T.	Lester Behrns	Lester Behrns	AG 1980	3
172 3/8	42 7/8	41 6/8	14 2/8	14 2/8	6 5/8	6 1/8	21 1/8	21 1/8	Granite Lake, Yukon	William E. Medley, II	William E. Medley, II	AG 1980	4
171 3/8*	42 2/8	42 3/8	14	14	5 6/8	5 7/8	32 2/8	32 2/8	Carcajou River, N. W. T.	Colin J. Kure	Colin J. Kure	OT 1980	5
170 2/8	42 7/8	42 7/8	13 4/8	13 4/8	5 7/8	6	29 2/8	29 2/8	Snake River, Yukon	Norman M. Thachuk	Norman M. Thachuk	SE 1982	6

*Final Score subject to revision by additional verifying measurements.

Stone's Sheep
Ovis dalli stonei

Minimum Score 170
World's Record 196 7/8

Score	Length of Horn R.	Length of Horn L.	Circumference of Base R.	Circumference of Base L.	Circumference at Third Quarter R.	Circumference at Third Quarter L.	Greatest Spread	Tip to Tip Spread	Locality Killed	By Whom Killed	Owner	Date Killed	Rank
181 3/8*	40 3/8	41 3/8	14 3/8	14 3/8	9	8 3/8	24 3/8	24 3/8	Tuchodi Lakes, B. C.	Romeo Leduc	Romeo Leduc	OT 1981	1
178 7/8**	42 3/8	43 3/8	15 3/8	15	5 3/8	5 3/8	25 3/8	25 3/8	Racing River, B. C.	Dick Sullivan	Dick Sullivan	OT 1982	2
176 3/8	45 3/8	44 3/8	14 3/8	14 3/8	5 3/8	5 3/8	28 3/8	28 3/8	Gataga River, B. C.	David C. Coleman	David C. Coleman	AG 1980	3
175 3/8	38 3/8	38	15	15	8	8	23 3/8	21 3/8	Muskwa River, B. C.	Robert M. Case	Robert M. Case	OT 1980	4
172 3/8	41 3/8	41 3/8	15 3/8	15 3/8	6	6 3/8	28 3/8	28 3/8	Mile Creek, B. C.	H. D. Miller	H. D. Miller	SE 1980	5
171 3/8	39 3/8	41 3/8	14 3/8	14 3/8	6	6 3/8	23 3/8	23 3/8	Dease Lake, B. C.	Michaux Nash, Jr.	Michaux Nash, Jr.	AG 1965	6
171 3/8	37 3/8	45 3/8	14 3/8	14 3/8	6	6 3/8	24	21 3/8	Prophet River, B. C.	John Whitcombe	John Whitcombe	AG 1981	7
170 3/8	36 3/8	37	14 3/8	14 3/8	8 3/8	8	20 3/8	19 3/8	Townsley Creek, B. C.	Robert L. Williamson	Robert L. Williamson	AG 1981	8

*Final Score subject to revision by additional verifying measurements.

Score Charts of the Official Scoring System for North American Big Game Trophies

OFFICIAL SCORING SYSTEM FOR NORTH AMERICAN BIG GAME TROPHIES

Records of North American Big Game

BOONE AND CROCKETT CLUB

205 South Patrick Street
Alexandria, Virginia 22314

Minimum Score:
  Alaska brown 28
  black 21
  grizzly 24
  polar 27

BEAR

Kind of Bear grizzly

Sex male

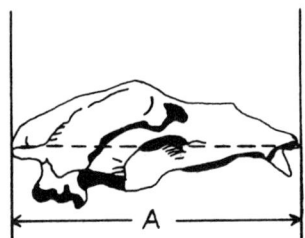
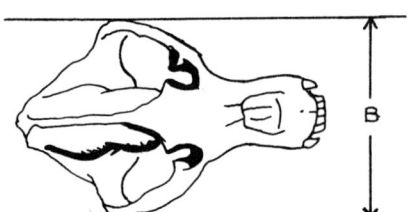

SEE OTHER SIDE FOR INSTRUCTIONS	Measurements
A. Greatest Length without Lower Jaw	16 11/16
B. Greatest Width	10 2/16
TOTAL AND FINAL SCORE	26 13/16

Exact locality where killed junction of Attway and Wakeman River, B. C.
Date killed 2Oct80 By whom killed Harry Leggett, Jr.
Present owner Harry Leggett, Jr.
Address
Guide's Name and Address
Remarks: (Mention any abnormalities or unique qualities)

I certify that I have measured the above trophy on 20 June 1983
at (address) Dallas Museum of Natl. Hist. City Dallas State Texas
and that these measurements and data are, to the best of my knowledge and belief, made in accordance with the instructions given.

Witness: Frank Cook Signature: Ed Williamson
  Official Measurer

INSTRUCTIONS FOR MEASURING BEAR

Measurements are taken with calipers or by using parallel perpendiculars, to the nearest one-sixteenth of an inch, without reduction of fractions. Official measurements cannot be taken for at least sixty days after the animal was killed. All adhering flesh, membrane and cartilage must be completely removed before official measurements are taken.

A. Greatest Length is measured between perpendiculars parallel to the long axis of the skull, without the lower jaw and excluding malformations.

B. Greatest Width is measured between perpendiculars at right angles to the long axis.

* * * * * * * * * * * * *

FAIR CHASE STATEMENT FOR ALL HUNTER-TAKEN TROPHIES

To make use of the following methods shall be deemed as UNFAIR CHASE and unsportmanlike, and any trophy obtained by use of such means is disqualified from entry for Awards.
 I. Spotting or herding game from the air, followed by landing in its vicinity for pursuit;
 II. Herding or pursuing game with motor-powered vehicles;
 III. Use of electronic communications for attracting, locating or observing game, or guiding the hunter to such game;
 IV. Hunting game confined by artificial barriers, including escape-proof fencing; or hunting game transplanted solely for the purpose of commercial shooting.

I certify that the trophy scored on this chart was not taken in UNFAIR CHASE as defined above by the Boone and Crockett Club. I further certify that it was taken in full compliance with local game laws of the state, province, or territory.
Date_____Signature of Hunter_____
(Have signature notarized by a Notary Public)

Copyright © 1981 by Boone and Crockett Club
(Reproduction strictly forbidden without express, written consent)

OFFICIAL SCORING SYSTEM FOR NORTH AMERICAN BIG GAME TROPHIES

Records of North American Big Game

BOONE AND CROCKETT CLUB

205 South Patrick Street
Alexandria, Virginia 22314

Minimum Score:
  cougar 15
  jaguar 14½

COUGAR and JAGUAR

Kind of Cat cougar

Sex male

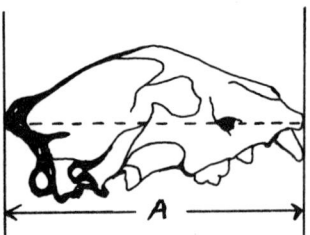
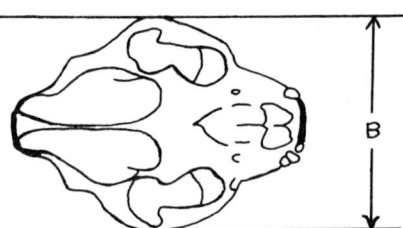

SEE OTHER SIDE FOR INSTRUCTIONS	Measurements
A. Greatest Length without Lower Jaw	8 13/16
B. Greatest Width	6 10/16
TOTAL AND FINAL SCORE	15 7/16

Exact locality where killed Cranbrook, B. C.	
Date killed 28Dec81 By whom killed Donovan W. Ellis	
Present owner Donovan W. Ellis	
Address	
Guide's Name and Address	
Remarks: (Mention any abnormalities or unique qualities)	

I certify that I have measured the above trophy on 22 June 19 83
at (address) Dallas Museum of Natl. Hist.   City Dallas   State Texas
and that these measurements and data are, to the best of my knowledge and belief, made in accordance with the instructions given.

Witness: Frank Cook   Signature: Steve Kubasek
                                      Official Measurer

INSTRUCTIONS FOR MEASURING COUGAR AND JAGUAR

Measurements are taken with calipers or by using parallel perpendiculars, to the nearest one-sixteenth of an inch, without reduction of fractions. Official measurements cannot be taken for at least sixty days after the animal was killed. All adhering flesh, membrane and cartilage must be completely removed before official measurements are taken.

A. Greatest Length is measured between perpendiculars parallel to the long axis of the skull, without the lower jaw and excluding malformations.

B. Greatest Width is measured between perpendiculars at a right angle to the long axis.

* * * * * * * * * * * *

FAIR CHASE STATEMENT FOR ALL HUNTER-TAKEN TROPHIES

To make use of the following methods shall be deemed as UNFAIR CHASE and unsportmanlike, and any trophy obtained by use of such means is disqualified from entry for Awards.
    I. Spotting or herding game from the air, followed by landing in its vicinity for pursuit;
    II. Herding or pursuing game with motor-powered vehicles;
    III. Use of electronic communications for attracting, locating or observing game, or guiding the hunter to such game;
    IV. Hunting game confined by artificial barriers, including escape-proof fencing; or hunting game transplanted solely for the purpose of commercial shooting.

I certify that the trophy scored on this chart was not taken in UNFAIR CHASE as defined above by the Boone and Crockett Club. I further certify that it was taken in full compliance with local game laws of the state, province, or territory.
Date_____ Signature of Hunter_____
(Have signature notarized by a Notary Public)

Copyright © 1981 by Boone and Crockett Club
(Reproduction strictly forbidden without express, written consent)

OFFICIAL SCORING SYSTEM FOR NORTH AMERICAN BIG GAME TROPHIES

Records of North American Big Game

BOONE AND CROCKETT CLUB

205 South Patrick Street
Alexandria, Virginia 22314

Minimum Score:
Atlantic 95
Pacific 100

WALRUS

Kind of Walrus _Pacific_

Sex _male_

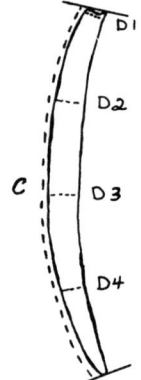
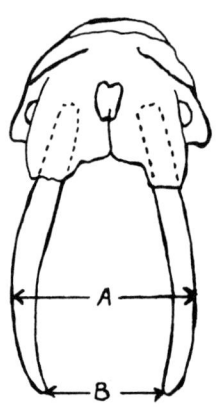

SEE OTHER SIDE FOR INSTRUCTIONS	Column 1	Column 2	Column 3
A. Greatest Spread	Right Tusk	Left Tusk	Difference
B. Tip to Tip Spread			
C. Entire Length of Loose Tusk	32 6/8	32 4/8	2/8
D-1. Circumference of Base	9 5/8	9 3/8	2/8
D-2. Circumference at First Quarter	10 4/8	10 2/8	2/8
D-3. Circumference at Second Quarter	9 2/8	8 7/8	3/8
D-4. Circumference at Third Quarter	7 4/8	7 2/8	2/8
TOTALS	69 5/8	68 2/8	1 3/8

ADD	Column 1	69 5/8	Exact locality where killed _Port Moller, Alaska_
	Column 2	68 2/8	Date killed _Oct81_ By whom killed _Picked up_
	Total	137 7/8	Present owner _Larry R. Rivers_
SUBTRACT Column 3		1 3/8	Address
FINAL SCORE		136 4/8	Guide's Name and Address
			Remarks: (Mention any abnormalities or unique qualities)

I certify that I have measured the above trophy on 28 Feb. 1982
at (address) 109 W. 6th Ave., Room 201   City Anchorage   State Alaska
and that these measurements and data are, to the best of my knowledge and belief, made in accordance with the instructions given.

Witness: _Craig A. Cook_   Signature: _Frank Cook_
                                             Official Measurer

INSTRUCTIONS FOR MEASURING WALRUS

All measurements must be made with a ¼-inch flexible steel tape to the nearest one-eighth of an inch. Enter fractional figures in <u>eighths</u>, without reduction. Tusks <u>must</u> be removed from mounted specimens for measuring. Official measurements cannot be taken for at least sixty days after the animal was killed.

A. Greatest Spread is measured between perpendiculars at a right angle to the center line of the skull.

B. Tip to Tip Spread is measured between tips of tusks.

C. Entire Length of Loose Tusk is measured over outer curve from base to a point in line with tip.

D-1. Circumference of Base is measured at a right angle to axis of tusk. Do not follow edge of contact between tusk and skull.

D-2-3-4. Divide measurement C of LONGER tusk by four. Starting at base, mark <u>both</u> tusks at these quarters (even though other tusk is shorter) and measure circumferences at these marks.

* * * * * * * * * * * *

FAIR CHASE STATEMENT FOR ALL HUNTER-TAKEN TROPHIES

To make use of the following methods shall be deemed as UNFAIR CHASE and unsportsmanlike, and any trophy obtained by use of such means is disqualified from entry for Awards.
  I. Spotting or herding game from the air, followed by landing in its vicinity for pursuit;
  II. Herding or pursuing game with motor-powered vehicles;
  III. Use of electronic communications for attracting, locating or observing game, or guiding the hunter to such game;
  IV. Hunting game confined by artificial barriers, including escape-proof fencing; or hunting game transplanted solely for the purpose of commercial shooting.

I certify that the trophy scored on this chart was not taken in UNFAIR CHASE as defined above by the Boone and Crockett Club. I further certify that it was taken in full compliance with local game laws of the state, province, or territory.
Date_____ Signature of Hunter_____
(Have signature notarized by a Notary Public)

Copyright © 1981 by Boone and Crockett Club
(Reproduction strictly forbidden without express, written consent)

OFFICIAL SCORING SYSTEM FOR NORTH AMERICAN BIG GAME TROPHIES

Records of North American Big Game

BOONE AND CROCKETT CLUB

205 South Patrick Street
Alexandria, Virginia 22314

Minimum Score:
Roosevelt 290
American 375

WAPITI

Kind of Wapiti: Roosevelt's elk

DETAIL OF POINT MEASUREMENT

		Column 1 Spread Credit	Column 2 Right Antler	Column 3 Left Antler	Column 4 Difference
A. Number of Points on Each Antler	R. 7 L. 7				
B. Tip to Tip Spread	23 7/8				
C. Greatest Spread	42				
D. Inside Spread of Main Beams 37 1/8 — Credit may equal but not exceed length of longer antler		37 4/8			
IF Spread exceeds longer antler, enter difference.					
E. Total of Lengths of all Abnormal Points					
F. Length of Main Beam			50 3/8	53	2 5/8
G-1. Length of First Point			15 6/8	16 5/8	7/8
G-2. Length of Second Point			15	15 4/8	4/8
G-3. Length of Third Point			15	15 6/8	6/8
G-4. Length of Fourth (Royal) Point			17 4/8	15 2/8	2 2/8
G-5. Length of Fifth Point			19	12 4/8	6 4/8
G-6. Length of Sixth Point, if present			12 7/8	5 6/8	7 1/8
G-7. Length of Seventh Point, if present					
H-1. Circumference at Smallest Place Between First and Second Points			9	8 5/8	3/8
H-2. Circumference at Smallest Place Between Second and Third Points			7 7/8	7 4/8	3/8
H-3. Circumference at Smallest Place Between Third and Fourth Points			7 5/8	7 1/8	4/8
H-4. Circumference at Smallest Place Between Fourth and Fifth Points			9 3/8	6 3/8	3
TOTALS		37 4/8	179 3/8	164	24 7/8

ADD	Column 1	37 4/8	Exact locality where killed Clatsop Co., Oreg.
	Column 2	179 3/8	Date killed Nov59 By whom killed Pravomil Raichl
	Column 3	164	Present owner Pravomil Raichl
Total		380 7/8	Address
SUBTRACT Column 4		24 7/8	Guide's Name and Address
FINAL SCORE		356	Remarks: (Mention any abnormalities or unique qualities)

I certify that I have measured the above trophy on 20 June 1983
at (address) Dallas Museum of Natl. Hist. City Dallas State Texas
and that these measurements and data are, to the best of my knowledge and belief, made in accordance with the instructions given.
Witness: Frank Cook Signature: Ed Williamson
OFFICIAL MEASURER

INSTRUCTIONS FOR MEASURING WAPITI

All measurements must be made with a ¼-inch flexible steel tape to the nearest one-eighth of an inch. Wherever it is necessary to change direction of measurement, mark a control point and swing tape at this point. Enter fractional figures in eighths, without reduction. Official measurements cannot be taken for at least sixty days after the animal was killed.

A. Number of Points on Each Antler. To be counted a point, a projection must be at least one inch long and its length must exceed the width of its base. All points are measured from tip of point to nearest edge of beam as illustrated. Beam tip is counted as a point but not measured as a point.

B. Tip to Tip Spread is measured between tips of main beams.

C. Greatest Spread is measured between perpendiculars at a right angle to the center line of the skull at widest part whether across main beams or points.

D. Inside Spread of Main Beams is measured at a right angle to the center line of the skull at widest point between main beams. Enter this measurement again in Spread Credit column if it is less than or equal to the length of longer antler; if longer, enter longer antler length for Spread Credit.

E. Total of Lengths of all Abnormal Points. Abnormal points are those nontypical in location (such as points originating from a point or from bottom or sides of main beam) or pattern (extra points, not generally paired). Measure in usual manner and enter in appropriate blanks.

F. Length of Main Beam is measured from lowest outside edge of burr over outer curve to the most distant point of what is, or appears to be, the main beam. The point of beginning is that point on the burr where the center line along the outer curve of the beam intersects the burr, then following generally the line of the illustration.

G-1-2-3-4-5-6-7. Length of Normal Points. Normal points project from the top or front of the main beam in the general pattern illustrated. They are measured from nearest edge of main beam over outer curve to tip. Lay the tape along the outer curve of the beam so that the top edge of the tape coincides with the top edge of the beam on both sides of the point to determine the baseline for point measurement. Record point length in appropriate blanks.

H-1-2-3-4. Circumferences are taken as detailed for each measurement.

* * * * * * * * * * *

FAIR CHASE STATEMENT FOR ALL HUNTER-TAKEN TROPHIES

To make use of the following methods shall be deemed as UNFAIR CHASE and unsportsmanlike, and any trophy obtained by use of such means is disqualified from entry for Awards.

I. Spotting or herding game from the air, followed by landing in its vicinity for pursuit;
II. Herding or pursuing game with motor-powered vehicles;
III. Use of electronic communications for attracting, locating or observing game, or guiding the hunter to such game;
IV. Hunting game confined by artificial barriers, including escape-proof fencing; or hunting game transplanted solely for the purpose of commercial shooting.

****

I certify that the trophy scored on this chart was not taken in UNFAIR CHASE as defined above by the Boone and Crockett Club. I further certify that it was taken in full compliance with local game laws of the state, province, or territory.

Date_____ Signature of Hunter_____
(Have signature notarized by a Notary Public)

Copyright © 1981 by Boone and Crockett Club
(Reproduction strictly forbidden without express, written consent)

OFFICIAL SCORING SYSTEM FOR NORTH AMERICAN BIG GAME TROPHIES

Records of North American Big Game

BOONE AND CROCKETT CLUB

205 South Patrick Street
Alexandria, Virginia 22314

Minimum Score:
mule 195
blacktail 130

TYPICAL
MULE AND BLACKTAIL DEER

Kind of Deer mule

DETAIL OF POINT MEASUREMENT

Abnormal Points	
Right	Left
Total to E	

SEE OTHER SIDE FOR INSTRUCTIONS			Column 1	Column 2	Column 3	Column 4
			Spread Credit	Right Antler	Left Antler	Difference
A. Number of points on Each Antler	R. 5	L. 5				
B. Tip to Tip Spread		19 7/8				
C. Greatest Spread		26 3/8				
D. Inside Spread of Main Beams	23 4/8	Credit may equal but not exceed length of longer antler	23 4/8			
IF Spread exceeds longer antler, enter difference						
E. Total of Lengths of Abnormal Points						
F. Length of Main Beam				24 3/8	24 3/8	
G-1. Length of First Point, if present				3	3 6/8	6/8
G-2. Length of Second Point				18	18 5/8	5/8
G-3. Length of Third Point, if present				13 2/8	13 3/8	1/8
G-4. Length of Fourth Point, if present				13 6/8	12 4/8	1 2/8
H-1. Circumference at Smallest Place Between Burr and First Point				5 4/8	5 4/8	
H-2. Circumference at Smallest Place Between First and Second Points				5 2/8	5 1/8	1/8
H-3. Circumference at Smallest Place Between Main Beam and Third Point				4 3/8	4 3/8	
H-4. Circumference at Smallest Place Between Second and Fourth Points				5 4/8	5	4/8
TOTALS			23 4/8	93	92 5/8	3 3/8

ADD	Column 1	23 4/8	Exact locality where killed Eagle Co., Colo.
	Column 2	93	Date killed 10Nov81 By whom killed Mark A. McCormick
	Column 3	92 5/8	Present owner Mark A. McCormick
TOTAL		209 1/8	Address
SUBTRACT Column 4		3 3/8	Guide's Name and Address
FINAL SCORE		205 6/8	Remarks: (Mention any abnormalities or unique qualities)

284

I certify that I have measured the above trophy on 21 June   1983
at (address) Dallas Museum of Natl. Hist.   City Dallas   State Texas
and that these measurements and data are, to the best of my knowledge and belief, made in accordance with the instructions given.

Witness: Dean A. Murphy   Signature: George Tsukamoto
                                                       OFFICIAL MEASURER

INSTRUCTIONS FOR MEASURING MULE AND BLACKTAIL DEER

All measurements must be made with a ¼-inch flexible steel tape to the nearest one-eighth of an inch. Wherever it is necessary to change direction of measurement, mark a control point and swing tape at this point. Enter fractional figures in eighths, without reduction. Official measurements cannot be taken for at least sixty days after the animal was killed.

A. Number of Points on Each Antler. To be counted a point, a projection must be at least one inch long and its length must exceed the width of its base. All points are measured from tip of point to nearest edge of beam as illustrated. Beam tip is counted as a point but not measured as a point.

B. Tip to Tip Spread is measured between tips of main beams.

C. Greatest Spread is measured between perpendiculars at a right angle to the center line of the skull at widest part whether across main beams or points.

D. Inside Spread of Main Beams is measured at a right angle to the center line of the skull at widest point between main beams. Enter this measurement again in Spread Credit column if it is less than or equal to the length of longer antler; if longer, enter longer antler length for Spread Credit.

E. Total Lengths of all Abnormal Points. Abnormal points are those nontypical in location such as points originating from a point (exception: G-3 originates from G-2 in perfectly normal fashion) or from sides or bottom of main beam or any points beyond the normal pattern of five (including beam tip) per antler. Measure each abnormal point in usual manner and enter in appropriate blanks.

F. Length of Main Beam is measured from lowest outside edge of burr over outer curve to the tip of the main beam. The point of beginning is that point on the burr where the center line along the outer curve of the beam intersects the burr, then following generally the line of the illustration.

G-1-2-3-4. Length of Normal Points. Normal points are the brow and the upper and lower forks as shown in the illustration. They are measured from nearest edge of beam over outer curve to tip. Lay the tape along the outer curve of the beam so that the top edge of the tape coincides with the top edge of the beam on both sides of the point to determine baseline for point measurement. Record point lengths in appropriate blanks.

H-1-2-3-4. Circumferences are taken as detailed for each measurement. If brow point is missing, take H-1 and H-2 at smallest place between burr and G-2. If G-3 is missing, take H-3 halfway between the base and tip of second point. If G-4 is missing, take H-4 halfway between the second point and tip of main beam.   * * * * * * * * * * * *

FAIR CHASE STATEMENT FOR ALL HUNTER-TAKEN TROPHIES

To make use of the following methods shall be deemed as UNFAIR CHASE and unsportsmanlike, and any trophy obtained by use of such means is disqualified from entry for Awards.
   I. Spotting or herding game from the air, followed by landing in its vicinity for pursuit;
  II. Herding or pursuing game with motor-powered vehicles;
 III. Use of electronic communications for attracting, locating or observing game, or guiding the hunter to such game;
  IV. Hunting game confined by artificial barriers, including escape-proof fencing; or hunting game transplanted solely for the purpose of commercial shooting.
****
I certify that the trophy scored on this chart was not taken in UNFAIR CHASE as defined above by the Boone and Crockett Club. I further certify that it was taken in full compliance with local game laws of the state, province, or territory.

Date_____ Signature of Hunter_____
(Have signature notarized by a Notary Public)

Copyright © 1981 by Boone and Crockett Club
(Reproduction strictly forbidden without express. written consent)

OFFICIAL SCORING SYSTEM FOR NORTH AMERICAN BIG GAME TROPHIES

Records of North American Big Game

BOONE AND CROCKETT CLUB

205 South Patrick Street
Alexandria, Virginia 22314

Minimum Score: 240

NON-TYPICAL
MULE DEER

Abnormal Points	
Right	Left
1	2 1/8
1 4/8	2 5/8
1 3/8	8 3/8
3 4/8	5 5/8
2	3 3/8
10 6/8	2 4/8
3 7/8	2
1 3/8	2
1 4/8	5 4/8
4 2/8	
Total to E	65 2/8

SEE OTHER SIDE FOR INSTRUCTIONS			Column 1	Column 2	Column 3	Column 4
A. Number of Points on Each Antler	R. 15	L. 14	Spread Credit	Right Antler	Left Antler	Difference
B. Tip to Tip Spread			16 5/8			
C. Greatest Spread			34 6/8			
D. Inside Spread of Main Beams	23 4/8	Credit may equal but not exceed length of longer antler	23 4/8			
IF Spread exceeds longer antler, enter difference						
E. Total of Lengths of Abnormal Points			65 2/8			
F. Length of Main Beams				27	26 6/8	2/8
G-1. Length of First Point, if present				3 2/8	3	2/8
G-2. Length of Second Point				19 3/8	18 6/8	5/8
G-3. Length of Third Point, if present				14 6/8	12 6/8	2
G-4. Length of Fourth Point, if present				14 5/8	14 2/8	3/8
H-1. Circumference at Smallest Place Between Burr and First Point				6	6	
H-2. Circumference at Smallest Place Between First and Second Points				5 2/8	5 2/8	
H-3. Circumference at Smallest Place Between Main Beam and Third Point				4 3/8	4 3/8	
H-4. Circumference at Smallest Place Between Second and Fourth Points				4 6/8	5	2/8
TOTALS			65 2/8	23 4/8	99 3/8	96 1/8	3 6/8

ADD	Column 1	23 4/8	Exact locality where killed Gem Co., Idaho
	Column 2	99 3/8	Date killed 20Oct82 By whom killed Ronald S. Holbrook
	Column 3	96 1/8	Present Owner Ronald S. Holbrook
	TOTAL	219	Address
SUBTRACT	Column 4	3 6/8	
	Result	215 2/8	Guide's Name and Address
Add Line E Total		65 2/8	Remarks: (Mention any abnormalities or unique qualities)
FINAL SCORE		280 4/8	

I certify that I have measured the above trophy on 22 June 19 83
at (address) Dallas Museum of Natl. Hist. City Dallas State Texas
and that these measurements and data are, to the best of my knowledge and belief, made in accordance with the instructions given.
Witness: Dean A. Murphy   Signature: George Tsukamoto
                                             OFFICIAL MEASURER

INSTRUCTIONS FOR MEASURING NON-TYPICAL MULE DEER

All measurements must be made with a ¼-inch flexible steel tape to the nearest one-eighth of an inch. Wherever it is necessary to change direction of measurement, mark a control point and swing tape at this point. Enter fractional figures in eighths, without reduction. Official measurements cannot be taken for at least sixty days after the animal was killed.

A. Number of Points on Each Antler. To be counted a point, a projection must be at least one inch long and its length must exceed the width of its base. All points are measured from tip of point to nearest edge of beam as illustrated. Beam tip is counted as a point but not measured as a point.

B. Tip to Tip Spread is measured between tips of main beams.

C. Greatest Spread is measured between perpendiculars at a right angle to the center line of the skull at widest part whether across main beams or points.

D. Inside Spread of Main Beams is measured at a right angle to the center line of the skull at widest point between main beams. Enter this measurement again in Spread Credit column if it is less than or equal to the length of longer antler; if longer, enter longer antler length for Spread Credit.

E. Total of Lengths of all Abnormal Points. Abnormal points are those nontypical in location or points beyond the normal pattern of five (including beam tip) per antler. Mark the points that are normal, as defined below. All other points are considered abnormal and are entered in appropriate blanks, after measurement in usual manner.

F. Length of Main Beam is measured from lowest outside edge of burr over outer curve to the tip of the main beam. The point of beginning is that point on the burr where the center line along the outer curve of the beam intersects the burr, then following generally the line of the illustration.

G-1-2-3-4. Length of Normal Points. Normal points are the brow and the upper and lower forks, as shown in the illustration. They are measured from nearest edge of beam over outer curve to tip. Lay the tape along the outer curve of the beam so that the top edge of the tape coincides with the top edge of the beam on both sides of the point to determine baseline for point measurement. Record point lengths in appropriate blanks.

H-1-2-3-4. Circumferences are taken as detailed for each measurement. If brow point is missing, take H-1 and H-2 at smallest place between burr and G-2. If G-3 is missing, take H-3 halfway between the base and tip of second point. If G-4 is missing, take H-4 halfway between the second point and tip of main beam.
* * * * * * * * * * *

FAIR CHASE STATEMENT FOR ALL HUNTER-TAKEN TROPHIES

To make use of the following methods shall be deemed as UNFAIR CHASE and unsportsmanlike and any trophy obtained by use of such means is disqualified from entry for Awards.
  I. Spotting or herding game from the air, followed by landing in its vicinity for pursuit;
 II. Herding or pursuing game with motor-powered vehicles;
III. Use of electronic communications for attracting, locating or observing game, or guiding the hunter to such game;
 IV. Hunting game confined by artificial barriers, including escape-proof fencing; or hunting game transplanted solely for the purpose of commercial shooting.
****

I certify that the trophy scored on this chart was not taken in UNFAIR CHASE as defined above by the Boone and Crockett Club. I further certify that it was taken in full compliance with local game laws of the state, province, or territory.

Date_____Signature of Hunter_____
(Have signature notarized by a Notary Public)

Copyright © 1981 by Boone and Crockett Club
(Reproduction strictly forbidden without express, written consent)

OFFICIAL SCORING SYSTEM FOR NORTH AMERICAN BIG GAME TROPHIES

Records of North American Big Game

BOONE AND CROCKETT CLUB

205 South Patrick Street
Alexandria, Virginia 22314

Minimum Score:
whitetail 170
Coues' 110

TYPICAL
WHITETAIL AND COUES' DEER

Kind of Deer Coues'

DETAIL OF POINT MEASUREMENT

Abnormal Points	
Right	Left
1 3/8	1
1 5/8	
Total to E 4	

SEE OTHER SIDE FOR INSTRUCTIONS		Column 1	Column 2	Column 3	Column 4
		Spread Credit	Right Antler	Left Antler	Difference
A. Number of Points on Each Antler	R. 8 L. 6				
B. Tip to Tip Spread	6 3/8				
C. Greatest Spread	19 4/8				
D. Inside Spread of Main Beams 15 6/8	Credit may equal but not exceed length of longer antler	15 6/8			
IF Spread exceeds longer antler, enter difference.					
E. Total of Lengths of all Abnormal Points					4
F. Length of Main Beam			20 6/8	20 6/8	
G-1. Length of First Point, if present			3 3/8	3 3/8	
G-2. Length of Second Point			10	7 3/8	2 5/8
G-3. Length of Third Point			5 7/8	6 3/8	4/8
G-4. Length of Fourth Point, if present			3	8	5
G-5. Length of Fifth Point, if present			1 3/8		1 3/8
G-6. Length of Sixth Point, if present					
G-7. Length of Seventh Point, if present					
H-1. Circumference at Smallest Place Between Burr and First Point			4 6/8	4 5/8	1/8
H-2. Circumference at Smallest Place Between First and Second Points			4 5/8	4 1/8	4/8
H-3. Circumference at Smallest Place Between Second and Third Points			4 4/8	4 6/8	2/8
H-4. Circumference at Smallest Place between Third and Fourth Points (see back if G-4 is missing)			5 6/8	8	2 2/8
TOTALS		15 6/8	64	67 3/8	16 5/8

ADD	Column 1	15 6/8	Exact locality where killed Pima Co., Ariz.
	Column 2	64	Date killed 21Nov81 By whom killed Kim J. Poulin
	Column 3	67 3/8	Present owner Kim J. Poulin
	Total	147 1/8	Address
SUBTRACT Column 4		16 5/8	Guide's Name and Address
FINAL SCORE		130 4/8	Remarks: (Mention any abnormalities or unique qualities)

I certify that I have measured the above trophy on ___21 June___ ___1983___
at (address) __Dallas Museum of Natl. Hist.__ City __Dallas__ State __Texas__
and that these measurements and data are, to the best of my knowledge and belief, made in accordance with the instructions given.
Witness: ___Frank Cook___ Signature: __Ed Williamson__
OFFICIAL MEASURER

INSTRUCTIONS FOR MEASURING WHITETAIL AND COUES' DEER

All measurements must be made with a ¼-inch flexible steel tape to the nearest one-eighth of an inch. Wherever it is necessary to change direction of measurement, mark a control point and swing tape at this point. Enter fractional figures in eighths, without reduction. Official measurements cannot be taken for at least sixty days after the animal was killed.

A. Number of Points on Each Antler. To be counted a point, a projection must be at least one inch long and its length must exceed the width of its base. All points are measured from tip of point to nearest edge of beam as illustrated. Beam tip is counted as a point but not measured as a point.

B. Tip to Tip Spread is measured between tips of main beams.

C. Greatest Spread is measured between perpendiculars at a right angle to the center line of the skull at widest part whether across main beams or points.

D. Inside Spread of Main Beams is measured at a right angle to the center line of the skull at widest point between main beams. Enter this measurement again in Spread Credit column if it is less than or equal to the length of longer antler; if longer, enter longer antler length for Spread Credit.

E. Total of lengths of all Abnormal Points. Abnormal points are those nontypical in location (points originating from points or from sides or bottom of main beam) or extra points beyond the normal pattern of up to eight normal points, including beam tip, per antler. Measure in usual manner and enter in appropriate blanks.

F. Length of Main Beam is measured from lowest outside edge of burr over outer curve to the most distant point of what is, or appears to be, the main beam. The point of beginning is that point on the burr where the center line along the outer curve of the beam intersects the burr, then following generally the line of the illustration.

G-1-2-3-4-5-6-7. Length of Normal Points. Normal points project from the top of the main beam. They are measured from nearest edge of main beam over outer curve to tip. Lay the tape along the outer curve of the beam so that the top edge of the tape coincides with the top edge of the beam on both sides of the point to determine baseline for point measurements. Record point lengths in appropriate blanks.

H-1-2-3-4. Circumferences are taken as detailed for each measurement. If brow point is missing, take H-1 and H-2 at smallest place between burr and G-2. If G-4 is missing, take H-4 halfway between G-3 and tip of main beam.

* * * * * * * * * * *

FAIR CHASE STATEMENT FOR ALL HUNTER-TAKEN TROPHIES

To make use of the following methods shall be deemed as UNFAIR CHASE and unsportsmanlike, and any trophy obtained by use of such means is disqualified from entry for Awards.
  I. Spotting or herding game from the air, followed by landing in its vicinity for pursuit;
  II. Herding or pursuing game with motor-powered vehicles;
  III. Use of electronic communications for attracting, locating or observing game, or guiding the hunter to such game;
  IV. Hunting game confined by artificial barriers, including escape-proof fencing; or hunting game transplanted solely for the purpose of commercial shooting.
****

I certify that the trophy scored on this chart was not taken in UNFAIR CHASE as defined above by the Boone and Crockett Club. I further certify that it was taken in full compliance with local game laws of the state, province, or territory.

Date_____Signature of Hunter_____
(Have signature notarized by a Notary Public)

Copyright © 1981 by Boone and Crockett Club
(Reproduction strictly forbidden without express, written consent)

OFFICIAL SCORING SYSTEM FOR NORTH AMERICAN BIG GAME TROPHIES

Records of North American Big Game

BOONE AND CROCKETT CLUB

205 South Patrick Street
Alexandria, Virginia 22314

Minimum Score:
whitetail 195
Coues' 120

NON-TYPICAL
WHITETAIL AND COUES' DEER

Kind of Deer __whitetail__

Abnormal Points	
Right	Left
3 3/8	1 3/8 2 1/8
5 5/8 8	4 7/8
4 3/8 7	1 1/8 1 1/8
2 7/8 7	2 1/8 2 7/8
5 1/8	9 1/8 7 3/8
12 5/8	2 4/8 7 4/8
11 3/8	7 3/8 4
4 5/8	1 6/8 3
3 7/8 10	4 5/8
7 6/8	5 5/8 6 7/8
5 3/8	1 4/8
Total to E	184

			Column 1	Column 2	Column 3	Column 4
	SEE OTHER SIDE FOR INSTRUCTIONS					
A.	Number of Points on Each Antler	R. 19 L. 25	Spread Credit	Right Antler	Left Antler	Difference
B.	Tip to Tip Spread	27				
C.	Greatest Spread	33 3/8				
D.	Inside Spread of Main Beams 23 3/8 Credit may equal but not exceed length of longer antler		23 3/8			
	IF Spread exceeds longer antler, enter difference.					
E.	Total of Lengths of Abnormal Points	184				
F.	Length of Main Beam			24 1/8	23 3/8	6/8
G-1.	Length of First Point, if present			8 1/8	7	1 1/8
G-2.	Length of Second Point			7 1/8	8 1/8	1
G-3.	Length of Third Point			6 3/8	7 6/8	1 3/8
G-4.	Length of Fourth Point, if present					
G-5.	Length of Fifth Point, if present					
G-6.	Length of Sixth Point, if present					
G-7.	Length of Seventh Point, if present					
H-1.	Circumference at Smallest Place Between Burr and First Point			5 1/8	5 1/8	
H-2.	Circumference at Smallest Place Between First and Second Points			4 4/8	4 4/8	
H-3.	Circumference at Smallest Place Between Second and Third Points			7 6/8	6 5/8	1 1/8
H-4.	Circumference at Smallest Place Between Third and Fourth Points			3 1/8	3 7/8	6/8
	TOTALS		184	23 3/8	66 2/8	66 3/8	6 1/8

ADD	Column 1	23 3/8	Exact locality where killed St. Louis Co., Mo.
	Column 2	66 2/8	Date killed 15Nov81 By whom killed Picked Up
	Column 3	66 3/8	Present owner Missouri Dept. of Conservation
	Total	156	Address
SUBTRACT	Column 4	6 1/8	
	Result	149 7/8	Guide's Name and Address
Add line E Total		184	Remarks: (Mention any abnormalities or unique qualities)
FINAL SCORE		333 7/8	

I certify that I have measured the above trophy on __22 June__ 19__83__
at (address) __Dallas Museum of Natl. Hist.__ City __Dallas__ State __Texas__
and that these measurements and data are, to the best of my knowledge and belief, made in accordance with the instructions given.

Witness: __George Tsukamoto__ Signature: __Glen C. Sanderson__
OFFICIAL MEASURER

INSTRUCTIONS FOR MEASURING NON-TYPICAL WHITETAIL AND COUES' DEER

All measurements must be made with a ¼-inch flexible steel tape to the nearest one-eighth of an inch. Wherever it is necessary to change direction of measurement, mark a control point and swing tape at this point. Enter fractional figures in eighths, without reduction. Official measurements cannot be taken for at least sixty days after the animal was killed.

A. Number of Points on Each Antler. To be counted a point, a projection must be at least one inch long and its length must exceed the width of its base. All points are measured from tip of point to nearest edge of beam as illustrated. Beam tip is counted as a point but not measured as a point.

B. Tip to Tip Spread is measured between tips of main beams.

C. Greatest Spread is measured between perpendiculars at a right angle to the center line of the skull at widest part whether across main beams or points.

D. Inside Spread of Main Beams is measured at a right angle to the center line of the skull at widest point between main beams. Enter this measurement again in Spread Credit column if it is less than or equal to the length of longer antler; if longer, enter longer antler length for Spread Credit.

E. Total of Lengths of all Abnormal Points. Abnormal points are those nontypical in location (points originating from points or from sides or bottom of main beam) or extra points beyond the normal pattern of up to eight normal points, including beam tip, per antler. Measure in usual manner and enter in appropriate blanks.

F. Length of Main Beam is measured from lowest outside edge of burr over outer curve to the most distant point of what is, or appears to be, the main beam. The point of beginning is that point on the burr where the center line along the outer curve of the beam intersects the burr, then following generally the line of the illustration.

G-1-2-3-4-5-6-7. Length of Normal Points. Normal points project from the top of the main beam. They are measured from nearest edge of main beam over outer curve to tip. Lay the tape along the outer curve of the beam so that the top edge of the tape coincides with the beam on both sides of the point to determine baseline for point measurement. Record point lengths in appropriate blanks.

H-1-2-3-4. Circumferences are taken as detailed for each measurement. If brow point is missing, take H-1 and H-2 at smallest place between burr and G-2. If G-4 is missing, take H-4 halfway between G-3 and tip of main beam.

* * * * * * * * * * *

FAIR CHASE STATEMENT FOR ALL HUNTER-TAKEN TROPHIES

To make use of the following methods shall be deemed as UNFAIR CHASE and unsportsmanlike, and any trophy obtained by use of such means is disqualified from entry for Awards.

I. Spotting or herding game from the air, followed by landing in its vicinity for pursuit;
II. Herding or pursuing game with motor-powered vehicles;
III. Use of electronic communications for attracting, locating or observing game, or guiding the hunter to such game;
IV. Hunting game confined by artificial barriers, including escape-proof fencing; or hunting game transplanted solely for the purpose of commercial shooting.

****

I certify that the trophy scored on this chart was not taken in UNFAIR CHASE as defined above by the Boone and Crockett Club. I further certify that it was taken in full compliance with local game laws of the state, province, or territory.

Date_____ Signature of Hunter_____
(Have signature notarized by a Notary Public)

Copyright © 1981 by Boone and Crockett Club
(Reproduction strictly forbidden without express, written consent)

OFFICIAL SCORING SYSTEM FOR NORTH AMERICAN BIG GAME TROPHIES

Records of North American Big Game

BOONE AND CROCKETT CLUB

205 South Patrick Street
Alexandria, Virginia 22314

Minimum Score:
Alaska-Yukon 224
Canada 195
Wyoming 155

MOOSE   Kind of Moose Canada

SEE OTHER SIDE FOR INSTRUCTIONS	Column 1	Column 2	Column 3	Column 4
		Right Antler	Left Antler	Difference
A. Greatest Spread	63			
B. Number of Abnormal Points on Both Antlers				
C. Number of Norman Points		15	16	1
D. Width of Palm		21 6/8	23	1 2/8
E. Length of Palm including Brow Palm		44 5/8	45	3/8
F. Circumference of Beam at Smallest Place		8 1/8	9 2/8	1 1/8
TOTALS	63	89 4/8	93 2/8	3 6/8

ADD
Column 1 63   Exact locality where killed Vizer Creek, B.C.
Column 2 89 4/8   Date Killed 19 Oct 80 By whom killed Michael E. Laub
Column 3 93 2/8   Present Owner Michael E. Laub
Total   245 6/8 Address
SUBTRACT Column 4 3 6/8   Guide's Name and Address
FINAL SCORE 242   Remarks: (Mention any abnormalities or unique qualities)

I Certify that I have measured the above trophy on 21 June 1983
at (address) Dallas Museum of Natl. Hist.   City Dallas   State Texas
and that these measurements and data are, to the best of my knowledge and belief, made in accordance with the instructions given.

Witness: Frank Cook   Signature: Ed Williamson
                                        Official Measurer

INSTRUCTIONS FOR MEASURING MOOSE

All measurements must be made with a ¼-inch flexible steel tape to the nearest one-eighth of an inch. Wherever it is necessary to change direction of measurement, mark a control point and swing tape at this point. Enter fractional figures in eighths, without reduction. Official measurements cannot be taken for at least sixty days after the animal was killed.

A. Greatest Spread is measured between perpendiculars in a straight line at a right angle to the center line of the skull.

B. Number of Abnormal Points on Both Antlers - Abnormal points are those originating from normal points or from the upper or lower palm surface, or from the inner edge of palm (see illustration). Abnormal points must be at least one inch long, with length exceeding width at one inch or more of length.

C. Number of Normal Points - Normal points originate from the outer edge of palm. To be counted a point, a projection must be at least one inch long, with the length exceeding width at one inch or more of length.

D. Width of Palm is taken in contact with the under surface of palm, at a right angle to the length of palm measurement line. The line of measurement should begin and end at the midpoint of the palm edge, which gives credit for the desirable character of palm thickness.

E. Length of Palm including Brow Palm is taken in contact with the surface along the under side of the palm, parallel to the inner edge, from dips between points at the top to dips between points (if present) at the bottom. If a bay is present, measure across the open bay if the proper line of measurement parallel to inner edge, follows this path. The line of measurement should begin and end at the midpoint of the palm edge, which gives credit for the desirable character of palm thickness.

F. Circumference of Beam at Smallest Place is taken as illustrated.

* * * * * * * * * * * *

FAIR CHASE STATEMENT FOR ALL HUNTER-TAKEN TROPHIES

To make use of the following methods shall be deemed as UNFAIR CHASE and unsportsmanlike, and any trophy obtained by use of such means is disqualified from entry for Awards.

I. Spotting or herding game from the air, followed by landing in its vicinity for pursuit;

II. Herding or pursuing game with motor-powered vehicles;

III. Use of electronic communications for attracting, locating or observing game, or guiding the hunter to such game;

IV. Hunting game confined by artificial barriers, including escape-proof fencing; or hunting game transplanted solely for the purpose of commercial shooting.

I certify that the trophy scored on this chart was not taken in UNFAIR CHASE as defined above by the Boone and Crockett Club. I further certify that it was taken in full compliance with local game laws of the state, province, or territory.

Date_____ Signature of Hunter_____

(Have signature notarized by a Notary Public)

Copyright © 1981 by Boone and Crockett Club
(Reproduction strictly forbidden without express, written consent)

OFFICIAL SCORING SYSTEM FOR NORTH AMERICAN BIG GAME TROPHIES

Records of North American Big Game

BOONE AND CROCKETT CLUB

205 South Patrick Street
Alexandria, Virginia 22314

Minimum Score:
- barren ground 400
- mountain 390
- Quebec-Labrador 375
- woodland 295

CARIBOU   Kind of Caribou barren ground

DETAIL OF POINT MEASUREMENT

SEE OTHER SIDE FOR INSTRUCTIONS		Column 1 Spread Credit	Column 2 Right Antler	Column 3 Left Antler	Column 4 Difference
A. Tip to Tip Spread	43 2/8				
B. Greatest Spread	50				
C. Inside Spread of Main Beams	47 7/8	47 7/8			
IF Spread exceeds longer antler, enter difference.					
D. Number of Points on Each Antler excluding brows			15	12	3
Number of Points on Each Brow			7	1	
E. Length of Main Beam			51 3/8	52 6/8	1 3/8
F-1. Length of Brow Palm or First Point			20	8 1/8	
F-2. Length of Bez or Second Point			24 3/8	25 6/8	1 3/8
F-3. Length of Rear Point, if present			3 1/8	3 7/8	6/8
F-4. Length of Second Longest Top Point			22	26 2/8	4 2/8
F-5. Length of Longest Top Point			29 4/8	27 5/8	1 7/8
G-1. Width of Brow Palm			14 5/8	1/8	
G-2. Width of Top Palm			9 3/8	6 6/8	2 5/8
H-1. Circumference at Smallest Place Between Brow and Bez Points			6 3/8	6 3/8	
H-2. Circumference at Smallest Place Between Bez and Rear Point, if present			5 4/8	5 5/8	1/8
H-3. Circumference at Smallest Place Before First Top Point			5 7/8	5 7/8	
H-4. Circumference at Smallest Place Between Two Longest Top Palm Points			13 4/8	11 3/8	2 1/8
TOTALS		47 7/8	227 5/8	193 4/8	17 4/8

ADD	Column 1	47 7/8	Exact locality where killed Wood River, Alaska
	Column 2	227 5/8	Date killed 7Sept80 By whom killed Q. Odell Robinson
	Column 3	193 4/8	Present owner Q. Odell Robinson
TOTAL		469	Address
SUBTRACT Column 4		17 4/8	Guide's Name and Address
FINAL SCORE		451 4/8	Remarks: (Mention any abnormalities or unique qualities)

I certify that I have measured the above trophy on ___22 June___ 19_83_
at (address) ___Dallas Museum of Natl. Hist.___ City ___Dallas___ State ___Texas___
and that these measurements and data are, to the best of my knowledge and belief, made in accordance with the instructions given.
Witness: ___Philip L. Wright___ Signature: ___George Tsukamoto___
OFFICIAL MEASURER

INSTRUCTIONS FOR MEASURING CARIBOU

All measurements must be made with a ¼-inch flexible steel tape to the nearest one-eighth of an inch. Wherever it is necessary to change direction of measurement, mark a control point and swing tape at this point. Enter fractional figures in eighths, without reduction. Official measurements cannot be taken for at least sixty days after the animal was killed.

A. Tip to Tip Spread is measured between tips of main beams.

B. Greatest Spread is measured between perpendiculars at a right angle to the center line of the skull at widest part, whether across main beams or points.

C. Inside Spread of Main Beams is measured at a right angle to the center line of the skull at widest point between main beams. Enter this measurement again in Spread Credit colum if it is less than or equal to the length of longer antler; if longer, enter longer antler length for Spread Credit.

D. Number of points on each antler. To be counted a point, a projection must be at least one-half inch long, with length exceeding width at the point of measurement. Beam tip is counted as a point but not measured as a point. There are no "abnormal" points in caribou.

E. Length of Main Beam is measured from lowest outside edge of burr over outer curve to the most distant point of what is, or appears to be, the main beam. The point of beginning is that point on the burr where the center line along the outer curve of the beam intersects the burr.

F-1-2-3. Length of Points are measured from nearest edge of beam on the shortest line over outer curve to tip. Lay the tape along the outer curve of the beam so that the top edge of the tape coincides with the top edge of the beam on both sides of the points to determine baseline for point measurement. Record point lengths in appropriate blanks.

F-4-5. Length of points are measured from the tip of the point to the top of the beam, then at a right angle to the lower edge of beam. The Second Longest Top Point cannot be a point branch of the Longest Top Point.

G-1. Width of Brow is measured in a straight line from top edge to lower edge, as illustrated, with measurement line at a right angle to main axis of brow.

G-2. Width of Top Palm is measured from midpoint of lower rear edge of main beam to midpoint of a dip between points, at widest part of palm. The line of measurement begins and ends at mid-points of palm edges, which gives credit for palm thickness.

H-1-2-3-4. Circumferences are taken as described for measurements. If rear point is missing, take H-2 and H-3 measurements at smallest place between bez and first top point.

* * * * * * * * * * *

FAIR CHASE STATEMENT FOR ALL HUNTER-TAKEN TROPHIES

To make use of the following methods shall be deemed as UNFAIR CHASE and unsportsmanlike, and any trophy obtained by use of such means is disqualified from entry for Awards.

I. Spotting or herding game from the air, followed by landing in its vicinity for pursuit;
II. Herding or pursuing game with motor-powered vehicles;
III. Use of electronic communications for attracting, locating or observing game, or guiding the hunter to such game;
IV. Hunting game confined by artificial barriers, including escape-proof fencing; or hunting game transplanted solely for the purpose of commercial shooting.

****

I certify that the trophy scored on this chart was not taken in UNFAIR CHASE as defined above by the Boone and Crockett Club. I further certify that it was taken in full compliance with local game laws of the state, province, or territory.

Date_____Signature of Hunter_____
(Have signature notarized by a Notary Public)

Copyright © 1981 by Boone and Crockett Club
(Reproduction strictly forbidden without express, written consent)

OFFICIAL SCORING SYSTEM FOR NORTH AMERICAN BIG GAME TROPHIES

Records of North American Big Game

BOONE AND CROCKETT CLUB

205 South Patrick Street
Alexandria, Virginia 22314

Minimum Score: 82   PRONGHORN

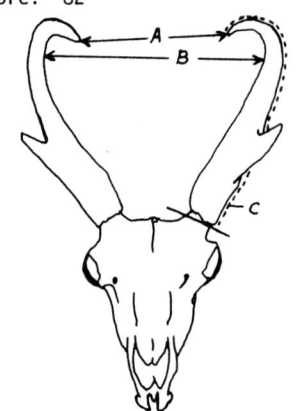 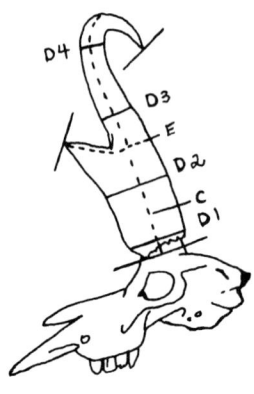

SEE OTHER SIDE FOR INSTRUCTIONS		Column 1	Column 2	Column 3
A. Tip to Tip Spread	9 4/8	Right Horn	Left Horn	Difference
B. Inside Spread of Main Beams	11 4/8			
IF inside Spread exceeds longer horn, enter difference.				
C. Length of Horn		17 2/8	17 3/8	1/8
D-1. Circumference of Base		6 6/8	6 3/8	3/8
D-2. Circumference at First Quarter		7	6 2/8	6/8
D-3. Circumference at Second Quarter		3 6/8	3 7/8	1/8
D-4. Circumference at Third Quarter		2 7/8	2 7/8	
E. Length of Prong		6 7/8	6 2/8	5/8
TOTALS		44 4/8	43	2

ADD	Column 1	44 4/8	Exact locality where killed Mora Co., N. M.
	Column 2	43	Date killed 29Aug82 By whom killed Roger B. Heemeier
	Total	87 4/8	Present owner Roger B. Heemeier
SUBTRACT Column 3		2	Address
FINAL SCORE		85 4/8	Guide's Name and Address
			Remarks: (Mention any abnormalities or unique qualities)

I certify that I have measured the above trophy on 20 June 1983
at (address) Dallas Museum of Natl. Hist.   City Dallas   State Texas
and that these measurements and data are, to the best of my knowledge and belief, made in accordance with the instructions given.

Witness: Glen C. Sanderson   Signature: Steve Kubasek
                                                Official Measurer

INSTRUCTIONS FOR MEASURING PRONGHORN

All measurements must be made with a ¼-inch flexible steel tape to the nearest one-eighth of an inch. Wherever it is necessary to change direction of measurement, make a control point and swing tape at this point. Enter fractional figures in <u>eighths</u>, without reduction. Official measurements cannot be taken for at least sixty days after the animal was killed.

A. Tip to Tip Spread is measured between tips of horns.

B. Inside Spread of Main Beams is measured at a right angle to the center line of the skull, at widest point between main beams.

C. Length of horn is measured on the outside curve on the general line illustrated. The line taken will vary with different heads, depending on the direction of their curvature. Measure along the center of the outer curve from tip of horn to a point in line with the lowest edge of the base, using a straight edge to establish the line end.

D-1. Measure around base of horn at a right angle to long axis. Tape must be in contact with the lowest circumference of the horn in which there are no serrations.

D-2-3-4. Divide measurement of longer horn by four. Starting at base, mark <u>both</u> horns at these quarters (even though other horn is shorter) and measure circumferences at these marks. If the prong interferes with D-2, move the measurement down to just below the swelling of the prong. If the prong interferes with D-3, move the measurement up to just above the swelling of the prong.

E. Length of Prong- Measure from the tip of the prong along the upper edge of the outer curve to the horn; then continue around the horn to a point at the rear of the horn where a straight edge across the back of both horns touches the horn, with the latter part being at a right angle to the long axis of horn.

* * * * * * * * * * * *

FAIR CHASE STATEMENT FOR ALL HUNTER-TAKEN TROPHIES

To make use of the following methods shall be deemed as UNFAIR CHASE and unsportsmanlike, and any trophy obtained by use of such means is disqualified from entry for Awards.

I. Spotting or herding game from the air, followed by landing in its vicinity for pursuit;
II. Herding or pursuing game with motor-powered vehicles;
III. Use of electronic communications for attracting, locating or observing game, or guiding the hunter to such game;
IV. Hunting game confined by artificial barriers, including escape-proof fencing; or hunting game transplanted solely for the purpose of commercial shooting.

I certify that the trophy scored on this chart was not taken in UNFAIR CHASE as defined above by the Boone and Crockett Club. I further certify that it was taken in full compliance with local game laws of the state, province, or territory.

Date_____Signature of Hunter_____
(Have signature notarized by a Notary Public)

Copyright © 1981 by Boone and Crockett Club
(Reproduction strictly forbidden without express, written consent)

OFFICIAL SCORING SYSTEM FOR NORTH AMERICAN BIG GAME TROPHIES

Records of North American Big Game
BOONE AND CROCKETT CLUB
205 South Patrick Street
Alexandria, Virginia 22314

Minimum Score: 115   BISON   Sex male

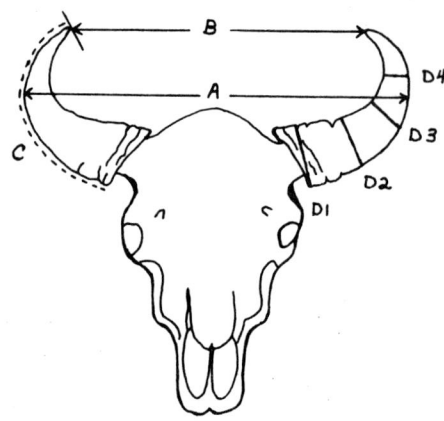

SEE OTHER SIDE FOR INSTRUCTIONS		Column 1	Column 2	Column 3
A. Greatest Spread	28	Right Horn	Left Horn	
B. Tip to Tip Spread	20 3/8			Difference
C. Length of Horn		19 7/8	20	1/8
D-1. Circumference of Base		14 4/8	14 4/8	
D-2. Circumference at First Quarter		12	12	
D-3. Circumference at Second Quarter		10 2/8	10 1/8	1/8
D-4. Circumference at Third Quarter		6 1/8	6	1/8
TOTALS		62 6/8	62 5/8	3/8

ADD	Column 1	62 6/8	Exact locality where killed Manitoba
	Column 2	62 5/8	Date killed 1928 By whom killed Unknown
	Total	125 3/8	Present owner James Fredrick
SUBTRACT Column 3		3/8	Address
FINAL SCORE		125	Guide's Name and Address
			Remarks: (Mention any abnormalities or unique qualities)

I certify that I have measured the above trophy on 22 June 19 83
at (address) Dallas Museum of Natl. Hist. City Dallas   State Texas
and that these measurements and data are, to the best of my knowledge and belief, made in accordance with the instructions given.

Witness: Steve Kubasek   Signature: Ed Williamson
                                                Official Measurer

INSTRUCTIONS FOR MEASURING BISON

All measurements must be made with a ¼-inch flexible steel tape to the nearest one-eighth of an inch. Wherever it is necessary to change direction of measurement, mark a control point and swing tape at this point. Enter fractional figures in eighths, without reduction. Official measurements cannot be taken for at least sixty days after the animal was killed.

A. Greatest Spread is measured between perpendicular at a right angle to the center line of the skull.

B. Tip to Tip Spread is measured between tips of horns.

C. Length of Horn is measured from lowest point on under side over outer curve to a point in line with tip. Use a straight edge, perpendicular to horn axis, to end the measurement, if necessary.

D-1. Circumference of Base is measured at a right angle to axis of horn. Do not follow the irregular edge of horn; the line of measurement must be entirely on horn material, not the jagged edge often noted.

D-2-3-4. Divide measurement C of longer horn by four. Starting at base, mark both horns at these quarters (even though the other horn is shorter) and measure circumferences at these marks, with measurements taken at right angles to horn axis.

* * * * * * * * * * * * *

FAIR CHASE STATEMENT FOR ALL HUNTER-TAKEN TROPHIES

To make use of the following methods shall be deemed as UNFAIR CHASE and unsportmanlike, and any trophy obtained by use of such means is disqualified from entry for Awards.

I. Spotting or herding game from the air, followed by landing in its vicinity for pursuit;
II. Herding or pursuing game with motor-powered vehicles;
III. Use of electronic communications for attracting, locating or observing game, or guiding the hunter to such game;
IV. Hunting game confined by artificial barriers, including escape-proof fencing; or hunting game transplanted solely for the purpose of commercial shooting.

I certify that the trophy scored on this chart was not taken in UNFAIR CHASE as defined above by the Boone and Crockett Club. I further certify that it was taken in full compliance with local game laws of the state, province, or territory.
Date_____ Signature of Hunter_____
(Have signature notarized by a Notary Public)

Copyright © 1981 by Boone and Crockett Club
(Reproduction strictly forbidden without express, written consent)

OFFICIAL SCORING SYSTEM FOR NORTH AMERICAN BIG GAME TROPHIES

Records of North American Big Game

BOONE AND CROCKETT CLUB

205 South Patrick Street
Alexandria, Virginia 22314

Minimum Score: 50   ROCKY MOUNTAIN GOAT   Sex _male_

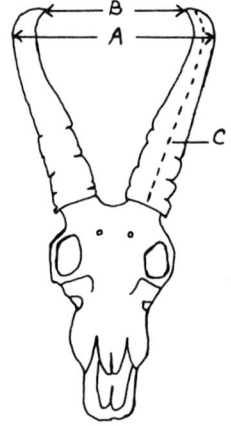 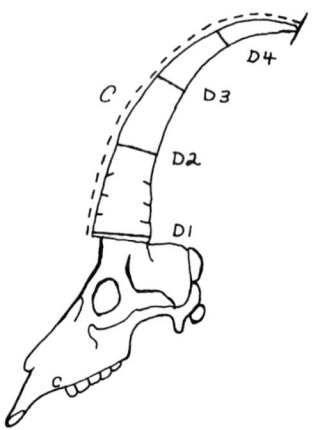

SEE OTHER SIDE FOR INSTRUCTIONS		Column 1 Right Horn	Column 2 Left Horn	Column 3 Difference
A. Greatest Spread	7			
B. Tip to Tip Spread	5 2/8			
C. Length of Horn		10 6/8	10 3/8	3/8
D-1. Circumference of Base		6 2/8	6 2/8	
D-2. Circumference at First Quarter		4 7/8	4 7/8	
D-3. Circumference at Second Quarter		3 2/8	3 2/8	
D-4. Circumference at Third Quarter		2	2	
TOTALS		27 1/8	26 6/8	3/8

ADD	Column 1	27 1/8	Exact locality where killed Mt. Horetzky, B. C.
	Column 2	26 6/8	Date killed 11Sept80 By whom killed Jackie O. Arnold
	Total	53 7/8	Present owner Jackie O. Arnold
SUBTRACT Column 3		3/8	Address
			Guide's Name and Address
FINAL SCORE		53 4/8	Remarks: (Mention any abnormalities or unique qualities)

I certify that I have measured the above trophy on 21 June 1983
at (address) Dallas Museum of Natl. Hist. City Dallas State Texas
and that these measurements and data are, to the best of my knowledge and belief, made in accordance with the instructions given.

Witness: _Frank Cook_   Signature: _Ed Williamson_
                                     Official Measurer

INSTRUCTIONS FOR MEASURING ROCKY MOUNTAIN GOAT

All measurements must be made with a ¼-inch flexible steel tape to the nearest one-eighth of an inch. Wherever it is necessary to change direction of measurement, mark a control point and swing tape at this point. Enter fractional figures in eighths, without reductions. Measurements are most accurately taken before mounting of the trophy. Official measurements cannot be taken for at least sixty days after the animal was killed.

A. Greatest Spread is measured between perpendiculars at a right angle to the center line of the skull.

B. Tip to Tip Spread is measured between tips of horns.

C. Length of Horn is measured from lowest point in front over outer curve to a point in line with tip.

D-1. Circumference of Base is measured at a right angle to axis of horn. DO NOT follow irregular edge of horn.

D-2-3-4. Divide measurement C of longer horn by four. Starting at base, mark both horns at these quarters (even though other horn is shorter) and measure circumferences at these marks.

* * * * * * * * * * * * *

FAIR CHASE STATEMENT FOR ALL HUNTER-TAKEN TROPHIES

To make use of the following methods shall be deemed as UNFAIR CHASE and unsportsmanlike, and any trophy obtained by use of such means is disqualified from entry for Awards.
    I. Spotting or herding game from the air, followed by landing in its vicinity for pursuit;
    II. Herding or pursuing game with motor-powered vehicles;
    III. Use of electronic communications for attracting, locating or observing game, or guiding the hunter to such game;
    IV. Hunting game confined by artificial barriers, including escape-proof fencing; or hunting game transplanted solely for the purpose of commercial shooting.

I certify that the trophy scored on this chart was not taken in UNFAIR CHASE as defined above by the Boone and Crockett Club. I further certify that it was taken in full compliance with local game laws of the state, province, or territory.
Date_____ Signature of Hunter_____
(Have signature notarized by a Notary Public)

Copyright © 1981 by Boone and Crockett Club
(Reproduction strictly forbidden without express, written consent)

OFFICIAL SCORING SYSTEM FOR NORTH AMERICAN BIG GAME TROPHIES

Records of North American Big Game

BOONE AND CROCKETT CLUB

205 South Patrick Street
Alexandria, Virginia 22314

Minimum Score: 90   MUSKOX   Sex male

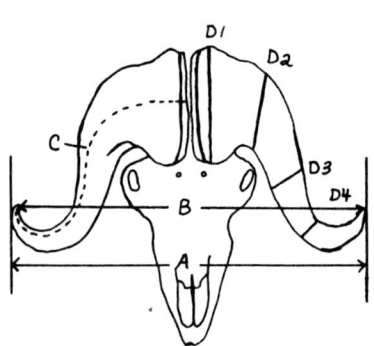 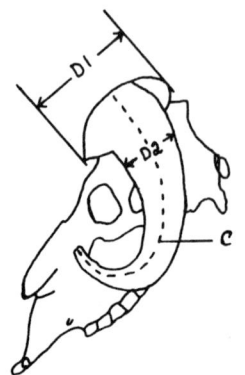

SEE OTHER SIDE FOR INSTRUCTIONS		Column 1	Column 2	Column 3
A. Greatest Spread	27	Right Horn	Left Horn	Difference
B. Tip to Tip Spread	25 6/8			
C. Length of Horn		25	26 5/8	1 5/8
D-1. Width of Boss		9 4/8	9 4/8	
D-2. Width at First Quarter		6 1/8	6 4/8	3/8
D-3. Circumference at Second Quarter		9 3/8	10	5/8
D-4. Circumference at Third Quarter		4 6/8	5 7/8	1 1/8
TOTALS		54 6/8	58 4/8	3 6/8

ADD	Column 1	54 6/8	Exact locality where killed Banks Island, N. W. T.
	Column 2	58 4/8	Date killed 2Mar81 By whom killed James M. Domokos
	Total	113 2/8	Present owner James M. Domokos
SUBTRACT Column 3		3 6/8	Address
FINAL SCORE		109 4/8	Guide's Name and Address
			Remarks: (Mention any abnormalities or unique qualities)

I certify that I have measured the above trophy on 22 June 19 83
at (address) Dallas Museum of Natl. Hist. City Dallas   State Texas
and that these measurements and data are, to the best of my knowledge and belief, made in
accordance with the instructions given.

Witness: Frank Cook   Signature: George Tsukamoto
                                   Official Measurer

INSTRUCTIONS FOR MEASURING MUSKOX

All measurements must be made with a ¼-inch flexible steel tape and adjustable calipers to the nearest one-eighth of an inch. Whenever it is necessary to change direction of measurement, mark a control point and swing tape at this point. Enter fractional figures in eighths, without reduction. Official measurements cannot be taken for at least sixty days after the animal was killed.

A. Greatest Spread is measured between perpendiculars at a right angle to the center line of the skull.

B. Tip to Tip Spread is measured between tips of horns by using large calipers, which are then read against a yardstick.

C. Length of Horn is measured along center of upper horn surface, staying within curve of horn as illustrated, to a point in line with tip. Attempt to free the connective tissue between the horns at the center of the boss to determine the lowest point of horn material on each side, near the top center of the skull. Hook the tape under the lowest point of the horn and measure the length of horn, with the measurement line maintained in the center of the upper surface of horn following the converging lines to the horn tip.

D-1. Width of Boss is measured with calipers at greatest width of base, with measurement line forming a right angle with horn axis. It is often helpful to measure D-1 before C, marking the midpoint of the boss as the correct path of C.

D-2-3-4. Divide measurement C of longer horn by four. Starting at base, mark both horns at these quarters (even though other horn is shorter). Then, using calipers, measure width of boss at D-2, making sure the measurement is at a right angle to horn axis and in line with the D-2 mark. Circumferences are then measured at D-3 and D-4, with measurements being taken at right angles to horn axis.

* * * * * * * * * * * *

FAIR CHASE STATEMENT FOR ALL HUNTER-TAKEN TROPHIES

To make use of the following methods shall be deemed as UNFAIR CHASE and unsportsmanlike, and any trophy obtained by use of such means is disqualified from entry for Awards.
- I. Spotting or herding game from the air, followed by landing in its vicinity for pursuit;
- II. Herding or pursuing game with motor-powered vehicles;
- III. Use of electronic communications for attracting, locating or observing game, or guiding the hunter to such game;
- IV. Hunting game confined by artificial barriers, including escape-proof fencing; or hunting game transplanted solely for the purpose of commercial shooting.

I certify that the trophy scored on this chart was not taken in UNFAIR CHASE as defined above by the Boone and Crockett Club. I further certify that it was taken in full compliance with local game laws of the state, province, or territory.
Date_____ Signature of Hunter_____
(Have signature notarized by a Notary Public)

Copyright © 1981 by Boone and Crockett Club
(Reproduction strictly forbidden without express, written consent)

OFFICIAL SCORING SYSTEM FOR NORTH AMERICAN BIG GAME TROPHIES

Records of North American Big Game

BOONE AND CROCKETT CLUB

205 South Patrick Street
Alexandria, Virginia 22314

Minimum Score:
bighorn 180
desert 168
Stone 170
white or Dall 170

SHEEP

Kind of Sheep bighorn

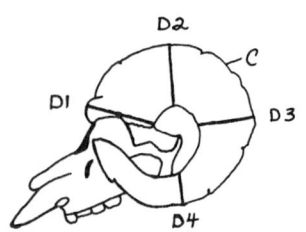
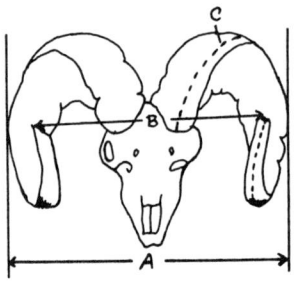

MEASURE TO A POINT IN LINE WITH HORN TIP

SEE OTHER SIDE FOR INSTRUCTIONS		Column 1	Column 2	Column 3
A. Greatest Spread (Is often Tip to Tip Spread)	28 6/8	Right Horn	Left Horn	Difference
B. Tip to Tip Spread	28 6/8			
C. Length of Horn		44 3/8	45 4/8	
D-1. Circumference of Base		15 7/8	15 5/8	2/8
D-2. Circumference at First Quarter		15 6/8	15 2/8	4/8
D-3. Circumference at Second Quarter		14 2/8	14 1/8	1/8
D-4. Circumference at Third Quarter		8 5/8	9 4/8	7/8
TOTALS		98 7/8	100	1 6/8

ADD	Column 1	98 7/8	Exact locality where killed Sanders Co., Mont.
	Column 2	100	Date killed 19Nov79 By whom killed Armand H. Johnson
TOTAL		198 7/8	Present owner Armand H. Johnson
SUBTRACT Column 3		1 6/8	Address
FINAL SCORE		197 1/8	Guide's Name and Address
			Remarks: (Mention any abnormalities or unique qualities)

I certify that I have measured the above trophy on 21 June 1983
at (address) Dallas Museum of Natl. Hist. City Dallas   State Texas
and that these measurements and data are, to the best of my knowledge and belief, made in accordance with the instructions given.

Witness: George Tsukamoto   Signature: Ed Williamson
                                              Official Measurer

INSTRUCTIONS FOR MEASURING SHEEP

All measurements must be made with a ¼-inch flexible steel tape to the nearest one-eighth of an inch. Wherever it is necessary to change direction of measurement, mark a control point and swing tape at this point. Enter fractional figures in eighths, without reduction. Official measurements cannot be taken for at least sixty days after the animal was killed.

A. Greatest Spread is measured between perpendiculars at a right angle to the center line of the skull.

B. Tip to Tip Spread is measured between tips of horns.

C. Length of Horn is measured from the lowest point in front on outer curve to a point in line with tip. Do not press tape into depressions. The low point of the outer curve of the horn is considered to be the low point of the frontal portion of the horn, situated above and slightly medial to the eye socket (not the outside edge). Use a straight edge, perpendicular to horn axis, to end measurement on "broomed" horns.

D-1. Circumference of Base is measured at a right angle to axis of horn. Do not follow irregular edge of horn; the line of measurement must be entirely on horn material, not the jagged edge often noted.

D-2-3-4. Divide measurement C of longer horn by four. Starting at base, mark both horns at these quarters (even though the other horn is shorter) and measure circumferences at these marks, with measurements taken at right angles to horn axis.

* * * * * * * * * * * * *

FAIR CHASE STATEMENT FOR ALL HUNTER-TAKEN TROPHIES

To make use of the following methods shall be deemed as UNFAIR CHASE and unsportsmanlike, and any trophy obtained by use of such means is disqualified from entry for Awards.
  I. Spotting or herding game from the air, followed by landing in its vicinity for pursuit;
  II. Herding or pursuing game with motor-powered vehicles;
  III. Use of electronic communications for attracting, locating or observing game, or guiding the hunter to such game;
  IV. Hunting game confined by artificial barriers, including escape-proof fencing; or hunting game transplanted solely for the purpose of commercial shooting.

I certify that the trophy scored on this chart was not taken in UNFAIR CHASE as defined above by the Boone and Crockett Club. I further certify that it was taken in full compliance with local game laws of the state, province, or territory.
Date_____ Signature of Hunter_____
(Have signature notarized by a Notary Public)

Copyright © 1981 by Boone and Crockett Club
(Reproduction strictly forbidden without express, written consent)

This book was:

Compiled with able assistance of: Jack Reneau
Paige L. Chandler
Margo P. Kline
Suzanne L. Eaker
Rita B. Johnsos

Designed by: Wm. H. Nesbitt

Typeset by: Compolith Graphics
Indianapolis, Indiana

Printed and bound by: Haddon Craftsmen
Scranton, Pennsylvania